The MAILBOX®

The Idea Magazine For Teachers®

INTERMEDIATE

1997–1998

YEARBOOK

Becky S. Andrews, Editor

The Education Center, Inc.
Greensboro, North Carolina

The Mailbox® 1997–1998 Intermediate Yearbook

Editor In Chief: Margaret Michel
Magazine Director: Karen P. Shelton
Editorial Administrative Director: Stephen Levy
Senior Editor: Becky S. Andrews
Associate Editors: Irving P. Crump, Peggy W. Hambright
Contributing Editors: Elizabeth H. Lindsay, Debra Liverman, Thad H. McLaurin, Cindy Mondello, Stephanie Willett-Smith
Copy Editors: Lynn Bemer Coble, H. Amanda Dixon, Karen L. Huffman, Scott Lyons, Jennifer Rudisill, Debbie Shoffner, Gina Sutphin
Staff Artists: Jennifer Tipton Bennett, Cathy Spangler Bruce, Pam Crane, Clevell Harris, Susan Hodnett, Sheila Krill, Mary Lester, Rob Mayworth, Kimberly Richard, Rebecca Saunders, Barry Slate, Donna K. Teal
Editorial Assistants: Mickey Hjelt, Laura Slaughter, Wendy Svartz
Librarian: Elizabeth A. Findley

ISBN 1-56234-213-4
ISSN 1088-5552

The Education Center, Inc.
P.O. Box 9753
Greensboro, NC 27429-0753

Contents

Teacher Resource Ideas

Getting Back In The Swim Of Things!

Back-To-School Ideas For A "Fin-tastic" Year

Fishing for some new ideas to add to your back-to-school plans? Dive into the first few weeks of the school year with the following catch of creative ideas, tips, and reproducibles!

ideas by Marcia Barton

Tony

I like pizza more than any other food.

I'm a good soccer player.

I hope to improve my handwriting this year.

Fishing For New Friends

Fishing for a fun, back-to-school icebreaker? Duplicate one fish pattern (see page 10) on brightly colored paper for each student. Have each student label his fish with his name at the top. Next divide students into pairs. Set a timer for two minutes; then tell each student to ask his partner one "getting-to-know-you" question. Have each student share the answer with his partner before writing it in a complete sentence on his fish.

When the time is up, divide students into different pairs. Have members of each group meet together and read the sentences on each other's fish. Then have them come up with a new question to ask each other, following the same steps as before. At the end of the time period, change groupings if desired and continue. When the fish have been covered with facts, hold a session during which students share interesting information they've learned about their new classmates. Then have each student cut out his fish and attach it to a "Fishing For New Friends" bulletin board.

Prepared To Care

Who hasn't had one of those days when nothing seems to go right? As a welcome-back treat—one that also lets students know that you understand what it's like to have a bad day—duplicate the coupons on page 8. On the first day of school, present each student with "An Elephant Never Forgets..." coupon, which grants the right to turn in an assignment one day late without penalty. Surprise a student who's having a rough day with a "Rainy Day Card." Allow the student to trade in this card for five minutes of computer time, a chocolate candy kiss, the privilege of keeping the class mascot on his desk for an hour, or any other special treat. What an easy way to help break the cycle that a bad start to a day can create!

Pam Crane

Say Cheese, Please!

Here's a tip that's so useful it just might make you smile! During the first week of school, pair your students; then have each pair stand side by side while you take a photo of them. Be sure to line up the photo so that each student is centered in one half of the lens. Have double prints made of the photos; then cut them in half, resulting in two wallet-sized pictures of each student. Use the photos in any of the following ways:

- Glue each child's photo on a hot-air balloon cutout. Mount the cutouts on your classroom door with the title "Look Who's Landed In Room 202!"
- Cut holes in a strip of bulletin-board border that is designed with animals or other artwork as shown. Glue each child's photo on the back of the border so her face shows through a hole. Use the border to decorate a "Class News" bulletin board.
- Purchase an inexpensive package of play money. Cut out the center of each bill; then glue or tape a child's photo behind the bill at the hole. Laminate the bills to use as rewards. Allow students to turn in their earned bucks at the end of the week to "buy" classroom privileges or small treats.
- Attach the photos to a piece of poster board; then laminate the poster and cut out the photo cards. Use the cards in drawings for classroom contests or to assign helpers.
- Label the backs of one set of photos with student names. Place them in your substitute-teacher folder for easy identification.
- Save one set of photos to attach to paper ornaments mounted on a bulletin-board Christmas tree.

Go Fish When You're Finished!

Collect student papers in a snap with this fishy idea! Obtain a box that is divided in compartments from a local liquor store. Paint the outside of the box with blue paint. Next cut apart an old cardboard box so that it lies flat. On the box, trace the outlines of several fish with tabs as shown; then cut out the fish. During the first week of school, have student volunteers paint the fish at an art center. When the fish have dried, bend each at its tab and attach it to the box with clear packing tape or hot glue as shown. Stick a file-folder label for each child on the inside of the cubbies; then position the box on a table in your classroom.

While establishing your class routines during the first week, teach students to "go fish when you're finished" by having them place any completed classwork or tests in their cubbies. A quick glance at the cubbies will tell you who hasn't finished yet. If you teach more than one class of students, number the cubbies; then assign a number to each child in a particular class, making sure to clear out the cubbies between classes.

While You Were Out

Keeping up with work for absent students can make any teacher feel as if she's drowning in paperwork! Pass this task on to your students by duplicating the "While You Were Out" forms on page 9 on pink paper. Cut out the forms; then punch a hole at the top left corner of each. Use a pushpin to hang the forms on a bulletin board. Each day choose a student to serve as class scribe. Have the scribe take a form from the board for each absent student and fill it out as assignments are given during the day. At the end of the day, have the scribe pin the completed forms on the bulletin board for absent students to pick up upon their return. Thank the scribe by presenting her with a copy of the special coupon on page 9, which can be stapled on any paper to earn an extra point.

Patterns

Use with "Prepared To Care" on page 6. Fill in the Rainy Day Card with a special treat or privilege before duplicating; or duplicate the card and let the student fill it in with the treat of his choice.

An
Elephant
Never
Forgets,

But in case
you do...

...attach this coupon to one assignment and turn it in one day late without penalty.

Name: _____

Date used: _____

An
Elephant
Never
Forgets,

But in case
you do...

...attach this coupon to one assignment and turn it in one day late without penalty.

Name: _____

Date used: _____

©1997 The Education Center, Inc.

Rainy
Day
Card

Having one of *those* days? Is something raining on your parade? Then chase the blues away by trading in this card for the following special pick-me-up:

_____

Hope your day brightens soon!

Name _____

Rainy
Day
Card

Having one of *those* days? Is something raining on your parade? Then chase the blues away by trading in this card for the following special pick-me-up:

_____

Hope your day brightens soon!

Name _____

©1997 The Education Center, Inc.

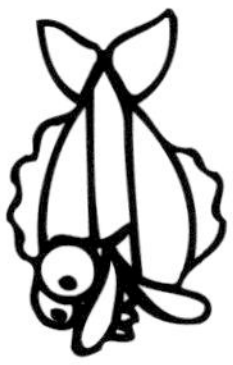

While You Were Out

Name: _____

Date of absence: _____

You missed:

__ an activity: _____

__ these assignments: _____

__ a quiz/test on: _____

__ an announcement: _____

__ other: _____

_____ class scribe

Please hook up with me if you need help catching up!

©The Education Center, Inc. • *THE MAILBOX*® • Intermediate • Aug/Sept 1997

Thanks For Diving Right In...

...and serving as class scribe for the day. Staple this coupon to the paper of your choice to earn an extra point.

Name: _____

Assignment: _____

Date: _____

©1997 The Education Center, Inc.

Thanks For Diving Right In...

...and serving as class scribe for the day. Staple this coupon to the paper of your choice to earn an extra point.

Name: _____

Assignment: _____

Date: _____

©1997 The Education Center, Inc.

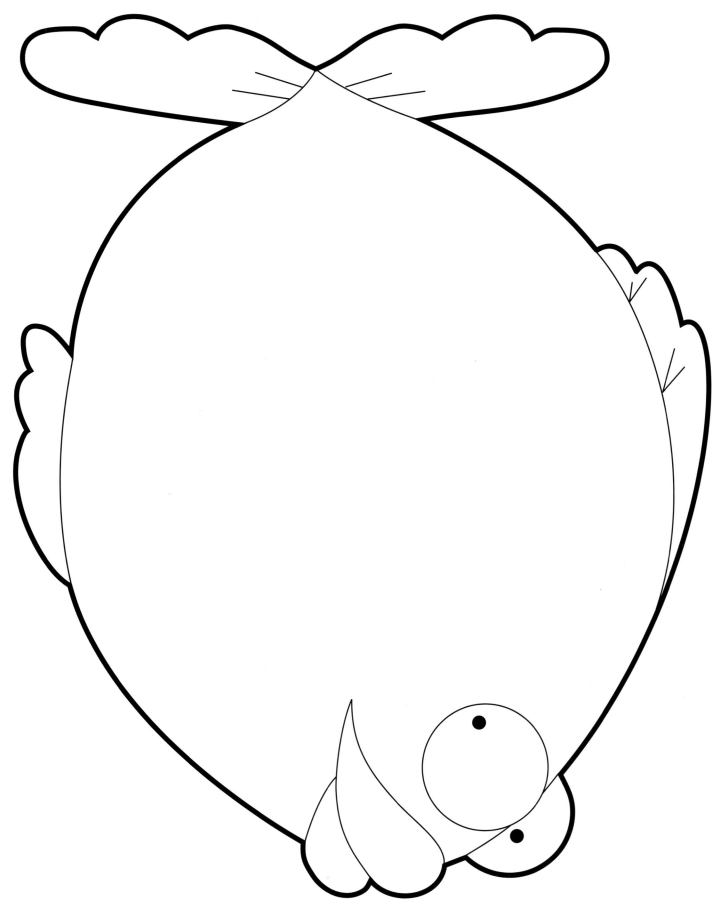

MAKING GROUP WORK "GRRREAT"!

Teaching children the value of working together—it's one of the most important tasks you do. But how do you make group work *really* work for you and your students? We asked some of our subscribers that question. With the help of their best ideas for promoting cooperation in the classroom, your students are sure to think that group work is "GRRREAT"!

TEAMWORK TALLY

Promote good behavior and cooperation in group settings with the following idea. Divide students into teams; then have each group decide on a team name. Give each group a large piece of poster board to decorate with its team name, team members' names, and any decorative pictures or symbols. Award points to teams that are on task or are ready first after a transition. Also award points for positive behaviors, such as working quietly, listening, completing work on time, following directions quickly, etc. Keep track of earned points. At the end of the week, reward the winning team with a special treat or privilege. You'll be amazed at how peer pressure and cooperation keep students on task and prepared for their lessons!

Sandi Norton—Gr. 4, Valley Springs Elementary, Harrison, AR

TEAM BOXES

Save class time by simplifying the organization and distribution of materials during cooperative group activities. Provide each group with a shoebox or another lidded container. Stock each box with items such as scissors, pens, pencils, markers, colored pencils, tape, glue, rulers, and small notepads. Not only will precious time be saved when preparing for group activities, but team members will also learn to practice sharing and patience!

Deedra Bignar—Gr. 6, Nebo Elementary, Jena, LA

JOB CARDS

Use the reproducible job cards on page 13 to help organize your cooperative groups. Duplicate one set of cards per group. Cut apart the cards, glue them on tagboard, and color and laminate if desired. Fold each card on the dotted line to create a stand-up card. Discuss with students the responsibilities described on each card. At the start of each group activity, give each team a set of cards to use as handy reminders. When you're ready for students to switch jobs, simply have them swap cards!

Maxine Pincott and Peggi Savage—Gr. 4
Oliver Ellsworth School, Windsor, CT

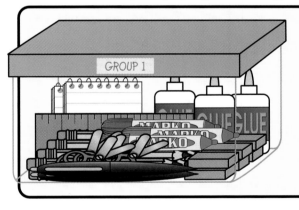

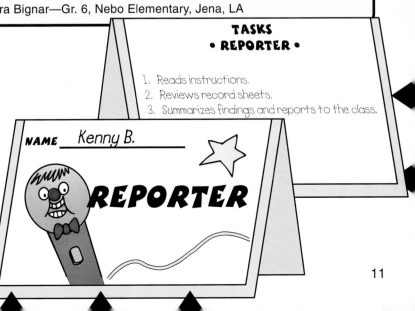

TASKS
• REPORTER •

1. Reads instructions.
2. Reviews record sheets.
3. Summarizes findings and reports to the class.

NAME Kenny B.

REPORTER

11

WHAT A DEAL!

Shuffle students into cooperative groups by using a deck of cards! Divide the deck into groups of four (four aces, four 8's, etc.) so that you have one card per child. Shuffle the cards; then give one to each student. Instruct him to find his three group mates according to the number/picture on his card. Then assign a job to each student based on his card's suit: spades—reader, diamonds—group leader, hearts—recorder, and clubs—timekeeper. With this method, groups and jobs can be changed easily. What a deal!

Kristi Gettelman—Gr. 5
St. Roman Grade School
Milwaukee, WI

Stop-Drop-Help!

1. Rephrase questions.
2. Give hints or clues.
3. Use encouraging words.

STOP-DROP-AND-HELP

Before using cooperative learning and peer teaching in the classroom, teach students *how* to help each other. Introduce the Stop-Drop-And-Help method: turn your paper over (stop), put your pencil down (drop), and turn to face the person who needs assistance (help). Teach students to coach one another by rephrasing questions, giving hints or clues, and using encouraging words. Display the method on a classroom poster, along with a sign on each student's desk, as reminders. Students will enjoy helping each other, and your job will become a little easier too!

Kimberly Marinelli—Gr. 5
La Barriere Crossings School
Winnipeg, Manitoba, Canada

But I can't erase!

But I can't divide the paper without a pencil!

THE PENCIL BOX

Help students see that they need each other's individual strengths with this eye-opening activity. Provide each group of four with the following materials: a pencil box (or other container) containing a ruler, scissors, an eraser, and a golf pencil; a sheet of paper for each group member. Then have students follow these steps:

1. Choose one object other than paper from the pencil box. This is your "strength."
2. Take one sheet of paper from the box.
3. Using *only* your strength, divide the paper into six equal parts. You are *not* allowed to share your strength with others in your group.

Next ask students, "How were you able to individually complete the task? Was it easy or hard? What would help you complete the task more accurately?"

Assign the same task again, giving only one sheet of paper to each group. Allow each student to share his strength with the rest of his group to complete the task. Students will quickly see that they need each other's strengths to get the job done accurately and effectively.

Tammy S. Edwards—Gr. 5
Stanwood Elementary
Scottdale, PA

PRINCIPAL INVESTIGATOR

NAME _____

TASKS • PRINCIPAL INVESTIGATOR •

1. Supervises assembly of materials and equipment.
2. First to put materials to use.
3. Makes sure all group members have an equal chance to participate.

MATERIALS MANAGER

NAME _____

TASKS • MATERIALS MANAGER •

1. Collects and returns materials.
2. Reports any damaged or missing materials to the teacher.
3. Gathers additional information from the teacher.

REPORTER

NAME _____

TASKS • REPORTER •

1. Reads instructions.
2. Reviews record sheets.
3. Summarizes findings and reports to the class.

DATA COLLECTOR

NAME _____

TASKS • DATA COLLECTOR •

1. Records data and observations on the group worksheet(s).
2. Returns the worksheet(s) to the teacher.
3. Checks activity results.

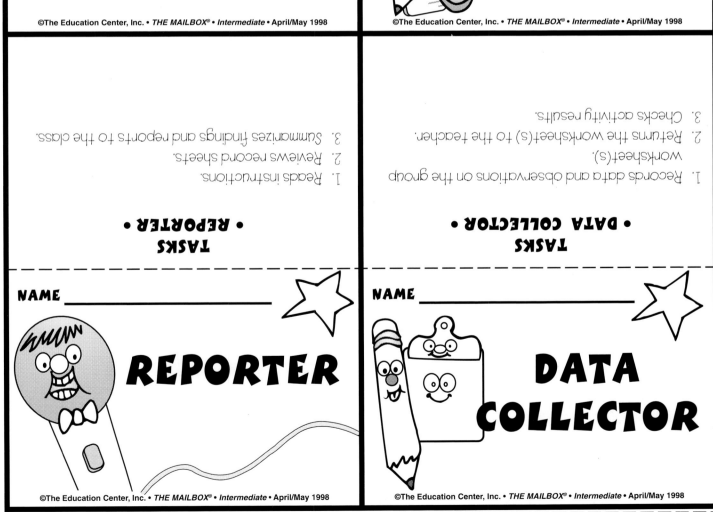

Note To The Teacher: Use with "Job Cards" on page 11.

A Treasure Chest Of Student-Teacher Tips

Favorite Student-Teacher Tips From Our Subscribers

Remember your first day as a student teacher? If you do, then you'll agree that the supervising teacher often holds the key to a successful intern experience. The following ideas from our readers are a treasure trove of ideas that will make your student teacher's time with your class a surefire success.

Great Greetings!

Ease your student teacher's first-day jitters by welcoming her with a student-made banner. A few days before the student teacher arrives, use a desktop-publishing program to make a banner, or have students design their own special banner welcoming her. Have each student sign the banner; then hang it in the front of your classroom.

Kelly A. Wong, Berlyn School, Ontario, CA

Introductory Bulletin Board

Looking for a unique way to introduce your student teacher to your class? Have him create an autobiographical bulletin board to share with your students. Encourage the student teacher to use the bulletin-board space to create a personal collage featuring pictures, mementos, and important information about his life. Provide time for the student teacher to discuss the bulletin board with students and answer questions.

Deborah Abrams Burroughs—Gr. 5, Laguna Elementary, Laguna, NM

Student-Teacher Survival Kit

This easy-to-make kit is sure to get your student teacher off to a great start! Cover a shoebox with brightly colored Con-Tact® paper; then apply apple or other school-related stickers. Next write "Student-Teacher Survival Kit" on the box lid. Place an assortment of handy items inside the box, such as a grader, red pens, incentive stickers, Band-Aids®, pencils, LifeSavers®, safety pins, a sewing kit, and a packet of aspirin. Give the box to your student teacher at your first meeting to start the experience off on a positive note!

Sandra Wilkin—Gr. 4
Parkview Elementary
Jackson, OH

Interactive Journal

A three-ring binder is all you need to provide your student teacher with important information and invaluable feedback. Fill a three-ring binder with useful information, such as schedules, school policies, and grade-level teaching objectives. Place stickers, awards, and sticky notes in the binder pockets; then put some paper in the rings. Record positive comments, questions, and suggestions on the pages during your student teacher's lesson. Have your student teacher respond on the page in the same way right after the lesson. What a great way to establish a productive dialogue!

Debbie Schneck—Gr. 4, Schnecksville, PA

Instant Activity File

It's a safe bet to say that almost every teacher has a file of favorite, tried-and-true activities. Help your student teacher start her own such file by placing one additional copy of each of your favorite activities in a file folder labeled "For The Student Teacher." Add an activity to the folder each time you place one in your own files. When you are assigned a student teacher, invite her to look through the file and select any activities that she would like to copy. Your student teacher will truly appreciate having her own personal collection of activities to take with her when she leaves.

Sandra Hill—Gr. 4, Brentwood Elementary, Sarasota, FL

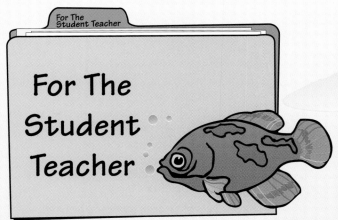

Tips To Student-Teach By

Making a student teacher's experience a positive one is easy with the help of the handy tips listed on page 17. Duplicate the tips for yourself and your student teacher, and read over them prior to beginning the student-teaching experience. You're sure to gain some valuable insights!

Dianne Kinard—Gr. 4 and Shannon L. Cravens—Student Teacher
Westminster Elementary, Westminster, SC

Video Hail And Farewell

If a picture is worth a thousand words, then this video for your student teacher will be priceless! Use a video camera to have your students introduce themselves to a new student teacher or say good-bye to one who is leaving soon. Videotape a short message from each of your students. Or, if you have a limited amount of time, take a photograph of each child and have her write a personalized message to the student teacher. Mount the photos and accompanying messages in a decorated photo album. Also provide the student teacher with an inexpensive single-use camera for taking pictures of the class, bulletin boards, and projects before he leaves.

Patricia E. Dancho—Gr. 6
Apollo-Ridge Middle School
Spring Church, PA

FAREWELL, MR. CLEMENTS

A Box Of Great Ideas

As a veteran teacher, one of the most valuable things you can give your student teacher is the benefit of your years of classroom experience. Take advantage of that experience to create this handy, inexpensive going-away gift for your student teacher. Label several file card dividers with categories, such as five-minute fillers, bulletin boards, games, and arts-and-crafts activities. Then record your favorite ideas on index cards and file them behind the appropriate dividers. Give the file box to your student teacher on her last day with your class.

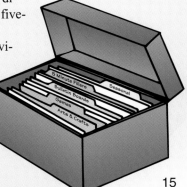

Sandra Hill—Gr. 4

Capture The Moment

Keep an annotated record of your student teacher's teaching experiences with the help of a disposable camera. Take photographs of day-to-day activities throughout the practicum. Then mount the photos in a scrapbook along with artwork and testimonials written by each student. Present the completed scrapbook at a farewell potluck luncheon in honor of your student teacher. Be sure to invite the student teacher's family to the luncheon to help you wish her the best of luck!

Deborah Abrams Burroughs—Gr. 5, Laguna Elementary, Laguna, NM

Student-Teacher Hope Chest

Send your student teacher off to her first job with a gift she'll love! Explain to students that they will be creating a hope chest for your student teacher as a going-away gift. Then send home a copy of the bottom half of page 17 with each child. Ask each student to consult with his parents and select an item from the list to include in the chest. Place students' contributions in a plastic tub decorated with the student teacher's name along with the students' signatures. Present the hope chest to the student teacher at a shower, complete with cake and punch. Your student teacher will leave your classroom with lots of wonderful memories and a container of useful items to get her off to a great start in her own classroom!

Dr. Shirley Jacob, Southeastern Louisiana University, Hammond, LA

Top It Off With A Tape

End your student teacher's experience on a high note with the help of a tape recorder and an audiocassette. Record each child telling the student teacher the special memories he has of their experience together. Give the tape to the student teacher and remind him to listen to it whenever he needs to lift his spirits.

Susan C. Russell—Grs. 3–4 Gifted and Talented
Susie E. Tolbert Elementary
Jacksonville, FL

Journal Of Inspiration

Show your student teacher just how much he meant to your class with the following idea. Purchase an unlined journal with a decorative cover; then glue a photograph of each child on a separate page in the book. Next have each student write a personal message to the student teacher on the page with her picture. Remind the student to mention the things she enjoyed about the student teacher's time in your class and to wish the student teacher well. The result will be a keepsake that will be an inspiration for your student teacher for years to come!

Brenda Shumake—Gr. 4, North Jackson Elementary, Jefferson, GA

12 Simple Tips
For A Successful Student-Teaching Experience

1. Take time to meet your student teacher before the first day.

2. Designate a work area the student teacher can call her own.

3. Introduce the student teacher to all faculty and staff. Make your student teacher feel like part of the faculty by including her in conversations with others.

4. Allow the student teacher to take over responsibilities as he feels comfortable, being careful not to overload him.

5. Make yourself available and approachable to talk with the student teacher.

6. Allow the student teacher to offer suggestions and comments to help you with your own planning and classroom decoration.

7. When the student teacher begins to teach, lessen anxiety on his part by working on something and not looking as if you are watching every move he makes.

8. After each lesson, begin by having the student teacher give her impressions, remembering that most often her worst critic is herself. Then offer any advice or suggestions you have, and always compliment her on the things she does well.

9. Always keep the student teacher informed as to how you think he is doing. Tell him both his strengths and areas that need improvement. Be sure to let him know when you see improvement in his techniques.

10. Get other perspectives by having other teachers observe the student teacher.

11. Enable the student teacher to see all that is involved in the profession of teaching by including her in all professional events, such as conferences, meetings, and in-services.

12. End the student-teaching experience with a gift made especially by the students.

A B C D E F G H I J K L M N O P Q R S T U V W X Y Z

Dear Parent,
On _____ our class will be hosting a new teacher shower for our student teacher. If you would like to contribute an item for the hope chest we are putting together, please consider any one of the following items. Please have your child bring your item to school by
_____.

Thank you,

_____

New Teacher Gift Registry

- file folders
- index cards
- postage stamps
- paper
- pens
- pencils
- stapler
- staples
- paper clips
- three-ring binder
- construction paper
- scissors
- nametags
- felt-tipped pens

- Band-Aids®
- plastic storage containers
- tissues
- three-hole puncher
- ruler
- stencils
- rubber bands
- clear tape
- masking tape
- clear Con-Tact® paper
- desk calendar
- wall calendar
- minute timer
- hand lotion

- chalk
- transparency markers
- two-sided tape
- staple remover
- sticky notes
- baby wipes
- plastic bags
- reward stickers
- rubber stamps
- brads
- cotton swabs
- spray bottle
- glue stick
- breath mints

To My Student Teacher

A B C D E F V W X Y Z

Note To The Teacher: Use tips with "Tips To Student-Teach By" on page 15 and note with "Student-Teacher Hope Chest" on page 16.

Helping Hands

Our Subscribers' Ideas For Working With Volunteers

How do our subscribers deal with the ever-growing demands of teaching? An extra pair of hands in the classroom is sure to lighten the load! Keep the following ideas handy as you recruit, use, and honor your classroom volunteers.

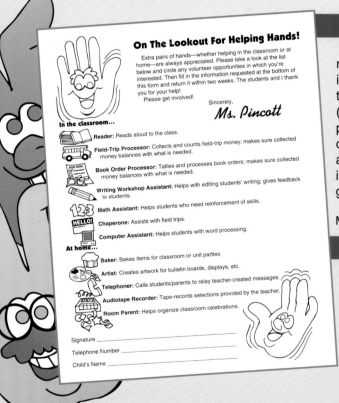

On The Lookout For Helping Hands!

Extra pairs of hands—whether helping in the classroom or at home—are always appreciated. Please take a look at the list below and circle any volunteer opportunities in which you're interested. Then fill in the information requested at the bottom of this form and return it within two weeks. The students and I thank you for your help!

Please get involved!

Sincerely,

Ms. Pincott

In the classroom...

Reader: Reads aloud to the class.

Field-Trip Processor: Collects and counts field-trip money; makes sure collected money balances with what is needed.

Book Order Processor: Tallies and processes book orders; makes sure collected money balances with what is needed.

Writing Workshop Assistant: Helps with editing students' writing; gives feedback to students.

Math Assistant: Helps students who need reinforcement of skills.

Chaperone: Assists with field trips.

Computer Assistant: Helps students with word processing.

At home...

Baker: Bakes items for classroom or unit parties.

Artist: Creates artwork for bulletin boards, displays, etc.

Telephoner: Calls students/parents to relay teacher-created messages.

Audiotape Recorder: Tape-records selections provided by the teacher.

Room Parent: Helps organize classroom celebrations.

Signature _____

Telephone Number _____

Child's Name _____

Sign Up Here, Please!

I like parent volunteers to help during the year. However, many parents are not sure what a job entails or the extent of involvement needed. In order to help parents decide what they can do to help, I developed a volunteer sign-up sheet (see page 20). It includes both classroom and at-home opportunities that are available, along with job descriptions. I distribute the sheets to students on the first day of school and ask that they be returned within two weeks. Parents like this informational sheet because it helps them know what they're getting into!

Maxine Pincott—Gr. 4, Oliver Ellsworth School, Windsor, CT

Calling All Volunteers

An easy but invaluable task that a volunteer can do is to make telephone calls. Some helpful calls include finding out where to buy classroom supplies; contacting businesses for donations of items, awards, or employees' time; and confirming plans with other parent volunteers regarding field trips, guest speakers, and party supplies. My telephoner is a key link in my chain of volunteers!

Kelly A. Wong, Berlyn School, Ontario, CA

Parent Volunteers' Basket

When you find yourself spending too much time cutting out things, stapling packets, or publishing students' writings, just remember that parents love to help out! And having parents complete these tasks saves you valuable time. Just place the items that you need help with in a basket in your classroom, along with essentials such as scissors, markers, rulers, and a stapler. Everything will then be ready when a volunteer comes to your class. If you're in the middle of a lesson, you don't have to stop to explain what needs to be done. Parents will know to go to the basket and get started!

Debbie Schneck—Gr. 4, Schnecksville, PA

Pam Crane

Family Biographies

During the school year, my students write biographies about family members who have been influential in their lives. When the biographies have been completed, the individual whom each student wrote about is invited to our class to hear his or her life story. After listening to the stories, our guests offer advice and give encouragement to the students. We've been honored with visits from many parents and grandparents—and even a 96-year-old great-grandmother!

Deborah Abrams Burroughs—Gr. 5, Laguna Elementary Laguna, NM

Thanks For Your "Involve-mint"!

My parent volunteers help me in lots of ways. I encourage them to work with students because I feel it is another way to meet students' needs. Some parents work with individuals or with small groups to reinforce skills. Others have children read aloud to them and retell stories, while others assist with classroom projects in which extra pairs of hands are always needed. Volunteers are essential in a time when many school districts face cutbacks.

At the end of the year, I thank each volunteer with petunias or marigolds. But I always receive the most comments on my unique thank-you card, into which I attach a York® Peppermint Pattie (see the illustration).

Christine Snodgrass, Stephenson Elementary, Portland, OR

SUPER Volunteer

Thanks for your
"Involve-mint"!
"Commit-mint"!
"Excite-mint"!

This is for your
"enjoy-mint"!

york
Get the sensation!®
CHOCOLATE COVERED
PEPPERMINT PATTIE

Thank-You Baskets

At the end of each year, I like to thank the special people who have donated their time to my students—either in the classroom or outside. I buy a small basket for each volunteer and line it with colorful fabric, with the volunteer's child helping me choose a favorite color. I then fill each basket with a mug, some herbal tea bags, and homemade jam. I also write a card or letter to each individual. This idea works well for me because I can search for mugs, baskets, and fabric throughout the year. My volunteers love this pampering treat!

Christine Smyth—Gr. 5, Frank Jewett Elementary, West Buxton, ME

On The Lookout For Helping Hands!

Extra pairs of hands—whether helping in the classroom or at home—are always appreciated. Please take a look at the list below and circle any volunteer opportunities in which you're interested. Then fill in the information requested at the bottom of this form and return it within two weeks. The students and I thank you for your help!

Please get involved!

Sincerely,

In the classroom...

Reader: Reads aloud to the class.

Field-Trip Processor: Collects and counts field-trip money; makes sure collected money balances with what is needed.

Book Order Processor: Tallies and processes book orders; makes sure collected money balances with what is needed.

Writing Workshop Assistant: Helps with editing students' writing; gives feedback to students.

Math Assistant: Helps students who need reinforcement of skills.

Chaperone: Assists with field trips.

Computer Assistant: Helps students with word processing.

At home...

Baker: Bakes items for classroom or unit parties.

Artist: Creates artwork for bulletin boards, displays, etc.

Telephoner: Calls students/parents to relay teacher-created messages.

Audiotape Recorder: Tape-records selections provided by the teacher.

Room Parent: Helps organize classroom celebrations.

Signature _____

Telephone Number _____

Child's Name _____

Note To The Teacher: See "Sign Up Here, Please!" on page 18. Make a photocopy of this page. Customize the copy by adding the approximate time commitment required after each job description. Add your signature below "Sincerely" before duplicating.

READY, AIM, ASSESS!

On-Target Ideas For Evaluating Student Progress

Assessment—it's one of the most challenging aspects of teaching. When we wanted to know what's working, we called on the experts—our subscribers! Read on to find out how teachers across the nation evaluate their students' progress.

TEST FEEDBACK FORMS

My students are learning to process their study skills, analyze tests, and write in complete sentences. How? I attach a Test Feedback form to each major test that I give. On the form I ask the student to write the grade she thinks she's earned on the test, give reasons for her choice, and explain why she thought the test was difficult or easy. If the student answers all the questions on the form, she earns bonus points. However, if she doesn't respond in complete sentences or give reasons for her answers, only partial credit is given. My Test Feedback form has been an excellent motivational tool. Students now process what they've done. And I can note who has recognized effective—as well as ineffective—study skills.

Gail Hooker—Reading Fleming Middle School, Flemington, NJ

ASSESSMENT CALENDARS

Assessment is an ongoing part of my daily routine. One helpful tool that I use is a blank monthly calendar for each student. I store the calendars on a clipboard that I keep with me throughout the day. During group work or individual conferences, I jot down notes and comments for that day on the calendars. At the end of the month, I file the calendars and clip new copies to my clipboard. When it's time for parent conferences, I share my observations of each child. Now I don't have to rely so much on my memory!

Katie Kasar—Gr. 4, Carollton Elementary, Oak Creek, WI

WRITING CHECKLISTS

Both students and teachers sometimes find it difficult to evaluate writing. I describe the components of the writing piece we're currently working on and create a checklist for students to use as they write. I model the components emphasized on the checklist, usually on the overhead projector. Then the students work together to create some models on their own before starting on their individual pieces. Checklists take the mystery out of the grading process and help me focus more on the goals I want students to achieve. Parents especially prefer this outline format over a general grade.

Mary Gates—Gr. 4, Huckleberry Hill School Brookfield, CT

DESCRIPTIVE PARAGRAPH CHECKLIST

NAME_____ DUE DATE_____

Student Check	
	Write a topic sentence that stimulates the reader's imagination.
	Use different senses.
	Use 10 describing words, such as adjectives or adverbs.
	Put detail in the description to "paint a picture" for the reader.
	Use varied and appropriate vocabulary for your audience.
	Create a title that captures the reader's attention.

Content Grade:_____ Mechanics Grade:_____
Teacher Comment:_____

HELPING PARENTS HELP YOU

Many parents are willing to grade papers at home, but often can't come to school to get them. I purchased three 10" x 13" plastic, see-through envelopes, then punched a hole in the top of each one. I also bought some inexpensive locks with keys. Now whenever I need help with grading papers, I send them to a parent in an envelope secured with a lock. I also send the parent one key in a sealed envelope and keep one copy of the key at school. The parent can check the papers and return them to me in the locked envelope.

Marcia Lehrman, Maple Elementary, Avon, IN

Margo really participated in our problem-solving discussion.

ASSESSMENT NOTES

A grid of 2" x 1 1/2" boxes—one box for each student—and two-inch Post-It® notes help me organize my assessment comments. Each week I select a subject on which to observe students. During this time I make positive observations of several students on Post-It® notes. I place each note over that child's name on the grid, which I keep on a clipboard. When I observe during that subject again the next day, I can easily see which students I still need to write comments on. At the end of the week, when the grid is full, I transfer all of the notes to a binder that has a page for each child. At the end of the grading period, I can easily transfer each binder page to a student's portfolio or attach it to his report card.

Cindy Hamilton—Gr. 5, Baldwin Intermediate School
Quincy, IL

STUDENTS AS SELF-EVALUATORS

To help students become effective self-evaluators, I have them rate their projects before I grade them. When a project (such as a book report) is assigned, I give students the criteria that I will use to grade it. When the project is finished, each child rates her work on a copy of my evaluation sheet, adding anything that she wants me to know about her efforts to the bottom of her sheet. I grade the project on the same form the students use. Each child can then compare my opinions with hers. While my grade is the one recorded, I consider students' thoughts about their efforts, especially their written comments. Over time students develop a more critical eye when completing and evaluating projects. They also gain important insight about the qualities teachers look for in a finished project.

Phyllis Ellett—Grs. 3–4 Multiage, Earl Hanson Elementary
Rock Island, IL

I think I deserve at least a B on my science project.

Todd needs additional help with his multi. facts.

Amber asked several questions about the homework assignment.

QUESTIONNAIRE

1. Did you mispronounce words?
   Frequently   Sometimes   Never
2. Did you skip words?
   Frequently   Sometimes   Never
3. Did you pause in the middle of sentences?
   Frequently   Sometimes   Never
4. Did you use good expression?
   Frequently   Sometimes   Never
5. Did you understand the story as you read?
   Frequently   Sometimes   Never
6. What did you learn about your reading today?
   _____
   _____

DO I SOUND LIKE THAT?

Self-assessment is a powerful tool that has opened many of my students' eyes. I tape-record each student as he reads for 30 seconds or several paragraphs. The student must note the material he read so that he can easily locate it later. I tape about five students on one audiocassette, noting the order on the outside of the cassette. During a quiet, whole-class activity, each student listens to himself on a Walkman™ as he follows along in the book. As a student listens, he fills out a questionnaire like the one shown. Then that child passes the Walkman™ and tape to the next person listed on that cassette.

Lauri Wedel-Isaacs—Gr. 4, L'Ouverture Magnet School, Wichita, KS

SELF-EVALUATION REPORTS

When evaluating I often find that my best resources are the students themselves. I have each child keep a portfolio of his work in a classroom folder. At the end of each quarter, I distribute the folders and have the students organize their work. Students are then asked to reflect on their work of the last quarter and set goals for the next quarter. I guide them through this process by distributing copies of a self-evaluation form (see page 24). I always review this self-evaluation form with parents at the beginning of a conference.

Loraine Moore—Gr. 4, Pearl Prep, El Monte, CA

ANONYMOUSLY YOURS

At the end of each nine-week grading period, I invite my students to write anonymous letters to me. Each student must focus on three topics: the positive, the negative, and suggestions for the upcoming grading period. For each negative that a student includes, she must also write a positive comment or suggestion. As I read the letters, I highlight recurring topics such as too much homework, more homework exemptions, etc. It's often a real wake-up call for me! Sometimes I haven't been aware of some of the things students write about.

I also have each student write the grade she feels she deserves for the nine weeks on another sheet of paper. The student must also explain why she deserves that grade. It's always interesting to see how a student's perception of her progress aligns with mine! I keep these papers on file to share with parents during conferences.

Patricia Dancho—Gr. 6, Apollo-Ridge Middle School, Spring Church, PA

I think I deserve an A because

My
Self-Evaluation

Name_____ Date_____

Directions: After reviewing your portfolio for this grading period, complete the following statements:

1 During this grading period, I enjoyed _____ the

most because _____.

2 I think I made the most progress with _____.

3 I still need to work on _____

_____.

4 My effort on my assignments has been _____

_____.

5 My favorite book I read during this grading period was _____

_____.

6 One goal I have for the next grading period is to _____

_____.

7 I spend about _____ on homework each night.

8 I think I need to improve in the following areas*:

☐ following directions ☐ participating in class discussions

☐ completing work on time ☐ cooperating in groups

☐ bringing supplies to class ☐ listening in class

☐ neatness ☐ spending more time on homework

☐ obeying class rules ☐ _____

* Remember: We *all* have areas in which we need to improve. Be honest.

©The Education Center, Inc. • THE MAILBOX® Intermediate • Feb/Mar 1998 • written by Loraine Moore—Gr. 4, Pearl Prep, El Monte, CA

Fab Friday!

Favorite Activities For Celebrating The End Of The Week

Everyone looks forward to Friday, especially schoolkids (and their teachers)! How can you make it even more special? Take a look at this collection of our readers' ideas for turning Friday into a truly fabulous, fun-filled day.

Fabulous Friday Bingo

My weekly incentive plan culminates with a game of Multiplication Bingo during the last hour of each Friday. Students who turn in all of their required assignments get to play. I give each student markers and a bingo card labeled with the answers to 24 multiplication facts. I call out facts one at a time. A student wins each time she covers a row of correct answers on her card. Students who know their tables well may win several times before all of the 24 facts have been called. Each win is rewarded with a piece of sour candy—a prize my students love! Then, at the conclusion of the game, each child is given a bonus candy, ensuring that everyone wins at least one prize. I've seen amazing results with this incentive. No one wants to miss our Fabulous Friday bingo game!

Margo Moran—Grs. 4–5, Gordon Price Elementary
Hamilton, Ontario, Canada

With A Song In Our Hearts

All the fifth graders in our school join together to celebrate Fabulous Fridays. We integrate music and American history by gathering in the auditorium the last hour to sing patriotic songs and folk songs. Lyrics are displayed on an overhead projector as each song is played one time. A teacher then guides students through the lyrics, discussing vocabulary and the history behind the song or its writer(s). We begin with familiar songs such as "Yankee Doodle" and "This Land Is Your Land." Then we learn songs from the colonial period, the Revolutionary War, the War of 1812, and the westward movement. Students learn about history in a unique way that also promotes cultural literacy. At the end of the year, we culminate our history-through-music study with a musical show. Each class presents a skit and a few songs from a historical period. It's a fun way to showcase hidden talents, and everyone leaves school humming a song!

Alice Boles—Gr. 5, Riley Elementary, Lakewood, CA

Fruity Friday

Every Friday is Fruity Friday in my classroom! Each student brings a piece of fresh fruit from home. Then I choose a time during the day when students may eat their fruit. We've had everything from lemons to mangoes! While students are eating, we play Nutrition Baseball, watch nutrition videos, or play Food-Guide Pyramid games. Sometimes we just chat about what we've learned during the week and discuss our plans for the upcoming weekend. Parents are excited that their children are eating a healthful snack, and the kids love it too! (Keep some raisins on hand for students who forget.)

Amy Miller, Jefferson Elementary, Lincoln, IL

Lollipop Friday

Friday afternoons take a lickin' in my classroom! To celebrate Friday my students have 30 minutes of sustained silent reading, a time when they may choose whatever they would like to read. During this time students are allowed to enjoy lollipops while they read. Each student is encouraged to BYOL—"bring your own lollipop"—for this Friday activity.

Patricia Dancho—Gr. 6, Apollo-Ridge Middle School
Spring Church, PA

Goodie Lottery

I keep a goodie lottery box in my classroom. Whenever I catch a student being nice to a classmate or going out of his way to help someone, I have him write his name on a slip of paper and drop it in the box. Then, on Friday afternoon, I draw a name from the box. The student whose name is drawn gets to choose our Fun Friday activity (from my master list) for the end of the day. Students really work hard to get their names in the lottery box—everyone wants to be the leader of Fun Friday!

Debbie Patrick—Gr. 5, Park Forest Elementary
State College, PA

Book Sharing

My favorite Fabulous Friday activity is a simple one that requires no special materials or advance planning. I have each student make sure that he has his latest library book with him on Friday. Then I divide the class into small groups. Each group gathers in a different site in the classroom. Students spend about 30 minutes sharing their books with one another. What a great way to promote reading and end the week on a positive note!

Faye K. Wells, Marion County Elementary
Buena Vista, GA

Sponge Toss

At a workshop for teachers, I learned a unique stress-management technique that's also perfect for students. I collected several bucketfuls of the very softest foam sponges that I could find. For about ten minutes at the end of each Friday, students are allowed to throw the sponges at one another. The only rule is that the sponges must be thrown below the head. The kids have a blast!

Patricia Dancho—Gr. 6, Apollo-Ridge Middle School
Spring Church, PA

Priority Mail

To help end the week on a positive note, I deliver "priority mail" to my students on Friday morning. I fill a priority mail envelope—such as those from the post office—with positive notes, awards, and all kinds of affirmations. Also inside the envelope is a small musical card that plays a lively tune as an introduction to this Friday ritual. My students and I always look forward to Fridays and the delivery of priority mail!

Pat Madden, Corpus Christi School, Lansdale, PA

It's Game Time!

For a Friday afternoon that's quiet and soothing, I've gotten my students into playing chess and checkers. These tried-and-true strategy games are the perfect solution for providing students with activities that are both fun and enriching. After several weeks of play, the students hold tournaments. Winners of our chess and checkers tournaments are awarded prizes, such as inexpensive chess and checkers games or books from my classroom library.

Patricia Dancho—Gr. 6

Fabulous Friday Quiz Bowl

Get your classroom buzzing with excitement as you review the week's skills with a Friday Quiz Bowl! During the week I collect problems and questions that have been introduced or discussed. I write these questions on notecards and add them to my data bank. On Friday I divide the class into teams of four, with two teams competing at a time. Each team member is given a noisemaker such as a bell or a child's squeak toy. To begin I ask a question or present a problem. The first student to sound off gets a chance to answer it. If the answer is correct, a point is awarded to that player's team. If the answer is incorrect, the other team has 30 seconds to respond. Rounds are five minutes long; then the teams are switched until everyone has played. Fridays ring with excitement as students review the week's skills.

Terry Healy—Gifted K–6, Eugene Field Elementary
Manhattan, KS

Winding Down Another Great Year!

Creative Activities For Ending The School Year

Wow! Another successful school year is winding down. Be sure to save a few ticks on the clock for this great collection of end-of-the-year ideas!

with ideas by Debra Liverman, Karen Martino, Gail Peckumn, and Cynthia Wurmnest

Can Do!

Motivate students to maintain good behavior during the last days of school with this incentive plan. Give each student a slip of paper; then have him write on the slip a reward, such as playing a class game or getting extra recess, that he'd like the class to receive for good behavior. Collect and review the slips before putting them into a large can. Display a poster outlining what is required for you to draw a reward from the can. For example, draw a slip after the class has five successive days of not more than one person turning in a late assignment. Then, every time the class meets the requirements, draw a reward from the can and celebrate the class's can-do attitude!

I'd like to have some free time!

A volcano is a mountain or a hill formed around a crack in the earth's crust. When a volcano erupts, molten rock and other hot materials are thrown out of the crack.

Tube-Time Memories

Turn an end-of-the-year review into a big-screen event! Gather a cardboard box, an art knife, tape, and two wooden dowels slightly longer than the box's width. Next have each student think of one new fact or concept he's learned during the school year. Give each child an 8 1/2" x 11" sheet of white paper on which to briefly but thoroughly explain and illustrate that concept. Direct him to position his paper horizontally as he works. Collect the completed papers and tape them together side to side. Next tape the left edge of the first paper to one dowel and the right edge of the last paper to the other dowel. Wind the papers around the left dowel until all that shows is the last paper. Cut an opening that's slightly smaller than the paper in the bottom of the box. Punch four holes in the box near this opening, one at each corner as shown. Insert the dowels from inside the box so that the paper resembles a TV screen. To view, position the box just over the front edge of a table so that the lower ends of the dowels hang over the table. Turn the right dowel to make the pictures pass across the screen for a fun review of the year's studies. No channel surfing, please!

Two-Way Binoculars

Look two ways at once—back at the past school year and into the future—with this fun project. Give each student crayons or markers, scissors, and a duplicated copy of the binoculars pattern on page 34. Have each student think of one event, such as a field trip or a special project, from the current school year that was especially memorable for him and illustrate it inside the left lens. Next ask him to predict something he anticipates doing during the next school year and illustrate it inside the right lens. Finally have each student color and cut out his binoculars to display on a bulletin board titled "Sighted: Two Great School Years!"

Golden Memories

This school year is almost a memory—so why not ask students to reminisce about it (and practice an important writing skill) through personal narratives? Pique students' interest by reading aloud Mem Fox's *Wilfrid Gordon McDonald Partridge* (Kane/Miller Book Publishers, 1985), a picture book about a boy who wants to know the meaning of *memory* so he can help an elderly friend remember. After sharing the book, have students supply definitions for *memory*. Record the definitions on the board. Then ask each student to write a personal narrative that includes a memory about this year's first day of school, about something in class that made him laugh, or about any other school-year event that—for him, at least—is unforgettable. If desired, allow students to decorate the edges of their papers with gold crayons and share their writings at the end-of-the-year party.

Remember the time Alice Alarm Clock's ringer got stuck?

OHIO

1. The Buckeye State
2. State capital: Columbus
3. Natural borders: Ohio River and Lake Erie
4. Known as the Mother of Presidents
5. First state formed from the Northwest Territory

Name That State!

Fifty is nifty—at least with this review game on the 50 states! Give each student two index cards and assign her two different states to research. Have her write five facts about one state on one card and five facts about the other state on the other card. Collect, shuffle, and place the completed cards in a deck. Form teams of four or five students. Direct Team 1 to draw a card from the deck and read the clues on it to Team 2 one at a time. Give Team 2 five points if the state is guessed on the first clue, four points if it's guessed on the second clue, and so on until the state is correctly identified. Then have Team 2 draw a card and read clues to Team 3 and so on until all 50 states have been guessed. Declare the team with the most points the winner.

From Kudos To Keepsakes

Send students off at the close of this school year with letters they'll treasure! Duplicate a copy of the letter on page 31 for each student. Then personalize a copy of the letter for each child by filling its lines with positive comments. Distribute the letters on the last day of school. The positive impact of these personal notes will be felt longer than you may think!

Trivia Time

Evaluate just how much your students have learned this year by playing a kid-pleasin' trivia game. Form teams of four students per team. Assign each team a different number. Have each team write one question for each subject your class has studied on a different slip of paper; then have the team members store the slips in a small bag labeled with the team's number.

To play, have each team, in turn, draw and answer a question from another team's bag. Award five points for each correct answer. If a question is not answered correctly, allow another team to steal that question, lowering the point value to four, then three, and so on until a team answers correctly. Play until all the questions have been answered. Then declare the team with the most points the winner.

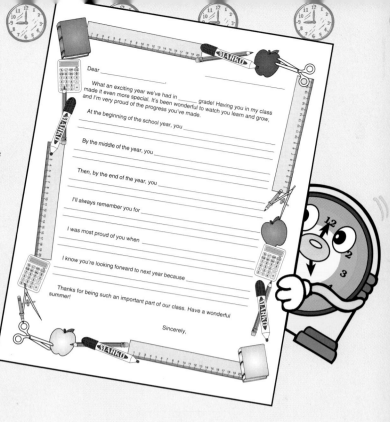

Dear _____,

What an exciting year we've had in _____ grade! Having you in my class made it even more special. It's been wonderful to watch you learn and grow, and I'm very proud of the progress you've made.

At the beginning of the school year, you _____

By the middle of the year, you _____

Then, by the end of the year, you _____

I'll always remember you for _____

I was most proud of you when _____

I know you're looking forward to next year because _____

Thanks for being such an important part of our class. Have a wonderful summer!

Sincerely,

Who invented the grandfather clock?

Father Time?

I Wish I'd Said That!

Invite a few famous people—via their profound quotes—to host an end-of-the-year review of inference skills. Give each student or group of students one copy of page 32. Have students read the quotes on the sheet one at a time, challenging them to dig below the surface for what they think is really being said. After students have completed the sheet, discuss their answers, including what they have written for the Bonus Box.

Follow up by having each student select one quote from page 32 to copy and illustrate on drawing paper. Mount the resulting projects on larger sheets of black construction paper for display. Or have each student illustrate his advice from the Bonus Box on drawing paper. Then bind the papers into a booklet titled "Words Of Wisdom From [your name]'s Students" to give to next year's class.

The Clock Is Ticking!

Use this activity on the last day of school to get in some fun practice with computation. Give each student a calculator, a copy of page 33, and the total number of days he's been absent during the year. Work the first few problems on the sheet with the class; then have students complete the rest of the page as directed.

____

Dear ______________________,

What an exciting year we've had in ______ grade! Having you in my class made it even more special. It's been wonderful to watch you learn and grow, and I'm very proud of the progress you've made.

At the beginning of the school year, you ______________________________
____
____

By the middle of the year, you ______________________________
____
____

Then, by the end of the year, you ______________________________
____
____

I'll always remember you for ______________________________
____
____

I was most proud of you when ______________________________
____
____

I know you're looking forward to next year because ______________________
____
____

Thanks for being such an important part of our class. Have a wonderful summer!

Sincerely,

Note To The Teacher: Use with "From Kudos To Keepsakes" on page 30.

Timeless Quotes

People are often remembered for the things they say. Several quotes from famous people are shown below. Read each quote carefully and think about its meaning. Then write what you think each quote means on the back of this sheet.

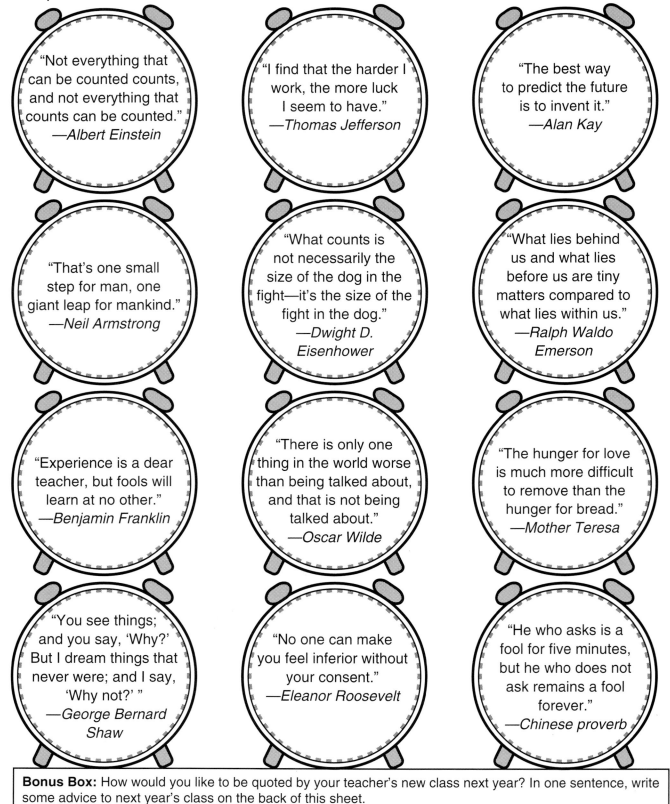

"Not everything that can be counted counts, and not everything that counts can be counted."
—Albert Einstein

"I find that the harder I work, the more luck I seem to have."
—Thomas Jefferson

"The best way to predict the future is to invent it."
—Alan Kay

"That's one small step for man, one giant leap for mankind."
—Neil Armstrong

"What counts is not necessarily the size of the dog in the fight—it's the size of the fight in the dog."
—Dwight D. Eisenhower

"What lies behind us and what lies before us are tiny matters compared to what lies within us."
—Ralph Waldo Emerson

"Experience is a dear teacher, but fools will learn at no other."
—Benjamin Franklin

"There is only one thing in the world worse than being talked about, and that is not being talked about."
—Oscar Wilde

"The hunger for love is much more difficult to remove than the hunger for bread."
—Mother Teresa

"You see things; and you say, 'Why?' But I dream things that never were; and I say, 'Why not?' "
—George Bernard Shaw

"No one can make you feel inferior without your consent."
—Eleanor Roosevelt

"He who asks is a fool for five minutes, but he who does not ask remains a fool forever."
—Chinese proverb

Bonus Box: How would you like to be quoted by your teacher's new class next year? In one sentence, write some advice to next year's class on the back of this sheet.

©The Education Center, Inc. • THE MAILBOX® • Intermediate • June/July 1998

Note To The Teacher: Use with "I Wish I'd Said That!" on page 30. As a research activity, have students use reference materials to find out the occupation or major accomplishments of each person quoted above.

The Clock Is Ticking!

The school year is almost over! Just how much time *do* you think you've actually spent in school? To find out, solve the problems below. Use a calculator for help.

1. Find the number of days you've been in school this year (subtract the number of days you've been absent from the total number of days in your school year):

   _____ – _____ = _____

2. Write the number of hours in your school day: _____
   Minutes in your school day (multiply the hours by 60): _____
   Seconds in your school day (multiply the minutes by 60): _____
   No wonder you're so smart!

3. Write the number of hours you've been in school this year (multiply the answer to Number 1 by the hours in Number 2): _____
   Minutes you've been in school this year (multiply the hours by 60): _____
   Seconds you've been in school this year (multiply the minutes by 60): _____
   You're getting good at this!

4. Write the number of years you've been in school (including kindergarten and this year): _____
   Days you've been in school (forgetting about absences, multiply the years by the days in your school year): _____
   Hours you've been in school (multiply the days by the hours in Number 2): _____
   Minutes you've been in school (multiply the hours by 60): _____
   Seconds you've been in school (multiply the minutes by 60): _____
   Impressive, isn't it?

5. Write the number of years until you graduate from high school: _____
   Days until graduation (multiply the years by 365): _____
   Hours until graduation (multiply the days by 24): _____
   Minutes until graduation (multiply the hours by 60): _____
   Seconds until graduation (multiply the minutes by 60): _____
   Mind-boggling, huh?

6. Write the total number of school days from kindergarten through 12th grade (multiply the number of years by the number of days in your school year): _____
   Hours (multiply the days by the hours in Number 2): _____
   Minutes (multiply the hours by 60): _____
   Seconds (multiply the minutes by 60): _____
   That's a bunch of brainpower, isn't it?

Bonus Box: How many months will you have for fun this summer? Weeks? Days? Hours? Minutes? Seconds? Write your answers on the back of this page.

Note To The Teacher: Use with "The Clock Is Ticking!" on page 30. Before distributing the sheet, tell each student the number of days in the school year and the number of days he/she has been absent during the year.

Pattern

Use with "Two-Way Binoculars" on page 29.

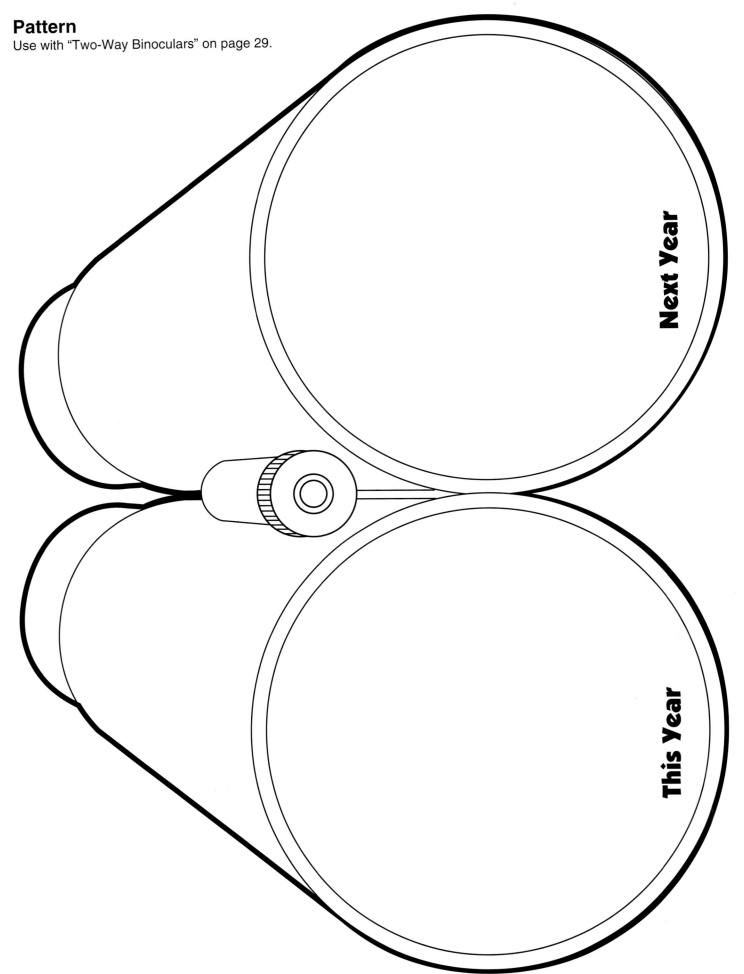

Next Year

This Year

Bulletin Boards

Serve Up A Great Year!

THIS YEAR'S MENU
- mouthwatering map skills
- delectable decimals
- tasty, top-rated novels
- appetizing parts of speech
- savory science topics
- palatable punctuation

AND MORE!

Want to present a mouthwatering glimpse of what the year holds for your new class? Cover a bulletin board with a paper tablecloth; then add paper placemats, napkins, plastic plates and utensils, and empty milk cartons or drink boxes as shown. In the center, add a large menu labeled with a sampling of topics you'll be studying this year or a list of school clubs and activities.

Kari Weston—Gr. 5, Centerville Elementary, Virginia Beach, VA

Motivate students to lend a hand with this colorful helpers display! On a small bulletin board, post library pockets labeled with your classroom jobs. Have each student trace one hand on a sheet of construction paper; then have him cut out the tracing and label it with his name. Assign jobs daily or weekly simply by inserting a hand cutout in each pocket. Decorate the board further with additional hand cutouts. Now isn't that a handy way to assign jobs?

Kathy Hillsman—Gr. 5
Douglas School
Danville, IL

HELPING HANDS

Michael — Pledge
Tisha — Line Leader
Katie — Playground
Clarence — Plants
Charlotte — Papers
Mickey — Assignments
Krista — Lunch Tickets
Andy — Messenger
Min — Windows
Pia — Boards

Pep up a back-to-school discussion of class rules by posting the cheerleader pattern on page 48 on a board as shown. Ask students to brainstorm a list of elements needed for a safe, happy, and productive school year; then have each student write a short cheer on a pennant-shaped cutout. Post the pennants, adding tissue-paper pom-poms to the corners of each. Use the display as a springboard to a discussion of class rules for the year.

Tina Genay—Gr. 4, Winchester School District, Winchester, VA
Ann Wasko—Gr. 4, Windsor School District, Windsor, NY

For a "tree-riffic" back-to-school display, mount a large tree trunk labeled as shown on a bulletin board. Add a green body of leaves labeled with the names of your new students. Also add to the display an enlarged copy of the squirrel pattern on page 48. During the second week of school, select one student to highlight. Duplicate a supply of the nut pattern on page 48 on light brown construction paper. Give a pattern to each child to fill in with a compliment about the student of the week. Pin the nut cutouts along the base of the tree. At the end of the week, send the cutouts home with the special student; then select a new student to feature the following week. Continue until all students have been honored.

Eileen James—Grs. 3–4
St. Matthews Elementary
Louisville, KY

Bulletin Boards ....

Celebrate class birthdays with the help of a doggie that's long on fun! Duplicate the patterns on page 49 onto brown paper. Connect the head and tail with a long strip of brown paper labeled as shown. Have each student write his name and birthdate on a colorful card; then have students arrange the cards as shown to make a giant bar graph. Add balloons, confetti, and streamers for a display that's hot diggity done!

Perry Stio, M. L. King School, Piscataway, NJ

If you're looking for a way to motivate reading, pop this board up in your classroom! Enlarge the popcorn bucket shown and mount it on a bulletin board. Duplicate a class supply of the popcorn cutout on page 50 onto white paper. Have each student fill out his pattern with a brief review of a favorite book; then have him outline the pattern with a yellow marker before cutting it out and pinning it on the board. Use the same idea to make a "Good Work Is Popping Up All Over!" display.

Julie Eick Granchelli—Gr. 4, Towne Elementary, Medina, NY

Recognize good work this fall with a display that's definitely something to crow about! Duplicate several copies of the crow pattern on page 50. Color the beak of each crow yellow; then cut out the crows and mount them with construction paper as shown. Provide each child with art supplies to make a colorful sunflower labeled with his name. Each week post several papers and student sunflowers on the display as shown.

Colleen Dabney—Grs. 6–7, Williamsburg Christian Academy, Williamsburg, VA

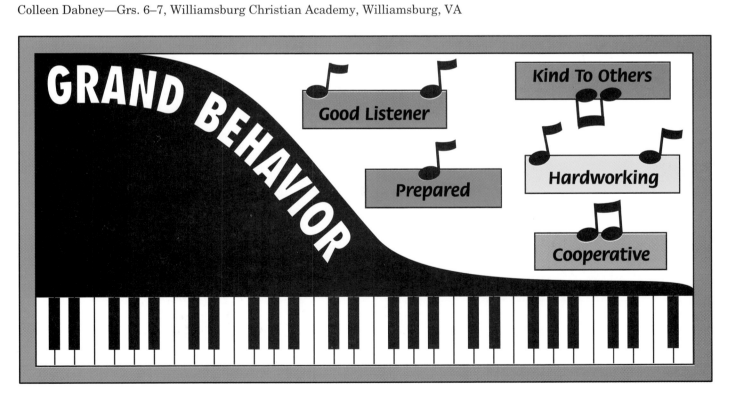

Good behavior is music to any teacher's ears! Decorate a board as shown to resemble a grand piano. Ask your class, "What makes a good student?" List their responses on the board; then have students select the top five. Write these noteworthy qualities on tagboard strips to mount on the board with cut-out notes. Use this idea to display "Grand Work," "Grand Writing," or other student projects.

Colleen Dabney—Grs. 6–7

Bulletin Boards

No time to make a holiday display? No problem! Mount large, white letters as shown on a background of red foil paper. Ask students, "What is it about the holidays that makes you happy?" Let each child write his answer on a letter using a red or green felt-tipped pen. Have students add shiny gold and green self-sticking stars to the background for a simply dazzling display.

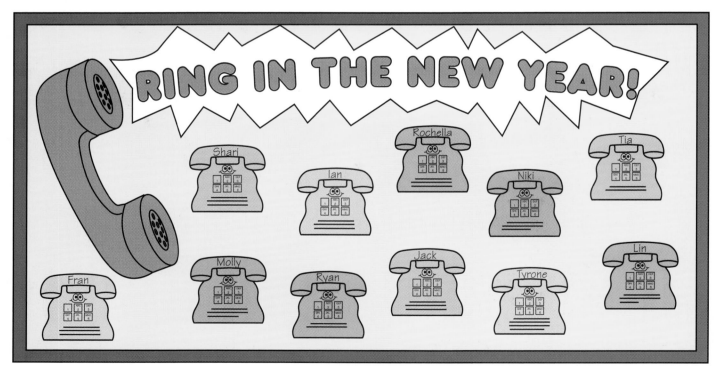

To ring in the New Year, enlarge the phone receiver shown and mount it on a board. Duplicate the pattern on page 51 on light-colored construction paper for each student. Have the student complete the pattern, cut it out, and add it to the board. When you take down the display, keep the patterns. Then return them one morning in February so students can discuss the progress they've made on their goals.

These Are Great Books —
And "Dots" The Truth!

Here's a board that will have your co-workers exclaiming, "Now 'dots' a great idea!" Have each student mount a book report on a large dot cut from neon-colored paper. Decorate the board further with smaller cut-out or self-sticking dots. Change the reports frequently to give students plenty of information about the great books "dot" are in your library!

Marilyn Gill, Noble, OK

For this self-esteem display, enlarge the take-out box shown. Have each student cut a fortune cookie from manila paper and label a white paper strip with his name. Collect the strips; then write a compliment on the back of each. Mount the cookies with the strips as shown. Adapt this for a terrific back-to-school display by writing welcome messages on the backs of the strips.

Colleen Dabney—Grs. 6–7, Williamsburg Christian Academy, Williamsburg, VA

Bulletin Boards ....

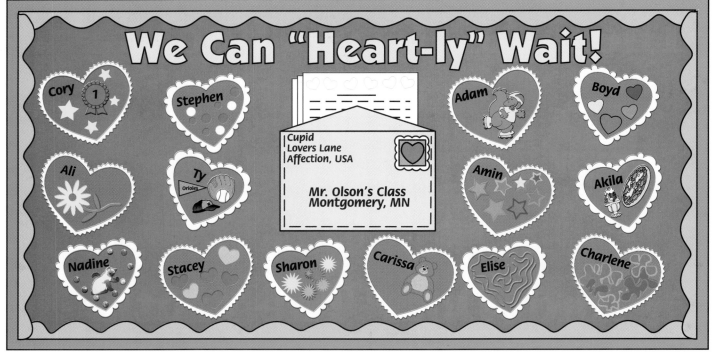

Need a display that "heart-ly" takes any time to make? Staple an envelope cutout to a board as shown to hold seasonal activities. Give each student a heart cutout labeled with his name. Have him decorate his heart at home with family members. Mount finished hearts on doilies. Encourage students to fill their waiting time before Valentine's Day by completing an activity from the board.

David M. Olson—Gr. 5, Montgomery-Lonsdale Middle School, Montgomery, MN

Shine the spotlight on great work! Laminate a yellow circle for each student. Cut a slit in each circle and attach two paper clips. Have each student use stencils to trace his name—connecting all letters—on tagboard. After coloring and cutting out his name, have the student staple it atop his circle. Periodically have each child select a paper to clip on his spotlight, along with a completed copy of the form on page 52.

Bonnie Gibson—Gr. 5, Kyrene Monte Vista School, Tempe, AZ

For a St. Pat's display, duplicate the shamrock on page 52 on green paper for each student. Have each student write about a time when she was lucky—without revealing her identity—on her shamrock. Then have her write her name lightly in pencil on the back of the cutout. Number the cutouts; then pin them to the board. Challenge students to guess the identity of each lucky person. Increase the mystery by adding shamrocks completed by staff members too!

Caroline Chapman, Vineland, NJ

Encourage teamwork with a nifty acronym and this cheery display! Draw slanting lines on a board as shown. Staple cut-out pennants labeled with student names to the lines. Discuss the acronym TEAM (Together Everyone Achieves More!); then post the motto on the board. Each time a student successfully teams up with a classmate, have him describe the situation on an index card to post on the board.

Perry Stio, M. L. King School, Piscataway, NJ

Bulletin Boards ....

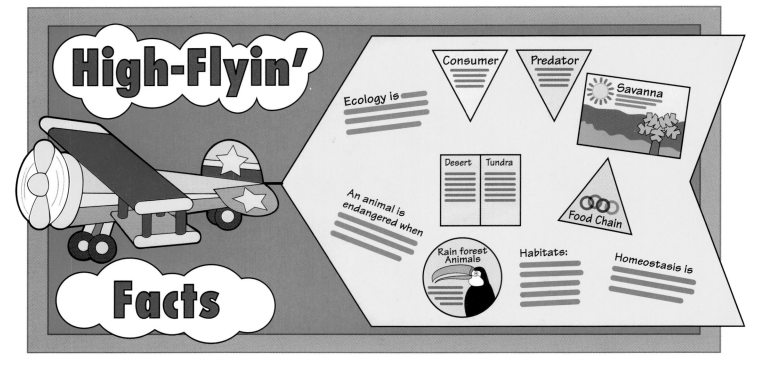

High-Flyin' Facts

Ecology is ____

An animal is endangered when ____

Consumer

Predator

Savanna

Desert | Tundra

Food Chain

Rain forest Animals

Habitats: ____

Homeostasis is ____

Review any topic with this high-flyin' display! Enlarge and color a copy of the plane pattern on page 54. Mount it on a board with a banner-shaped piece of bulletin-board paper. At the end of a unit, have students decorate the banner with facts about the topic. Attach a new banner when you're ready to review the next unit.

adapted from an idea by Jeri Daugherity—Gr. 5, Mother Seton School, Emmitsburg, MD

Our Work Is Tops!

Good! Bryan

Ⓐ Jamal

✓++ Tia

A+ Robbie

✓+ Alexa

✓ Shara

Great! Molly

Ⓐ Kim

Highlight top-notch work with an easy student-made display! Have each student group decorate a copy of the pattern on page 53 together. Post the tops on a bulletin board as shown. Each week ask one group's members to choose their favorite papers to post on the board. When you change groups, remove the tops and have teams decorate new ones for the display.

Colleen Dabney—Grs. 6–7, Williamsburg Christian Academy, Williamsburg, VA

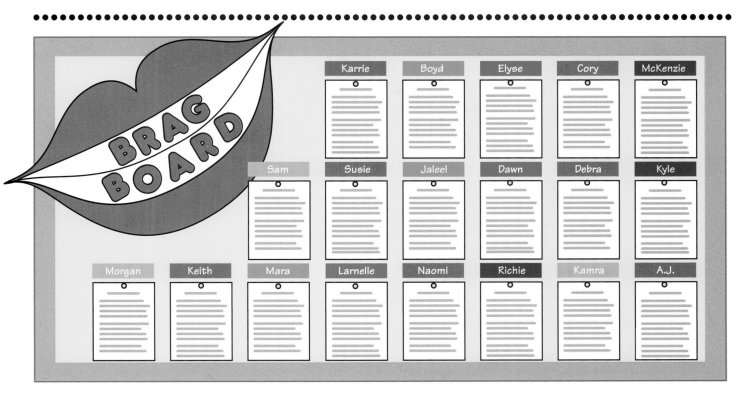

Looking for a display that stays up all year long? Here's one that will put a smile on your face! Post a nameplate for each student on a board decorated with a giant grin. Place a thumbtack under each nameplate. Then let each student post any paper he wants to brag about under his nameplate.

Shannon Hillis—Gr. 5, La Maddalena American School, Italy

Give everyone a "squeak" preview of the week ahead with this year-round display. Label five yellow triangular wedges with the days of the week; then laminate the wedges and post them with a large mouse cutout. Each week use a wipe-off marker to label the cheeses with special events, due dates, and reminders. On Friday simply wipe the display clean and reprogram it for the upcoming week.

Colleen Dabney—Grs. 6–7, Williamsburg Christian Academy, Williamsburg, VA

Bulletin Boards ....

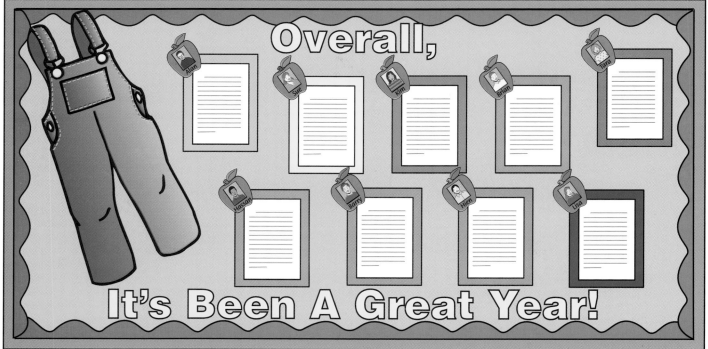

Highlight essays of the school year's most memorable moments with this eye-catching board. Pin a pair of child's overalls to the board. Then have each student color a copy of the apple pattern on page 55, cut it out, and tape a photo of himself on the cutout. Position each child's apple at the corner of his essay.

Tammy D. Taylor—Gr. 6, Franklin Elementary, Mt. Airy, NC

"Orange" you glad this end-of-the-year display is so simple to make? On an orange circle, have each student write a poem telling why one particular event, project, or activity made the year so much fun. Then display the circles with an enlarged orange cutout as shown. Or combine students' poems—each written on a purple grape cutout—into a bunch on a board titled "Fifth Grade Was A Bunch Of Fun!"

Theresa Hickey—Gr. 4, St. Ignatius School, Mobile, AL

Looking for a "bee-utiful" way to encourage good character? Write qualities of good character on bees duplicated from the pattern on page 56. Post the bees as shown. Place a basket of white precut flowers, duplicated from the pattern on page 55, near the board. Each time a student exhibits one of the qualities, have her write her name on a flower cutout, color it, and staple the blossom to the board.

Colleen Dabney—Grs. 6–7, Williamsburg Christian Academy, Williamsburg, VA

Round out the school year with a rollicking year-end review! Give each student construction paper, scissors, markers, and glue for creating any type of ball—a basketball, a playground ball, etc. Next have him write a question that reviews a concept he's learned during the year on the front of his ball and its answer on the flip side. Pin the balls to the board. Read one ball each day during the final weeks of school, challenging students to give the correct answer.

Patterns

Use with the bulletin boards on page 37.

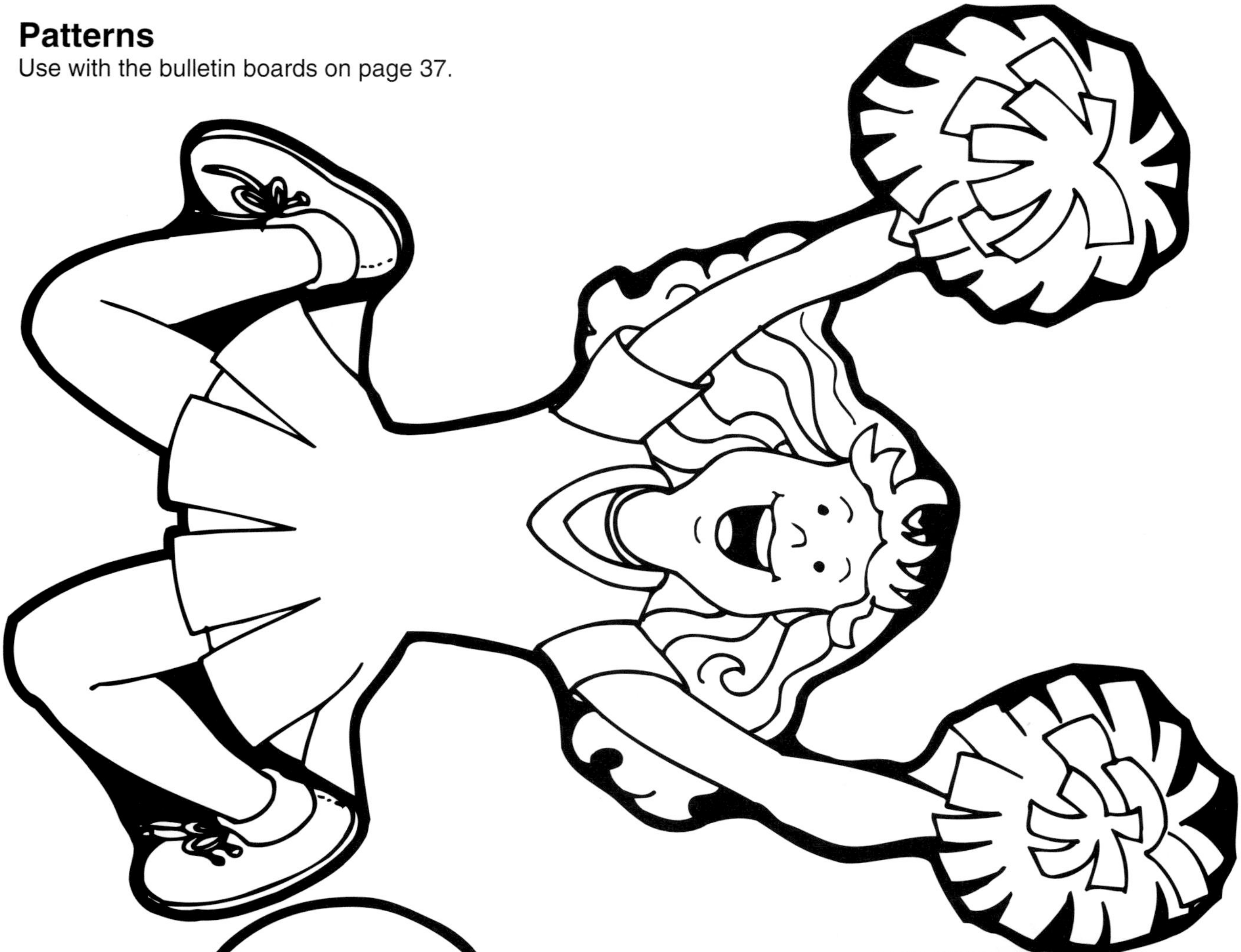

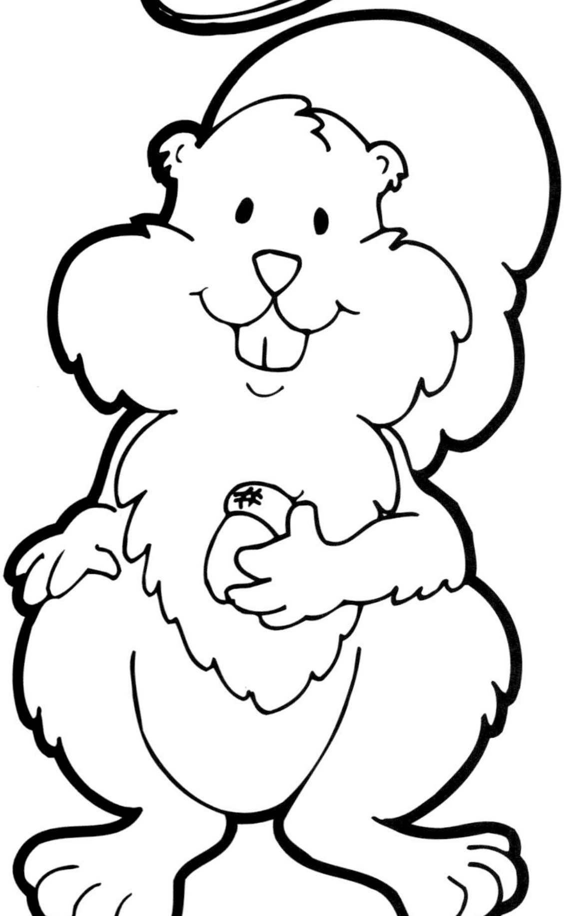

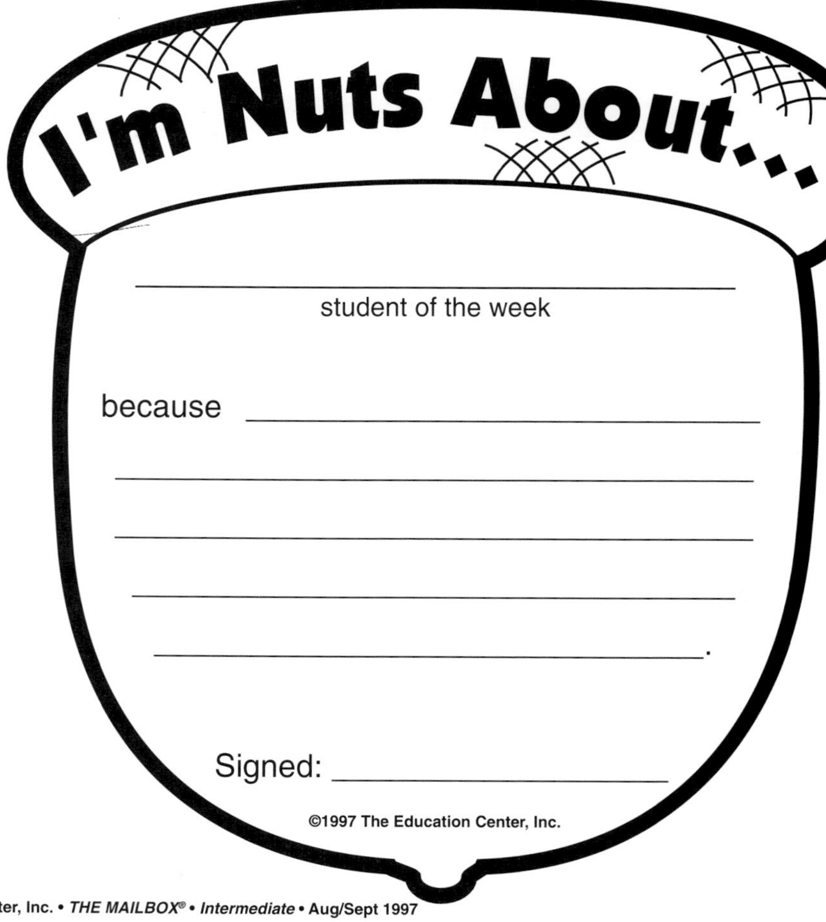

I'm Nuts About...
student of the week
because
Signed:
©1997 The Education Center, Inc.

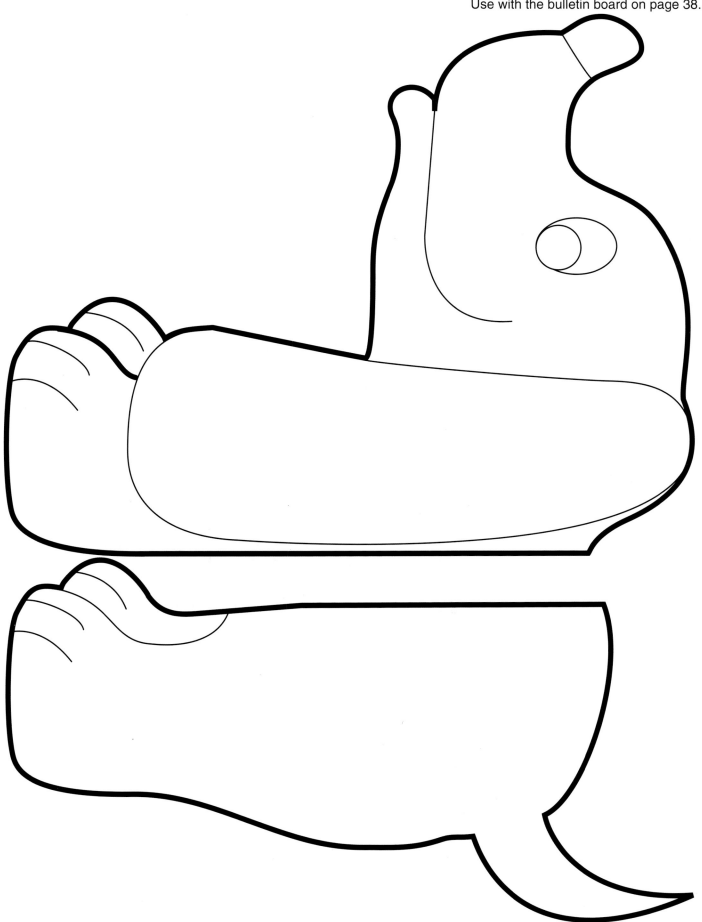

Pattern

Use with the bulletin board on page 40.

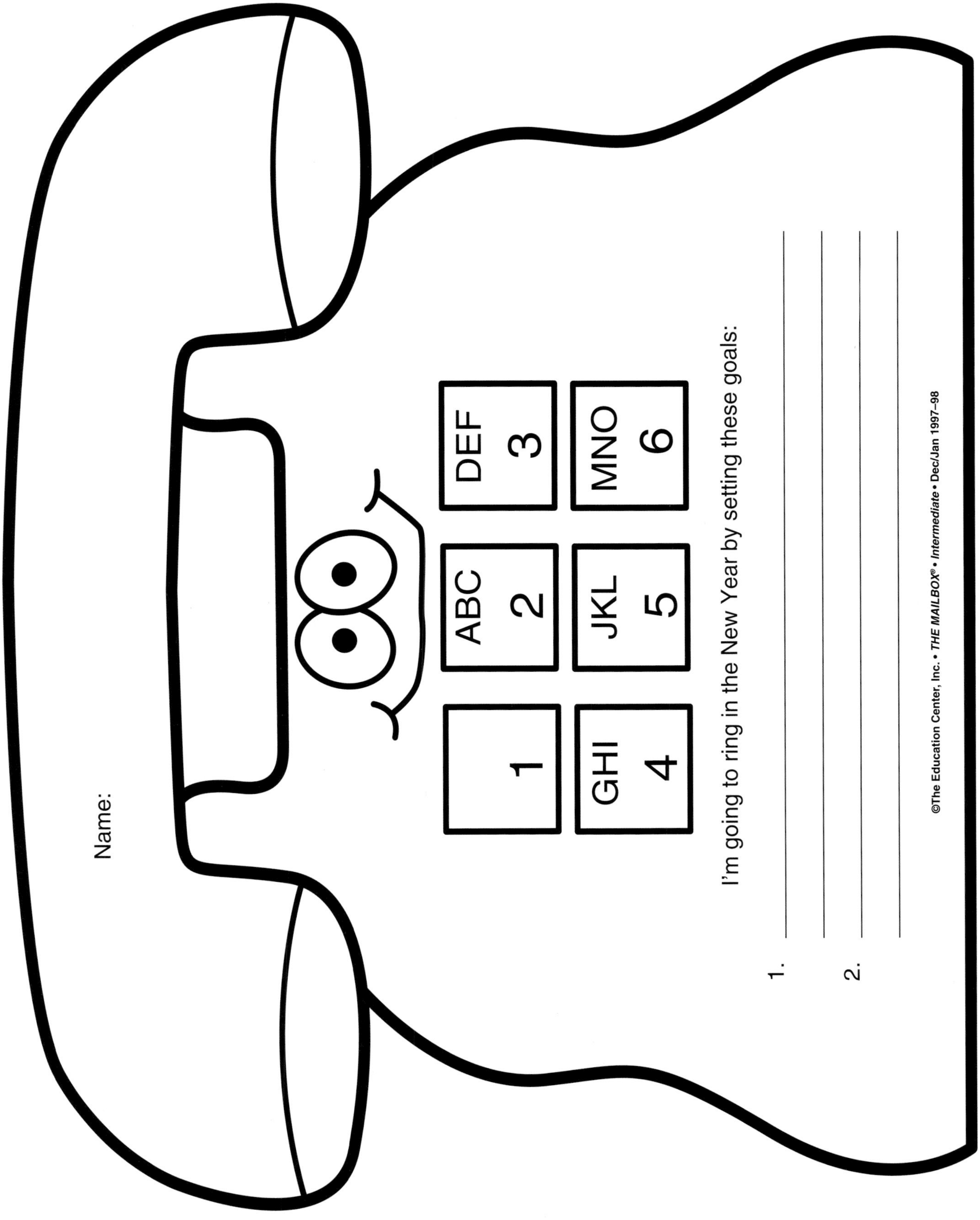

Name:
1
ABC 2
DEF 3
GHI 4
JKL 5
MNO 6
I'm going to ring in the New Year by setting these goals:
1.
2.

Patterns

Use with the bulletin boards on pages 42 and 43.

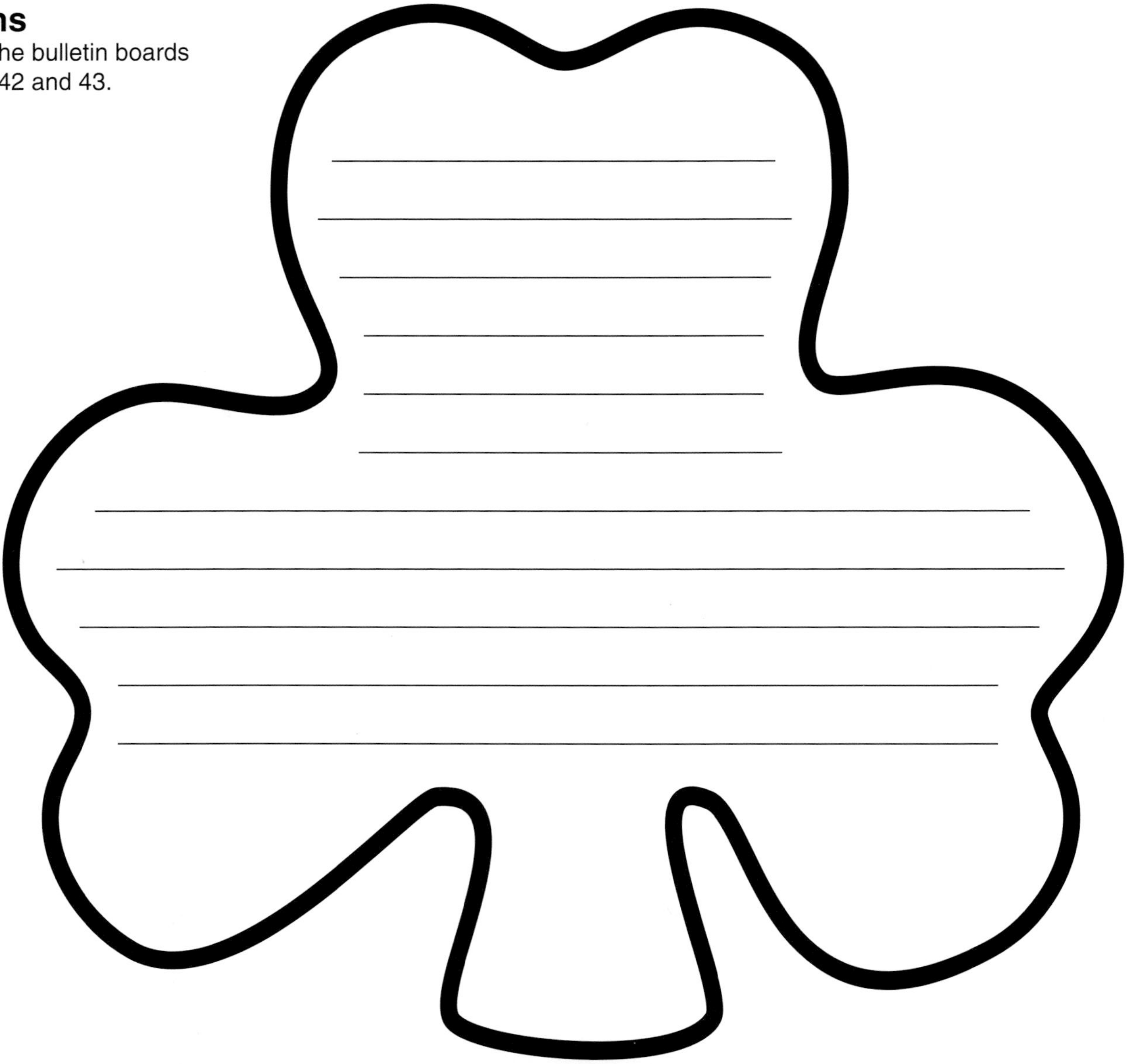

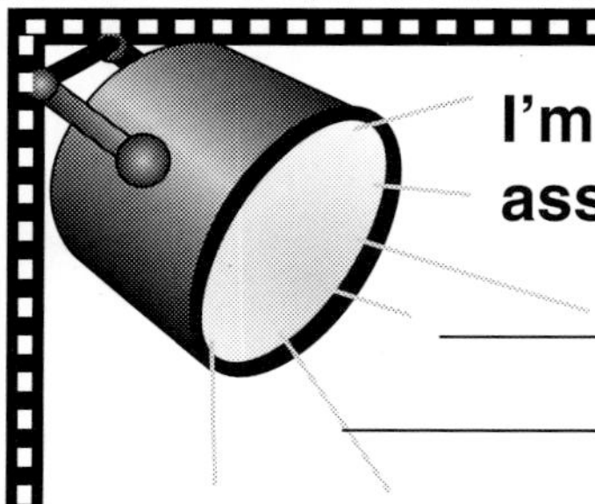

I'm spotlighting this assignment because

_____

_____

_____

_____

_____

_____

Name _____

Date _____

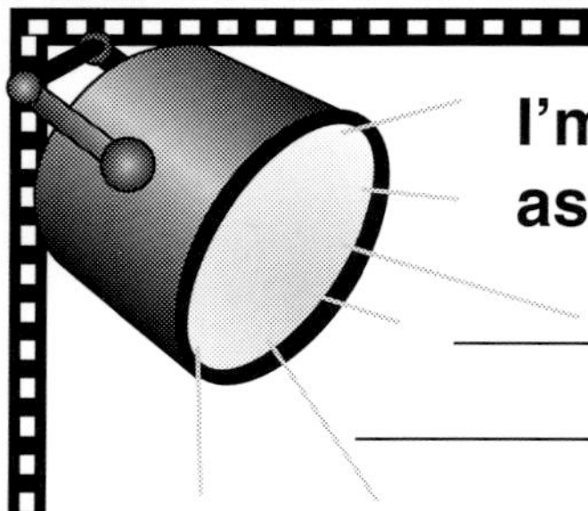

I'm spotlighting this assignment because

_____

_____

_____

_____

_____

_____

Name _____

Date _____

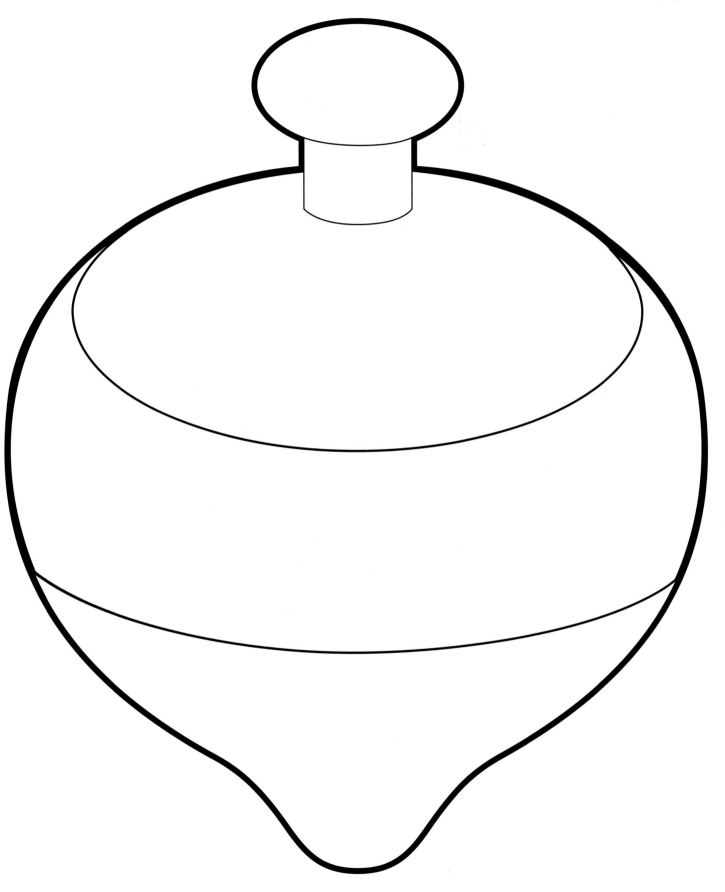

Pattern

Use with the bulletin board on page 44.

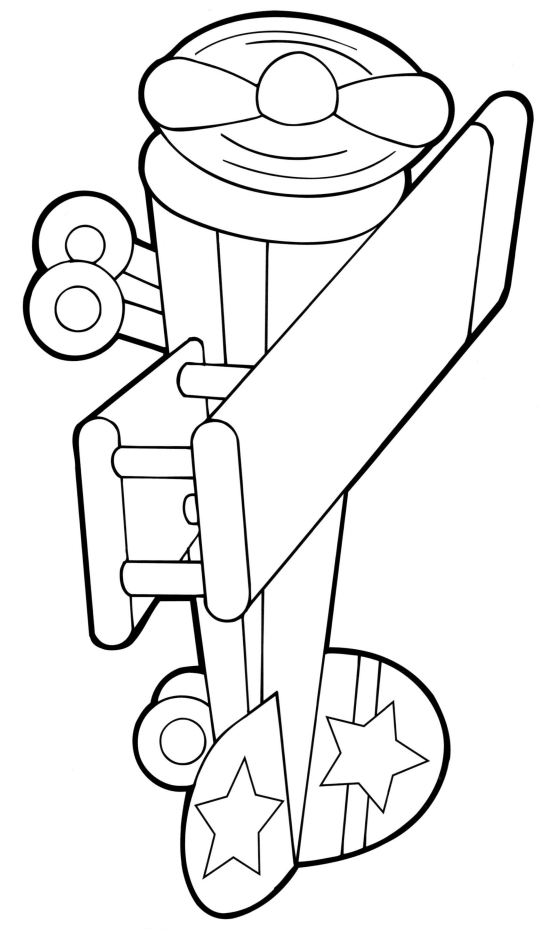

Pattern

Use with the bulletin board on page 47.

ARTS & CRAFTS

Arts & Crafts

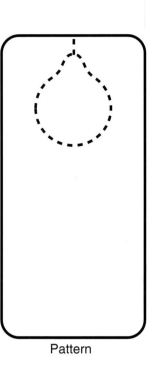

Pattern

Homework Hanger

Introduce this easy arts-and-crafts project to help your students send the message that they're serious about homework! Enlarge the doorknob hanger shown to make a pattern. Then have each student trace the pattern onto a sheet of lightweight cardboard. Direct the student to cut out the hanger and write his name on the back. Collect and paint the front of each hanger with brightly colored spray paint. Allow the hangers to dry; then return them to students. Have each child use cut-out shapes and glitter to decorate his hanger with a design and message to promote a quiet working area. Encourage each student to use the doorknob hanger at home to create a homework-friendly environment.

Paper-Towel Tie-Dye

Your students will be "dye-ing" to take part in this fun, colorful project!

Materials for each student:
one plain, white paper-towel sheet pulled from a roll
newspaper
glue
12" x 14" sheet of construction paper

Setting up the dyeing station: Cover a tabletop with newspaper; then place four 8-oz. clear plastic cups—each filled with a different color of food coloring—on the table. Use more cups and food coloring if you desire additional colors.

Directions for each student:
1. Fold your paper towel in half several times.
2. At the dyeing station, dip each corner of the folded paper towel into food coloring.
3. Unfold the towel and spread it out to dry on a sheet of newspaper.
4. Glue the dried dyed paper towel to a piece of construction paper.

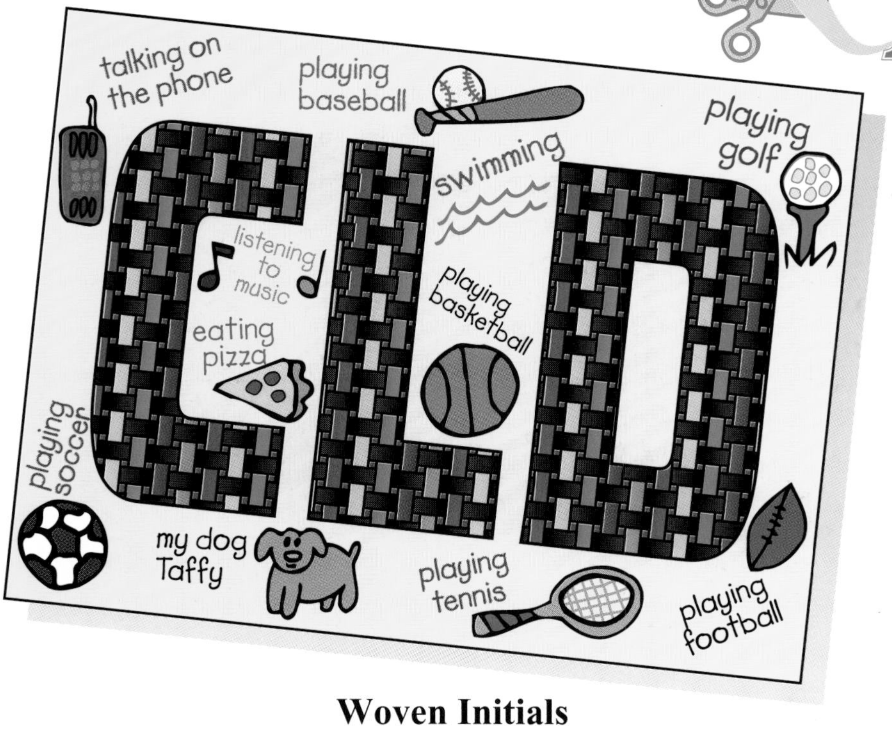
talking on the phone
playing baseball
playing golf
swimming
listening to music
eating pizza
playing basketball
playing soccer
my dog Taffy
playing tennis
playing football

Steps for each student:

1. Trace the letters of your three initials on the pastel paper; then cut them out. Save any center pieces (from an *O, D, P,* etc.) for later use.
2. Glue just the ends of the colored strips to the bright-colored paper in a repeating pattern.
3. Weave the black strips through the colored strips one strip at a time to make a checkerboard pattern.
4. Glue down the loose ends of the black strips.
5. Apply glue to the back of the initials sheet. Glue it on top of the woven sheet (also gluing down any center pieces of letters).
6. Trim away excess ends.
7. Write or illustrate your favorite things with markers in the spaces around each initial.

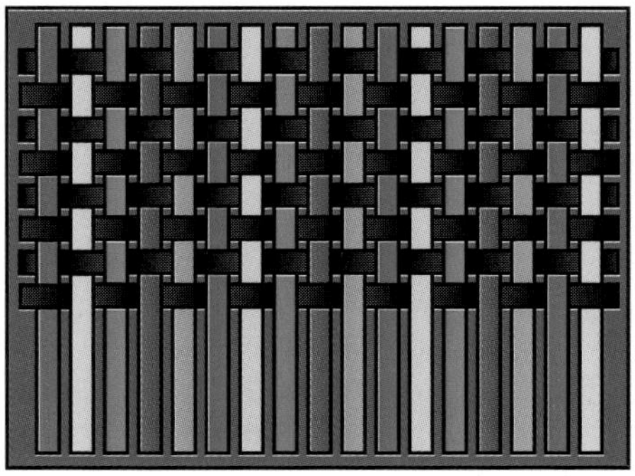

Woven Initials

Help students learn more about one another—and practice the Native American art of weaving—with this attractive back-to-school art project!

Materials for each student:
one 9" x 12" sheet of black construction paper cut lengthwise into 1/2" strips
thirty 1/2" x 9" strips of construction paper: six of each of five different colors
two 9" x 12" sheets of colored construction paper—one pastel, one bright
scissors
glue stick
six-inch block letters for tracing the student's initials
colorful markers
pencil

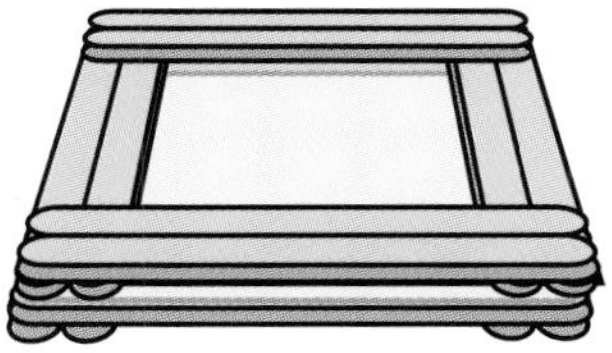

Framed Nature Prints

Take advantage of the abundance of plant life outside during this time of year with an earthy art project. Go on a playground expedition, directing each child to collect interesting plant leaves and flower petals. After returning to your room, provide each student with two 4 1/2" x 4 1/2" pieces of waxed paper. Set up a pressing station in a safe location—complete with an iron, a towel, and a supply of newsprint. Have each student arrange his leaves on the waxy side of one of his pieces of waxed paper. Then have him gently lay the other piece—waxy side down—on top of the arrangement. Ask one student at a time to bring his arrangement to you. Lay a piece of newsprint over the arrangement and place it on the towel. Then, using a warm iron, press gently until the waxed-paper sheets melt together.

After the waxed paper cools, have each student return to his seat with his print. Give each student 16 craft sticks with which to make two eight-stick frames, each with four pairs of sticks glued together as shown. Direct the student to glue the print in between the two frames so that it is enclosed. Then provide paint pens, glitter, and other art materials for each student to use to personalize his frame.

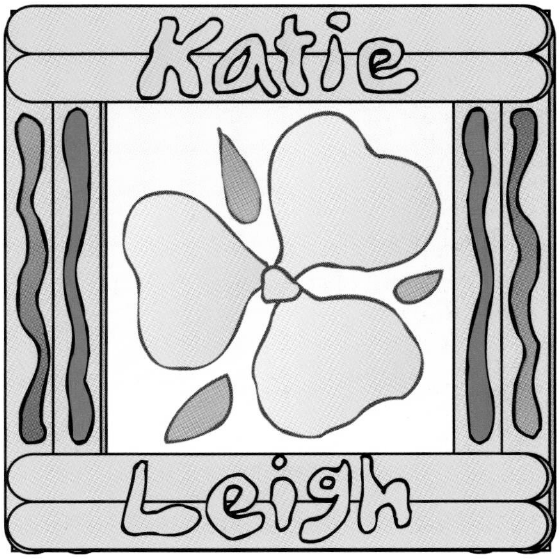
Katie
Leigh

Not-So-Scary Scarecrows

This creative arts-and-crafts project makes a great centerpiece for the harvest season.

Materials for each student:
one cardboard toilet-paper roll with slitted sides
    (see "Materials for the teacher")
one craft stick
one oaktag circle 2" in diameter
raffia
3" segment of wide seasonal craft
    ribbon
mustard (or yellow), green, black, pink,
    white, and orange acrylic craft paint
one thin, black permanent marker
miniature straw hat (purchased inex-
    pensively at a craft store)
glue
scissors
paintbrush
pencil

Materials for the teacher:
hot glue gun with glue sticks
X-acto® knife (use to cut two identical slits—large enough to
    fit a craft stick through—opposite one another approxi-
    mately halfway down each student's toilet-paper roll)

Directions for making the scarecrow:
1. Slide a craft stick through the slits in the toilet-paper roll to
   make arms.
2. Use a pencil to mark off the area for a face on the roll.
3. Next paint the arms and paper roll—except for the face area—using green paint.
4. Paint the face with mustard (or yellow) paint.
5. Glue raffia inside the straw hat to make hair and at the ends of the craft stick to make hands.
6. Have your teacher use a hot glue gun to attach the hat with hair to the top of the toilet-paper roll.
7. Cut the large section of craft ribbon into a triangle shape to make a bandana. Glue the bandana onto the
   roll below the face.
8. Draw the facial features—eyes, nose, and mouth—on the facial area. Then paint the features with white,
   pink, and black craft paint.
9. Next paint the oaktag circle to look like a pumpkin using the orange paint. Add green paint to make a stem
   and let it dry.
10. Write "Happy Harvest!" on the circle with a permanent black marker. Glue the circle with the message
    side outward to the bottom front of the roll.

Jacquelyn Miller—Gr. 6, Townsend School, Vickery, OH

Spooky Spiderwebs

Oh, what webs will be woven by your students with this "spider-iffic" Halloween project! Staple a sheet of black construction paper to a same-sized sheet of oaktag for each student. Direct the student to draw eight radial lines outward from a center point on the oaktag side. Next have the student use a pencil to connect the eight radial lines with line segments to make a web. Give each student a generous length of white yarn and a yarn needle. Have the student knot his thread and bring the needle up through the center point so that the knot is on the oaktag side. Direct the student to stretch the yarn from the center point to the end of each radial line, returning through the center point before beginning a new line. After the student stitches the eighth line, instruct him to stitch the eight connecting segments by bringing the needle up through the midway point of one radial line and down through the midway point of the next. When finished, have the student tie off the yarn on the oaktag side. Finally, provide the student with pipe cleaners for creating a spider to attach to the web.

Joan Mary Macey—Art
Binghamton City Schools
Binghamton, NY

Halloween Sunset

Don't let the sun set on another fall without doing this simple project! Provide each student with a set of watercolor paints and an 11" x 14" sheet of construction paper. Direct the student to select a point on his paper to paint the setting sun. Have students use yellow, red, orange, purple, and blue for the sky. Encourage students to use the lightest of these colors closest to the setting sun and the darker colors farther from it. Next tell students to use the earth tones—brown, green, and black—to paint the earth's terrain. Once the watercolors are dry, have students use black crayons or charcoal to add seasonal silhouetted shapes, such as bats and haunted houses, to the scene.

Phyllis Ellett—Grs. 3–4, Earl Hanson Elementary
Rock Island, IL

Harvest Pets

Fill your classroom with delightful gourd guys and gals this fall! Provide each student with a small gourd, decorative fabric scraps, felt, rubber cement, wiggle eyes, pipe cleaners, and yarn. Direct the student to use the materials to decorate her gourd, taking advantage of the gourd's unique markings and bumps, to reveal its own special personality. Use the decorated gourds as subjects of a narrative writing assignment, having each student describe her gourd's life and adventures. Display the gourds with the narrative writing pieces in your school's media center.

When harvesttime has passed, store the gourds in a dry place for several months to allow them to dry out. Then give them back to students to use as decorative musical instruments.

Susan White, Cranston Johnston Catholic Regional School
Cranston, RI

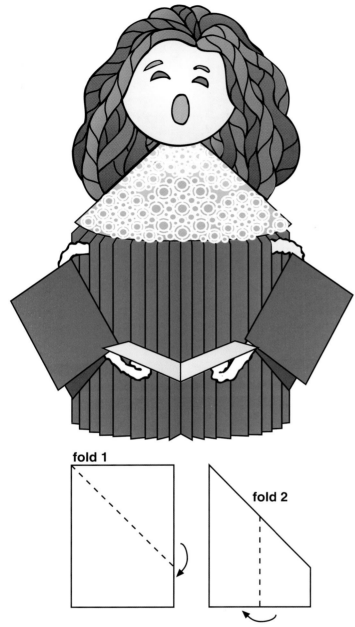

fold 1

fold 2

Christmas Caroler

Sing a song of fun as your students turn old magazines into a choir of Christmas carolers!

Materials for each student: one magazine (preferably the size of a *Reader's Digest*®); spray paint—red, green, or gold; one toothpick; one 3" Styrofoam® ball; yarn—brown, black, or yellow; felt—blue, red, brown, and black; two white pipe cleaners; construction paper; one 5" paper doily; hot glue gun; scissors; ruler

Steps:

1. Fold over the top right-hand corner of each magazine page into the binding as shown.
2. After all pages have been folded, fold them in lengthwise as shown.
3. Fold the magazine until the front cover touches the back cover. With your teacher's help, use hot glue to glue the two covers together.
4. Spray-paint the form red, green, or gold.
5. Glue a pipe cleaner on each side of the figure for arms; then cut construction-paper sleeves to lay over the pipe cleaners.
6. Stick the toothpick in the top of the form. Attach the doily at its base to make a collar.
7. Attach the foam ball to the toothpick for a head.
8. Glue yarn to the head to make hair.
9. Cut facial features from felt and glue them to the head.
10. Cut out a 3" x 2" sheet of construction paper. Fold it in the middle to make a songbook.
11. Glue the songbook to the pipe cleaners.

Shari Medley—Gr. 5
Lakeshore Elementary
Fond du Lac, WI

Snowman Pin

When the weather outside is frightful, try this craft activity to make your day truly delightful! Have each student paint a craft stick white to make a snowman's body. Then direct the student to draw or paint a face at the top of the snowman, leaving enough room to attach a hat. Have the student cut a black top hat from construction paper and glue it on the craft stick. Then have the student wrap a piece of colorful ribbon around the snowman's neck and add additional accessories. Attach a pin back to each finished snowman. Have each student wear his pin or give it as a gift.

Andrea Troisi—Librarian
LaSalle Middle School, Niagara Falls, NY

Holiday Package Pins

Wrap up your holiday arts-and-crafts activities with this easy-to-make gift idea.

Materials for each student: holiday wrapping-paper scraps; three cardboard rectangles of various sizes, no larger than 1 1/2" in length or width; glue; one pin back; clear tape; assortment of 1/8-inch-wide satin ribbon in Christmas colors; scissors

Steps:

1. Wrap each cardboard rectangle in wrapping paper.
2. Tie a bow on each package using 1/8-inch-wide satin ribbon.
3. Overlap the edges of the three rectangles and glue them together.
4. Attach the pin back to the back of the arrangement.

Donna Vanaselja—Gr. 6
Sherwood Elementary
Melbourne, FL

body

Crafty Christmas Mouse

This is one mouse your students will be happy to have stirring around the house this holiday season!

Materials for each mouse: one red or green felt square; one candy cane; two wiggle eyes; one red or green pom-pom; glue; scissors; ruler

Steps:

1. Use the patterns shown to cut the two mouse body parts from the felt.
2. Cut two 3/4" slits 1/2 inch apart in the middle of the mouse body where indicated.
3. Slide the oval shape through the slits in the body to make mouse ears.
4. Glue the wiggle eyes and the pom-pom nose at the pointy end of the mouse body.
5. Insert the straight end of the candy cane through the portion of the mouse ears that is located on the mouse's underside.

Merrill Watrous
Eugene, OR

ears

63

Crayon Ornament

Use an old standby from your art cabinet—crayons—in this fun ornament-making project.

Materials for each student: small wooden or heavy cardboard star; yellow craft paint; paintbrush; fishing line; craft glue or a hot glue gun; scissors; three crayons; black permanent marker

Steps:

1. Paint the wooden star yellow.
2. Glue three crayons together into a pyramid shape as shown.
3. Write your name and the year on the star using a black permanent marker.
4. Glue the star to one side of the crayon pyramid.
5. Glue a loop of fishing line to the star to use as a hanger.

Marcia Miller—Gr. 4, Merritt Elementary, Mt. Iron, MN

Candy-Cane Centerpiece

Brighten your school cafeteria or teachers' lounge this holiday season with these cheery seasonal centerpieces.

Materials for each pair of students: one red or green 14" taper candle; eight candy canes; one thick rubber band; one 12" length of one-inch-wide satin ribbon with a seasonal pattern; one 3" x 6" sheet of paper; markers

Steps:

1. Hold the eight candy canes in a bundle with the curved portion of each one facing outward.
2. Tightly wrap the rubber band around the candy canes about halfway down.
3. Slip a 14" taper candle into the middle of the arrangement.
4. Arrange the candy canes so that they are evenly spaced.
5. Tie a bow of satin ribbon around the arrangement to cover the rubber band.
6. Fold the piece of 3" x 6" paper in half to make a gift card for the centerpiece. Decorate the card with markers.

Merrill Watrous
Eugene, OR

Seasonal Scenes

For a "can-do" holiday activity that's as fun as it is unique, try this teacher-tested project!

Materials: Pringles® can; art knife; holiday wrapping paper; glue; scissors; lace or rickrack; white tissue paper; assorted colors of construction paper and other art supplies; ruler

Steps:

1. Cut a four-inch-tall oval in the middle of the Pringles® can as shown.
2. Cut a 9" x 11" sheet of wrapping paper; then glue it to the can.
3. Trim the wrapping paper from the cut-out oval section.
4. Decorate around the cut-out oval and the top and bottom of the can using lace or rickrack.
5. Stuff the bottom portion of the can with white tissue paper to make snow.
6. Decorate the inside of the can with a special winter scene, such as a snowman or Christmas tree. Or use a pinecone to create a winter animal to place in the can.

English Valentine Crackers

Crack open one of these fun Valentine's Day favors for an extraspecial holiday!

Materials for each cracker:
one toilet-paper tube
white paint
one 2" heart-shaped cookie cutter
one 9" x 12" sheet of red tissue paper
two 6" lengths of white curling ribbon
conversation hearts or other Valentine's Day candy
aluminum pie pan or foam meat tray

Steps:
1. Pour a small amount of white paint into the pan or tray.
2. Dip the cookie cutter into the paint; then use it to stamp outlines on the tissue paper.
3. Let the tissue paper dry overnight.
4. Place an empty toilet-paper tube in the center of one 9-inch end of the paper.
5. Roll up the tube in the paper.
6. Tie one end of the paper together with curling ribbon.
7. Fill the tube with conversation hearts or other candy.
8. Use a length of ribbon to tie up the paper at the open tube end.
9. When you're ready, pull on the two tied ends to crack open your valentine cracker!

Use different cookie cutters, candy, and colors of tissue paper to make crackers for other holidays throughout the year.

Ann Scheiblin—Gr. 6
Oak View Elementary
Bloomfield, NJ

Irish Garden

You'll love this St. Patrick's Day project that's great on the eyes, yet easy on the supplies! Give each student a sheet of 9" x 12" white paper. Divide your class into groups of four. Direct each group member to use a green marker or crayon to cover his entire sheet with a St. Patrick's Day pattern that resembles a wrapping-paper design. When he's finished, have each student cut his paper into four equal rectangles. Direct the student to give one rectangle to each member of his group and keep one for himself. Have the student trace a flower petal on each of his four rectangles and cut out the petals. Then have him glue his petals, a green-paper stem and leaves, and a decorative center to construction paper. Finally have the student cut out his flower. Attach the completed flowers to a bulletin board to create a display that's sure to make Irish—and non-Irish—eyes smile!

Barbara Samuels
Rockaway, NJ

Valentine Bags

Help students transport their Valentine's Day goodies home from school with these sturdy, easy-to-make bags!

Materials for each student:
one plain, white lunch bag
one two-foot length and one one-foot length of rug yarn
scissors
glue
construction paper
marker
ruler

Steps:

1. Fold down the top two inches of the lunch bag toward the inside of the bag.
2. Cut a 1/4-inch notch at the top of each of the two shorter sides of the bag as shown.
3. Tie the two-foot length of rug yarn into a loop.
4. Place the yarn loop around the bag underneath the folded edge.
5. To make a handle, tie the ends of the one-foot yarn length to the parts of the yarn loop sticking out from the notches on the bag's sides.
6. Pull up on the handle and glue down the edges of the bag to seal in the yarn loop.
7. Glue heart-shaped, construction-paper cutouts to the bag's front. Write your name on the bag.

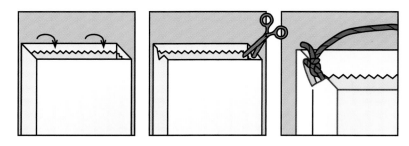

Glow-In-The-Dark Art

This fluorescent art project is sure to brighten up your classroom! Cut different-colored fluorescent paper into squares measuring 1 1/2 inches and larger. Give each student a 9" x 12" sheet of black construction paper and several of the squares. Have the student fold each square in half along the diagonal; then have him fold the two endpoints so that they meet in the middle as shown. Next direct the student to glue the folded shapes onto the black paper to make a 3-D design. Provide additional fluorescent paper so students can cut out shapes to mix in among the folded figures.

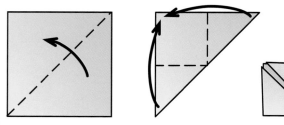

Joan M. Macey—Grs. 4–5
Benjamin Franklin School, Binghamton, NY

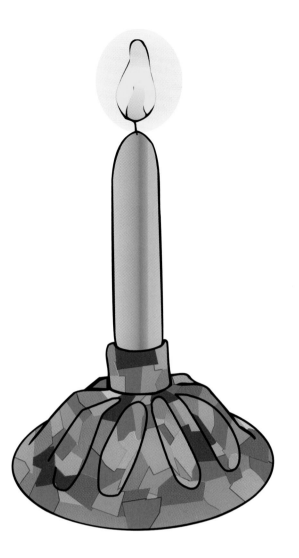

Arts & Crafts

Colorful Candleholder

Show Mom how much she lights up your life with the following art activity.

Materials for each student:
empty 1-gallon Gatorade® bottle
plastic top from a syrup bottle
colorful tissue paper
art glue

water
paintbrush
paper cup
scissors

Steps for the teacher:
1. Several weeks prior to this art activity, have students bring in the Gatorade® bottle and plastic top from home.
2. Carefully cut off the bottom of each Gatorade® container. Trim it into a circular shape around the flower-shaped bottom.

Steps for the student:
1. Pour a small amount of glue into a paper cup; then thin the glue by adding a few drops of water.
2. Tear the tissue paper into small pieces.
3. Using the paintbrush, apply glue to a tissue piece and place it on the underside of the Gatorade® piece. Continue until the piece is completely covered with tissue.
4. Glue tissue paper to the inside of the syrup bottle top.
5. Let the Gatorade® piece and syrup top dry completely. Then glue the syrup top to the center of the Gatorade® piece as shown.
6. After the project dries, place a candle in the holder.

Colleen Dabney—Grs. 6–7, Williamsburg Christian Academy, Williamsburg, VA

Mother's Day Flowerpot

Plant a smile on Mom's face this Mother's Day with this easy gift idea.

Materials for each student:
one 4-inch clay flowerpot, prepainted with any color spray paint
paintbrush
stencil craft paint (variety of colors)
acrylic sealant
1 sheet of tissue paper
1-foot length of thin ribbon
10 Hershey's® Hugs® and Kisses® candies
optional—small sponges or stencils

Steps:
1. Paint your pot with colorful designs. If desired, sponge-paint or stencil your pot.
2. After the paint dries, have the teacher spray your pot with acrylic sealant to protect it and add shine.
3. Place ten Hershey's® Hugs® and Kisses® candies in the center of the tissue-paper sheet.
4. Gather the edges of the tissue together and tie it with the ribbon; then put it inside the flowerpot.
5. Fluff the tissue paper; then deliver your hugs and kisses to Mom with love!

Christine Smyth—Gr. 5, Frank Jewett Elementary, West Buxton, ME

Big Is Better!

Need a simple art activity to liven up a class struck by spring fever? Draw a square grid on a page from a coloring book. Cut on the grid lines; then give each student one piece of the picture. Have each child proportionally draw and color the design from his piece onto a nine-inch square piece of paper. Mount the students' enlarged drawings together on a bulletin board or classroom wall to re-create the original picture. You can bet that the interesting result will make a BIG impression on everyone!

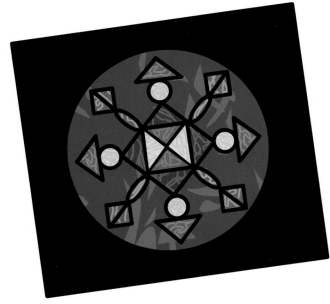

Glorious Stained Glass

Add a little color to a unit on medieval times or geometry (see pages 123–128) with the following activity.

Materials for each student:
1 sheet of graph paper
1 pencil
one 8" x 11 1/2" sheet of clear (transparency-quality) plastic
Sharpie® markers, various colors including black
aluminum foil
tagboard
tape
scissors
2 paper clips

Steps:
1. Draw a large circle on the graph paper with the pencil. In the circle's center, draw a basic geometric shape.
2. Continue the design by adding to the top, bottom, and sides of the original shape. Use straight and curved lines, allowing the graph paper to be your guide.
3. After the pencil design is complete, place the clear plastic sheet on top of the graph paper. Clip the sheets together.
4. Using a black Sharpie® marker, trace the design onto your plastic.
5. Use a variety of colored Sharpie® markers to color in the design.
6. Crinkle a piece of foil; then smooth it out. Tape the plastic sheet atop the foil.
7. Draw a circle slightly smaller than your design on the tagboard. Cut out the circle.
8. Tape the plastic/foil sheet behind the tagboard frame.

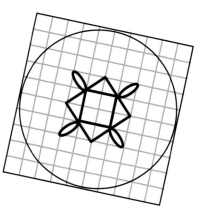

Merrill Watrous, Eugene, OR

My, How
Elizabeth
Has Grown!

My, How We've Grown!

Plant the seed for some great memories with this end-of-the-year art activity! Have each student follow the directions at the right to make a flowerpot flip book. Display students' completed books on a bulletin board titled "We've Really Grown This Year!"

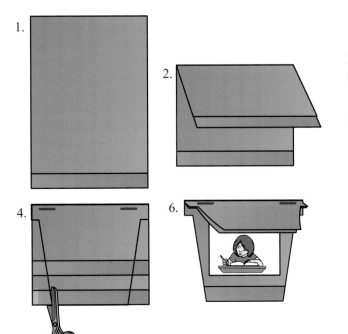

Materials for each flower: eight 6" x 6" pieces of different-colored tissue paper, 1 green pipe cleaner, green construction paper, scissors, transparent tape

Directions for making the flower:
1. Stack the eight pieces of colored tissue paper on top of each other.
2. Fold the tissue-paper sheets accordion style, like a fan.
3. Secure the arrangement in the middle with one end of the green pipe cleaner. Leave the remaining portion of the pipe cleaner for a flower stem.
4. Spread out the tissue paper on either side of the pipe cleaner.
5. Carefully pull each layer toward the middle to make a flower.
6. Cut out two leaves from green construction paper.
7. Tape the leaves to the flower stem.

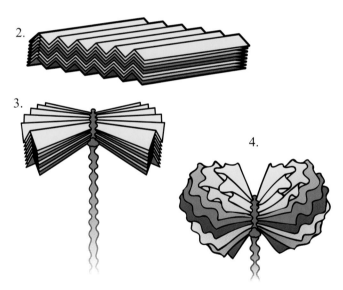

Materials for each flowerpot: two 6" x 8" sheets of brown construction paper, three 4" x 5" sheets of white paper, 1 stapler, 1 pencil, crayons, glue, scissors, transparent tape, 1 ruler

Directions for completing the project:
1. Stack the two 6" x 8" sheets of brown construction paper so that the top edges are three-quarters of an inch apart.
2. Fold over the top half to form four layers as shown.
3. Staple the book at each side near the top of the fold.
4. Draw the outline of a flowerpot on the flip book and cut it out.
5. Draw and color a memorable event from the school year on each of the three white paper sheets.
6. Glue each drawing to one of the bottom three flaps of the book.
7. Decorate the cover of the flip book with a title as shown.
8. Tape the pipe-cleaner stem to the back of the flowerpot.

Cindy Campbell
Boswell Elementary
Lebanon, MO

69

Beauty And The Beach

Re-create the beauty of the ocean with an arts-and-crafts idea that's "shore" to be a hit with your students!

Materials for each student:

sand—natural and blue; craft glue; shaving cream; 1 paintbrush; 1 small paper cup; 1 craft stick; 3 small seashells; one 5" x 8" sheet of watercolor paper or poster board; 1 pencil; scrap paper; water

Water on the beach,
washing over grains of sand,
flowing back to sea.

Directions:

1. Cover the bottom half of the watercolor paper with a layer of glue. If necessary add water to the glue for easier spreading. Evenly spread out the glue using the paintbrush.
2. Sprinkle natural-colored sand at the bottom of the paper to create a layer of beach sand.
3. Sprinkle blue sand above the natural sand to create a layer of ocean water as shown.
4. Glue small shells on the natural sand.
5. Using the craft stick, mix equal parts of shaving cream and craft glue in the small paper cup.
6. Add a couple of lines of the shaving-cream mixture along the top edges of the blue sand to create ocean spray and breaking waves. Let the picture dry.
7. Write a haiku poem about the ocean on a sheet of scrap paper. Copy the final version of the poem in the space above the ocean scene.

Colleen Dabney—Grs. 6–7
Williamsburg Christian Academy
Williamsburg, VA

Personalized Pencils

Are your students getting restless? Never fear! This end-of-the-year craft activity will have them pushing pencils again in no time!

Materials for each student:

1 sharpened pencil; transparent tape; embroidery floss in three different colors; 1 ruler; assorted small beads; scissors; craft glue

Directions:

1. Cut a four-inch length of embroidery floss. Tie a double knot near one end. String a small bead on the floss; then add additional beads. Tape the unknotted end of the floss to the top of the pencil, right below the metal band.
2. Cut a five-foot length of floss. Tape one end to the top of the pencil beside the string of beads. Wrap the floss tightly around the pencil ten times, being sure to cover the taped ends.
3. String a small bead on the floss; then push it up to the pencil. Keep winding the floss tightly, adding a bead about every ten times around. When about a third of the pencil is covered, tape the floss to the pencil and trim off any excess floss.
4. Choose a different-colored piece of floss and cut a five-foot length. Tape the end of the new floss right where the end of the old one is taped. Begin winding the floss, continuing to add a bead about every ten times around.
5. When the middle third of the pencil is covered, choose another color of floss and repeat Step 4 with the remainder of the pencil.
6. Dab a small amount of glue at the bottom of the pencil to hold the final floss in place.
7. Let the pencil dry.

Note: To sharpen the pencil, first unstick the glued end of the floss. Then unwind the floss, trim off the excess, and sharpen the pencil. Glue the end of the floss back in place.

LANGUAGE ARTS UNITS

Blueprints For Building A Better Paragraph

How is a well-constructed house similar to a well-written paragraph? To be structurally sound, a house must have a roof—just as an effective paragraph needs a topic sentence. Serving the same purpose as the walls in a house are the supporting details that give a paragraph its form. Finally, a house has a foundation to pull things together just as the concluding sentence does in a paragraph. Use the fun-filled activities in this unit to get your students writing paragraphs that are sure to hit the nail right on the head!

with ideas by Simone Lepine

Building The Basic Paragraph

Shoring Up The Details

Use this fun exercise to emphasize the importance of writing paragraphs that contain strong details supporting the topic sentence. Fill a paper grocery bag with items commonly found in a kitchen—a measuring cup, mixing spoon, saltshaker, wire whisk, etc. Then add a toothbrush or other nonkitchen item to the bag. Point out to students that successful paragraph writing involves having supporting details that relate to the topic sentence. Empty the bag and ask students to describe what the contents share in common. Then ask them to point out anything that does not belong. Explain that a good paragraph's supporting details are directly related to its topic sentence—just as the items in the kitchen bag should all relate to the kitchen. As a follow-up to this activity, provide practice writing a paragraph by giving each student a copy of page 77 to complete.

Framing A Good Paragraph

Show your students the building blocks for an effective paragraph with this hands-on activity. Have each student bring a shoebox from home. Instruct the student to write a paragraph about his favorite room in his house, making sure to include the three parts of a paragraph—a topic sentence, supporting details, and a concluding sentence.

Next provide a supply of cardboard, scissors, tape, glue, and markers. Explain to each student that he will be constructing a model home from his shoebox. Demonstrate that each shoebox should have three or four rooms, made by inserting cardboard pieces into the box as walls. After each student has constructed his walls, have him use additional cardboard to make a removable peaked roof to rest on top of the box. Have each student place his lid underneath the box without attaching it; then have him decorate his box. Next direct the student to record each sentence of his paragraph on a separate strip of paper. Have him glue the topic sentence on the box roof, each supporting detail to the floor in one of the rooms, and his concluding sentence inside the box lid. Then hold an Open House, allowing students to tour all of the model homes.

My favorite room in my house is the kitchen.

I like it best because it is very comfortable.

These are the many reasons the kitchen is my favorite room.

I also like the kitchen because I enjoy baking.

Each night my family eats dinner together in the kitchen.

The Fab Four

There are four basic types of paragraphs, each serving a different purpose:
expository—explains how to do something; provides sequential instructions
persuasive—expresses an opinion; offers evidence to support the opinion
descriptive—describes something using sensory-related details
narrative—tells a story: beginning, problem, and resolution
Below and on the following pages, you'll find creative, easy-to-do activities to help you teach your students how to write each of these types of paragraphs.

Building Expository Paragraphs

Brick By Brick

Build a wall of sequence words to support your students' expository writing with this easy idea. Cut a supply of rectangular bricks from red paper. Then gather several how-to books containing sequence words—arts-and-crafts books, cookbooks, etc. Pair students and provide each pair with a how-to book, a blank overhead transparency, and a dry-erase marker. Direct each pair to select an expository, or how-to, page in its book. Have the partners lay the transparency on top of the page and highlight any sequence words they locate. As pairs share their highlighted words, record each new sequence word on a brick. Attach tape to each brick's back; then brick by brick, build a wall of sequence words by attaching the bricks to a wall or bulletin board. Discuss with students how sequence words serve as the building blocks for a well-written expository paragraph. Encourage students to refer to the sequence-word wall as they write their own expository paragraphs.

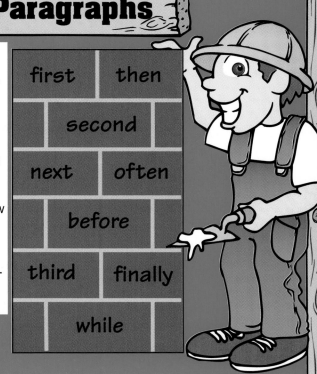

first | then
second
next | often
before
third | finally
while

At Home With Your Students

Martha Stewart will be green with envy when she gets a load of the at-home expository paragraphs your students write! Provide each student with a copy of page 78; then review the directions for writing a how-to paragraph on the sheet. After each student has completed her sheet, have her share her how-to paragraph with the rest of the class.

Wringing Out Great Writing

Use this creative lesson to equip students with the skills they need to write effective how-to paragraphs. Challenge each student to write an expository paragraph about one of these topics: making a milk shake, sharpening a pencil, riding a bike, playing a card game, making lemonade, writing a friendly letter, making a sandwich, or heading a paper. Check each student's paragraph to ensure he has included the necessary elements as well as sequence words.

Next provide each student with one copy of page 79 (giving any student whose paragraph is longer than five sentences an additional copy). Have each student cut out the clothing on his sheet; then have him record one sentence from his paragraph on each garment. Give each student a paper clip for each garment along with a length of yarn. Direct the student to clip the clothing to the yarn in random order. Pair students; then have one student hold his clothesline up while the other reads the sentences and rearranges them in the correct order. Have the partners switch and repeat the procedure. For more practice, place each student's paragraph parts, yarn, and paper clips in an envelope at a center.

73

Building Persuasive Paragraphs

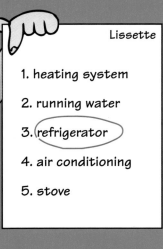

Lissette

1. heating system
2. running water
3. refrigerator
4. air conditioning
5. stove

Can't Live Without It!

There's no doubt many of your students are probably already schooled in the fine art of persuasion. This activity will help them transfer that expert ability to their written work. Ask each student to list five things every home must have, circling the most important item. Next direct the student to record at least three reasons his circled item is essential to the home, numbering these reasons from most to least important. After students have completed this step, point out that a persuasive paragraph's main idea—stated in the topic sentence—is always an opinion. Explain that the topic sentence is followed by logical, ordered statements that support the opinion and a concluding sentence that restates the opinion. Have each student write a persuasive paragraph in support of the one item he feels is most essential to the home; then invite the student to read aloud his paragraph to the class. Afterward have the class vote on the top five items students think every home should have.

Words To Build On

Lay a solid foundation for persuasive writing by teaching your students the importance of careful word selection. Divide your class into groups of three to five students. Call out a word from the word list below and allow each group three minutes to list as many synonyms for the word as it can. When the time expires, award a point to the group that has listed the most synonyms. Then make a larger synonym list by combining each individual group's list. Discuss each synonym and its connotations—the feelings or emotions it suggests. Find words within the list to which especially strong positive and negative feelings are associated, discussing specific cases in which each word would be useful in persuading an individual. Repeat the game with additional words, reviewing the importance of careful word selection in persuasive writing.

Suggested words: *good, bad, small, big, nice, mean, happy, sad*

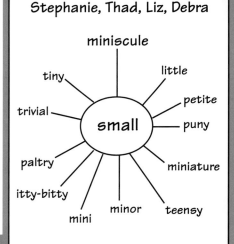

Stephanie, Thad, Liz, Debra

miniscule · little · tiny · petite · trivial · small · puny · paltry · miniature · itty-bitty · mini · minor · teensy

New And Improved!

Turn your students into savvy product developers by challenging them to design the next miracle household products. Have each student develop a product and accompanying sales pitch in the form of a well-written persuasive paragraph. Once each student has written her sales pitch, encourage her to build a model of the new product. Invite each student to read aloud her sales pitch to the class, using the model as a visual aid. Display student models along with their written descriptions for others to enjoy.

Try new Kid Flakes, good for goodness sake!

KID FLAKES

Clevell Harris

Building Descriptive Paragraphs

Spice It Up!

With the help of their five senses, your students can cook up some great writing! Label each of five clear plastic jars with one of the five senses—smell, taste, touch, sight, and sound. Provide each student with five strips of paper. Beginning with the sense of smell, have each child record on a strip a word that relates to that sense. Collect student responses in the jar labeled "Smell," and continue through the other senses until each child has responded with a word for every sense. Next shake the jars and have each student pull one strip from each. Challenge the student to use her five words to write a creative paragraph about a day when she woke up in a strange, unfamiliar house. Remind the student to include the three elements of a paragraph in her writing: a topic sentence, supporting details, and a concluding sentence.

On the day when students will share their paragraphs, provide each child with a copy of page 80. Have each student share her paragraph, encouraging her classmates to add new sensory words to their copies of page 80 as she does. Direct students to store these sheets in their writing portfolios as a reference for future writing.

This house is pretty as a peacock!

Dream Home

Your students will be right at home with this descriptive-writing activity! Begin by asking each student the following questions about her dream home: "What features would the home have? What types of rooms would it contain? How would the home be decorated?" Explain that good architects work from detailed floor plans. Show your students an example of a floor plan from the newspaper's real-estate section, pointing out how items are labeled with sizes specified. Then direct each student to design a floor plan for her dream home. After each student has completed her floor plan, have her describe it in a descriptive paragraph. Have each student display her paragraph, floor plan, and a two-column "Bid Sheet" (as shown) on her desk. Challenge students to read about their classmates' homes and estimate what each house would cost. Encourage each student to put in a bid on the house she most likes by recording her name in one column of the house's bid sheet, followed by the amount she'd be willing to pay in the second column.

As Big As A House

Sometimes a well-placed simile can describe something much better than a series of colorful adjectives. Provide each student with a copy of the top half of page 81. Explain that students will be embarking on a unique search for items that match the description of a specific simile.

After students have completed the reproducible, have each child bring in several pictures of houses cut from magazines or newspapers. Have the student select one house about which to write a descriptive paragraph. Direct the student to include a minimum of four similes in his paragraph. Provide each student with an 11" x 14" sheet of construction paper on which to glue his paragraph and house picture. Mount student work on a bulletin board titled "Descriptive Writing With Similes—As Easy As Pie!"

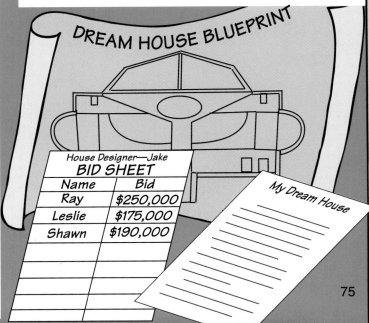

DREAM HOUSE BLUEPRINT

House Designer—Jake
BID SHEET

Name	Bid
Ray	$250,000
Leslie	$175,000
Shawn	$190,000

My Dream House

75

Building Narrative Paragraphs

Home Is Where...

Narrative writing hits very close to home with this student-driven activity! On Friday, give each student a copy of the bottom half of page 81. Direct the student to record on the sheet anything he does—no matter how trivial—over the weekend. On Monday, explain that each student will use the information he gathered to write a narrative paragraph about his weekend. Tell each student that the main idea should be what he thought of his weekend, while the supporting details should identify the specific events that directly influenced his overall feelings about the weekend. Review with students sequence words as well as the three parts of a paragraph; then have each student write his narrative paragraph.

Next sharpen students' listening and paraphrasing skills by having one student at a time read aloud his narrative. Select a volunteer to retell in his own words what the author's weekend was like and give reasons why his classmate did or did not enjoy the weekend.

Name————
Weekend Journal
Narrative writing

Friday After School————

Saturday————

Sunday————

The Big, Bad Narrative

We're all aware that the mighty breath of the Big, Bad Wolf revealed some serious structural problems in the homes of two of the three little pigs. To weave this classic tale into a lesson on narrative writing and point of view, read aloud a version of *The Three Little Pigs*. Then plot on the board the basic sequence of events in a story map. Ask your students how the events would vary if told through the eyes of the Big, Bad Wolf instead of the impartial narrator. Have students come up with a topic sentence that reveals the main idea from the wolf's perspective, and record it on chart paper. Then have them do the same thing for the supporting details and the concluding sentence.

Continue the activity by having each student write a narrative paragraph from the perspective of one of the three pigs. Ask student volunteers to share their paragraphs. Discuss how changing the point of view altered the story. Also talk about the ways in which the stories remained the same. Extend the activity by having each student make finger puppets and perform her revised version of the tale for a group of younger students.

Home Sweet Home

A well-written paragraph is like a well-designed house. A house always has a roof on top. A paragraph always starts "at the top" with a topic sentence stating the main idea. Within a house are rooms that provide structural support. In the same way, a paragraph contains details that support the main idea. Finally, the foundation is always at the bottom of a house—much like the concluding sentence is at the end of a paragraph.

Directions: Write a paragraph containing a topic sentence, supporting details, and a concluding sentence. Record each part of the paragraph in its corresponding section of the house. Then decorate and cut out the house.

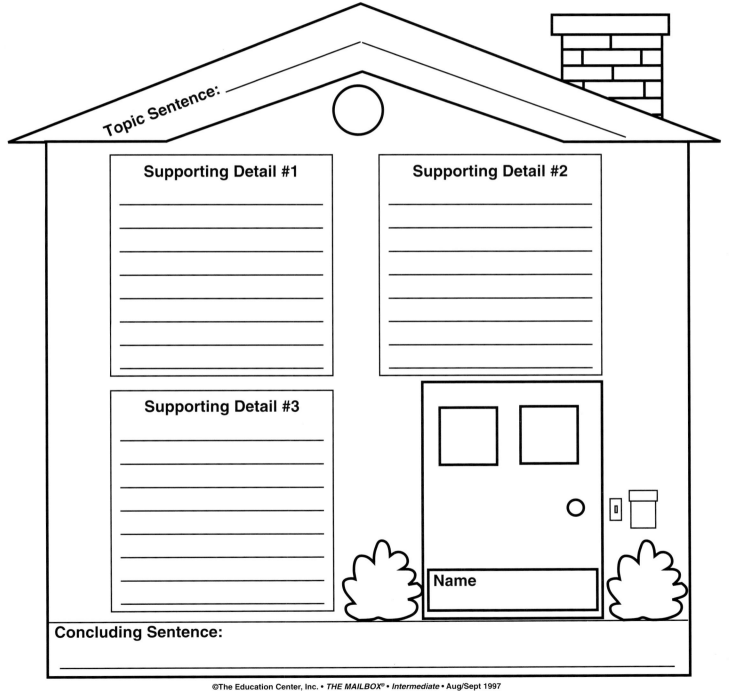

Topic Sentence: _____

Supporting Detail #1
_____
_____
_____
_____
_____
_____
_____
_____

Supporting Detail #2
_____
_____
_____
_____
_____
_____
_____

Supporting Detail #3
_____
_____
_____
_____
_____
_____
_____

Name

Concluding Sentence:
_____

Note To The Teacher: Use with "Shoring Up The Details" on page 72. Provide students with scissors. Display the students' cut-out houses on a "Building Better Paragraphs" bulletin board in your classroom.

Hammering Out A How-To

An effective *expository,* or how-to, paragraph has a topic sentence; supporting details that include step-by-step, time-ordered details; and a concluding sentence. The paragraph below tells the steps for writing an expository paragraph. It also gives an example of what an expository paragraph should sound like.

How To Write A How-To Speech

Expository writing, often called how-to writing, is easy if you follow a few simple steps! Begin by selecting a task on which you would like to give a how-to speech. Come up with a topic sentence that clearly states the main idea of your paragraph. Next record in order each of the steps a person must do to complete the task you selected. Then write a concluding sentence to summarize what you have gone over in your paragraph. Practice delivering your paragraph as a speech and gather any visual aids you might need during your presentation. Finally, present your how-to paragraph to your classmates. As you can see, writing and delivering a how-to paragraph is not difficult.

Directions: Select a chore, repair task, or craft that you have taken part in at home. Use the space below to organize an expository paragraph explaining how to do that project.

Topic Sentence: _____
_____

Supporting Details (step-by-step instructions): _____
_____
_____
_____
_____
_____
_____
_____
_____
_____
_____

Concluding Sentence: _____
_____

Bonus Box: On the back of this sheet, write an expository paragraph detailing how to make an ice-cream sundae.

Note To The Teacher: Use with "At Home With Your Students" on page 73.

Hangin' It Up!

Directions: Cut out each laundry item below. Then write the topic sentence of your expository paragraph on one garment. Select three more garments and record one of the supporting details on each one. Finally, write the concluding sentence on the remaining garment. Shuffle the clothing; then use paper clips to attach each garment to your length of yarn.

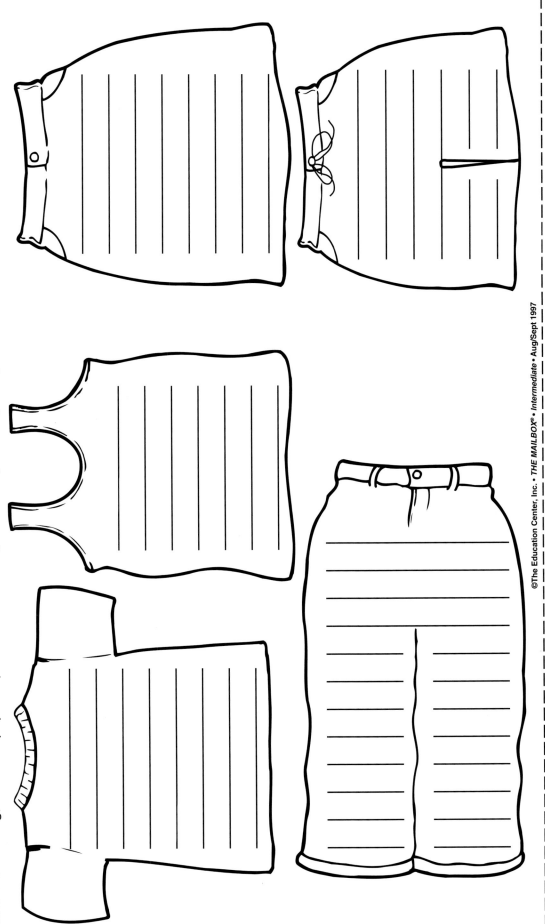

©The Education Center, Inc. • *THE MAILBOX*® • *Intermediate* • Aug/Sept 1997

Note To The Teacher: Use with "Wringing Out Great Writing" on page 73. Duplicate one copy for each student, giving the student an additional sheet if his expository paragraph is more than five sentences long. Provide each student with at least one paper clip for each cut-out garment, scissors, and an 18-inch length of yarn.

Spicing Up Your Vocabulary

Use the jars to stock up on some sensory words. They're just the thing you need to turn boring writing into a feast for the senses! Refer to the list often when you need those extraspecial ingredients guaranteed to tickle your reader's taste buds.

Taste

Smell

Touch

Sight

Sound

Note To The Teacher: Use with "Spice It Up!" on page 75. Direct each student to place this list of sensory words in his writing portfolio for future reference.

Name____ Descriptive writing

Simile Scavenger Hunt

Read each of the similes below. Then, in the blank beside each, list items that fit the simile's description.

Example: slippery as soap: a muddy pig, a salamander, my driveway after it rains

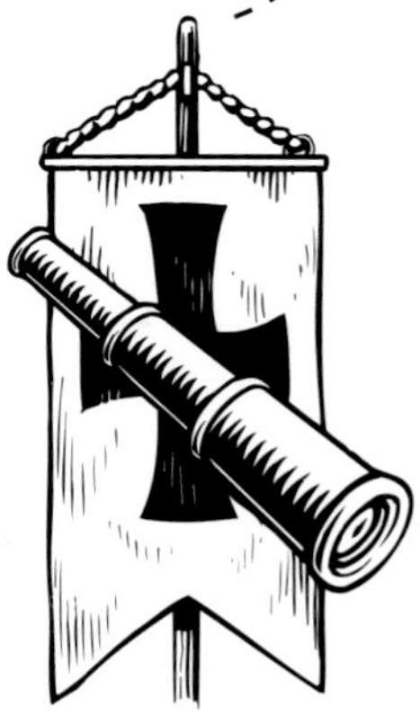

as big as a house: ____________________

red like a brick: ____________________

as hard as a rock: ____________________

as tough as nails: ____________________

as cold as ice: ____________________

as clear as glass: ____________________

as quiet as a mouse: ____________________

as soft as a kitten: ____________________

as black as coal: ____________________

as light as a feather: ____________________

as sweet as sugar: ____________________

bright like the sun: ____________________

as clear as crystal: ____________________

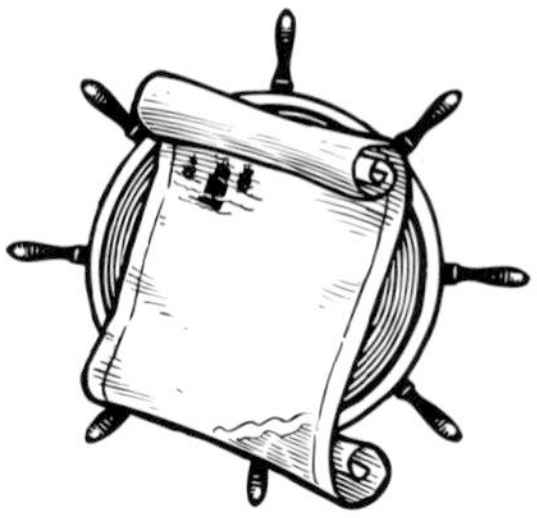

Bonus Box: On the back of this sheet, record three additional similes.

Name____ Narrative writing

Weekend Journal

Hip, hip, hooray—it's finally Friday! Use this journal to keep track of what you do over the weekend. Record all activities in which you participate in the correct section below. Return the journal to school on Monday.

Friday After School ____________________

Saturday ____________________

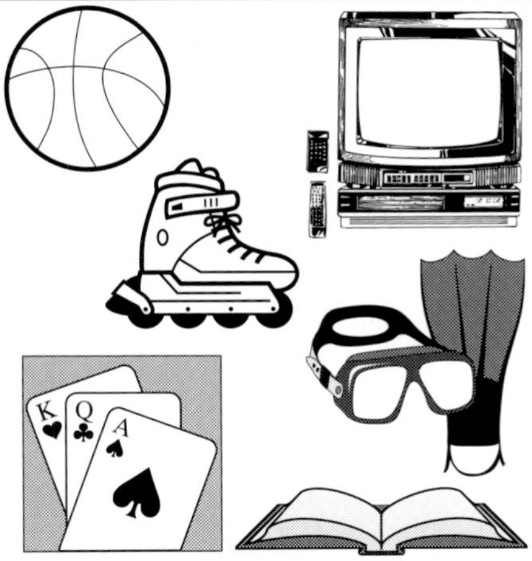

Sunday ____________________

Note To The Teacher: Use the top half of this page with "As Big As A House" on page 75. Use the bottom half with "Home Is Where…" on page 76.

Grammar's Bare Necessities
Creative Activities For Teaching Parts Of Speech

Students who can barely wait for English class—sound impossible? Not anymore! Use the following kid-pleasin' activities and reproducibles to reinforce the bare necessities of sentences—the parts of speech. We guarantee grammar lessons that are almost "un-bear-ably" fun!

by Marcia Barton and Hellen Harvey

Nonsense Nouns

Review common and proper nouns with help from a classic poem. Duplicate one copy of "Jabberwocky" by Lewis Carroll on page 87 for each student. Read the poem aloud; then take a few minutes to discuss students' opinions of its meaning. Next divide your class into pairs. Challenge each pair to underline all the common nouns in the poem with a *red* crayon and all the proper nouns with a *blue* crayon. Reread the poem aloud, this time stopping after each verse. Call on different students to share their underlined words from that verse and explain why they classified each noun as common or proper. Collect students' copies of page 87 and redistribute them for the next activity, "Portmanteau Adjectives."

Follow up this activity by reading aloud *Jabberwocky: From Through The Looking Glass* by Lewis Carroll (Harry N. Abrams, Inc.; 1989), accented by the imaginative illustrations of talented artist Graeme Base.

Portmanteau Adjectives

Why use two words when one will do the trick? Lewis Carroll's "Jabberwocky" is filled with *portmanteaus*—words whose form and meaning are derived by blending two or more words. For example, the word *slithy* was made by combining *lithe* and *slimy*. Duplicate and distribute one copy of "Jabberwocky" on page 87 to each student. Pair your students; then direct each pair to list all the adjectives found in the poem on a sheet of paper. Next challenge the pair to guess which two words were used to make each portmanteau adjective. Tell the pairs to be creative in their choices and that you will accept any justifiable answer. Allow the pairs to share their word choices. Finally instruct each pair to create its own portmanteau using two or more adjectives. Have the pair write and illustrate a sentence using its new portmanteau adjective, then share its creation with the class.

Follow up this activity by reading aloud poems from *Animal Fare: Zoological Nonsense Rhymes* by Jane Yolen (Harcourt Brace & Company, 1994). In this entertaining book, animal names are portmanteaus that are explained through clever rhymes.

"Snickersnack"

Assess each student's knowledge of parts of speech with this whole-class game that's sure to become everyone's favorite! Use a hole puncher to make 20 red, 20 blue, and 20 yellow paper candies for each student. Next cut out and laminate one red, one blue, and one yellow two-inch paper circle. Use a wipe-off marker to label each circle as shown; then attach a small piece of Sticky-Tac to the back of each one.

To play, write a sentence on the board and have each student copy it onto a sheet of paper. Then have her place a blue dot above the subject, and either a yellow dot above the action verb or a red dot above the linking verb(s) in that sentence. Circulate around the classroom to assess students' understanding. Next select a student volunteer to use the two-inch circles to label the parts of speech in the sentence on the board. Have each student check her work, then collect the used candies into a pile on the corner of her desk. Continue the game by writing a new sentence on the board. Once a student has collected 20 paper candies, have her call out, "Snickersnack!"; then reward her with a snack-sized Snickers® candy bar. After the game, save the paper candies in Ziploc® bags and reuse them when teaching other parts of speech such as adjectives, adverbs, or prepositions.

The Search Is On!

I spy a great parts-of-speech learning center in your classroom! Have student or parent volunteers peruse old magazines and cut out pictures of busy places such as cities, markets, or malls. Laminate each picture and store it in a learning center. When a student has free time, direct him to examine one of the pictures, then identify and list as many nouns and verbs in the picture as he can. For practice with other parts of speech, have the student list adjectives and adverbs that describe each of the nouns and verbs that he found in the picture. Soon you'll spy a classroom full of parts-of-speech experts!

Mouthwatering Menus

Help your students see the difference an adjective makes with this tasty idea! Enlist the help of parents and students to collect menus from different restaurants. Then distribute one menu, drawing paper, and crayons to each student. Instruct the student to list on a sheet of paper all the adjectives found on her menu. Point out how unappetizing the menu would be without the adjectives in the descriptions. Next have each student create a menu for an imaginary restaurant with a specific theme such as *The Doggy Diner, Hawaiian Hula Hut,* or *Candy Cafe.* Instruct each student to include on her menu appetizers, main courses, side dishes, desserts, and beverages that go along with the theme of her restaurant. Display the completed menus on a bulletin board titled "Mouthwatering Menus."

Clevell Harris

"Charade" A Phrase

Introduce prepositional phrases with this new twist on an old favorite. Make a list of prepositional phrases that can be acted out by a student (such as *under the desk* or *behind the chair*); then write each one on a different slip of paper. Fold up each slip and place it in a paper bag. Have a student pull a phrase from the bag and act it out for her classmates. Call on students to guess the prepositional phrase being dramatized. Direct the student who guesses correctly to pull the next slip of paper from the bag and "charade" the phrase!

Morning Rituals

Every child's morning is full of action! Use these morning rituals to introduce action verbs. Instruct each student to write ten sentences, in sequential order, that tell what he did before arriving at school. For example, *I turned off my alarm clock* or *I rolled out of bed.* Next pair your students and have each pair swap papers. Direct each partner to underline the verb in each sentence on the paper, then return the paper to the author. Allow each child to share his sentences while you make a list on the chalkboard of all the verbs used. Encourage students to list favorite verbs from the board in their writing journals.

Put On Your Thinking Caps!

Just as people can wear many proverbial hats, so can words! To help students understand that words can be used as more than one part of speech, write on separate tagboard strips sentences for each word listed below—first using the word as a noun, then as a verb. Underline the listed word in each sentence. Next designate one side of the classroom as the *noun* area and the other side as the *verb* area. Identify each area by labeling an old hat with the correct part of speech for each area of the room. One at a time, call on a student to choose a sentence strip, decide how the underlined word is used in the sentence, and then go to the area of the classroom labeled for that part of speech. Direct the child to place the labeled thinking cap on his head and read his sentence aloud. If he is in the correct area, allow him to call on the next person. Continue play until each student has had a turn. End the game by having pairs of students whose sentences highlight the same word explain the clues they used to identify their word's part of speech.

Word list:

dream	hammer
paint	ice
ship	sound
duck	park
picture	ride
water	run
light	line
turn	copy

I had a **dream** about a jar of honey!

84

"Adverbots"

Increase your students' understanding of adverbs with this fun project. Use various geometric figures to draw a robot (see the illustration) on the chalkboard or an overhead transparency. Tell your students that you designed this robot to help you with your teaching responsibilities. Then use adverbs to label and explain what the different parts of your robot can do (see the illustration). Next have each student imagine that he can design his own robot to do anything. Have a few students explain what they would like their robots to do for them. Then give each student a sheet of drawing paper on which to design his own robot. Have him use adverbs to label and explain all of his robot's functions just as you did. On the back of his paper, have him write all the adverbs that he used to explain his robot. Use pushpins to post the finished robots on a bulletin board titled "Adverbots!" Allow a few students at a time to visit the display and identify the adverbs used in each explanation. Have them check their answers by removing the pushpins and turning each picture over to reveal the adverb list.

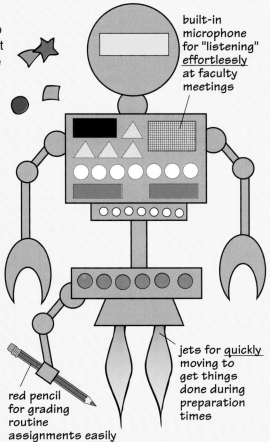

built-in microphone for "listening" <u>effortlessly</u> at faculty meetings

red pencil for grading routine assignments <u>easily</u>

jets for <u>quickly</u> moving to get things done during preparation times

Creature Quest

Focus on recognizing prepositional phrases with this class question-and-answer game. Duplicate and cut out several copies of the creature pattern below onto colored paper. While your students are out of the room, hide the creature cutouts around the classroom. When your students return, review prepositional phrases by sharing several examples. Next explain that they are going on a Creature Quest. Tell students that you have hidden several creatures around the classroom and that their job is to find each one by using prepositional phrases to ask questions. In turn, have each student ask you three questions about the location of the creatures. For example, a student may ask, "Is there a creature *under the computer chair?*" Respond by answering *yes* or *no;* then write the preposition used on the chalkboard. If a student repeats a question already asked, he forfeits the remaining questions in his turn. Any student who locates a hidden creature should capture it, then trade it in for a privilege or treat. Continue play until all the creatures have been found; then erase the board and challenge your students to list as many prepositions as they can.

Pattern
Use with "Creature Quest" above.

Student Teachers

When reviewing parts of speech, let your students do the teaching! Divide your class into seven cooperative groups; then assign each group a part of speech—noun, verb, adjective, adverb, pronoun, preposition, or conjunction. Tell each group that it is responsible for learning about its assigned part of speech and presenting the information to the class in lesson format. Explain that the lesson must include: a definition of the part of speech; examples of the part of speech in use; a song or rhyme to help students remember the part of speech; a strategy for locating the part of speech in a sentence; and a game, puzzle, or reproducible to evaluate how well the class learned the part of speech from the group's presentation. You'll be surprised how much your students will learn from one another!

Time's Up!

Help your students review adverbs with this suspenseful game. Obtain an inexpensive kitchen timer or an old alarm clock. Arrange your students in a circle and announce an action verb that has many possible modifiers such as *runs*. Then set the timer for three or four minutes and pass it to a student. Instruct that student to name an adverb that answers one of the following questions: runs *where?* runs *how?* or runs *when?* If he correctly names an adverb, have him pass the timer to the student on his right, who then has to name another adverb. If he is incorrect or names an adverb already used, or if the timer goes off while he is holding it, he is "out." Reward the last student not called "out" with a coupon for free time or another special privilege. Vary this activity by announcing a noun and having students name a correct adjective.

Nouns Abound All Around

Give your students a break from the classroom and lead them on a noun tour! Divide your class into four groups—(1) people; (2) places; (3) things; and (4) ideas, thoughts, and emotions. Designate three members in each group as the Recorder, Noise Monitor, and Reporter. As you walk around the school, have the Recorder from each group write down all the nouns that are spotted by his teammates and fit in his group's category. Instruct the Noise Monitor to keep down his group's noise level. Upon returning to the classroom, have the Reporter read aloud his group's noun list.

Follow up this activity by instructing each group to write a pronoun that can take the place of each noun it listed.

Places

restroom
playground
cafeteria
media center
hallway
art closet
office

Nonsense!

Several nouns—both common and proper—are hidden deep within this poem, some cleverly disguised as nonsense words. Circle each common noun with a *red* crayon and each proper noun with a *blue* crayon. Good luck—after all, you're going up against the Jabberwock!

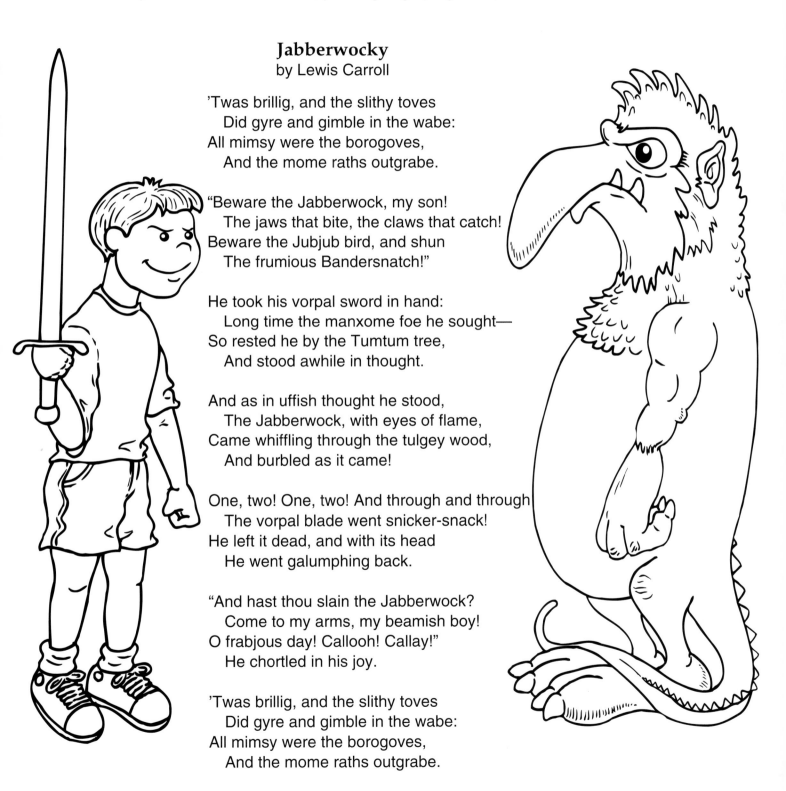

Jabberwocky
by Lewis Carroll

'Twas brillig, and the slithy toves
    Did gyre and gimble in the wabe:
All mimsy were the borogoves,
    And the mome raths outgrabe.

"Beware the Jabberwock, my son!
    The jaws that bite, the claws that catch!
Beware the Jubjub bird, and shun
    The frumious Bandersnatch!"

He took his vorpal sword in hand:
    Long time the manxome foe he sought—
So rested he by the Tumtum tree,
    And stood awhile in thought.

And as in uffish thought he stood,
    The Jabberwock, with eyes of flame,
Came whiffling through the tulgey wood,
    And burbled as it came!

One, two! One, two! And through and through
    The vorpal blade went snicker-snack!
He left it dead, and with its head
    He went galumphing back.

"And hast thou slain the Jabberwock?
    Come to my arms, my beamish boy!
O frabjous day! Callooh! Callay!"
    He chortled in his joy.

'Twas brillig, and the slithy toves
    Did gyre and gimble in the wabe:
All mimsy were the borogoves,
    And the mome raths outgrabe.

Bonus Box: Use your own nonsense words to write and illustrate a story about the Jubjub bird, the Bandersnatch, or the Jabberwock.

The Frame Game

Are you ready for a challenge? The frame below has four nouns listed across the top. Your job is to write nine different adjectives to modify each noun. The challenge? The first letter of each adjective you write must match the letters in the word *ADJECTIVE*. If you get stuck, use a dictionary or a thesaurus. Your teacher will explain how you can score points. A few examples have been done for you.

	creature	friend	school	spaceship
A		*angry*		
D				
J				
E	*eccentric*			
C				
T				
I				
V			*vibrant*	
E				

Bonus Box: Make your own Frame Game by drawing a grid on the back of this page and writing the word *ADVERB* down the left side of it. Write four *verbs* across the top of the frame. Challenge a friend to write adverbs to modify the verbs in the frame.

Note To The Teacher: A player earns one point for each classmate who did *not* write the same word as he did in a space. For example, if you have 12 players and a student wrote an adjective that wasn't repeated by anyone, award that student 11 points. If five students wrote the same word, then those five students would each be awarded 7 points—one point for each player who didn't use that word. The student with the highest point total is the winner.

A Patchwork Of Poetry

When asked "What is a poem?", your students might respond that it's just a bunch of words that rhyme. Put an end to that common misconception with the help of this patchwork of activities on writing inventive poetry!

by Simone Lepine

Poet's Toolbox

Supply students with the tools they need for building wonderful poems. Give each child a copy of page 92. Then have him cut out the minipages, stack them in order, and staple them together to make a booklet. Explain that each page describes a specific poetic technique and features a short writing assignment. Have the student complete each assignment on the blank page to the left of the printed page. As you complete the activities in this unit, encourage each student to keep his booklet handy so he has the tools needed to build his poetry.

A Poet's Toolbox
Name KATIE GORHAM

List Poetry

In addition to keeping us organized, lists are a great resource for writing poetry! On separate strips of paper, have each student list the foods she usually eats for lunch. Then direct her to arrange the slips, deciding where each phrase should end and what words sound good together. Have the student write her poem on the side of a paper lunch bag, adding a title. Cover a bulletin board with a checkered tablecloth background. Title the board "Poetry Picnic"; then pin the bags on it.

Definition Poems

Put a poetic twist on the often tedious task of writing definitions! Read Ralph Waldo Emerson's poem "Success" (shown at the right). Look up *success* in the dictionary with your students; then have the class compare and contrast the poem and dictionary definitions. Next brainstorm a list of human emotions or traits. Have each student select one of the words to use as the subject of a *definition poem*—a poem that defines an idea or a word creatively. Have the student follow the pattern shown, writing her final copy on a sheet of white paper. Then have her write the word's dictionary definition on another piece of paper. Direct the student to glue both writings to a sheet of construction paper. After students have shared their work, discuss why they preferred the dictionary or poem definitions.

(Title)
To _____
To _____
To _____
To _____
To _____
To _____
This is to _____.

Success
To laugh often and much; to win the respect of intelligent people and affection of children; to earn the appreciation of honest critics and endure the betrayal of false friends; to appreciate beauty, to find the best in others; to leave the world a bit better, whether by a healthy child, a garden patch or a redeemed social condition; to know even one life has breathed easier because you have lived. This is to have succeeded.
—*Ralph Waldo Emerson*

Picture-Perfect Sensory Poetry

A picture can say a thousand words, but poetry can capture a picture in just a few! Have each student bring in a picture that shows an interesting image. Have the student paper-clip her picture to a paper lunch bag placed on her desk. Next give the student a copy of page 93. Have her cut the strips and place them next to her bag. Then rotate students from one bag to the next. When a student arrives at a bag, have her look at the picture clipped to it, fill out one of the strips beside it with a phrase describing the picture, and then drop the strip in the bag. The phrase should relate to the sense pictured on the strip. For example, if a student views a picture of a beach and selects the "smell" strip, she might write "The smell of salt and suntan lotion fills the air." After five rotations, have each student return to her seat, take the sentences from her bag, and arrange them in any order. Then have her write the sentences in poetic form. Display each poem with its matching picture.

Pyramid Poetry

Take a tip from the ancient Egyptians with this unique activity! Explain to students that a *pyramid poem* has one word—the title—in the first line. An additional word is added to each successive line. A pyramid poem is great for describing a person or thing. Have each student write a pyramid poem about himself. After each student writes his poem, give him one construction-paper square for each word in his poem. Direct the student to write each word on a separate square, then arrange and glue his squares, as shown, on a sheet of construction paper. Display the poems under the heading "Poetry Amid The Pyramids."

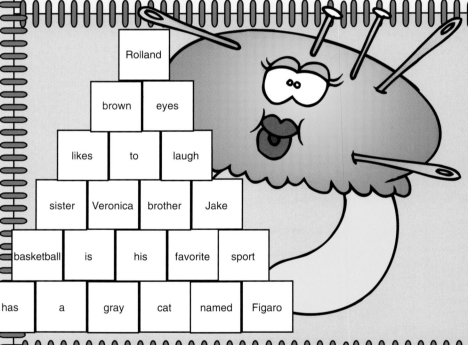

Terse Verse

What is a short poem called? A *terse verse!* Explain to students that they will be writing poems containing only two words. This may seem easy, but it's finding the right word combination that's the real trick. After sharing the examples shown, have each student list rhyming words. Next have the student try to combine two words that have the same number of syllables and then write a definition describing the combination. Have each student share his terse verse; then have students complete the reproducible on page 94.

30-Pound Feline =
Fat Cat

Toy Reptile =
Fake Snake

Feverish Child =
Hot Tot

Poetry With Emotion

Encourage students to get emotional in this next poetry activity! Brainstorm a list of emotions. Have each student select an emotion from the list. Display the pattern shown below for students to follow as they write poems about their emotions. Explain that lines 2 through 5 can be arranged in any order. After each student has finished his poem, have him display it in a flip book. To make a flip book, have the student stagger three equal-sized pages and fold them as shown. Then have the student staple along the top edge as shown and write each sentence of his poem in order on the six minipages. *Kimberly Branham—Gr. 5, Wateree Elementary, Lugoff, SC, and Simone Lepine*

Line 1—[Emotion] is [color].
Line 2—It smells like _____.
Line 3—It looks like _____.
Line 4—It tastes like _____.
Line 5—It sounds like _____.
Line 6—[Emotion] feels like _____.

5 in.

1½ in.

1½ in.

Happiness is purple.
It smells like cotton candy.
It looks like a circus.
It tastes like an ice-cream sundae.
It sounds like a laughing baby.
Happiness feels like a feather tickling my soul.

Character Clerihews

Clerihews masterfully prove the point that poetry can be found just about anywhere—even in social studies! A *clerihew*—originated by the British writer Edmund Clerihew Bentley—is a four-lined humorous poem about a real or fictitious person. Show students the following clerihew pattern and sample poem:

Line 1 ends with a person's name.
Line 2 rhymes with line 1.
Lines 3 and 4 rhyme with each other.

Abraham Lincoln
was always thinkin'
that slavery was wrong
and freedom should be everyone's song.

Next direct each student to select a historical figure about whom to write a clerihew. Have each student share his poem with the class; then combine the poems in a binder labeled "Need Something To Do? Read A Clerihew Or Two!"

Alphabet Poetry

Looking for a poetry activity that's as easy as *A, B, C?* An *alphabet poem* features a sequence of letters and words that begin with those letters. This type of poem is often silly. Share the example shown that uses the sequence *E, F, G,* and *H.* Write sets of four sequential letters on index cards, putting a different set of four letters on each card. Pair students and give each pair a card. Direct the pair to come up with a silly sentence or phrase using words that begin with the letters on its card. Challenge students to continue the sequence by adding on additional alphabet letters and corresponding words. Have each pair share its finished sentence with the class.

Elephants
Fly
Giant
Helicopters

E F G H

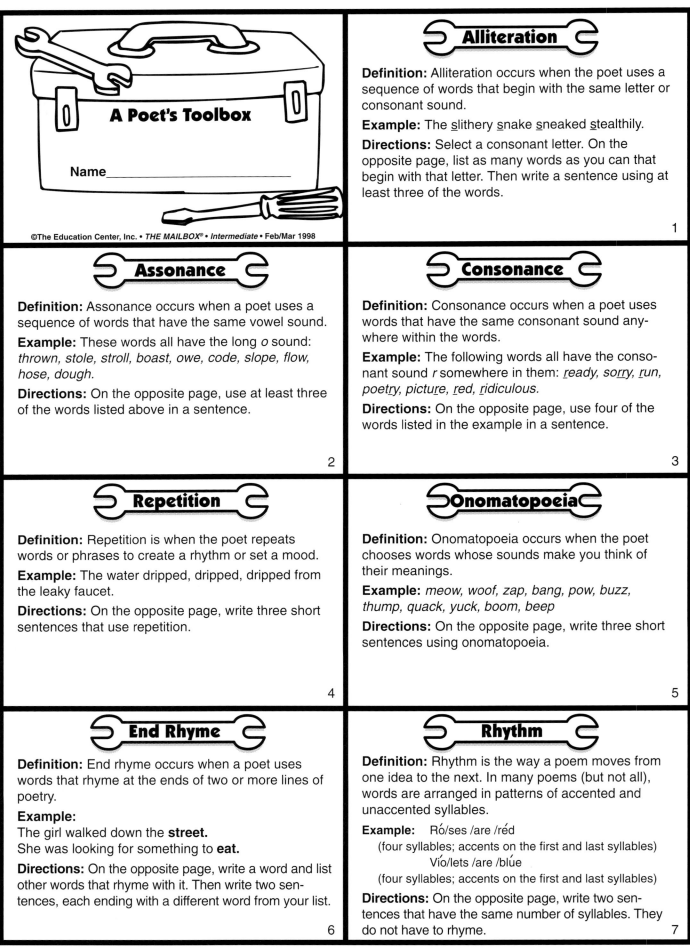

A Poet's Toolbox

Name_____

Alliteration

Definition: Alliteration occurs when the poet uses a sequence of words that begin with the same letter or consonant sound.

Example: The slithery snake sneaked stealthily.

Directions: Select a consonant letter. On the opposite page, list as many words as you can that begin with that letter. Then write a sentence using at least three of the words.

1

Assonance

Definition: Assonance occurs when a poet uses a sequence of words that have the same vowel sound.

Example: These words all have the long *o* sound: *thrown, stole, stroll, boast, owe, code, slope, flow, hose, dough.*

Directions: On the opposite page, use at least three of the words listed above in a sentence.

2

Consonance

Definition: Consonance occurs when a poet uses words that have the same consonant sound anywhere within the words.

Example: The following words all have the consonant sound *r* somewhere in them: *ready, sorry, run, poetry, picture, red, ridiculous.*

Directions: On the opposite page, use four of the words listed in the example in a sentence.

3

Repetition

Definition: Repetition is when the poet repeats words or phrases to create a rhythm or set a mood.

Example: The water dripped, dripped, dripped from the leaky faucet.

Directions: On the opposite page, write three short sentences that use repetition.

4

Onomatopoeia

Definition: Onomatopoeia occurs when the poet chooses words whose sounds make you think of their meanings.

Example: *meow, woof, zap, bang, pow, buzz, thump, quack, yuck, boom, beep*

Directions: On the opposite page, write three short sentences using onomatopoeia.

5

End Rhyme

Definition: End rhyme occurs when a poet uses words that rhyme at the ends of two or more lines of poetry.

Example:
The girl walked down the **street.**
She was looking for something to **eat.**

Directions: On the opposite page, write a word and list other words that rhyme with it. Then write two sentences, each ending with a different word from your list.

6

Rhythm

Definition: Rhythm is the way a poem moves from one idea to the next. In many poems (but not all), words are arranged in patterns of accented and unaccented syllables.

Example: Ró/ses /are /réd
   (four syllables; accents on the first and last syllables)
      Vío/lets /are /blúe
   (four syllables; accents on the first and last syllables)

Directions: On the opposite page, write two sentences that have the same number of syllables. They do not have to rhyme.

7

Sentences That Make "Sense"

Directions: Cut along the dotted lines to make five strips—one for each of the five senses. Place the strips beside your paper bag. After your classmates help you fill in each strip, arrange the strips to create a poem about the picture.

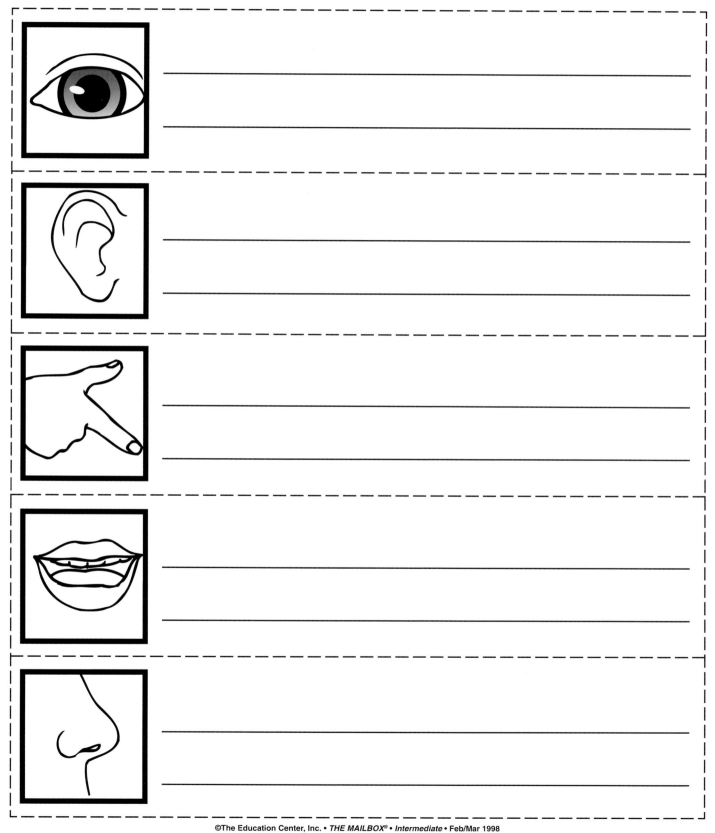

©The Education Center, Inc. • THE MAILBOX® • Intermediate • Feb/Mar 1998

Terse Verse

What is a short poem called? A *terse verse!* This type of poem is made up of a title and two words that rhyme and have the same number of syllables. The rhyming words describe the title. **Examples:**

A Funny Baby Horse—Silly Filly
A Feverish Child—Hot Tot

Directions: Think of four terse verses of your own to write on scrap paper. Use the dictionary or thesaurus if you need help. Then follow these easy steps:

1. Write the title of one of your terse verses (such as "A Feverish Child") on the two solid lines in one of the boxes on the right.
2. Cut along each of the dotted lines.
3. Fold back the flap on the solid line so it opens like a door.
4. After you've completed Steps 1–3 for all four boxes, fold this paper in half along the center line.
5. Use clear tape to attach the two sides together where it says TAPE.
6. Write the two-word terse verse in the space underneath each flap. Then fold the flap back down.
7. Give your completed page to a classmate. See if your classmate can guess each terse verse before he or she opens the flap.

Directions For Solving The Verses: Read the titles below. See if you can guess each terse verse before you open its flap.

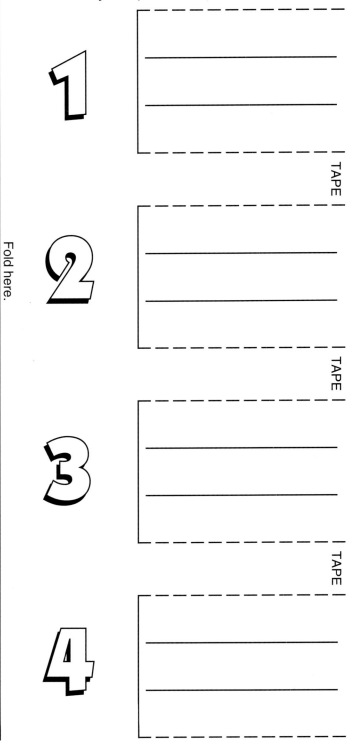

©The Education Center, Inc. • *THE MAILBOX®* • *Intermediate* • Feb/Mar 1998

　Note To The Teacher: Use with "Terse Verse" on page 90. Provide each student with a copy of this page, scissors, and transparent tape.

Picture Books And Writing—
A DYNAMIC DUO!

Using Picture Books To Teach Writing Skills

Looking for a way to make writing workshop a super success? Then pick up a picture book—"write" now! Use the following ideas from our readers to teach key writing skills through the pages of picture books.

Miss Yonkers Goes Bonkers

written by Mike Thaler and illustrated by Jared Lee
Avon Books

Skill: Descriptive writing

What kid wouldn't love a book about a teacher who wears a baseball cap and dances on her desk while humming "Girls Just Wanna Have Fun"? Use this hilarious tale about a teacher gone completely crazy to give students practice with descriptive writing. After reading the book to your class, challenge each student to write his own version titled "[your name] Goes Bonkers." Encourage students to include lots of details as they describe the day when *you* went a bit crazy at school. Bind the pages in a book that's sure to become a class favorite! *Jeffrey J. Kuntz—Grs. 4–6, West End Elementary, Punxsutawney, PA*

The Talking Eggs: A Folktale From The American South

retold by Robert D. San Souci
illustrated by Jerry Pinkney
Scholastic Inc.

Skill: Writing a fairy tale

When I want to introduce a unit on writing fairy tales, I pick up Robert D. San Souci's *The Talking Eggs*. It tells the story of two sisters—one kind, one selfish—and their very different encounters with an old woman and her magical talking eggs. After sharing the book with students, we discuss the elements of fairy tales. The next day I give each student a plastic Easter egg in which I've placed a small object, such as a penny, a pebble, or a bean. Each student then writes a brief fairy tale that incorporates his egg's item as a magical element in the story. It's a writing activity that's all it's cracked up to be! *Anita Perez—Gr. 5, Clyde Intermediate School, Clyde, TX*

Using Wordless Picture Books

Skill: Descriptive writing

Turn to wordless books the next time you want to sharpen descriptive-writing skills. Divide students into groups; then give each group a wordless picture book (ask your media specialist for good examples). Have each student in the group list verbs, adjectives, and adverbs that could be used to describe the story. Then have students in the group go over one another's lists, crossing out any repeated words. Finally have each group work together to write text for the book, using words from their lists. Encourage students to include as many descriptive details as possible.
adapted from an idea by Marie Altenburg—Gr. 6, Lindenhurst Middle School, Lindenhurst, NY

The Day I Finally Rode My Bike

Sidney: The Story Of A Kingfisher

written by John Mooy and Jane Stroschin
illustrated by Jane Stroschin
Henry Quill Press

Skill: Writing a personal narrative

In this lovely picture book, Sidney must learn to dive headfirst into the water to catch fish—but he's afraid. He tries different ways to catch fish, but none of them work for him. Finally Sidney develops the confidence to be himself and catch fish like a kingfisher. After I read this book to my students, we talk about skills we've gained through practice and perseverance (such as riding a bike and learning to ski). At the end of the discussion, I have each student write a personal narrative about a skill he has learned and become confident at doing. *Marian Kender—Gr. 6, St. Hugo Of The Hills School, Bloomfield Hills, MI*

The Pain And The Great One

written by Judy Blume
illustrated by Irene Trivas
Simon & Schuster Children's Books

Skill: Writing a personal narrative

To give students practice with writing personal narratives, I turn to Judy Blume's tale of sibling rivalry, *The Pain And The Great One*. First I tell students about my relationship with my own brother: even though we fought as kids, we still loved each other. Then I ask volunteers to share about their relationships with loved ones who sometimes annoy them. Next I read aloud *The Pain And The Great One*. I ask each student to think of a close friend or relative who also sometimes bothers her. Then I have the student write a paragraph describing how this person sometimes annoys her (without naming the person). In a second paragraph, the student gives reasons why she misses this person when he/she is not around. After students have finished writing, we discuss how similar we all are to the Pain and the Great One. *Michelle Sewing-Sohn—Media Specialist, Forest Park Elementary, Dix Hills, NY*

Our Life Missions

Miss Rumphius

written and illustrated by Barbara Cooney
The Viking Press

Skill: Writing a personal essay

Motivate students to look into their futures with this tale of a young girl who grows up to fulfill her life's mission: see the world, retire by the sea, and leave the world a nicer place. Read this gentle story aloud to your class; then ask each student to ponder his life's mission. Next have each student write a personal essay in which he shares about his life's mission. Encourage students to answer the five *W*s in their essays:

Whom do you hope to become?
What mission would you like to accomplish?
When would you like to accomplish this mission?
Where would you like to accomplish your mission?
Why would you like to accomplish this mission?

Bind the finished essays into a class book titled "Our Life Missions." Then watch as students take their first steps into the future—just by dreaming! *Patricia Twohey—Gr. 4, Old County Road School, Smithfield, RI*

Earrings!

written by Judith Viorst
illustrated by Nola Langner Malone
Aladdin Books

Skill: Persuasive writing

Give students practice in writing persuasively with this story about a girl trying to coerce her parents into letting her get her ears pierced. Begin by discussing times when students have tried to persuade their parents to give them something they really wanted. Then read *Earrings!* aloud to the class. After reading, list on the board the reasons the little girl gave her parents for allowing the piercing. Also discuss how she elaborated on each reason. Next have each child think of something he wants very badly. Then have him write a letter in which he tries to persuade a parent to give him what he wants. Remind students to elaborate on their reasons as the girl in the story did. You can bet you won't have to persuade students to finish this fun assignment! *La Tonne Leftwich—Gr. 4, Lake Dallas Elementary, Lake Dallas, TX*

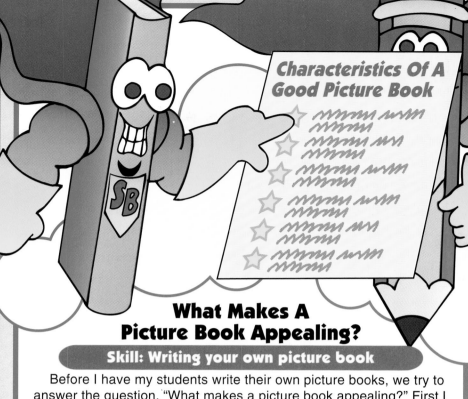

What Makes A Picture Book Appealing?

Skill: Writing your own picture book

Before I have my students write their own picture books, we try to answer the question, "What makes a picture book appealing?" First I divide students into groups. Then I give each group several outstanding picture books. Each group reads its books together and discusses the characteristics that make them appealing (for example: easy-to-read text, interesting illustrations, good dialogue, colorful characters, etc.). As a class, we then create a list titled "Characteristics Of A Good Picture Book." I post this list in our classroom for students to refer to when they begin writing their own picture books. *Sharon Sobeck—Gr. 5, Saint Elizabeth Elementary, Pittsburgh, PA*

If You Give A Mouse A Cookie

written by Laura Joffe Numeroff
illustrated by Felicia Bond
Scholastic Inc.

Skill: Cause and effect

Provide practice with writing cause-and-effect statements with a story about a mouse who begins a comical chain of events simply by taking a cookie. After reading this book and Numeroff's follow-up, *If You Give A Moose A Muffin*, have each student fill in this sentence starter: "If you give a _____ a _____…". Then have the student use the starter to create a chain of events following Numeroff's pattern. Once the student has listed a chain of at least ten cause-and-effect statements, have her use them to write and illustrate her own picture book. Provide time for students to share their creations with a class of younger students. *Debbie Erickson, Waterloo Elementary, Waterloo, WI,* and *Leigh Taylor Bowman, David Youree Elementary, Smyrna, TN*

Pam Crane

The Napping House

written by Audrey Wood and illustrated by Don Wood
Harcourt Brace & Company

Skill: Using a thesaurus when writing

Find a good writer and you'll find a thesaurus close by! Teach students how to use this handy tool with Audrey Wood's delightful tale about a whole household asleep on a lazy afternoon. After reading the book aloud once, read it again, pointing out the synonyms for *sleeping*—such as "a *dreaming* child" and "a *dozing* dog." Then divide students into groups of four or five. Give each group a thesaurus and a card labeled with one of the following words: *eating, happy, sad, big, pretty, talking.* Have each student use a thesaurus to find two synonyms for his group's word; then have him create a sentence and illustration for each synonym. Have each team bind its pages together between a cover to create its own variation of *The Napping House* (i.e., "The Eating House," "The Happy House," etc.). *Diane M. Oswald—Librarian, Parkland Elementary, El Paso, TX*

Postcards From Pluto: A Tour Of The Solar System

written and illustrated by Loreen Leedy
Holiday House, Inc.

Skill: Writing nonfiction

Each year we combine our study of the solar system with a unit on writing nonfiction. After looking at several of *The Magic School Bus®* books, we discuss how author Joanna Cole presents factual information in a way that makes her books fun to read. We then read *Postcards From Pluto.* This charming book includes postcards written from children who are touring the planets. The postcards are creative, yet also contain factual information. After examining this book, each child chooses a planet to research and designs a postcard that includes at least six facts about the planet. As a follow-up, each student then creates her own nonfiction picture book about a topic of her choice. We conclude by reading our original picture books to other classes. What a great way to combine science, reading, and writing! *Michelle Discenza—Gr. 5, Morrisville Year-Round Elementary, Morrisville, NC*

Will we miss the panda bear?

Will We Miss Them?: Endangered Species

written by Alexandra Wright
illustrated by Marshall Peck, III
Charlesbridge Publishing

Skill: Summarizing, writing a brief research report

Sharpen summarizing and report-writing skills with the help of a nonfiction picture book about endangered animals. After reading *Will We Miss Them?* aloud to the class, have each student research an endangered animal (ask your school's media specialist for a list or check the Internet). Then have the student write a brief summary of his animal, copying the format in *Will We Miss Them?:*

- a sentence that asks, "Will we miss the [name of animal]?"
- a paragraph that briefly describes the animal and its unique features
- a paragraph that tells why the animal is endangered and how it is currently being protected

Also have the student draw an illustration of his animal. Bind the finished pages together to make your own class version of this thought-provoking book. *Sherri Levitt—Gr. 4, Pembroke Elementary, Troy, MI*

It Takes Two!

Part 1: Choose two fiction picture books to compare.
Read each book; then fill in the blanks below.

Title of Book #1: _____

Title of Book #2: _____

Theme: What did the main character learn by the end of the story? What was the author's main purpose in writing the book?

Book #1: _____

_____

Book #2: _____

_____

Setting: Where did the main action take place?

Book #1: _____

_____

Book #2: _____

_____

Characters: Who were the central characters in the story?

Book #1: _____

_____

Book #2: _____

_____

Plot: What happened to the main characters in the story?

Book #1: _____

_____

Book #2: _____

_____

Writing Style: What did you notice about the author's writing style? Was the author really good at describing things or people? Making you laugh? Writing dialogue?

Book #1: _____

_____

Book #2: _____

_____

Illustrations: What art medium was used? How did the pictures add to the story? Did the author also do the illustrations?

Book #1: _____

_____

Book #2: _____

_____

Part 2: On another sheet of paper, write a paragraph that tells how the two picture books are alike. Write a second paragraph that tells how the two books are different. Write a third paragraph that tells which book you liked best and why.

Note To The Teacher: You may wish to have students complete this activity over several days.

Name _____

100

If I Had My Way,...

Books—good ones, that is—are full of great characters who seem to jump off the page. Well, what if a character jumped off the page of the picture book you just read? What would he/she have to say about how the author wrote the story? How would the character rewrite the book? What suggestions would the character give the author?

Directions: Pretend that you are a character from a picture book you have read. Think about that character's personality. Then, in the speech bubble, write about how you would change the book's plot. Include suggestions you would give the author to improve the book. In the box, draw a picture of the character.

Picture Book: _____

Author: _____

Character: _____

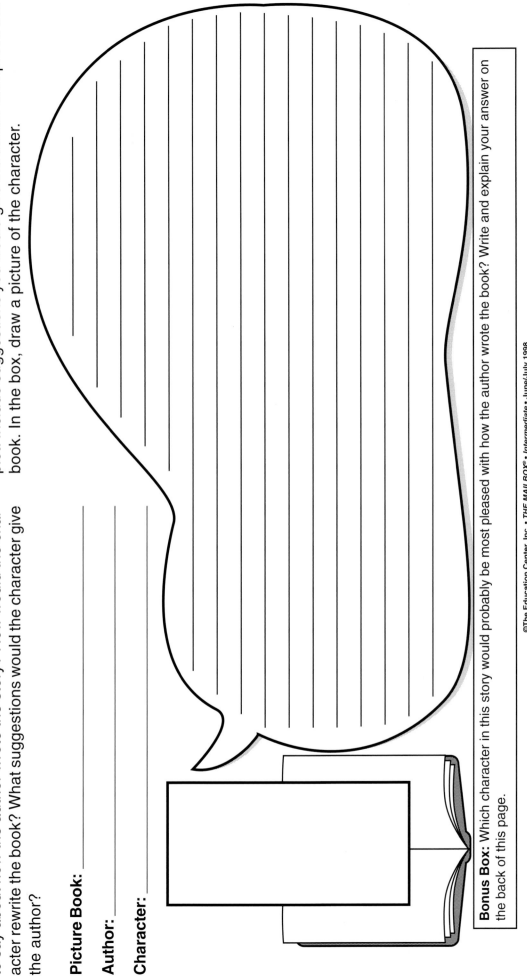

Bonus Box: Which character in this story would probably be most pleased with how the author wrote the book? Write and explain your answer on the back of this page.

©The Education Center, Inc. • *THE MAILBOX®* • *Intermediate* • June/July 1998

Note To The Teacher: Provide each student group with an assortment of picture books to read before completing this page. Also use this reproducible as a book-report project or as a writing activity for a novel your class is reading.

Digging For Inferences

Authors don't always tell everything. But they make up for it by providing plenty of clues that imply what's happening without directly stating it. If your students need to bone up on their inference skills, dig right into the creative activities below!

Ideas by Mary S. Gates—Gr. 4, New Milford, CT

Where Am I?

Challenge the class to brainstorm a list of story settings. Record students' ideas on chart paper as shown below. Then give each child a copy of the top half of page 102 to complete as directed. Have her share the resulting paragraph aloud, challenging the class to guess the setting. After this activity instruct each student to copy her paragraph onto an index card. File the cards in a "setting bank" for students to use in future writing assignments.

campsite
classroom
deserted island
racetrack
radio station
playground
pizza parlor
mall
skating rink
gym

Fabulous Feelings

Authors often imply a character's feelings by simply describing how he or she looks or acts. Give each child a card labeled with a feeling to pantomime (see the list below). Have the student use appropriate actions, gestures, and body language—but no words—to act out the feeling on his card. Accept suitable synonyms as correct answers.

Feelings To Pantomime:
embarrassed
exhausted
frightened
bored
disappointed
pleased
thrilled
worried
frustrated
desperate
uninterested
weak
disgusted
furious
puzzled
shy
surprised
lonely
sleepy
overwhelmed

Take A Guess!

Provide practice writing descriptive clues with a nifty team guessing game. Divide students into groups. Give each group one copy of the planning sheet at the bottom of page 102. After all sheets have been completed, instruct one group to share its first clue. If the feeling is guessed by another group on the first clue, award the team that shared the clue *0* points; then have the next team share its first clue. If a feeling hasn't been guessed after three guesses, direct that team to give a second clue and award points as shown. If an answer is a synonym, say, "Synonym," and allow that student to guess again without penalty. Play until each feeling has been guessed correctly. Declare the group with the *fewest* points at the end of the game the winner.

SCORING
Guessed after 1 clue: 0 points
Guessed after 2 clues: 1 point
Guessed after 3 clues: 2 points
Guessed after 4 clues: 3 points
…and so on.

S-T-R-E-T-C-H Your Senses

To write a really good description of a place, you should use all your senses. Follow the steps below to write a detailed description of a place without naming it. How? Simply s-t-r-e-t-c-h your senses!

1. Name a place. _____
2. Write five specific adjectives that describe how this place looks.
   _____
3. List at least six objects you can find in this place. _____
   _____
4. What can you smell, hear, or taste in this place? _____
   _____
5. Write at least five "ing" words that tell what can happen in this place. _____
   _____
6. List at least three short phrases to describe any special qualities about this
   place. _____
7. Describe how you feel when you're in or at this place. _____
   _____
8. Read over your answers to 1–7. On the back of this sheet, write a paragraph that describes the place *without* naming it.
9. Ask a classmate to read your paragraph and guess the place you described.

©The Education Center, Inc. • *THE MAILBOX®* • *Intermediate* • April/May 1998

Team members: _____ Inference
_____

Take A Guess!

Directions: Think of a feeling and write it on the bone. Below the bone, list words, people, and situations that could help others guess this feeling. Then number the clues in the order that you'll share them. (*Hint: Begin with the hardest clue and end with the easiest.*)

The feeling:

_____

Words (not synonyms) that describe this feeling: _____
_____

People who have experienced this feeling: _____
_____

Situations in which this feeling can be felt: _____
_____
_____

©The Education Center, Inc. • *THE MAILBOX®* • *Intermediate* • April/May 1998

Note To The Teacher: Use the top half of this page with "Where Am I?" on page 101. Use the bottom half with "Take A Guess!" on page 101.

Write On!

"In-spidered" Writing

"In-spider" your students to write this fall with the help of some eight-legged friends! Duplicate a spider pattern on black construction paper for each student. Give each student a spider and a piece of white chalk, directing him to write one writing topic on each leg of his spider. Next have each student cut out his spider and add wiggle or cut-out eyes to it. Draw a web outline on a covered bulletin board and post the spiders on it. Use an inexpensive, cotton spiderweb for a more authentic look. Encourage students to refer to the spiders for future writing inspiration.

Julie Eick Granchelli—Gr. 4
Towne Elementary
Medina, NY

Star Author

Reward a hardworking writer with this star treatment! Keep a supply of cut-out stars on hand in your classroom. When you find a student whose finished work is done particularly well, ask for permission to read it aloud to the class. After reading the selection, have each of your students write something positive about the work on a cut-out star. Display the featured writing along with the complimentary stars on a "Star Author" bulletin board. Students will love seeing their work displayed and receiving positive praise from their peers!

Jessica Nardi—Language Arts Resource
Hillsborough Elementary
Livingston, NJ

Synonym Trees

A pair of synonym trees are just the thing for students whose writing is growing short on word variety! Cut two large tree trunks—each with six large branches—from brown bulletin-board paper. Attach the trees to a classroom wall; then cut a generous supply of leaves from fall-colored construction paper. Next have your students brainstorm a list of words they feel are overused in their writing, such as *big, said,* and *good.* Instruct students to select the 12 most overused words from the list. Record each of the selected words on a tree branch; then direct students to use a thesaurus to find and share aloud synonyms for each overused word. Record each synonym on a cut-out leaf and attach it to the branch of the word it can replace. Remind each student to refer to the trees for a synonym whenever he finds himself stumped!

Nancy Oglevie Jaeger—Gr. 5
Sangre Ridge Elementary
Stillwater, OK

Write On!

Strange Visitor

Improve descriptive writing and character development with this fun activity. Secretly select one student to bring an unusual, mismatched outfit of clothing to school and put it on before writing class. Instruct him to enter the classroom, clap his hands to get everyone's attention, and walk out of the room. As a class, brainstorm a description of the student and record students' responses on the chalkboard. Invite the dressed-up child back into the room and check the class's description for accuracy. Follow up by having each student write a descriptive paragraph about himself so that someone would be able to use it to pick him out of a crowd. Collect and redistribute the papers; then have students guess whom each paragraph describes.

Betty Bowlin—Gr. 4, Henry Elementary, Ballwin, MO

Poetry Inspired By Art

Link haiku and symmetry with this simple art activity. Give each student a 9" x 12" sheet of construction paper to place on her desk. Drop a splash or two of paint on each student's paper. Have the student fold her paper in half greeting card–style, press the two halves together, then unfold the paper. Next instruct the student to write a haiku about what she sees in the paint blotch. After the paint dries, staple each poem to its artwork and post the project in the room.

Susan A. Ferguson—Gr. 5
Byram Intermediate School, Stanhope, NJ

> Whales in the ocean,
> Swimming around and around
> In the sea so blue.

My Buddy

Your next bulletin board is just a writing assignment away! Have each student bring in his "buddy"—a special blanket, a teddy bear, or another object—from his early childhood days. Then have the student write a paragraph explaining what his buddy meant to him. Take a picture of each student with his buddy. Display the pictures and paragraphs on a bulletin board titled "Meet My Buddy!"

James Embrescia—Gr. 4
Hilltop Elementary, Beachwood, OH

A "Write" Idea!

End those frequent complaints of "I don't know what to write about!" with this easy idea. Have each student bring in a small assignment pad. Throughout the day—whenever a topic comes up that would be good to write about—call out, "A 'write' idea!" Then have the class brainstorm two or three related topics to write about. Have each student record the topics in her assignment pad. After only a few such sessions, your students' pads will be packed with writing ideas!

Terry Healy—Gifted K–6, Eugene Field Elementary, Manhattan, KS

> Describe your favorite season of the year.
>
> Compare a tree in winter to a tree in summer.
>
> Tell about a time you experienced a severe storm.

MATH UNITS

Places, Everyone!

Creative Strategies For Teaching Place-Value Concepts

Putting numbers in their places—that's what place value is all about! Help students better understand this challenging math topic with the following hands-on games and learning activities.

by Irving P. Crump

This Must Be The Place!

Review basic place-value concepts and introduce new ones with this versatile, hands-on chart that students can make and keep. Provide each student with a 12" x 18" sheet of light-colored paper and a ruler. Also provide permanent markers for students to share. Then guide them through these steps:

1. With your sheet of paper lying horizontally, fold it in half and crease it. Then fold it in half and crease it again.
2. Open up your sheet. Using a permanent marker, draw lines along the three vertical creases.
3. Measure and draw a horizontal line one inch from the top edge of your sheet.
4. Beginning on the left side, label the four resulting boxes "billions," "millions," "thousands," and "ones."
5. Measure and draw another horizontal line one inch below the first one.
6. Beginning on the right side of your paper, measure and draw a vertical line 1 1/2 inches from the edge. Extend this line from the first horizontal line down to the bottom edge of the paper.
7. Measure and draw another vertical line 1 1/2 inches from the first one. Extend this line from the first horizontal line down to the bottom edge of the paper.
8. From left to right, label the three resulting small boxes "H" (hundreds), "T" (tens), and "O" (ones).
9. Continue measuring and drawing vertical lines (1 1/2 inches apart) across the paper so that the thousands, millions, and billions sections are exactly like the ones section.
10. Label the three column headings ("H," "T," and "O") in each section.

Next provide each student with a small (about 4" x 6") piece of construction paper in a color that contrasts with his chart. Have each student cut this sheet into small markers (about one square centimeter each). Share with students that our numeration system is based on groups, or multiples, of ten—thus it's a *decimal system.* Our numeration system is also known as a *place-value system.* In a place-value system, every digit in a numeral has two different values: the *value of the digit* and the *place value of the digit.* Students' charts show just some of the place values in our numeration system.

Then have students use their place-value charts and markers with the teacher-directed lessons on page 107.

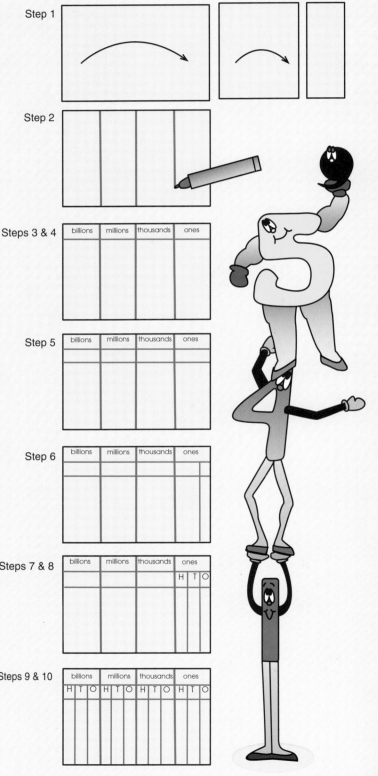

Introductory Activities

Number Families
Skill: vocabulary, basic skills

Write the numeral 123,456,789,246 on a chalkboard or transparency. Tell students to note that the digits are grouped in threes. Each group is called a *period.* (Students may wish to use the word *family* instead.) The periods are named—reading from left to right: *billions, millions, thousands,* and *ones.* Also have students observe that within each group the names are the same: *hundreds, tens,* and *ones.* Thus the *place value* of any digit is ones, tens, or hundreds followed by the group name. Ask students if the ones family is named when reading a numeral. *(no)* Help students see that to read a numeral, it's necessary to consider the *values* of the digits and the *positions* they occupy.

Breaking Down Big Numerals
Skill: simplifying large numerals

Cover all of the digits in the numeral written on the board (123,456,789,246) except for the 123 group. Ask a volunteer to read that group of digits *(one hundred twenty-three).* Next cover all of the digits except the 456 group and ask a volunteer to read that group of digits *(four hundred fifty-six).* Repeat this procedure with the last two groups of digits. Guide students to see that in reading (or writing) a large numeral, it's helpful to break it down into its periods—and read each period as a simple, three-digit numeral. Also help students see that the commas represent pauses when reading a numeral, just as they do in reading text. Whenever a student comes to a comma in reading or writing a large numeral, he knows to pause and say or write a period name. Ask volunteers to reread each group of three digits—this time adding the period name after each one.

In First Place
Skill: naming the first place value

Beginning from the right, have each student place one marker in each of the first eight columns of his chart. Ask a volunteer to read the numeral that is formed *(11 million, 111 thousand, 111).* Next have students clear their charts and place four markers in each of the first six columns. Ask a volunteer to read the numeral that is formed *(444 thousand, 444).* Have students observe that the first digit in a numeral represents the largest place value, and that it determines how to begin reading or writing the numeral. Continue with various other examples, extending all the way to the hundred billions place.

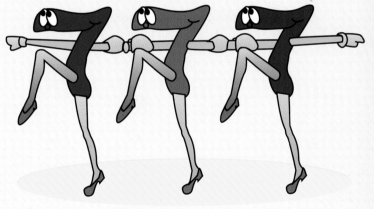

A Place For Nothing
Skill: zeros as placeholders

Have each student place six markers in the one millions place, five in the hundred thousands place, three in the one thousands place, one in the hundreds place, and seven in the ones place. Then ask the class, "How many digits will this numeral have when you write it?" *(seven)* Ask a volunteer to write the numeral on the board *(6,503,107).* Remind students that the value of the first digit's place *(millions)* determines how large the numeral will be and that any empty place to the right of that digit must have a zero placeholder. Continue with other similar examples. Have students write their resulting numerals on paper.

Place-Value Games

Place-Value Matchup
Whole-Class Game

Now have students put away their place-value charts for this fun game of skill and chance. First have each student draw five blanks on a sheet of paper to represent a five-digit number. Next pull ten cards from a deck of playing cards: one joker plus the 2–9 and an ace of any suit. The ace will represent *1* and the joker *0*. Also label five index cards as follows: "10,000s"; "1,000s"; "100s"; "10s"; and "1s."

To play, shuffle the ten playing cards. Draw a card and announce its value to the class. Each student writes that digit in one of his five blanks. After the digit is written, it cannot be moved. Lay that card aside, and continue drawing and announcing four more cards. Keep these cards together to use later. After you've drawn five cards, each student will have written a five-digit number.

Next mix up the five discarded cards. Draw one playing card and one index card. Announce the value of the playing card and the place value on the index card. If a student's digit matches both the digit *and* the place value you announce, he earns one point. Have each student who has a match draw a circle around it. Continue drawing four more pairs of cards: one each of the discarded playing cards and one of the index cards. If all five of a student's digits match, he earns a bonus of five points for a total of ten altogether. Extend this game to include hundred thousands and millions by making additional matching place-value cards.

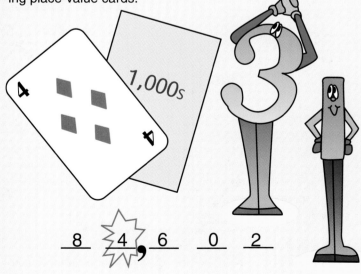

Match!

The Great Place-Value Race
Game For Two

Provide each pair of students with one copy of the gameboard on page 109, the directions on the top half of page 110, and a pair of dice. Give Player One ten markers (paper squares, buttons, checkers, etc.) of the same color; give his opponent ten markers of a different color. Read and discuss the directions with the entire class. Then have each pair of students determine who begins the game by rolling the dice. The student in each pair who rolls the larger number begins play.

Take A Chance!
Whole-Class Game

Provide each student with a copy of page 111. Have each student cut the sheet in half and save the bottom half to use later. Have students follow steps 1–3 in the directions to prepare for playing "Take A Chance!"

While students prepare, pull ten cards from a deck of playing cards: one joker plus the 2–9 and an ace (any suit). The ace will represent *1* and the joker *0*. Mix up the cards. When everyone is ready, draw a card and announce its value to the class. (Remind students that you have the digits 0–9, but will call out only nine of them.) Each student must decide in which of the nine places to write that digit. Continue play until you've drawn and announced nine digits. Then instruct each student to write the nine-digit numeral that results from matching each digit to its place value on the octagon. Determine who has the greatest numeral.

To play again, have each student move his octagon to a blank space on his paper. Mix up the cards and follow the same directions above, or try one of the following variations:

- Students must leave the center box blank until the ninth card is announced. Every student will write that digit in the box.
- After a card is drawn and its value announced, put the card back in the deck and reshuffle. Then draw a second card. Repeat this process until nine cards have been drawn.

The Great Place-Value Race

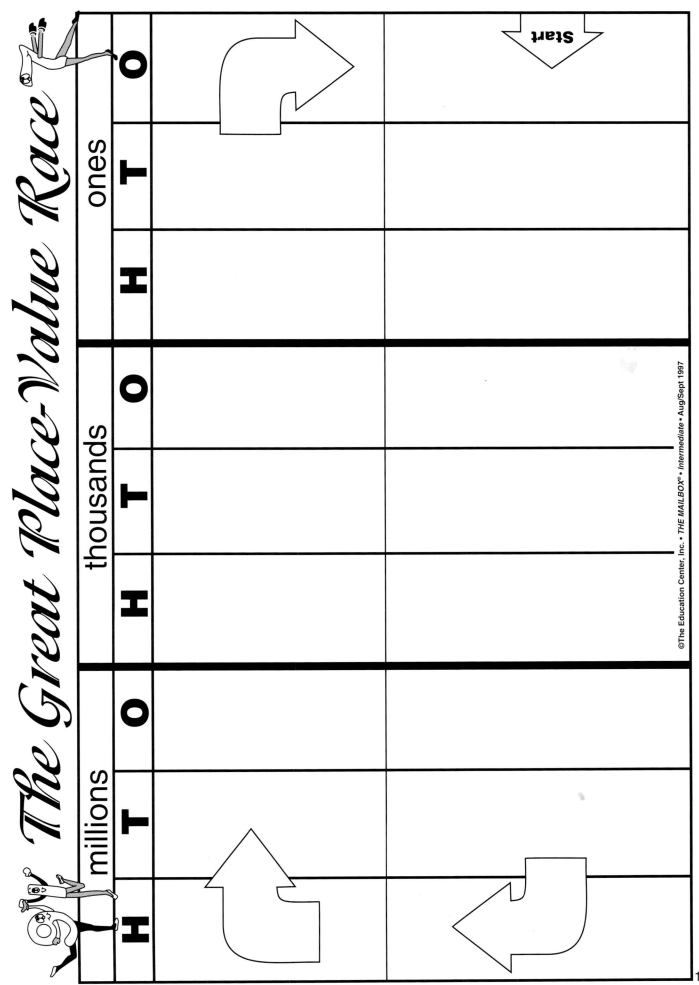

millions			thousands			ones		
H	T	O	H	T	O	H	T	O

Start

©The Education Center, Inc. • *THE MAILBOX® • Intermediate • Aug/Sept 1997*

Note To The Teacher: Use with "The Great Place-Value Race" on pages 108 and 110.

109

The Great Place-Value Race

Materials needed:
for each pair of players: one gameboard (page 109), pair of dice
for each player: ten same-colored game markers, pencil and paper

Directions for two players:
1. Place your ten game markers beside the gameboard near *Start.*
2. Player One rolls the dice and moves one of his or her game markers that number of spaces. If he or she rolls a *10, 11,* or *12,* Player One follows the arrows and continues to the top half of the gameboard. Example: If *12* is rolled, the marker will land in the one millions space.
3. Player Two then takes a turn.
4. Play continues until all ten of each player's markers have been moved onto the gameboard.
5. The object of the game is to build the largest number possible.
   —A player may have more than one marker in a space.
   —If a player lands in a space occupied by one or more of his or her opponent's markers, the player may bump one marker and remove it from the gameboard. That marker is no longer in play.
6. BONUS ROLL! After all markers of both players are on the gameboard, each player gets one bonus roll of the dice. A player may move any one of his or her markers on the gameboard the same number of spaces as his or her roll. (If that marker reaches the ones place, it follows the arrow on into the bottom half of the gameboard.)
7. Each player writes the numeral he or she created by counting his or her markers in both halves of the gameboard. Be sure the player includes any zero placeholders. The winner is the student with the greater numeral.

Note To The Teacher: Use with "The Great Place-Value Race" on pages 108 and 109.

- -

Name_____Patterns

Place-Value Patterns

Can you complete each pattern below? Pay close attention to place value—especially how each numeral is different from the one to its left. Fill in each blank with the numeral that fits the pattern.

1. 148; 158; 168; _____; 188; 198; _____

2. 605; 705; 805; _____; _____; 1,105; 1,205

3. 6,734; 5,734; 4,734; _____; _____; 1,734; _____

4. 76,485; 81,485; 86,485; _____; 96,485; _____; 106,485

5. 18,000; _____; _____; 24,000; 26,000; 28,000; _____

6. 156; 166; 266; 276; 376; _____; _____; _____; 596

7. 85; 185; 285; 385; 1,385; 2,385; 3,385; _____; _____; 33,385

8. 12,612; 12,617; 12,667; 13,167; _____; 68,167

9. 1,487,329; 487,329; 387,329; 377,329; 376,329; _____; _____

10. 512,479; 512,478; 512,468; 512,368; _____; 501,368; _____

11. 614,375; 614,376; 614,386; 614,486; 615,486; _____; _____

BONUS CHALLENGE: 364,237; 364,240; 364,300; 365,000; _____; 400,000

Take A Chance!

Feeling lucky? See what happens in this game of skill and chance!

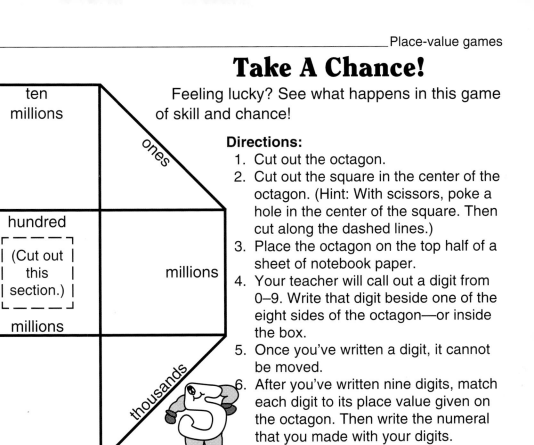

Directions:
1. Cut out the octagon.
2. Cut out the square in the center of the octagon. (Hint: With scissors, poke a hole in the center of the square. Then cut along the dashed lines.)
3. Place the octagon on the top half of a sheet of notebook paper.
4. Your teacher will call out a digit from 0–9. Write that digit beside one of the eight sides of the octagon—or inside the box.
5. Once you've written a digit, it cannot be moved.
6. After you've written nine digits, match each digit to its place value given on the octagon. Then write the numeral that you made with your digits.
7. The student with the greatest numeral is the winner.

The octagon labels (clockwise from top): ten millions, ones, millions, thousands, tens, hundreds, ten thousands, hundred thousands. Center box: hundred millions (Cut out this section.)

©The Education Center, Inc. • THE MAILBOX® • Intermediate • Aug/Sept 1997

Note To The Teacher: See page 108 for information on playing this game.

Top row: 9 4 8 2 0 3 | S T A R T → | 3 9 4 1 6 8 5

Left column: 1 8 5 9 0 6 8 2
Right column: 2 6 0 7 3 6 2 5

1,000,000 Or Bust!

See who can build the greatest number—without going over one million! Just follow the directions below.

Materials needed: paper and pencil for each player, one die

Directions for two players:
1. Player One rolls the die. Then Player One chooses and then announces either, "Digit," or "Place value."
   a. **If Player One chooses *digit:*** Count the same number of spaces as your roll and circle the digit you land on. Roll a second time. Match your second roll with the place value in the chart. Write the numeral that has the digit you circled in the matching place value. Example: If your circled number is 6 and you rolled a 3 on your second roll, your numeral would be 600. The digit 6 and the place value *100s* equal 600.
   b. **If Player One chooses *place value:*** Find the place value in the chart that matches your roll. Roll a second time. Count the same number of spaces as your second roll and circle the digit you land on. Write the numeral that has the digit you circled in the matching place value. Example: If you first rolled a 4, your place value is *1,000s*. If your second roll lands you on a 9, your numeral equals 9,000.
2. Player Two then takes a turn. (Don't land on a digit that has been circled. Just skip it and continue to the next one.)
3. Player One repeats Step 1. The player then adds this second numeral to the first one.
4. The object of the game is to see who can get closest to 1,000,000 without going over. A player may "freeze" after reaching 950,000. The opponent then continues play until he or she can top the frozen numeral without going over 1,000,000.

roll	place value
1	1s
2	10s
3	100s
4	1,000s
5	10,000s
6	100,000s

Bottom row: 7 1 7 0 8 3 6 1 9 4 5 1 0 7 4

LASSOING LISTS

Creative Ideas For Teaching Organized Listing

It's a student's worst math nightmare: a problem has more than one possible answer! What to do? A complete and organized list can help show all of the choices. Include the following creative ideas on *your* list of activities when you teach this useful problem-solving strategy.

by Irving P. Crump

Put It There, Pardner!

Introduce organized listing with this fun demonstration. Have two students come to the front of the classroom and shake hands with each other. Ask the class, "Is there any other possible combination of handshakes when two people shake hands with each other?" *(no)* Write the data shown on a chalkboard, replacing the letters with students' names.

A-B
1 handshake

• Invite a third student to join the pair. Then ask, "If *three* students shake hands with each other, how many different handshakes are possible?" Next have Student A shake hands with Students B and C. List these two combinations on the board as shown. Have Student B shake hands with Student C. Write this combination on the board. Ask, "Should Student B shake hands with Student A? Should Student C shake hands with either Student A or B?" *(No, these combinations have already been made.)* With three students, three different handshakes are possible.

A-B   B-C
A-C
3 handshakes

• Next have a *fourth* student join the three at the front of the class. Ask, "If *four* students shake hands with each other, how many different handshakes are possible?" Then have Student A shake hands with Students B, C, and D. Write these combinations on the board. Next have Student B shake hands with Students C and D, and write these combinations on the board. Ask why Student B shouldn't shake hands with Student A. *(They have already shaken hands with each other.)* Lastly have Student C shake hands with Student D and write that combination on the board. Ask, "Should Student D shake hands with any of the other three students?" *(No, students A, B, and C have already shaken hands with student D.)* Six different handshakes are possible with four students.

A-B   B-C   C-D
A-C   B-D
A-D
6 handshakes

- Repeat the activity on page 112 with *five* students shaking hands, and then with *six*. List each combination (as shown) as students shake hands. Have students compare the number of students to the number of handshakes and look for a pattern. (See the table below.) Have students determine how many different handshakes are possible if *ten* people shake hands with each other.

- Remind students that a list needs to be *ordered* or *organized* in some way. Writing down all possible combinations in random order can be confusing: a combination may be left out or repeated. But most importantly, it takes more time, even if the answer is correct! See the ideas below and the reproducible on page 114 for more listing activities.

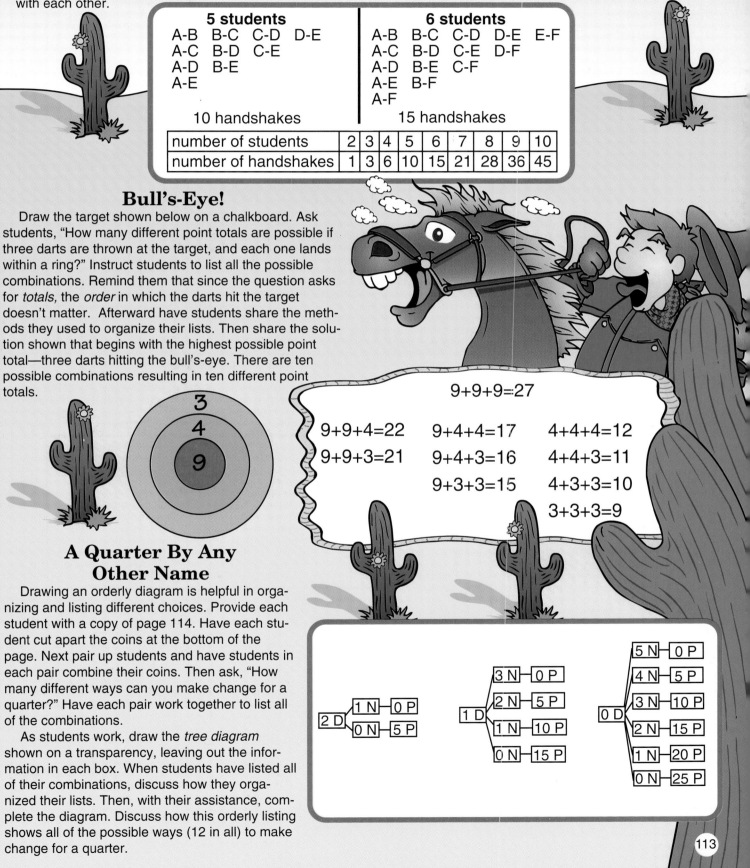

5 students

A-B B-C C-D D-E
A-C B-D C-E
A-D B-E
A-E

10 handshakes

6 students

A-B B-C C-D D-E E-F
A-C B-D C-E D-F
A-D B-E C-F
A-E B-F
A-F

15 handshakes

number of students	2	3	4	5	6	7	8	9	10
number of handshakes	1	3	6	10	15	21	28	36	45

Bull's-Eye!

Draw the target shown below on a chalkboard. Ask students, "How many different point totals are possible if three darts are thrown at the target, and each one lands within a ring?" Instruct students to list all the possible combinations. Remind them that since the question asks for *totals*, the *order* in which the darts hit the target doesn't matter. Afterward have students share the methods they used to organize their lists. Then share the solution shown that begins with the highest possible point total—three darts hitting the bull's-eye. There are ten possible combinations resulting in ten different point totals.

$$9+9+9=27$$

$$9+9+4=22 \quad 9+4+4=17 \quad 4+4+4=12$$
$$9+9+3=21 \quad 9+4+3=16 \quad 4+4+3=11$$
$$9+3+3=15 \quad 4+3+3=10$$
$$3+3+3=9$$

A Quarter By Any Other Name

Drawing an orderly diagram is helpful in organizing and listing different choices. Provide each student with a copy of page 114. Have each student cut apart the coins at the bottom of the page. Next pair up students and have students in each pair combine their coins. Then ask, "How many different ways can you make change for a quarter?" Have each pair work together to list all of the combinations.

As students work, draw the *tree diagram* shown on a transparency, leaving out the information in each box. When students have listed all of their combinations, discuss how they organized their lists. Then, with their assistance, complete the diagram. Discuss how this orderly listing shows all of the possible ways (12 in all) to make change for a quarter.

113

Rounding Up Lists

Why is making a list a good way to solve some math problems? An organized list helps you show all the possible answers. You can list all of the different answers, then find the one that works. Sometimes you may have to count all of the answers.

Solve each problem below by making an organized list. Show your work for problems 1–5 on another sheet of paper.

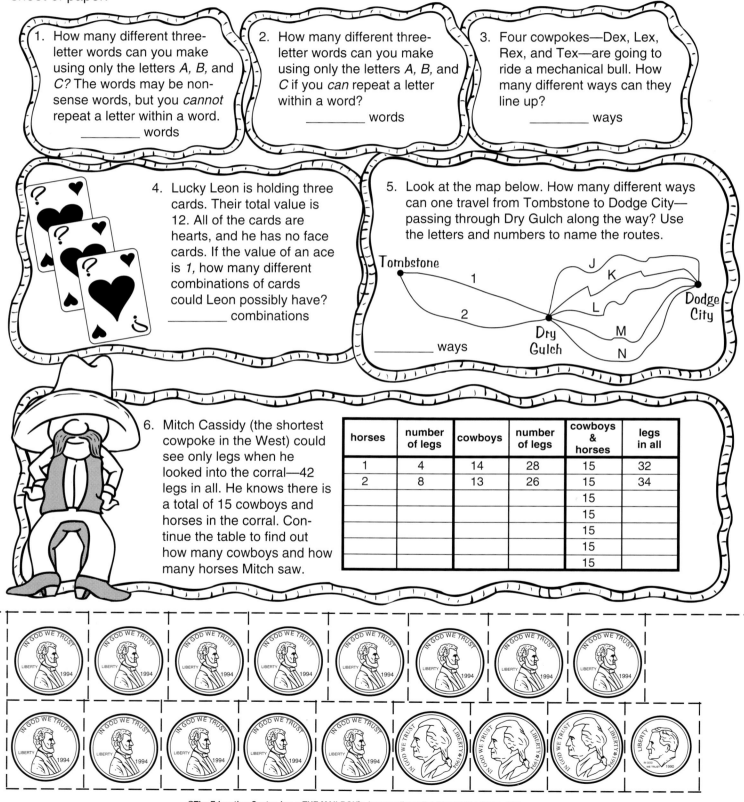

1. How many different three-letter words can you make using only the letters *A, B,* and *C?* The words may be non-sense words, but you *cannot* repeat a letter within a word.
   _____ words

2. How many different three-letter words can you make using only the letters *A, B,* and *C* if you *can* repeat a letter within a word?
   _____ words

3. Four cowpokes—Dex, Lex, Rex, and Tex—are going to ride a mechanical bull. How many different ways can they line up?
   _____ ways

4. Lucky Leon is holding three cards. Their total value is 12. All of the cards are hearts, and he has no face cards. If the value of an ace is *1,* how many different combinations of cards could Leon possibly have?
   _____ combinations

5. Look at the map below. How many different ways can one travel from Tombstone to Dodge City—passing through Dry Gulch along the way? Use the letters and numbers to name the routes.

   Tombstone
   1
   2
   J
   K
   L
   M
   N
   Dodge City
   Dry Gulch
   _____ ways

6. Mitch Cassidy (the shortest cowpoke in the West) could see only legs when he looked into the corral—42 legs in all. He knows there is a total of 15 cowboys and horses in the corral. Continue the table to find out how many cowboys and how many horses Mitch saw.

horses	number of legs	cowboys	number of legs	cowboys & horses	legs in all
1	4	14	28	15	32
2	8	13	26	15	34
				15	
				15	
				15	
				15	
				15	

Batter Up!

A Lineup Of Creative Math Activities On The World Series

Sure, the leaves are changing colors and there's a nip in the air. But ask any schoolchild for a sign of autumn, and you'll probably hear, "It's World Series time!" Celebrate the crown jewel of America's pastime with the following series of activities.

ideas by Kim C. Davis—Gr. 4, Fair Street Elementary, Gainesville, GA

Getting Ready

As the World Series approaches, begin collecting newspaper and magazine articles to share with your students. You're sure to find biographies on the players and coaches of the two teams involved. Plus there are always plenty of tables and charts filled with tons of data—such as the players' heights, weights, offensive and defensive statistics, hometowns, and family information. Use these statistics in a variety of teacher-directed and independent math lessons such as the suggestions that follow.

Suggested Activities:

- Have students list the players in order by jersey numbers.

- Have students find the *mean, median,* and *mode* of the players' weights and heights.

- Use the weight and height statistics in graphing exercises. Discuss the different relationships revealed by the data.

- Using a calculator, demonstrate how batting averages are computed. *(number of hits ÷ number of times at bat; then round the quotient to the nearest thousandth)*

- Have students plot batting averages, ERAs, RBIs, number of stolen bases, and home runs on bar graphs.

- On an appropriate map, plot the hometowns of players and coaches. Have students compute the distance between the two participating teams' home fields.

- Have students draw body outlines—to scale—of each team's players on butcher paper, from tallest to shortest. Then have students work in pairs to draw one another's outlines. Have students color both the student and player outlines to make them realistic. After students cut out all of the figures, attach the baseball players to a classroom or hallway wall. Then position your students' outlines in front of the players. Students will have a better idea of the meanings of proportion and size when they see for themselves just how tall 6 feet 3 inches is!

- Using a well-publicized salary of a professional athlete, calculate the player's pay per year, month, week, and day. Also compute the player's per-game earnings by dividing the salary by 162—the number of games during the regular pro baseball season.

- Find out the attendance per individual game for a local sports stadium for one sporting season. Have students find the average attendance per game and the total yearly attendance. Provide students with ticket prices; then have them find the average income taken in by the stadium for each game and for the entire season.

- Use the home run–hitting reproducible on page 116 to give students plenty of batting practice on reading tables.

50 Years Of The World Series

The World Series is one of the world's major sports events. It has been played every year since 1903, except in 1904 and 1994. The American and National League pennant winners play each other. The first team to win four games wins the world championship. The table below includes information about the World Series of the last 50 years.

year	winner/league	loser/league	games won-lost	year	winner/league	loser/league	games won-lost
1947	New York A*	Brooklyn N**	4–3	1972	Oakland A*	Cincinnati N**	4–3
1948	Cleveland A*	Boston N**	4–2	1973	Oakland A*	New York N**	4–3
1949	New York A*	Brooklyn N**	4–1	1974	Oakland A*	Los Angeles N**	4–1
1950	New York A*	Philadelphia N**	4–0	1975	Cincinnati N**	Boston A*	4–3
1951	New York A*	New York N**	4–2	1976	Cincinnati N**	New York A*	4–0
1952	New York A*	Brooklyn N**	4–3	1977	New York A*	Los Angeles N**	4–2
1953	New York A*	Brooklyn N**	4–2	1978	New York A*	Los Angeles N**	4–2
1954	New York N**	Cleveland A*	4–0	1979	Pittsburgh N**	Baltimore A*	4–3
1955	Brooklyn N**	New York A*	4–3	1980	Philadelphia N**	Kansas City A*	4–2
1956	New York A*	Brooklyn N**	4–3	1981	Los Angeles N**	New York A*	4–2
1957	Milwaukee N**	New York A*	4–3	1982	St. Louis N**	Milwaukee A*	4–3
1958	New York A*	Milwaukee N**	4–3	1983	Baltimore A*	Philadelphia N**	4–1
1959	Los Angeles N**	Chicago A*	4–2	1984	Detroit A*	San Diego N**	4–1
1960	Pittsburgh N**	New York A*	4–3	1985	Kansas City A*	St. Louis N**	4–3
1961	New York A*	Cincinnati N**	4–1	1986	New York N**	Boston A*	4–3
1962	New York A*	San Francisco N**	4–3	1987	Minnesota A*	St. Louis N**	4–3
1963	Los Angeles N**	New York A*	4–0	1988	Los Angeles N**	Oakland A*	4–1
1964	St. Louis N**	New York A*	4–3	1989	Oakland A*	San Francisco N**	4–0
1965	Los Angeles N**	Minnesota A*	4–3	1990	Cincinnati N**	Oakland A*	4–0
1966	Baltimore A*	Los Angeles N**	4–0	1991	Minnesota A*	Atlanta N**	4–3
1967	St. Louis N**	Boston A*	4–3	1992	Toronto A*	Atlanta N**	4–2
1968	Detroit A*	St. Louis N**	4–3	1993	Toronto A*	Philadelphia N**	4–2
1969	New York N**	Baltimore A*	4–1	1994	Not held		
1970	Baltimore A*	Cincinnati N**	4–1	1995	Atlanta N**	Cleveland A*	4–2
1971	Pittsburgh N**	Baltimore A*	4–3	1996	New York A*	Atlanta N**	4–2
A* = American League				N** = National League			

A. Use the table to answer the following:

1. How many series have been only four games long? _____
2. How many series have lasted seven games? _____
3. Which team has won the most series in a row? _____ How many? _____
4. In the last five years (excluding 1994), which league has won more series? _____
5. Before 1995, when was Cleveland last in the series? _____ How many years ago was that? _____
6. When was the last time that the same two teams played in the series for two straight years? _____
7. How many different teams won the series in the 1970s? _____

B. Label each statement T (true), F (false), or DK (don't know). Then for each statement that you marked T or F, tell whether you used the I (introduction), the T (table), or B (both) to help you. The first one is done for you.

__F__ 1. The World Series has been played every year since 1903. __B__
____ 2. The American League has won more series than the National League. ___
____ 3. A series consists of at least four games. ___
____ 4. The home team usually wins the World Series. ___
____ 5. Sometimes two teams from the same city play in the World Series. ___
____ 6. More people watch the World Series on TV than any other sports event. ___
____ 7. Since 1947, New York (A*) has been in more series than any other team. ___
____ 8. Some World Series games have been called off because of darkness. ___

Bonus Box: The 1947 World Series is especially memorable because of Jackie Robinson and television. Explain why on the back of this page.

©The Education Center, Inc. • THE MAILBOX® • Intermediate • Oct/Nov 1997 • Key p. 308

GRAPHS UNDER CONSTRUCTION

Creative, Hands-On Activities For Building Graphing Success

Collecting data—then graphing that data—is one way students can make sense of the tons of information in their lives. Include the following creative teaching suggestions and learning experiences to help your students build graphing skills.

by Irving P. Crump

Keeping It All Together

One key for successfully collecting and displaying data is *organizational skills.* Help students with this skill throughout your graphing activities by providing them each with a copy of the miniposter on page 120 and a blank folder. Have each student color and decorate his miniposter, then open his folder and paste the miniposter on the left side. On the side adjacent to the miniposter, have each student copy the math terms shown, allowing plenty of space for definitions and examples. Have students refer to their folders often, adding definitions and other terms as needed. Encourage students to store all related work and reproducibles in the folder as well.

—statistics
—tally sheet
—frequency table
—bar graph
—pictograph
—number scale
—interval
—vertical axis
—horizontal axis
—histogram
—line graph
—circle graph

Graphs In The News

Introduce the term *statistics* to your students, asking what it means to them. Then share that *statistics* is "the branch of math that deals with collecting, organizing, displaying, and analyzing data." Discuss with your students the different types of graphs they've seen. Then ask them to cut out and bring to class some of those graphs. Newspapers and newsmagazines—especially *USA Today®, Time®, Newsweek®,* and *U.S. News & World Report®*—regularly include bright, colorful graphs that display a variety of trends, information, and current events. Title a bulletin board "Picture This!" and post the graphs on it. Invite students to view the graphs and discuss them with each other.

On a sheet of chart paper, list the different types of data that are shown in the graphs. Ask students, "Why is a graph a useful way to display data?" *(A graph is concise and easy to read, and provides a pictorial display of information.)* Continue having students add graphs to the display throughout your unit.

117

Tally Up!

Tally Sheet

number of letters in name	number of students
2	
3				
4	ﬀﬀﬀ (tally marks)
5			
6	ﬀﬀﬀ |||
7			
8					

Using a *tally sheet* is a simple way to collect data. Ask students, "Who in our class has the longest first name? How many other students have names with that many letters?" Call on several volunteers to suggest how they would organize the data you're asking for. Their responses will likely include:

- List students' names. Then count the letters in each one. Write that number beside the name.
- Make columns with number headings (2 letters, 3 letters, etc.). Write each name in the matching column.
- List numbers (2 letters, 3 letters, etc.) in a column. Write each name beside the matching number.

Next make a tally sheet, like the one shown, on a transparency or the chalkboard, adding more numbers if necessary. In turn, have each child state his name and the number of letters it has. As each number is given, make a tally mark beside the corresponding number on the transparency. When finished, ask students if your original questions have now been answered. Also ask if this method was an efficient way to answer the questions. Then continue with the next activity to show a simple way to display this information.

Using A Frequency Table

Beside the tally sheet (from the preceding activity), make a *frequency table* like the one shown. Then ask, "Which number of letters on the tally sheet has the most matching names? How many names?" Write this information in the first line of the table. Continue with the number of letters that has the second-most matching names. Add this information in the second line of the table. Continue filling the table until every student is represented. Then ask, "Which display is easier to read: the tally sheet or the frequency table?" *(The frequency table is easier to read because the information is listed in an orderly fashion. Also there are no tally marks to count, and facts can be found more readily.)*

Frequency Table

number of letters in name	number of students
3	8
4	5
5	4
6	3
7	2
8	2

---

1. Let A be the *year* in which you were born.
   A = 1988
2. Let B be the *day of the year* on which you were born.
   January: 31 days
   February: 29 days (1988 was a leap year.)
   March: 31 days
   April: 12 days
   B =103rd day of the year (31+ 29 + 31+12 = 103)
   B = 103
3. Find C: C= (A − 1) ÷ 4. Ignore the remainder.
   C = (1988 − 1) ÷ 4 = 1987 ÷ 4 = 496 r. 3
   C = 496
4. Find D: D = A + B + C
   D = 1988 + 103 + 496
   D = 2,587
5. Divide D by 7.
   2,587 ÷ 7= 369 r. 4. Note the remainder: **4**

Use the table below to see which day of the week matches the remainder of the division problem in Step 5.

(The student born on April 12, 1988, was born on a Tuesday.)

Remainder:	Birthday:
0	Friday
1	Saturday
2	Sunday
3	Monday
4	Tuesday
5	Wednesday
6	Thursday

Bar Graphs And Pictographs

Ask students what kinds of graphs they see most often in magazines and textbooks, and they'll likely say *bar graphs* and *pictographs*. Share with students that these graphs show comparisons of data. And although a pictograph is usually colorful and eye-catching, it doesn't show specific data as well as a bar graph does. Have students collect data to display in a bar graph or pictograph by asking, "On which day of the week were you born?" Share the steps for determining one's day of birth shown in the chart at the left. Then, as you guide students, have them complete each step. (The chart includes a completed sample birthdate: April 12, 1988.) When everyone has finished, draw a tally chart and frequency table on the chalkboard. Ask each student to state his day of birth as you complete the tally sheet. Then organize the tally sheet results in the frequency table, beginning with the day of the week with the most tally marks.

To complete the activity, give each student a copy of page 122. Direct half of the class to make bar graphs—and the other half pictographs—of the information listed in the frequency table. Suggest that students review the information on their miniposters to help them.

Introducing The Histogram

A *histogram* is a special bar graph that shows the number of times data occurs within a certain range. While the bars in a bar graph and in a histogram are of the same width, the bars in a histogram are connected with no space between them. Another difference between the two is that a bar graph shows specific information and a histogram's information is much more general.

To collect data for students to use in a histogram, tape two yardsticks end-to-end on a wall so that each student can measure her height. Then divide students into pairs. Have the students in each pair measure each other's height to the nearest inch. When all heights are determined, have each student write her initials and her height on the chalkboard. Ask students to study the data and think about what intervals (ranges) should be included in a histogram to display the data (examples: 50–54 in., 55–59 in., 60–64 in., etc.). Stress that the intervals must all be equal. Next provide each student with a copy of page 122 on which to make a histogram of the class data.

Clevell Harris

hour	number of visitors
8:00 – 9:00	
9:00 – 10:00	
10:00 – 11:00	
11:00 – 12:00	
12:00 – 1:00	
1:00 – 2:00	
2:00 – 3:00	

On The Line

A *line graph* shows changes and variations over a period of time. To make a line graph, students follow the same guidelines as those for making a bar graph—except that lines are drawn instead of bars.

Early one morning before your instructional day begins, direct each student to label a sheet of paper as shown. Then tell students that they are going to keep a record of the number of visitors to your class during the day—both adults and children. Beginning with the 8:00 to 9:00 interval, have each student make a tally mark for each individual who comes to the classroom door during that hour. Even if the visitor does not enter the classroom, have students make a tally mark for him or her. Then, near the end of the day, instruct each student to make a line graph displaying the collected data for homework. Have each student draw his graph on a copy of the reproducible on page 122. Have student groups compare their graphs the next day.

A Piece Of The Pie

A *circle graph* (also called a pie chart) shows the parts of a whole and the relationships among those parts. Model a circle graph by sharing with students a typical Saturday in your life! Since a day has 24 hours, such a graph should be divided into 24 equal parts. Approximate the time you spend on each activity to the nearest hour; then list the data on the board. To get—and keep—your students' attention, embellish your day somewhat. For example, list the following data on the board: 7 hours—sleeping, 1 hour—schoolwork, 2 hours—meals, 3 hours—skateboarding, 4 hours—skydiving lessons, 5 hours—mountain climbing, and 2 hours—training your pet boa constrictor.

Next draw the 24-section circle graph shown on the chalkboard (or make a transparency of the one on page 121). Have students assist you as you complete your graph. As a follow-up, give each student a copy of page 121. Instruct each student to complete the 24-section circle graph to show a typical Saturday in his life—or perhaps one he would like to experience!

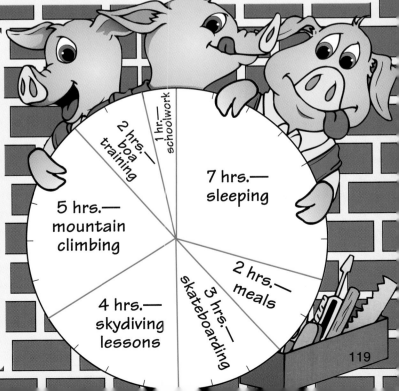

119

_____
(architect's name)

TIPS FOR BUILDING A GREAT GRAPH

1. Give your graph a title.
2. Label the *vertical axis*—from the base to the top.
3. Label the *horizontal axis*—from left to right at the bottom.
4. If you're making a *pictograph,* show the symbol and its value in a key.
5. If you're making a *bar graph,* make sure the bars are the same width. Also use equal space between the bars.
6. If you're making a *histogram,* all of the bars should be side by side.
7. Use the correct number scale. Make sure the intervals are equal (for example: 1–5, 6–10, 11–15, 16–20, etc.).

Tally Sheet

Best Building Materials*

straw	IIII
sticks	HHT II
bricks	HHT HHT II

*according to P.B.A. (Pig Builders Assoc.)

Frequency Table

Material	Number of Votes
bricks	12
sticks	7
straw	3

Bar Graph

Wolf Puffs Blown At Each House

number of puffs: 16, 14, 12, 10, 8, 6, 4, 2, 0

straw, sticks, bricks*

materials
*gave up after 16 puffs!

Circle Graph

A Wolf's Day

12 hours Exercising (to build up lungs!)
8 hours Sleeping
4 hours Eating

Pictograph

Wolf Exercises

aerobics, weights, running

♥ = 2 wolves

Histogram

Time It Takes P.B.A. Members To Build Houses

number of builders: 10, 9, 8, 7, 6, 5, 4, 3, 2, 1, 0

0–6, 7–12, 13–18, 19–24

hours

Line Graph

Pigs' Home Insurance Costs

hundreds of dollars: 6, 5, 4, 3, 2, 1, 0

May, June, July

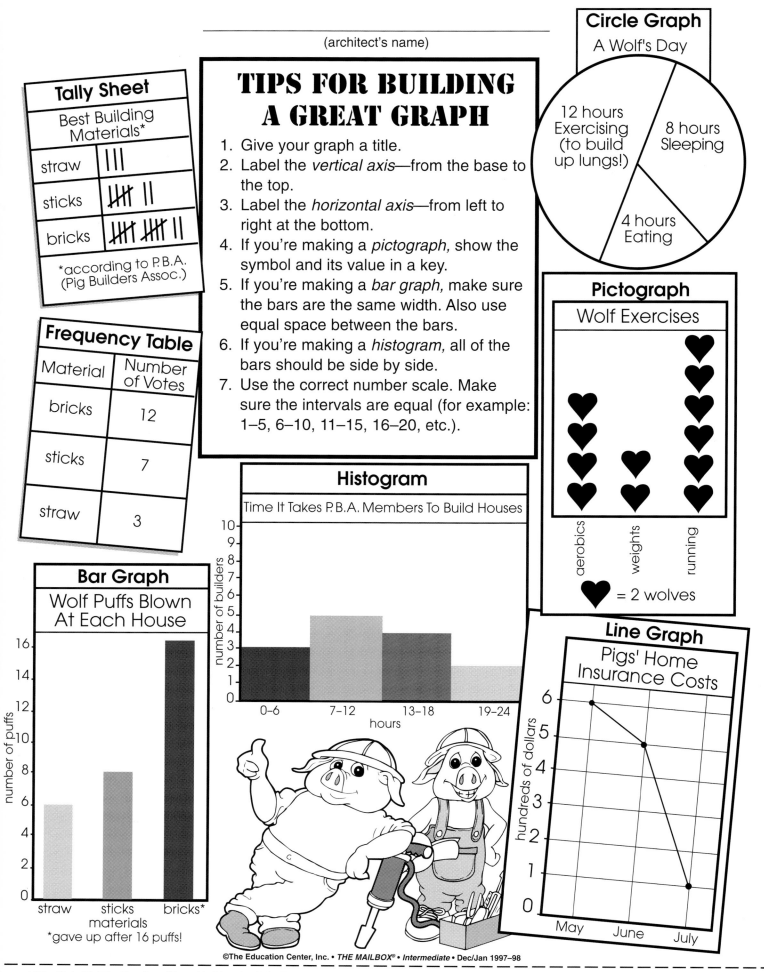

©The Education Center, Inc. • *THE MAILBOX*® • *Intermediate* • Dec/Jan 1997–98

Name _____

BUILDING CIRCLE GRAPHS

A circle graph divided into 24 equal sections can be used to show a variety of data:

- Use the graph to display data about a 24-hour day.
- Divide the graph into 3, 4, 6, 8, or 12 (all factors of 24) equal sections to display other data. For example: 1 of 12 equal sections equals 5 minutes of an hour.

A circle graph divided into 100 equal sections can be used to show a variety of data:

- Use the graph to display percentages, which are based on 100.
- Use the graph to show parts of a dollar. For example: 10 of 100 equal sections equals 10¢.
- Divide the graph into 5, 10, 20, 25, or 50 (all factors of 100) equal sections to display other data. For example: 8 of 50 equal sections equals 8 U.S. states.

Note To The Teacher: Use with "A Piece Of The Pie" on page 119.

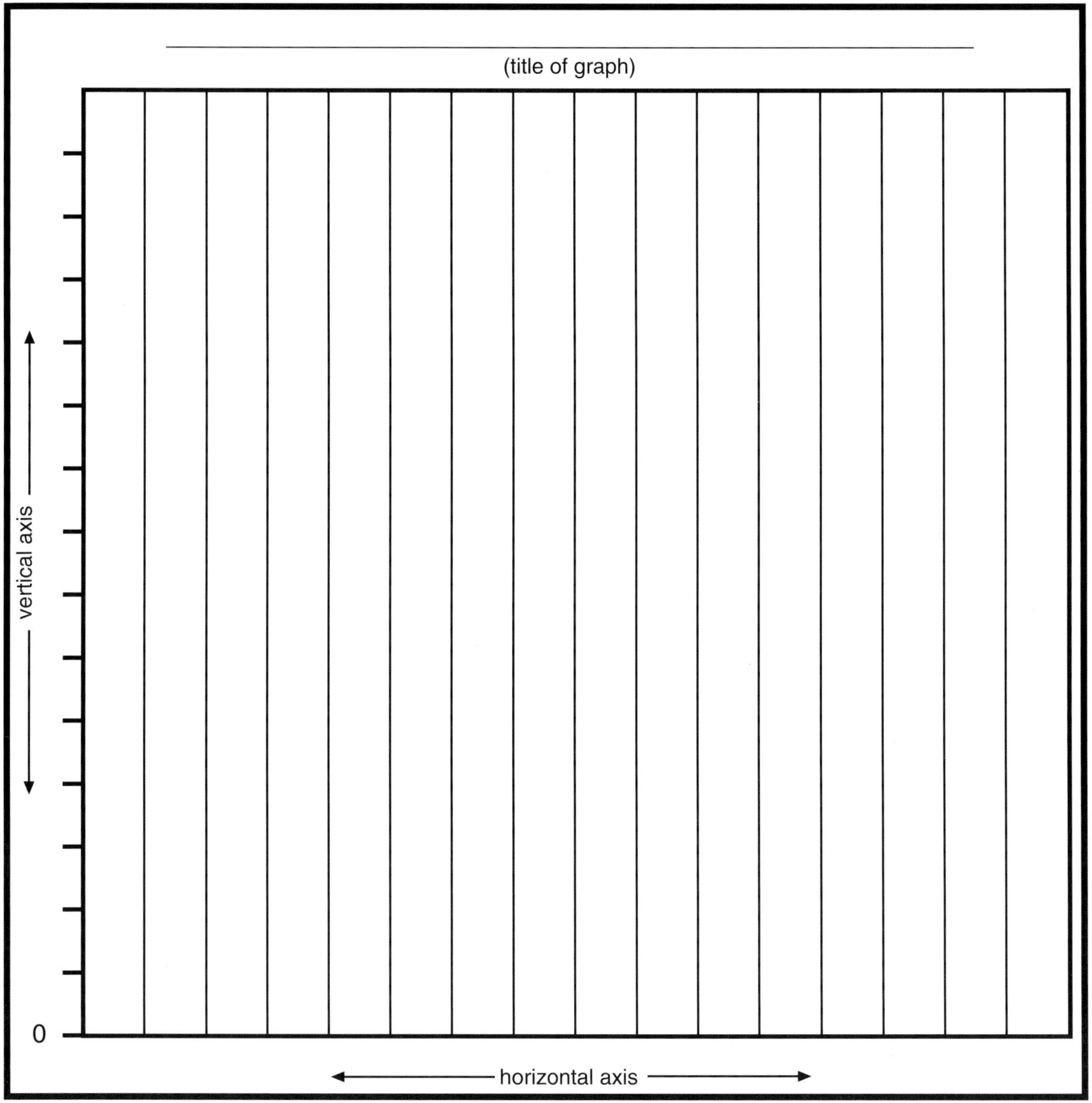

Name _____

A BLUEPRINT FOR BUILDING GRAPHS

Follow this plan to create graphs that are the envy of the neighborhood!

1. Title the graph.
2. Label the vertical axis: base to top.
3. Label the horizontal axis: left to right at the bottom.
4. *Bar Graph:*
   a. Bars should be of equal width.
   b. Use equal space between bars.
   c. Use a number scale with equal intervals (ranges).
   d. Use a ruler to make sure the bars are the right heights.
5. *Pictograph:*
   a. Use a key to show the symbol and its value.
   b. Label only one axis.
6. *Histogram:*
   a. Bars should be of equal width.
   b. Bars are connected. There is no space between them.
   c. A histogram gives general information. For example: the number of runners who finish a race between 50 and 60 minutes.
7. *Line Graph:*
   a. Make a bar graph, but leave off the bars!
   b. Mark points on a line graph.
   c. Connect the points with straight lines.

(title of graph)

← horizontal axis →

↕ vertical axis

0

©The Education Center, Inc. • THE MAILBOX® • Intermediate • Dec/Jan 1997–98

Note To The Teacher: Use with "Bar Graphs And Pictographs" on page 118 and "Introducing The Histogram" and "On The Line" on page 119.

Take A "Geo-Journey"!

Helping Students Discover Geometry In Their World

Why do intermediate students love geometry so much? Because there's lots of *doing*—classifying, putting shapes together, expanding patterns, and making three-dimensional shapes. Watch the beauty and logic of geometry come alive for your students with the following creative, hands-on activities and reproducibles.

ideas by Irving P. Crump and Gail Peckumn

Staying Organized With Geo-Folders

Our world is filled with patterns and shapes; in other words—geometry! Help students become more comfortable with the language of geometry by making geo-folders. Provide each student with a folder and a copy of page 126. Instruct the student to color and decorate the cover art, then cut it out and glue it to the front of his folder. Next have each student cut out the word list and glue it to the left side of his opened folder.

As you introduce geometry vocabulary, have each student list two or three words on each side of a sheet of notebook paper. After adding brief definitions and illustrations, have students store their sheets in their folders. The list covers a wide range of geometry concepts; include only those that you teach at your level.

Understanding Horizontal And Vertical

Help students better understand the concepts of *horizontal* and *vertical* with this simple demonstration. Fill a clear, clean, plastic two-liter soft-drink bottle about one-half full of water. Cap the bottle and set it upright on a tabletop. Ask a volunteer to describe the surface of the water. *(The surface of the water in the bottle is horizontal.)* Next hold the bottle by its top and tilt it about 45°. Ask someone to describe the surface of the water. *(It remains horizontal.)* Finally lay the bottle completely on its side, and ask a student to describe the surface of the water. *(It remains horizontal.)*

Tie a small stone or other weight to a piece of string and suspend it from the ceiling. Explain to the class that the string is vertical. Hold the bottle of water—as still as possible—behind the string. Ask students how vertical and horizontal relate to each other. *(They are at right angles to each other.)* Brainstorm with students different objects in the classroom, as well as outside the classroom, that are vertical and horizontal. Have students identify the objects in the list that have right angles. Ask the class, "Why are right angles so important?" *(Right angles are common in the environment. Walls are built at right angles to the ground. If they weren't they would tend to fall over.)*

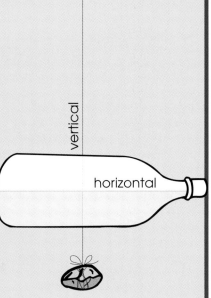

123

- Find three examples of congruent objects.
- Find an object that has a vertical line of symmetry.
- Find an object that is a perfect square.
- Find five different rectangles.
- List five different sets of car parts that are congruent.
- Find an object that has an acute angle.
- Find an object that has parallel line segments.
- Find a semicircle.
- Find two examples of spheres.
- Find an example of an octagon.

Schoolyard Geometry

Head to the great outdoors and take your students on a schoolyard geometry scavenger hunt! Duplicate a list (similar to the one shown) of various geometric concepts that are evident in your school environment. Is a water tower on your campus or nearby? Students should be able to identify different types of angles and shapes within its framework. Sidewalks, buildings, signs, playground equipment, fences, and vehicles all have distinct patterns and shapes that students will recognize. Give each student a copy of the list. Have students take their geo-folders with them and describe other examples of geometry concepts that they find.

Household Symmetry

Symmetry is everywhere—even in the mattress pads at home! To show students just how commonplace symmetrical designs are, bring in a mattress pad (or a copy of its pattern on a sheet of paper) and point out the symmetry in its pattern. Then, as a class, brainstorm other items found around the home that exhibit symmetry. For example: the pattern in a rug, a sofa, or the family china; the front panel of a boom box; or the design in a tiled kitchen floor.

For homework instruct each student to draw examples of five objects that have symmetry—one object per side of a sheet of paper—that he finds at home. The next day have each student share his examples with the class. Challenge class members to guess each design as it's presented. Afterward have each student reveal the identity of each design and use a marker to draw all the lines of symmetry. Display students' work on a bulletin board titled "Around-The-House Symmetry!"

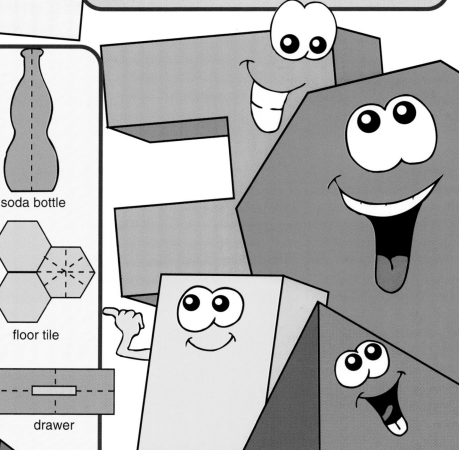

soda bottle

floor tile

drawer

What To Include On Your Map

- Three streets that are parallel to each other.
- Two avenues that are perpendicular to the three parallel streets.
- One boulevard that intersects three streets, but is not perpendicular to them.
- Five rectangular buildings, four square buildings, and six pentagon-shaped buildings.
- A park with two triangular sandboxes and two circular swimming pools.
- A name for your town.

Linking Geometry And Maps

Connect basic geometric concepts to real-life situations with this creative map activity for pairs. Give each pair of students a copy of the same city map. Ask each pair to look at the map's key, name the geometric shapes shown in it, and tell what each shape represents. Next have each pair use its map to answer questions—aloud or on paper—such as "Which street is parallel to Pentagon Street?" or "Which street intersects Octagon Avenue at an acute angle?"

Extend the activity by giving each student colored pencils, a ruler, and a sheet of drawing paper. Have him use the materials to design a city map that meets predetermined criteria that include geometric concepts (see the suggestions in the chart on the left). Encourage students to be creative in naming the items on their maps. Display the completed maps on a bulletin board titled "We're Mapping Our Way Through Geometry!"

Slide, Flip, Turn!

Geometry deals with movement, as well as patterns and shapes. Review the concepts of *slide, flip,* and *turn* with your students, copying the diagrams at the right onto a chalkboard if desired. Then have one student go to the chalkboard. Draw a simple design in one corner of the board. Direct the student to "move" the design across the board as you direct him to "slide," "flip," or "turn." Repeat this activity several times with other students and different designs.

Next divide students into groups of four. Give each group one copy of page 127, a die, scissors, and four different-colored crayons. Instruct students to follow the directions on the page to play the game. What a fun workout as the game pieces slide, flip, and turn on their way to the finish line!

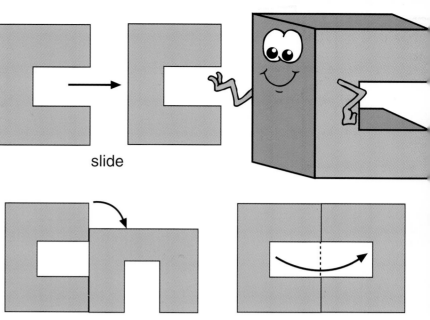

slide

turn

flip

Follow The Leader

Focus on following directions, listening skills, and geometry concepts with this fun drawing activity. Draw a simple picture like the one shown below on a transparency, without revealing it to your students. Instruct students to draw the picture on their own papers, as you give one geometric clue at a time. (See the list.) After students have finished their drawings, turn on the overhead so they can compare their pictures to yours. After completing two or three drawings with the entire class, divide students into pairs. Have each student make a geometric drawing without revealing it to his partner. Then have partners take turns describing and drawing each other's designs.

1. Draw a circle.
2. Draw a vertical diameter through the circle.
3. Draw a radius in the right semicircle that is horizontal.
4. Draw a square in the left semicircle.
5. Draw a chord that crosses the horizontal radius.

A Different Kind Of Grid

Encourage your young mathematicians to be copycats with this nifty idea! Provide each student with a copy of page 128. Ask students how the grid on this page is different from other grids they've used. *(The distances between any two successive horizontal dots, as well as any two successive diagonal dots, are the same.)* Make a transparency of the page and display it on an overhead. Ask students to describe the different kinds of shapes that can be drawn on the grid, such as right, equilateral, and isosceles triangles; rectangles; hexagons; trapezoids; rhombuses; and parallelograms. Draw each shape with a wipe-off marker as a student describes it. Next have students follow the directions on the bottom half of the page to complete the designs on the reproducible.

Hint: Make additional copies of the grid by gluing two copies of the top half of page 128 onto one sheet of paper. Then duplicate that sheet for each student.

Folder Cover Art

Geo-Folder

(name)

Geometry Word List

Geo-Words

- three-dimensional
- space figure
- plane figure
- plane
- point
- line
- line segment
- ray
- angle
- right angle
- acute angle
- obtuse angle

- straight angle
- line of symmetry
- symmetric figure
- congruent figures
- perimeter
- area
- volume
- horizontal
- edge
- face
- vertex (corner)
- vertical

- diagonal
- intersecting lines
- perpendicular lines
- parallel lines
- polygon
- quadrilateral
- square
- rectangle
- trapezoid
- parallelogram
- rhombus
- triangle

- right triangle
- scalene triangle
- isosceles triangle
- equilateral triangle
- acute triangle
- obtuse triangle
- circle
- radius
- diameter
- circumference
- arc
- chord

- pentagon
- hexagon
- octagon
- cube
- prism
- pyramid
- cone
- cylinder
- sphere
- slide
- turn
- flip

Note To The Teacher: Use with "Staying Organized With Geo-Folders" on page 123.

Geometric Aerobics

Ready for a real workout? Use your game pieces below to practice slides, flips, and turns—and try to be the first player to reach the finish line!

Directions for four players:

1. Cut out the four game pieces at the bottom of this sheet. Give one piece to each player. Each player chooses a crayon and colors both sides of his or her game piece.
2. Roll the die to see who goes first.
3. On your first turn, place your piece on START. Roll the die. Then follow the directions in the box at the right to find out how to move your game piece. The arrows indicate the direction in which you are to move. (Two or more game pieces can occupy a space on the gameboard at the same time.)
4. The first player to reach FINISH wins!

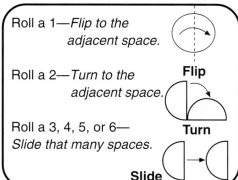

Roll a 1—*Flip to the adjacent space.*

Flip

Roll a 2—*Turn to the adjacent space.*

Turn

Roll a 3, 4, 5, or 6—*Slide that many spaces.*

Slide

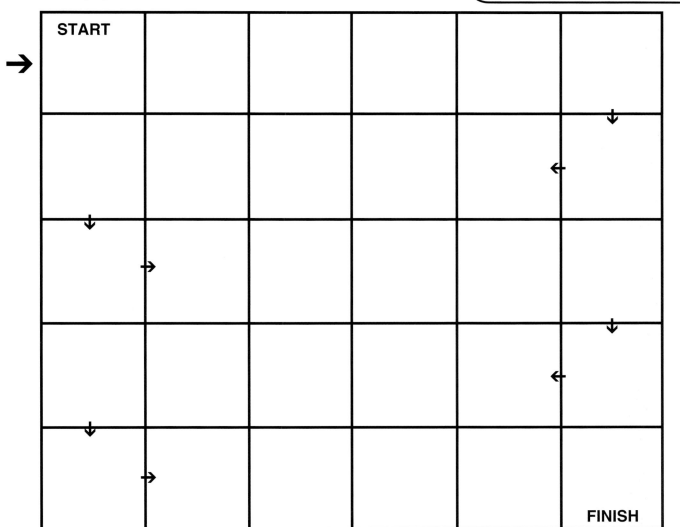

Note To The Teacher: Use with "Slide, Flip, Turn!" on page 125. Give each group of four students one die, scissors, four different-colored crayons, and one copy of this sheet.

Name _____ Geometry: visual thinking

Be A Copycat!

Copy each of the following designs on the grid above. Use colored pencils to decorate your designs.

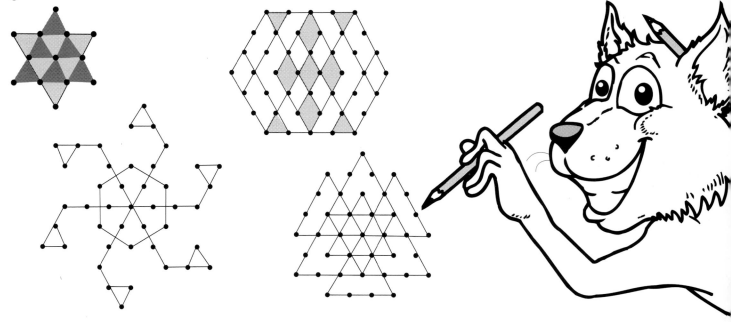

Note To The Teacher: See "A Different Kind Of Grid" on page 125 for additional information on how to use this page.

Picture Books And Math— ANOTHER DYNAMIC DUO!

Using Picture Books To Teach Math Skills

Picture books and math—a dynamic duo? You bet! Use the following suggestions from our readers to make picture books a powerful part of your math lessons!

Math Curse

written by Jon Scieszka and illustrated by Lane Smith
Viking

Skill: Writing equations

Just when you think it's safe to go to school, your teacher puts a math curse on you! At least that's what the child in this hilarious, high-speed picture book thinks as she finds out that "...you can think of almost everything as a math problem." I read this book to my students after a lesson on equations. After a discussion about how math can be found in everyday life, I instruct each student to list ten problems (along with their solutions) based on his activities for that day. The student displays or illustrates his problems on a sheet of construction paper as creatively as possible. My kids love comparing their work with one another. The equations also make a creative student-centered display. *Diane W. Lupia—Gr. 6, Mechanicsburg Area Intermediate School, Mechanicsburg, PA*

How Many Feet? How Many Tails?: A Book Of Math Riddles

written by Marilyn Burns and illustrated by Lynn Adams
Scholastic Inc.

Skill: Division

Part of the Hello Math Reader™ series, this book by renowned educator Marilyn Burns is the perfect springboard to review division skills. In the book, a grandfather challenges his grandkids with riddles such as "What has twelve feet, three tails, and sleeps under the porch?" *(one mother cat and two kittens).* After reading this book to students, have each child make up his own series of riddles using larger numbers. For example, "What has 48 feet, 12 tails, and 24 ears, and lives in India?" *(12 tigers).* Challenge students to try to include information currently being studied in other subjects in their problems. For example, if you're studying invertebrates, a student might ask "What has 36 legs, 18 body parts, and 12 antennae?" *(6 ladybugs).* Bind the students' riddles into a class math-riddle book. *Kelly A. Lu, Berlyn School, Ontario, CA*

Jim And The Beanstalk

written and illustrated by Raymond Briggs
Sandcastle Books

Skill: Measurement

For a picture book that measures up to all of its math potential, you can't beat this updated version of the famous beanstalk tale! In this story, Jim climbs a mysterious beanstalk only to find a giant with lots of problems—all involving measurement—that need solving. After sharing this book with students, I challenge them to create a suit for the book's gigantic character (to go with the new wig, glasses, and teeth that Jim helps him get in the story). First I choose one student to use as a model. After taking this student's measurements, we decide as a class whether to double or triple them for our giant's outfit. Then I divide students into groups, giving each team a large piece of butcher paper, measuring tools, and other art supplies. Each group then measures, draws, colors, and cuts out its giant-sized outfit. It's a math project that's always a gigantic success! *Kelly A. Lu*

Eating Fractions

written and illustrated by Bruce McMillan
Scholastic Inc.

Skill: Addition, multiplication of fractions, multiplication facts

In this photo-illustrated book, two children learn about simple fractions while whipping up some yummy foods. In the back of the book, the author gives recipes for the pictured foods. After I share this book with my class, I challenge my students to double or triple the recipes to make larger serving sizes. Then we make some of the dishes using the rewritten recipes. Who would have thought that math practice could be so delicious? *Kelly A. Lu, Berlyn School, Ontario, CA*

Pam Crane

1,000,000,000 BUNNIES!!

Bunches And Bunches Of Bunnies

written by Louise Mathews and illustrated by Jeni Bassett
Dodd, Mead & Company

Skill: Multiplication

Showing that multiplication is really a form of addition, bunches of bunnies cavort across the pages of this engaging picture book. Share the book with students; then discuss that the bunny bunches represent the numbers from one to twelve multiplied by themselves. Next divide students into small groups or pairs. Have each group rewrite the story using even larger numbers of bunnies. Provide oversized paper for students to illustrate their rewrites. The fun—and learning—are sure to multiply like rabbits! *Kelly A. Lu*

Anno's Magic Seeds

written and illustrated by Mitsumasa Anno
Philomel Books

Skill: Patterning

In this multilayered tale, a wizard gives Jack two mysterious seeds: one to eat and one to plant. And from that day forth, Jack's fortunes grow as rapidly as his magic seeds. After reading this book to students, we search together for a pattern to determine how many seeds Jack has over a ten-year period. Once we determine the pattern, we use it to predict the number of seeds over longer periods of time, such as 15, 20, and 50 years. When I'm sure students understand the pattern, I change the number of seeds Jack starts with and add circumstances that might affect the number eaten each year. *Stacey Roggendorff—Gr. 6, Union Sixth Grade Center, Tulsa, OK*

How many ways can you get to 25?
25+0,...24+1,...
23+2,...22+3,...
21+4,...

12 Ways To Get To 11

written by Eve Merriam and illustrated by Bernie Karlin
Aladdin Paperbacks

Skill: Writing equations

Bright illustrations of cut paper show that there's more than one way— 12, to be exact—to illustrate an addition sentence for the number 11. After sharing this preschool book with your students, group them into pairs and assign each pair a number greater than 20 (depending on the ability levels of your students). Also give each pair a sheet of chart paper and a marker. Have the pair title its chart paper "How many ways can you get to [assigned number]?" Then challenge each pair to list as many equations for their number as possible on their chart paper. As a follow-up, have each group transform its chart into an illustrated picture book. *Kelly A. Lu*

Social Studies Units

Setting The Stage For Social Studies

Get ready to draw back the curtain on exciting, new ideas for teaching U.S. geography and government. They're sure to leave students yelling, "Encore!"

Living Geography

Liven up a lesson on physical geography by having students act out the topography of different U.S. regions. Divide students into six groups. Arrange the groups in a right-to-left (east-to-west) order; then assign each group a different region from the chart shown. Beginning with the coastal lowlands, direct each group to perform its assigned part. When all the actions have been completed, ask students to observe the diversity of the resulting landscape.

Cathy Ogg—Gr. 4
Happy Valley Elementary
Johnson City, TN

Coastal Lowlands—lie flat on floor
Appalachian Highlands/Ozark-Ouachita Highlands—stand upright with hands clasped together above heads
Interior Plains—lie flat on floor
Rocky Mountains—stand upright on chairs with hands clasped together above heads
Western Plateaus, Basins, And Ranges—some lie flat on floor; others lie on floor on their backs, holding legs and arms up to make a U-shape
Pacific Ranges And Lowlands—some mimic the Rocky Mountains group; others lie flat on floor

Senator Jake Ribbet

Review Preview

Looking for a fun way for students to review U.S. states and capitals and important geography terms? Use the wordplay activity on page 133 and the challenging puzzle on page 134 to fill the bill!

Welcome To Congress!

Help students appreciate the role lawmakers play in our government by transforming your classroom into a mock Congress. Announce that you will act as president for the next three days. Assign each student a role as a U.S. senator or member of the House of Representatives from a different state. Then follow this three-day plan:

Day One: Have each student make a nametag that designates his title. Direct the senators to sit on one side of the classroom and the representatives on the other. Have each student write a *bill*—a brief proposal he hopes will become a law (a new classroom rule).

Day Two: Have each student present his bill. Direct the House of Representatives and the Senate to vote on each bill; then have Congress send on any bills receiving unanimous consent in both houses to you for approval. Sign or veto the bills, reminding students that Congress can override your presidential veto with a two-thirds majority vote in both houses.

Day Three: During this day, observe the laws that were voted into effect. Follow up by having each student write a paragraph explaining how a bill becomes a law.

Leslie Davidson—Gr. 4
New Caney Elementary
New Caney, TX

Director

Freddy

You Must Be Hearing Things!

Freddy has been studying hard for a geography quiz—so hard that he's beginning to hear things. In fact, he's even hearing the words he studied in other people's conversations! Look at the bold words and letters in the sentences below to help you figure out the words Freddy's hearing. Write each word in the blank provided. Then write the letter of the matching definition below in the blank beside each word. The first one has been done for you.

	Word	Definition
1. **I** saw the sky diver **land** in the field.		
2. Skiers flock to the **beaut**iful Rocky Mountains in winter.	1. _island_	_F_
3. Natalie's dog chewed on her dad's **golf** balls.	2. _____	___
4. Stan got a **base** hit **in** the third inning.	3. _____	___
5. The **sores** on the dog's paws were almost healed.		
6. Ned's song was a **tribute** to his friend **Carrie**.	4. _____	___
7. **Can Juan** identify the rock?	5. _____	___
8. The **mound** of sand must have weighed a **ton**.		
9. To**day's** game ended with no one getting **hurt**.	6. _____	___
10. Todd walked **straight** over to the game booth.	7. _____	___
11. Amy thought it was strange that the museum had a **plaque** of an elephant's **toe**.	8. _____	___
12. My uncle's air**plane** arrived on time at the airport.	9. _____	___
13. The **pens in** the box belonged to **Sue La** Grande.	10. _____	___
14. The main character in the book had to **save** his sister **Anna** from the bear.	11. _____	___
15. **His** bicycle **must** be brand-new.	12. _____	___
16. **Val** and **Lee** signed up for the talent show.	13. _____	___

A. small, flat-topped hill with steep sides

B. large or small depression in the land or the ocean floor

C. very deep valley with steep sides

D. very dry place, with little rainfall and few plants

E. part of the ocean that extends into the land

F. body of land completely surrounded by water

G. narrow strip of land joining two larger bodies of land

H. land with a broad base that rises sharply into a peak from the land around it

I. piece of land extending into the water from a larger body of land

J. large, high, rather level area that is raised above the surrounding land

K. treeless grassland, or a grassland with a few trees and bushes

L. place where a stream or river begins

M. narrow body of water that connects two larger bodies of water

N. stream that empties into a larger stream or lake

O. long, low area, usually between hills or mountains or along a river

P. wide area of flat or gently rolling land

14. _____ ___

15. _____ ___

16. _____ ___

Am I hearing things?

Bonus Box: On the back of this sheet, write sentences like the ones above for the words *canal, channel, continent, harbor, delta,* and *oasis.* Then have a classmate try to guess the geography word in each sentence and tell its meaning.

Name _____ Puzzle: U.S. capitals

Freddy's Capital Challenge

Freddy and his froggy friends are fried! They've been stumped by the states-and-capitals puzzle below. The states and capitals on the sides of the boxes do not match. To help Freddy and the gang, follow these steps:

1. Cut out the boxes and save the bottom portion of this page.
2. Arrange the boxes so that *all* their sides match a capital city with its state.
3. When you're finished, glue the boxes in place on a sheet of construction paper. Glue the bottom portion of this page to the construction paper below the boxes.
4. Look at the bold letter in the center of each box. Beginning with the box at the top right, copy the letters onto the blanks below the boxes in a left-to-right order. The resulting sentence will tell you one more thing to do.

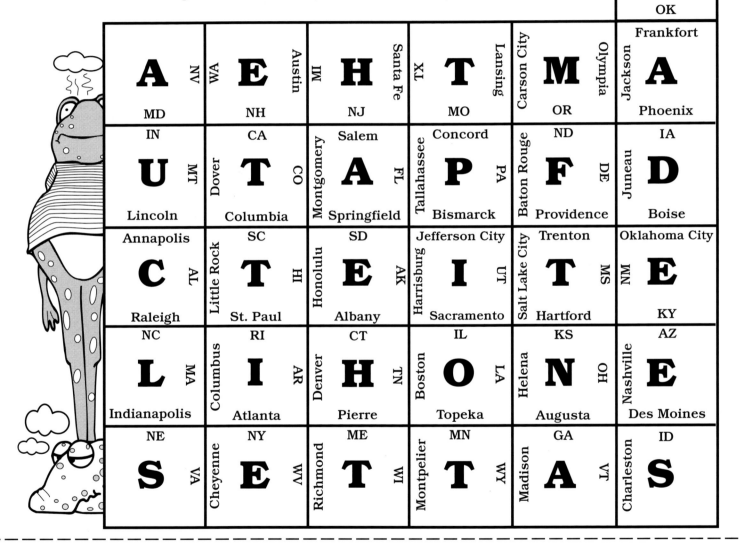

___ ___ ___ ___ ___ ___ ___ ___ ___ ___ ___

___ ___ ___ ___ ___ ___ ___ ___ ___

___ ___ ___ ___ ___ ___ ___ ___ ___.

___ ___ ___ ___ ___ ___ ___

Bonus Box: Name the two states that gave land for the site of our national capital.

©The Education Center, Inc. • THE MAILBOX® • Intermediate • June/July 1998 • Key p. 308

Note To The Teacher: Give each student scissors, glue, and a 9" x 12" sheet of construction paper.

A Map Skills Excursion

Get your students ready for an adventure into the charted world of map skills! Use this collection of ideas and activities to prepare your students for a yearlong journey with map skills.

ideas by Joy Kalfas

Pretravel Preparation

Demonstrate the significance of maps with this introductory activity. Direct each student to fold a sheet of paper in half. Instruct him to write explicit directions on how to get to school from his house on one half of the paper; then have him quickly sketch a map that includes street names and landmarks to show the same route on the other half. Direct each student to exchange maps with a classmate and determine which is easier to follow—the written directions or the map. Explain that maps provide a picture and are therefore easier for many people to follow. Reinforce this concept by having each student visualize the following location: "Laos is a country in Asia that is located south of China. It is just east of Thailand and directly west of Vietnam." Discuss why this task is difficult. Next display a world map and have a volunteer locate Laos on the map using the same set of directions. Point out that using a map often makes it easier to find a location.

Conclude this activity by dividing your class into groups of four or five students. Give each group a sheet of chart paper and a marker. Instruct each group to title its paper "Why We Use Maps"; then have the group brainstorm and list uses for maps and why they are important. Create a master list of "Why We Use Maps" on the chalkboard from the students' responses.

Tour Groups

No trip is complete without tour groups! Explain that tour groups travel together and often wear distinguishable colors so they can spot one another and prevent one member from being separated from the group. Divide your class into tour groups of four or five students. Then arrange each child's desk so that he is in a cluster with his assigned tour group. Give each group a few sheets of construction paper, one sheet of poster board, and markers. Challenge the students to select names and catchy slogans for their tour groups. Then instruct each group to use the construction paper to design name badges and the poster board to make a banner that represents its group. For example, a group that chooses the name and slogan "Cloud Riders—Our map skills are far above the rest!" might design blue nametags and a banner decorated with clouds.

For the first assignment, provide each tour group with a variety of maps and atlases. Allow the groups a few minutes to familiarize themselves with the maps. Then have each group create a list of items that most maps contain. Have each group share its list, avoiding repetitions, as you record the responses on chart paper titled "Items On A Map." Keep the chart posted in the classroom for reference throughout your map skills unit.

Cloud Riders

Our map skills are far above the rest!

Stephen
Katie
Leigh
David

Exploring Map Scales

Maps are never as large as the part of the earth that they show—and that's why knowing how to read a map scale is a must for young geographers! Introduce the concept of map scales by having each student fold a sheet of paper in half. Display a U.S. map; then instruct each student to quickly draw an outline map of the United States on the left side of his paper and an outline map of his state on the right side. Most likely students will draw the two maps relatively the same size. Explain that a state map can be just as large as a U.S. map. Then introduce the term *scale* and explain that cartographers use a scale to tell us the relationship between real distances and the distances on a map. Demonstrate the importance of scaling down each portion of the map proportionally by discussing a model airplane or car. Point out that if the wings were scaled down less than the rest of the plane, it would look funny and would not be an accurate model.

Next direct each student to a page that displays a map in his social studies text. Discuss where to look for the map's scale; then demonstrate how to measure a distance on a map using the scale and a sheet of paper (see the illustrations). For practice have each student find various distances on maps that are in his social studies text or on a wall map. Then duplicate a class set of page 138 and have each student complete the page as directed.

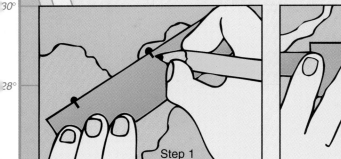
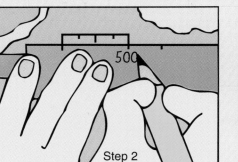
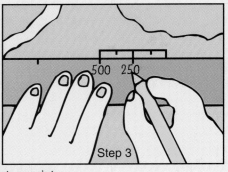

Step 1: Mark a piece of paper to show the distance between the two points.
Step 2: Place the paper along the map's scale. Line up the left mark with the zero on the scale. If the map scale is shorter than the distance, mark on the paper the endpoint of the scale and the distance it represents.
Step 3: Then line up that endpoint with the zero on the scale. Estimate the additional distance according to the scale. Add the two distances to find the total.

Battle Of The Brains

Pit your tour groups (see "Tour Groups" on page 135) against one another in this fast-paced challenge. Instruct each group to select a recorder; then announce one of the categories listed below. Give the groups two minutes to write down as many items that fit this category as possible on a sheet of paper. Encourage each tour group to whisper its responses to one another so that the other groups do not hear its answers. After two minutes call, "Pencils down" and have each group read aloud its written responses. Award each group one point for each correct response; then record the group's total points on the chalkboard. Continue the game by announcing a new category. The team with the most points at the end of the game is the winner.

Suggested categories: names of continents, names of oceans, states that begin with a specific letter, state capitals, foreign countries, foreign capitals, bodies of water, items found on a map

As The World Turns

When it's time to practice longitude and latitude, start spinning your classroom globe! Provide each student with a copy of a world map. Spin the globe; then stop it by placing your finger on a location. State the latitude and longitude of the location to which you are pointing. Then have each student find the called coordinates on her map and name the location of your secret vacation spot. For more latitude and longitude practice, duplicate one copy of page 139 for each student. Have each student fill in her bingo card as directed; then randomly call out the coordinates listed in the answer key on page 309 to play the game.

Visiting Various Symbols

Stars, dots, and lines—what would a map be without these symbols? Tell students that map *symbols* are pictures that stand for places that are too big to draw clearly on a map. Explain that a *legend* or *key* shows you what each symbol on the map means. Next have each tour group peruse a variety of atlases and maps in order to create a map legend for a town on a newly discovered planet. Have each group design a symbol for each of the following items: a mountain, a swamp, a river, a forest, a lake, an alien apartment building, a spaceship parking lot, a launchpad, and two other items of its choice. Give each group an 11" x 17" sheet of white construction paper on which to create its map legend. Instruct the group to use color on its legend and to be prepared to share each symbol with the class. As each group shares its legend, compare the different symbols used to show the same item. Display each group's legend on a wall. Or place each in a learning center; then challenge students to select a legend and use its symbols to draw a map of the imaginary town.

Venturing Across The Grid

Without a grid, finding a location on a map is like looking for a needle in a haystack! Relay this point to students by duplicating a section of a gridded street map for each child. Challenge each student to find a well-hidden road on the map. After students do some searching, explain how to find the location using the grid.

Next have students practice using grids by playing Cruise Ship. Label the vertical and the horizontal axes of a 10 x 10 grid as shown; then duplicate two copies per child. Have each student draw four cruise ships on one of his grids by coloring adjacent squares—two squares for his two-passenger cruise ship, three squares for his three-passenger cruise ship, four squares for his four-passenger cruise ship, and five squares for his five-passenger cruise ship. Divide your class into pairs. Instruct each pair to sit across from one another, but out of the view of one another's papers. In turn have each partner call out a grid location such as, "B7." Have his partner say, "Hit" if the student named a colored square and, "Miss" if he did not. Direct each partner to keep track of his called locations on the blank grid and the hits to his own ships on the colored grid. The first person to fill all four of his partner's ships (name each colored square) is the winner.

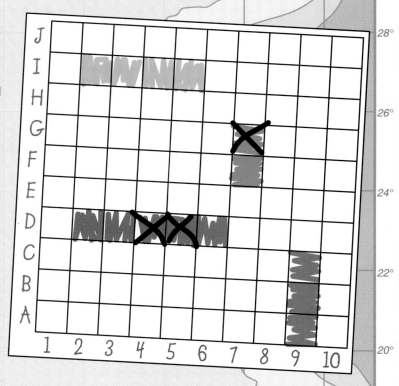

Final Destination

Wrap up your map skills adventure with a fun map-making project! Have each tour group apply its new map skills to create a map of a fictional city that is the perfect vacation spot for tourists. Provide each group with bulletin-board paper, rulers, pencils, several sheets of graph paper, and colored pencils or crayons; then write these steps on the chalkboard:

1. Name your vacation hot spot. Brainstorm at least seven tourist attractions in it.
2. Create a scale for your map. Use the scale to sketch the seven tourist attractions on a sheet of graph paper.
3. Draw a symbol for each attraction. Create a legend for your map.
4. Create and label a grid on your map.
5. Check your map for accuracy; then use the scale and your ruler to enlarge the map onto the bulletin-board paper.
6. Color your map and its legend.

Evaluate each group's map; then hang up each map for a classroom display.

Scaling Around Orangestone Park

Put on your hiking boots, because your tour group is planning a hike through Orangestone Park! Your job is to determine the distance of a hike to the various locations on the map. Study the map of Orangestone Park; then use the scale along with a ruler or a sheet of notebook paper to measure the distances asked for in each of the questions below. Write your answers on the lines provided.

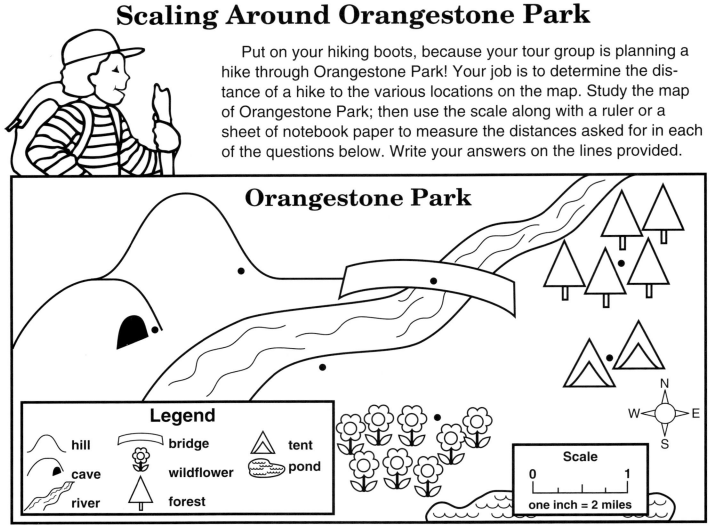

Orangestone Park

Legend

⌒ hill　　⌒ bridge　　△ tent
cave　　✿ wildflower　　pond
river　　△ forest

Scale
0 _____ 1
one inch = 2 miles

1. What distance does one inch equal on this map of Orangestone Park? _____
2. How far of a hike is it from the tents to the river? _____
3. How far will you have to hike to get to the hill from the tents? _____
4. If you hike from the wildflowers to the tents, then to the bridge, how many miles is your hike? ____
5. If you start at the bridge, is it shorter to hike to the hill or to the cave? _____ How much shorter? _____
6. If you start at the tents and hike across the bridge to the hill, then back across the bridge to the tents, how long is your hike? _____
7. How long is the hike from the hill to the cave? _____
8. If you hike from the tents to the forest, how many miles is your hike? _____
9. If you hike from the tents to the forest, then to the wildflowers, across the bridge, to the bottom of the hill, and finally to the cave, about how many miles will you hike? _____
10. One of your tour group members is lost in Orangestone Park. Follow these clues to find him.
    - From his tent, he hiked two miles north.
    - Then he hiked five miles southwest.
    - Finally he hiked about three miles northwest.
    Where is your friend? _____

Bonus Box: Pretend that you are lost somewhere in Orangestone Park. On the back of this paper, write clues to help your fellow hikers find you. Exchange your clues with a partner and see if he or she can rescue you.

Bingo With "L-attitude"

It's bingo time! Fill in each box of your bingo card with one of the cities listed below. Then listen for your teacher to call out a latitude and longitude coordinate. Look up each coordinate on your world map to find the city that is located there. If you have that city written on your bingo card, cover the square with a chip. Call out, "Bingo," if you cover five squares in a row vertically, horizontally, or diagonally.

LATITUDE

LONGITUDE

Amsterdam	Cairo	Helsinki	Milan	Rome
Athens	Calcutta	Johannesburg	Montreal	Santiago
Baghdad	Dublin	London	Moscow	Sydney
Beijing	Fairbanks	Madrid	Mumbai (Bombay)	Teheran
Brasília	Glasgow	Melbourne	Munich	Vienna
Buenos Aires	Harare	Mexico City	Oslo	

B I N G O

Note To The Teacher: Use this page with "As the World Turns" on page 136. For a listing of the cities' latitude and longitude coordinates, see page 309. Give each student a handful of dried beans to use as bingo chips.

The Road To Ancient Rome

Engineering brilliance, exquisite art and architecture, and military might—words that describe one of the most advanced civilizations and greatest powers the world has ever known. Lead your students on a journey to the fascinating world that was ancient Rome with the following innovative activities and reproducibles.

written by Cynthia Wurmnest and Elizabeth H. Lindsay

Background Information

Believed to have begun as a small village in 753 B.C., Rome soon grew into a magnificent and vast civilization. At its height in about 100 A.D., it spanned the entire area of the Mediterranean coast, parts of Central Europe, North Africa, and the Middle East. This great empire—filled with the rich and diverse cultures of its nearly 80 million citizens—was linked together by an impressive network of roads (some of which still exist today). Thus the saying "All roads lead to Rome" was truly fitting.

"Rome-in' " Through The Library

Get your study of ancient Rome moving with a challenging scavenger hunt that will polish even the rustiest of library skills! Give a quick review of how to use an index, a table of contents, and an alphabetically arranged resource like an encyclopedia or biographical index. Then divide the class into teams of four. Give each team a copy of "On The Road To Rome" on page 143. Then direct each team to scavenge reference materials like those discussed to find the answers to the listed questions. Emphasize the need to identify a key word or words in helping locate information. Check the answers of the first team to finish; then continue the competition for the remaining teams. Reward the first team to answer all of the questions accurately with a special treat or prize.

The Roman Wall Of Fame

Legendary people—are they always good, or are they sometimes not-so-good? Direct students to identify legendary people throughout history who exhibit either positive or negative characteristics, such as Davy Crockett and Jesse James. Then discuss the characteristics of each one.

Next write the names of some famous Romans like those listed below on the board. Pair students; then supply each pair with a 4" x 6" index card, a six-foot sheet of bulletin-board paper, and markers or colored pencils. Direct the pair to choose a person from the list to research for information such as who he was, when and where he lived, and why he was famous. Have the pair record its information on its index card. Next have the pair create a life-size portrait of the person in action. Instruct one student to lie on the bulletin-board paper while the other student traces an outline of his body. Finally have the pair add detail and color to its figure. (See the example shown on the left.) After each pair has shared its information, display the figures and summaries on a large wall in the classroom or hallway titled "The Roman Wall Of Fame."

- Romulus and Remus
- Trajan
- Spartacus
- Julius Caesar
- Augustus
- Tiberius
- Nero
- Hadrian
- Mark Antony
- Constantine The Great
- Virgil
- Cicero
- Horace

Spartacus was a famous Thracian gladiator. He fought other gladiators and wild animals in an arena to entertain the Romans. When he fought, he wore a helmet and used a shield and sword. He later led many gladiators in a rebellion against the Roman forces. He died in battle in 71 B.C.

Amazing Aqueduct Engineering

The city of Rome had millions of gallons of water pumped daily to its households, bathhouses, fountains, and public toilets. This water was brought from high in the mountains by massive man-made channels called *aqueducts*. Some of the aqueducts that brought water to Rome still stand today and continue to service the city's fountains.

Demonstrate the principle of the aqueduct system with the following experiment. Provide each group of students with two small buckets and a six-foot piece of clear, plastic aquarium tubing. Fill one bucket with water; then add a small amount of food coloring to the water so that students may more easily see it flow through the tubing. Direct each group to place the water-filled bucket on a desk and the empty one on the floor beside the desk. Next direct one member in each group to place one end of the tubing into the water. Instruct the student to siphon the water from the bucket by gently sucking on the tubing until the water appears at the edge of the bucket. Then tell the student to quickly place the tubing into the empty bucket. Finally discuss how—like an aqueduct bringing water down from the mountains—the pressure brought on by the higher elevation of the water-filled bucket causes the continuous flow of water to the bucket placed at the lower level.

Cafe Roma!

Fast food in ancient Rome? You bet your *popinas!* Although wealthier Romans ate their dinners in the *triclinium* (a room with a dinner table surrounded by three couches), most ate at local "take-away bars" called *popinas* or bought food from street vendors. Their diet consisted of foods grown in their area and those imported from conquered lands. The result was a diverse menu of fruits, vegetables, meats, and grains, such as those listed at the right.

Invite your students to sample the flavor of the Roman diet by arranging your own take-away bar. About a week in advance, enlist the aid of parents in purchasing the foods and supplies for your bar. On the day of the activity, have students set up the bar and create posters advertising the foods being offered. Then feast in a fashion fit for an emperor!

Foods:

Eggs, nuts, cheese, breads, honey, wine (grape juice for students), figs, dates, apples, grapes, cabbages, carrots, cherries, peaches, pears, plums, leeks, olives, lettuces, beef, pork, chicken, fish; other special favorites included small birds, fattened snails, peacock brains, flamingo tongues, and a sauce made of fish guts called *liquamen!*

Trading Places

Roman citizens belonged to one of three main classes. These classes included the high-ranking *patricians,* wealthy landowners from the original families of Rome; the middle-ranking *equites,* rich merchants and traders; and the lower-ranking *plebeians,* the ordinary working class. Other people were allowed to live in the city, but did not have full-citizen's rights. This group included *slaves* who might be prisoners, captives of war, or people purchased from a slave dealer.

Divide students into groups of four. Direct each member of a group to research one of the classes for information on topics such as home, family life, work, leisure activities, and rights and privileges. Two good sources are Mike Corbishley's *Growing Up In Ancient Rome* (Troll Communications L.L.C., 1993) and *What Do We Know About The Romans?* (Peter Bedrick Books, Inc.; 1992). Then direct each member to prepare a two-minute talk for his group in which he becomes that member of society. If desired, give students time to construct props in order to enliven their speeches; then videotape them in action! After all speeches are shared, discuss students' findings as a class.

Mosaic Art

Roman walls and floors were covered with detailed pictures made from small, brightly colored glass, stone, or ceramic tile. These *mosaics* were a popular art form in ancient Rome and often detailed Roman life—a baker placing bread in the oven or a Roman god or goddess, for example. Challenge your students to become creators of their own mosaics. Provide each student with a variety of colorful half-inch-wide strips of construction paper, a sheet of 9" x 12" light-colored construction paper, scissors, glue, and a pencil. Direct each student to first draw a simple outline of a figure—such as a flower vase, an animal, or a hot-air balloon—onto the sheet of construction paper. Next instruct the student to cut the construction-paper strips into 1/4-inch squares. Have the student use glue to fill in the figure with the squares. Display the mosaics on a wall or bulletin board.

E Pluribus Unum (One Out Of Many)

Out of one language come many of the words in the English language—one-third to be exact! That language is none other than *Latin*—the language of ancient Romans. As the Romans conquered new lands and their empire grew, they brought their language with them.

Have each student bring in a brown paper grocery bag. Direct the student to cut out the bottom of her bag, cut along one side, and then lay the bag flat. If desired, have the student tear the outside edges of the bag to make it look like the papyrus paper on which the Romans often wrote. Next explain to students how to find the *etymology,* or origin, of a word in the dictionary. Share several examples of words that originate from Latin. Then direct each student to write the letters from *A* to *Z* on her bag. Instruct the student to search a dictionary to find a word that is of Roman origin for each letter. Have the student write the word, its Latin counterpart, and a definition in her own words next to each letter as shown. Display each student's collection of words. Before you know it, your students will be speakin' and writin' in Roman!

When In Rome—Do As The Romans Do!

Would you believe that graffiti written on public buildings is not just a problem of today's world? The ancient Romans were notorious for the messages they engraved on stone walls throughout their cities! Invite your students to take part in this Roman tradition—but in a more productive manner! Obtain a six-foot sheet of bulletin-board paper and draw a wall on it like the example shown. Post the paper on a large wall or bulletin board. Next direct each student to research a specific Roman contribution or achievement. Instruct each student to draw an illustration or symbol representing the contribution on the wall, then write a descriptive sentence or two beside his picture. After the wall is finished, have each student share his graffiti art.

A—abbreviate, abbreviatus, to shorten
B—beast, bestia, a four-footed animal
C—cellar, cellarium, basement
D—document, documentum, official paper
E—exceed, exedere, overdo
F—
G—
H—
I—
J—
K—
L—
M—
N—
O—
P—
Q—
R—

Latin phrases such as status quo (things as they are), and et cetera (and the rest) are still used today.

Civilians accused of a crime were tried by a jury. The jury listened to evidence about the crime, and then a judge passed a sentence according to the law.

OCTAVIAN WAS HERE, 13 A.D.!

Plants and animals are often classified using Latin names. **Ranunculus** is the scientific name for a buttercup.

Veni, vidi, vici! (I came, I saw, I conquered!)

On The Road To Rome

Looking to find some fascinating facts about ancient Rome? Then get ready to roam the library! First, underline the key word or words in each question that will help you start your hunt. Then, using the words, search through reference materials to find the answer to each question. Write your answers on another sheet of paper.

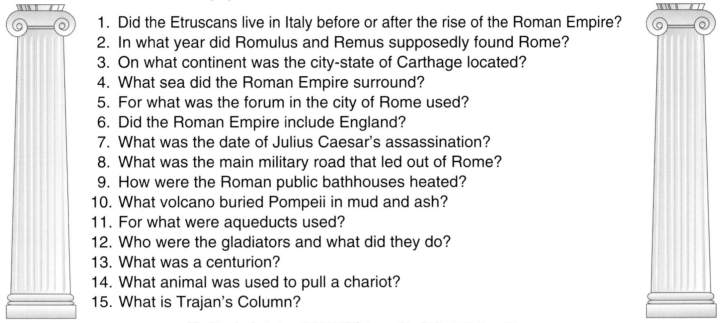

1. Did the Etruscans live in Italy before or after the rise of the Roman Empire?
2. In what year did Romulus and Remus supposedly found Rome?
3. On what continent was the city-state of Carthage located?
4. What sea did the Roman Empire surround?
5. For what was the forum in the city of Rome used?
6. Did the Roman Empire include England?
7. What was the date of Julius Caesar's assassination?
8. What was the main military road that led out of Rome?
9. How were the Roman public bathhouses heated?
10. What volcano buried Pompeii in mud and ash?
11. For what were aqueducts used?
12. Who were the gladiators and what did they do?
13. What was a centurion?
14. What animal was used to pull a chariot?
15. What is Trajan's Column?

Note To The Teacher: Use with " 'Rome-in' ' Through The Library" on page 140.

Name_____Critical thinking

Unearthing Your Bedroom

Would you believe that a whole city in ancient Rome was buried in 79 A.D. by a layer of volcanic mud and ash? When scientists finally dug up the city about 1,700 years later, they found things exactly as they were before the volcano erupted! Guard dogs were at doorways, bread was in ovens, and people were trying to escape with jewelry or money. This enabled scientists to piece together a picture of the day-to-day life of a typical Roman family.

Imagine that your house is completely covered by a strange and mysterious substance that will preserve it for years to come. Then, 1,700 years later, scientists uncover artifacts in your bedroom. What would they discover about you?

Directions: In the box below, draw and color pictures of ten items depicting you and your life that you would want scientists to uncover. Then, on the back of this sheet, write a sentence for each item explaining why you chose it.

1.	2.	3.	4.	5.
6.	7.	8.	9.	10.

144

A Month By Any Other Name...

In 46 B.C. the Roman emperor Julius Caesar decided to change the calendar that Rome was currently using. He named the calendar the *Julian calendar* (after himself). Caesar declared that the year would have 365 days, and that the first day of the year would begin in *Januarius*, named for the god *Janus*, who symbolized beginnings and endings.

Imagine that you are an emperor and have decreed that a new calendar is to be made. How would you name each month and whom would you honor—presidents, athletes, movie stars, family members, your dog? Write a new name for each month in the blanks provided. Then write a sentence explaining whom or what you are honoring each month and why on the back of this sheet.

CALENDAR NAME _____

JANUARY _____

FEBRUARY _____

MARCH _____

APRIL _____

MAY _____

JUNE _____

JULY _____

AUGUST _____

SEPTEMBER _____

OCTOBER _____

NOVEMBER _____

DECEMBER _____

Bonus Box: Choose two months of the year besides January. Research the months to find for whom or for what each one was named. Write your findings on the back of this sheet.

FIGHTING FOR INDEPENDENCE

CREATIVE IDEAS FOR STUDYING THE REVOLUTIONARY WAR

Freedom—it's a gift that we often take for granted. Not so the early Americans who fought fiercely to gain independence from the British during the Revolutionary War. Help your students catch the spirit of '76 as they study this classic conflict with the following creative ideas and activities!

by Lisa Waller Rogers

HOW IT ALL STARTED

War doesn't happen overnight, and this one was 12 years in the making! Use this research project to study the events leading up to the Revolutionary War. Divide your class into six groups. Assign each group one of the events leading up to the war listed below. Instruct each group to research the event, then prepare a short skit about it to teach the rest of the class. Have each group perform its skit for the class in chronological order.

Causes Of The American Revolution

- 1763—Parliament issued the Proclamation of 1763.
- 1765—Parliament passed the Stamp Act.
- 1767—Parliament passed the Townshend Acts.
- 1768—British soldiers moved into Boston, which eventually triggered the Boston Massacre in 1770.
- 1773—Boston colonists took part in the Boston Tea Party.
- 1774—The British passed strict laws that colonists called the Intolerable Acts.

THE MIDNIGHT RIDE

In 1775, British General Thomas Gage ordered Lieutenant Colonel Francis Smith and 700 men to Concord. They were to destroy colonists' military supplies there and arrest Samuel Adams and John Hancock for treason. This secret plan was discovered. On the morning of April 19, 1775, Paul Revere and William Dawes rode to Lexington and neighboring towns warning colonists that the British were coming. When the British arrived, they were met by alert colonists. No one knows who fired the first shot, but eight colonists were killed and the American Revolution had begun.

Paul Revere's feat inspired Henry Wadsworth Longfellow's "Paul Revere's Ride," one of the most popular poems in American literature. Share with your students *Paul Revere's Ride* by Nancy Winslow Parker (William Morrow & Company, Inc.), an illustrated version of Longfellow's famous poem. Point out how Longfellow makes his words almost gallop through the poem, like a horse's hooves. Discuss how history might have been different had news of the secret attack not leaked out.

I HAVE RIGHTS!

Thomas Jefferson wrote in the Declaration of Independence "that all Men are created equal, that they are endowed by their Creator with certain unalienable [unchangeable] Rights." Do kids also have rights that no one can take away? Challenge each student to make a list of "kids' rights." Then have the student turn his rights into short slogans. For example, if one student thinks that kids have the right to choose the food they eat, then his slogan might be "Our Food, Our Choice!"

After each student has chosen his slogan, give him two 18" x 24" sheets of light-colored construction paper, two 18-inch lengths of yarn, and markers. Instruct him to create the same slogan design on both sheets of paper, then punch two holes at the top of each sheet. Direct the student to use yarn to connect the two sides, making a sandwich board (see the illustration). Allow each student to wear his sandwich board as the class holds an impromptu Kids' Rights Parade through the school.

OUR FOOD, OUR CHOICE!

SIGN HERE, PLEASE!

Not only was John Hancock's signature the first on the Declaration of Independence, it was also the largest and most famous. He said he would sign his name large enough so that King George could read it without his glasses. Familiarize your students with the signing of the Declaration of Independence by reading aloud *Will You Sign Here, John Hancock?* by Jean Fritz (Putnam Publishing Group, 1982). Afterward have each student simulate how tedious writing was at that time by guiding him through the directions at the right for making a quill pen. Then cover a bulletin board with white paper and title it "Colonial-Graffiti Corner." Invite each student to sign his own John Hancock on the board using his quill pen. *(For more on using Jean Fritz's great biographies, see pages 151–153.)*

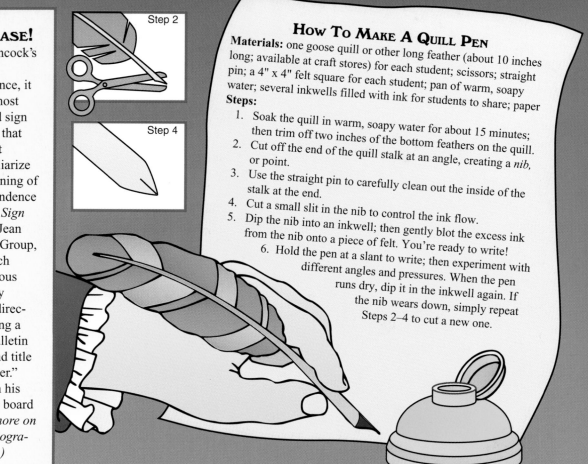

Step 2

Step 4

HOW TO MAKE A QUILL PEN

Materials: one goose quill or other long feather (about 10 inches long; available at craft stores) for each student; scissors; straight pin; a 4" x 4" felt square for each student; pan of warm, soapy water; several inkwells filled with ink for students to share; paper

Steps:

1. Soak the quill in warm, soapy water for about 15 minutes; then trim off two inches of the bottom feathers on the quill.
2. Cut off the end of the quill stalk at an angle, creating a *nib*, or point.
3. Use the straight pin to carefully clean out the inside of the stalk at the end.
4. Cut a small slit in the nib to control the ink flow.
5. Dip the nib into an inkwell; then gently blot the excess ink from the nib onto a piece of felt. You're ready to write!
6. Hold the pen at a slant to write; then experiment with different angles and pressures. When the pen runs dry, dip it in the inkwell again. If the nib wears down, simply repeat Steps 2–4 to cut a new one.

THE COLONIAL CITIES

Cities were the center of life in the 13 colonies. The largest cities—Boston, Baltimore, Charles Town (Charleston), Newport, New York City, and Philadelphia—lay along the Atlantic coast. Display a map showing the 13 colonies during this time. Point out each of the six cities listed above; then discuss why both the British and the colonists would want control of them. Next duplicate and distribute one copy of page 149 to each student. Divide your students into pairs; then challenge each pair to use reference materials to match the six cities with their descriptions.

HELP FROM THE HOME FRONT

Although a few women did fight alongside men in the war, most of them stayed home working in ways they never had before. In addition to their regular work, women ran farms and businesses, sewed uniforms for soldiers, and made gunpowder and cannonballs. When soldiers fought near their homes, women were expected to feed and nurse the wounded. Some women followed the army as cooks and laundresses, while others acted as spies.

Divide your class into pairs. Assign each pair to research one of the women listed at the right. Then give each pair a 9" x 24" sheet of white construction paper, a ruler, and colored pencils or crayons. Direct the pair to create a comic strip illustrating how its assigned woman aided the war effort. Display the completed strips on a bulletin board titled "Heroines Of The American Revolution."

WOMEN TO RESEARCH

Abigail Adams	Mary Pickersgill
Anne Bailey	Mary "Molly Pitcher" Hays
Margaret Corbin	Deborah Sampson
Lydia Darragh	Phillis Wheatley
Mary Katherine Goddard	Betsy Ross
Sybil Ludington	

WHO AM I?

In 1776, cities were the center of life in the 13 colonies. The big cities were the places to see a play or catch up on the latest fashions, news, or gossip. However each city was also different in its own way.

Read each of the clues below. Then use these clues along with reference materials to match each of the six cities listed with its correct description.

Cities
Boston
Charleston
Philadelphia
New York City
Newport
Baltimore

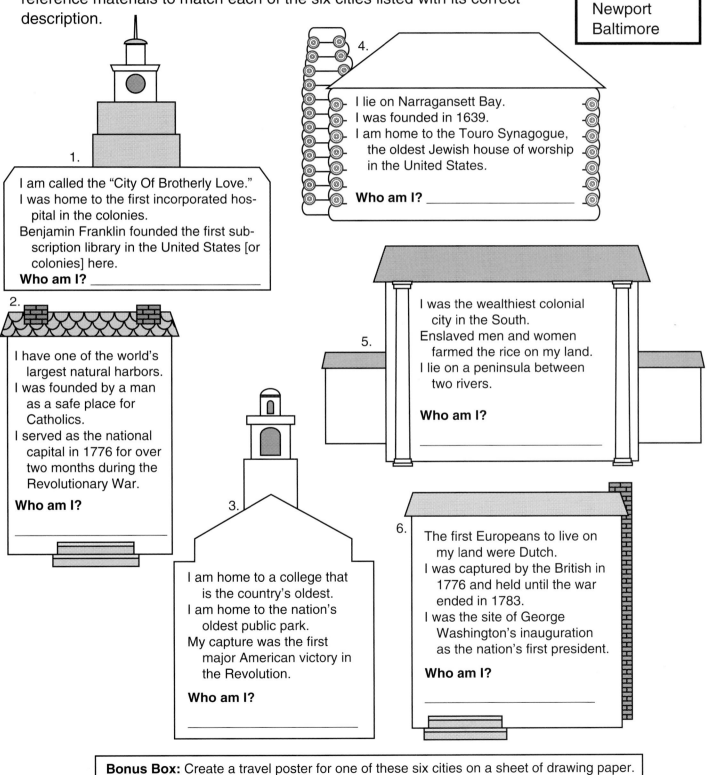

1.
I am called the "City Of Brotherly Love."
I was home to the first incorporated hospital in the colonies.
Benjamin Franklin founded the first subscription library in the United States [or colonies] here.
Who am I? _____

4.
I lie on Narragansett Bay.
I was founded in 1639.
I am home to the Touro Synagogue, the oldest Jewish house of worship in the United States.

Who am I? _____

2.
I have one of the world's largest natural harbors.
I was founded by a man as a safe place for Catholics.
I served as the national capital in 1776 for over two months during the Revolutionary War.

Who am I?

_____

5.
I was the wealthiest colonial city in the South.
Enslaved men and women farmed the rice on my land.
I lie on a peninsula between two rivers.

Who am I?

_____

3.
I am home to a college that is the country's oldest.
I am home to the nation's oldest public park.
My capture was the first major American victory in the Revolution.

Who am I?

_____

6.
The first Europeans to live on my land were Dutch.
I was captured by the British in 1776 and held until the war ended in 1783.
I was the site of George Washington's inauguration as the nation's first president.

Who am I?

_____

Bonus Box: Create a travel poster for one of these six cities on a sheet of drawing paper.

LETTERS TO HOME

Some colonists still had relatives living in England during the American Revolution. Pretend that you are one of these colonists in 1776. On another sheet of paper, write a draft of a letter to a relative who still lives in England. In the letter, explain your point of view on the Revolution. Then edit your draft and neatly copy it onto this page.

_____
(date)

Dear _____,

_____

_____

_____

_____

_____

_____

_____

_____

_____

_____

_____

_____

_____

Sincerely,

_____

Bonus Box: On the first draft of your letter, underline the sentence containing the statement that would be the most difficult for your relative to understand.

©The Education Center, Inc. • THE MAILBOX® • Intermediate • Dec/Jan 1997–98

Note To The Teacher: After each student completes this page, have him cut out the letter along the bold line. Collect and post the completed letters on a bulletin board titled "Letters To Home."

She Makes History A Hit!

Using Jean Fritz's Books To Teach U.S. History

With diverse casts of characters and story lines, author Jean Fritz skillfully weaves fact and fiction together to paint a picture of the past that delights young readers. Use the following activities based on Fritz's popular history books to introduce your students to the people and events that have helped shape history.

by Simone Lepine

Suggested Fritz Titles To Use With These Activities
(All books published by Putnam Publishing Group)

- *Can't You Make Them Behave, King George?*
- *Where Was Patrick Henry On The 29th Of May?*
- *Why Don't You Get A Horse, Sam Adams?*
- *Shh! We're Writing The Constitution*
- *Just A Few Words, Mr. Lincoln: The Story Of The Gettysburg Address*
- *And Then What Happened, Paul Revere?*
- *What's The Big Idea, Ben Franklin?*
- *Will You Sign Here, John Hancock?*
- *Who's That Stepping On Plymouth Rock?*

Activities To Use With Any Of Fritz's Historical Titles

Reading-Response Booklet

Use this easy-to-make booklet to custom-tailor your class's study of Jean Fritz's books. From the list on this page, choose the books that you want your students to read. Provide each student with one sheet of 5 1/2" x 8 1/2" paper for each book you selected and one additional sheet to use as a booklet cover. Have the student stack the sheets and staple them together to make a booklet; then have him decorate the cover of his booklet. Provide each student with a copy of page 153; then direct him to cut out the activity boxes of the books the class will be reading. Next have the student glue one activity box to the top of each right-hand page in his booklet. After the student reads one of the books, have him complete the activity page for it.

Fun With Jean Fritz's Books
Reading-Response Booklet

Name Roy

Why Do You Title Books With Questions, Jean Fritz?

Explore Jean Fritz's unique approach to titling her books with this activity. Show your students a collection of Jean Fritz's work. Ask students to point out the book titles that are questions. Have each student act as if he were the historical figure to whom each question is addressed. Then have the student write the book title along with the answer he thinks the character would give. For example, a student might respond that Patrick Henry—the main character in *Where Was Patrick Henry On The 29th Of May?*—would answer the question posed in his book's title by saying, "I was giving an emotional speech to my fellow countrymen!" Challenge your students to make up additional book titles based on historical events and people about which Jean Fritz has not written. Provide students with the example of a book about Harriet Tubman that could be titled *How Did You Find Your Way, Harriet Tubman?*

If I Knew Then What I Know Now!

Jean Fritz's books stand out in the sea of nonfiction because she has a knack for bringing well-known historical figures and events to life. Before reading one of Fritz's books, have each student make a two-column chart like the one shown. Instruct the student to record what she already knows about the individual or historical event from textbooks and other sources in the "Before Reading" column. Then have the student read Fritz's book that pertains to that subject or person. When the student finishes reading the story, have her list any new facts she has learned. Conclude by having the student explain how reading Fritz's story helped her better understand this topic or person.

What I Know About John Hancock	
Before Reading	**After Reading**
He was a patriot.	He was very wealthy and threw big parties.
He signed the Declaration of Independence.	He lived in a house with 54 windows.
He was from New England.	He signed the Declaration of Independence large so that King George, even without his glasses, was sure to see his signature.
He did not like the way England was treating the colonies.	He was disliked by King George because he refused to pay taxes.

Activities To Use With Fritz's Biographies

T-Shirt Trivia

Looking for a fun way for your students to share what they've learned from reading Jean Fritz's biographies? Divide your class into groups. Assign each group a Fritz biography the class has read. Provide each group with a T-shirt cut from construction paper. Direct each group to write the name of the person upon whose life the biography was based in the center of the T-shirt. On a separate sheet of paper, have the group list the things it learned about the person from reading the story. Then have the group draw symbols and write words to represent each fact on its T-shirt. Invite each group to share its shirt with the rest of the class and explain what each picture or symbol represents. Display the completed T-shirts on a bulletin board titled "Jean Fritz's Biographies Are 'Tee-rrific'!"

Famous Resumés

Ask your students the following question: "Which individual would you hire: Ben Franklin, King George, or Paul Revere?" Explain that one way an employer decides whom to hire is by looking over each person's *resumé*—a personal summary of job experience and accomplishments. Show students samples from a book on how to write a resume. Point out the information that each resume includes: *name, address, education, job experience,* and *achievements.* Next divide your students into seven groups. Provide each group with one of Fritz's biographies. Have each group read its book together and keep a record of the jobs, experience, and accomplishments of the person upon whose life the story is based. Then instruct each group to use the information it gathers to write a resumé for the individual.

Extend the activity by holding a job fair. Select several job advertisements from the newspaper's classified ads. Write the job titles on the board and have a member from each group copy them onto a sheet of paper. Read each job description aloud to your students one at a time. As you read each description, have each group write an explanation as to whether its famous person would be qualified for the job. Once you have read all the job descriptions aloud, have each group share its responses and explain its decisions.

Monuments-R-Us!

Your students will approach this "monumental" task with great enthusiasm! After reading several biographies by Jean Fritz, read aloud *Who's That Stepping On Plymouth Rock?,* the story of how Plymouth Rock became a national landmark. Ask the following questions: "Why did the people of Plymouth want to make a monument out of the rock? Why do nations create monuments, and why do people visit them? What are some monuments you have visited or heard about? What can people learn from monuments?" When the discussion is completed, have each student design a monument in honor of one of the individuals or historic events about which he has recently read. Explain that the monument's design should reflect the importance of the individual or event. Then have each student draw or construct a small-scale model of the monument. Provide time for each student to share his completed monument with the class and explain his design.

Reading-Response Booklet

Directions: Cut out the title box, glue it to your booklet cover, and decorate the cover. Then cut out the activity box for each book you will be reading. Glue one activity box to the top of each right-hand page in the booklet you made. After you finish reading a book, find its page in the booklet. Choose one activity from the box and complete it on that page.

Why Don't You Get A Horse, Sam Adams?
1. Draw a picture showing how Sam Adams dressed at the beginning of the book; then write a description of his appearance.
2. Why do you think Samuel Adams would not ride a horse? Name one thing you dislike doing and explain why you dislike it.
3. Pretend you are Samuel Adams. Write a short speech outlining your opinions on England's role in the colonies and America's independence.

Will You Sign Here, John Hancock?
1. List and describe John Hancock's nine *conveyances*, or vehicles. Why do you suppose he had so many?
2. Explain why you think the Continental Congress chose George Washington over John Hancock as Commander in Chief of the Army.
3. John Hancock was one of the richest men in the colonies. Find three details in the book that support that statement.

Shh! We're Writing The Constitution
1. Describe the government organization proposed in Edmund Randolph's Virginia Plan.
2. Why were some delegates opposed to organizing the government as proposed by Randolph?
3. Pretend you are a delegate at the convention. Write a letter home to your family describing the summer's events.

Who's That Stepping On Plymouth Rock?
1. Make a timeline that shows how Plymouth Rock got to its present location.
2. Do you think the first Pilgrims really stepped on Plymouth Rock? Explain your answer.
3. Name your favorite historical monument. Describe what the monument represents and why it is your favorite.

Just A Few Words, Mr. Lincoln: The Story Of The Gettysburg Address
1. Pretend you are living during the time of the Civil War. Write a letter to President Lincoln describing your feelings about the war.
2. List what you think are the two most important points covered in President Lincoln's speech.
3. Choose five words you are not familiar with from President Lincoln's speech. Look up each word in the dictionary and write its meaning in your own words.

Fun With Jean Fritz's Books
Reading-Response Booklet

©The Education Center, Inc. • THE MAILBOX® • Intermediate • Dec/Jan 1997–98

Name_____

Can't You Make Them Behave, King George?
1. Pretend you are King George. Explain why the colonists should pay taxes.
2. After reading pages 24–31, make up your own list of five rules that a good king should follow.
3. What do you think would have happened if the colonists had not won the war? Describe how things would have been different.

And Then What Happened, Paul Revere?
1. Make a list of Paul Revere's many jobs and skills.
2. Pretend you are Paul Revere. Write an entry in your journal describing the Boston Tea Party.
3. Make a map that shows the location of important events that occurred along the route of Paul Revere's famous ride.

Where Was Patrick Henry On The 29th Of May?
1. What were some of the jobs Patrick Henry tried and was unsuccessful at doing before he found out he had a gift for speaking?
2. Write out the words to Patrick Henry's famous speech on pages 36 and 37. Then reenact the speech with the help of several classmates.
3. Write a short speech on an issue you feel strongly about. Then deliver the speech to your class.

What's The Big Idea, Ben Franklin?
1. After reading Ben Franklin's list of rules for good behavior (page 21), make up your own list of ten rules for good behavior.
2. List some of Ben Franklin's inventions that are described in the book. Then plan an invention of your own by drawing a diagram of it. Write a paragraph describing what the invention can do.
3. Write a poem about Ben Franklin's interesting life.

HEADIN' WEST!
CREATIVE IDEAS FOR STUDYING AMERICA'S WESTWARD MOVEMENT

Restlessness, a desire for land, and an itch for adventure—sounds like Oregon Fever! For people in the mid- to late-1800s, the most common cure for this condition was to gather their belongings and head west. Use the following ideas and activities to get the wheels turning on your study of America's westward expansion.

by Wanda Helmuth and Debra Liverman

CALIFORNIA
**Land Of Beauty
And
Unlimited WEALTH
For ALL!**

**Land For Everyone!
GOLD
For The Taking!**

PACK YOUR WAGON

Imagine cramming your possessions and the necessary supplies for a six-month, 2,000-mile trek aboard a 10' x 4' wooden wagon! Obviously, selecting what to bring along on a westward trip was difficult. Travelers needed to be prepared not only for the trip, but also for life as settlers once they arrived.

Divide your class into groups of four or five students. Challenge each group to make a list of supplies—including food, clothing, tools, and cooking gear—that might have been taken on the trip west. Then have the group rank its list in order of importance. Next share the list below containing items that were typically taken on the trip west. Enlarge the pattern on page 157 to make a large wagon outline to mount on a bulletin board titled "Pack Your Wagon!" Invite each student to use a colorful marker to write a sentence on the display explaining one personal possession she would bring along (besides the necessary supplies).

TOO GOOD TO BE TRUE?

Was the West too good to be true? Those who encouraged others to move west often made it sound better than it really was. Stories were spread of abundant land, plentiful gold, mild winters, and no disease. With your class, brainstorm a list of words and phrases, such as "thousands of acres" and "rivers filled with fish," that may have been used to lure people westward. Write students' responses on the chalkboard. Then instruct each student to use items from the list to design an advertisement that might have been seen in an 1800s newspaper. Give the student a sheet of newsprint on which to re-create his final design. Hang the completed ads around the classroom. Have the class vote on the most persuasive ad.

flour	cows for milk and meat	
yeast	cloth	
crackers	needles	wax (for making candles)
cornmeal	thread	lanterns
bacon	pins	washbowls
eggs	scissors	tents
dried meat and fruit	leather	medicines
potatoes	saws	cooking supplies
rice	hammers	eating utensils and cups
beans	axes	pots and pans
coffee	nails	weapons
sugar	string	
salt	knives	
water	soap	

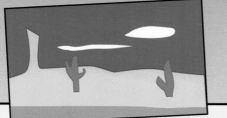

Landmarks Along The Oregon Trail

Scotts Bluff, Nebraska
Register Cliff, Wyoming
Independence Rock, Wyoming
Devil's Backbone, Oregon
Chimney Rock, Nebraska

Soda Springs, Idaho
Steamboat Springs, Idaho
Fort Laramie, Wyoming
Courthouse Rock, Nebraska

PIONEER LANDMARKS

The early trails that the pioneers traveled were just that—trails. There were no road signs or mile markers to help the travelers along. Instead the pioneers relied on landmarks. Assign each student to research one of the Oregon Trail landmarks listed above. Then give the student an index card on which to design a postcard illustrating that location. On the back of the card, have him write a message that might have been sent from a pioneer on the trail to a friend or relative back east. Display the postcards in a plastic-sleeved photo album for easy viewing or on a bulletin board.

HANG ON TO YOUR HAT!

Tip your hat to the history-making men and women of the westward movement with this research activity! Duplicate several copies of the hat and bonnet patterns on page 157. Assign each student to research one of the people listed at the right. Then give the student the appropriate pattern—a hat if his assigned person is male or a bonnet if the person is female. Instruct the student to write on his pattern a few sentences explaining his assigned person's contribution to the westward movement. Next direct the student to lightly color and cut out the pattern. Finally post the completed hats on a bulletin board titled "Hats Off To These History Makers!"

People To Research
Mary Achey
Antonio Armijo
William Becknell
Catharine Beecher
Daniel Boone
James Bowie
Jim Bridger
Evelyn Jephson Cameron
Kit Carson
William Clark
Davy Crockett
Marie Dorion
William George Fargo
John Charles Frémont
James Gadsden
Mary Anna Hallock
Sam Houston
Thomas Jefferson
Mary Jemison
Meriwether Lewis
Abraham Lincoln
James Marshall
Biddy Mason
John McLoughlin
Esther Morris
Carrie Roach
Sacajewea
Jedediah S. Smith
Eliza Spalding
Robert Stuart
Tecumseh
Marcus Whitman
Narcissa Prentiss Whitman
Sarah Winnemucca

James Marshall
He discovered gold while clearing out the stream near Sutter's sawmill where he worked. About one year later, news of his discovery reached the East Coast.

Name Sammy

NOW WHAT DO WE DO?

Traveling such a great distance was an exciting, but challenging experience. The pioneers were aware that they would face many problems and obstacles along their six-month journey, but being aware didn't make it any easier! Divide your class into groups of four or five students. Give each group one copy of page 158 and challenge its members to think like pioneers to answer each question. Afterward allow a few groups to share their answers. Next refer to the answer key on page 309 to explain to the class what the pioneers actually did in each situation. After this brain-boostin' activity, your students will feel ready to hit the trail!

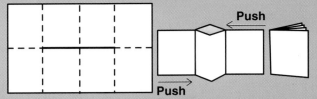

Begin with the basic eight-section fold. Cut along the boldface line as shown. Refold lengthwise. Push in the outer sides toward the center. Fold and close the book.

TRAVELING TIPS

Just as more Americans were hurrying west, publishers were rushing to print trail guides and manuals for these novice travelers. Many books proved very helpful. Unfortunately some of the printed guides were written by men who had never traveled west, and hence offered incorrect advice.

Give each student a 12" x 18" sheet of white construction paper; then guide the student through the steps above to create a blank booklet. Challenge her to use reference materials to create a trail guide filled with tips for traveling west. Each page of her guide should be on one of the following topics: Food, How To Stay Healthy, Landmarks Along The Trail, Crossing Rivers, How To Prevent Boredom, and Tricks Of The Trail. Have each student decorate the cover of her booklet; then post the completed guides on a bulletin board titled "Tips For Trail Travelers."

TRAIL OF TEARS

America's westward expansion led to conflicts over land between Native Americans and the white settlers. Some Native Americans fought for their land, but all of them were eventually forced to sign treaties giving more and more of it to white settlers. In 1830 Congress passed the *Indian Removal Act,* which gave the government the right to relocate the Native Americans. By the time the Cherokees moved the 800 miles to their new home, one-fourth of them had died from starvation, disease, or the cold weather. This journey became known as the *Trail Of Tears.* By 1900 all the remaining Native Americans had been forced from their homes and onto reservations.

Pose a "what if" situation to students. Suppose the Native Americans had won the right to retain their land, some of which contained gold. Have each student write a paragraph about how American history might have been different if Native Americans continued to live without any interference from the settlers. Let volunteers share their paragraphs with the class.

LITERATURE SUGGESTIONS

- *Caddie Woodlawn* by Carol Ryrie Brink (Simon & Schuster Children's Books, 1990)
- *Only The Names Remain: The Cherokees And The Trail Of Tears* by Alex W. Bealer (Little, Brown And Company; 1996)
- *Daily Life In A Covered Wagon* by Paul Erickson (National Trust For Historic Preservation, 1994)
- *Wagon Train: A Family Goes West In 1865* by Courtni C. Wright (Holiday House, Inc.; 1995)

Looking for a great novel to add to your study of the westward movement? See the literature unit on pages 234–238 featuring Jean Van Leeuwen's exciting book, *Bound For Oregon*!

Pattern
Use with "Pack Your Wagon" on page 154.

Patterns
Use with "Hang On To Your Hat!" on page 155.

Name

Name

NOW WHAT DO WE DO?

Traveling west was not easy! Along the way, settlers were faced with many problems and situations that were new to them. Put on your pioneer thinking cap to imagine what you would do in each of the situations below. Write your answers on the lines. Use the back of this page if you need more space.

1. When would be the best time of year to start your trip west? (Remember: the trip will take five to six months.)

   _____

   _____

   _____

2. How can you cross a river with your wagon without a bridge? _____

   _____

   _____

3. Pioneers brought along many foods, including eggs. How can you store the eggs so that they won't break on the bumpy trip? _____

   _____

   _____

4. A buffalo would provide a large amount of meat for the pioneers. How can you make the meat last a long time without allowing it to spoil?_____

   _____

   _____

5. Since pioneers were traveling on the plains, they might go days without seeing trees or wood. How can you build a fire without wood? _____

   _____

   _____

6. What could you do if you ran out of supplies? _____

   _____

   _____

7. What could you do if your oxen could not pull your wagon up a high mountain?

   _____

   _____

   _____

   _____

8. There were some very steep mountains along the trail. How could you prevent your wagon from rolling down the mountain too fast? _____

   _____

   _____

   _____

Bonus Box: How do you think we know so much about what it was like to travel west in a wagon? Write your answer on the back of this page.

©The Education Center, Inc. • *THE MAILBOX®* • *Intermediate* • Feb/Mar 1998 • Key p. 309

158   **Note To The Teacher:** Use with *"Now* What Do We Do?" on page 155.

The Inuit

The Inuit are among the most adaptable people on Earth. For hundreds of years, they have made their homes in the harsh Arctic climate. Introduce students to the traditional culture of these native people with the following creative activities and reproducibles.

by Lisa Waller Rogers and Debra Liverman

About These Activities

Inuit (IHN-yoo-iht) are people who live in and near the Arctic. Today more than 100,000 Inuit live in Russia, Alaska, Canada, and Greenland. Because the Inuit have always lived in groups scattered over this huge region, it is virtually impossible to describe a general way of life for all Inuit. The activities in this unit focus on the traditional way of life, much of which most Inuit people no longer follow.

Season To Season

From season to season, the Inuit used whatever resources were available in their area. They learned the yearly migration patterns of Arctic birds and animals. And they understood signs of changes in weather conditions and ice and snow formations.

Get students thinking about the seasonal activities in the traditional Inuit culture with the activity on page 163. Have each child complete the reproducible; then go over the correct answers with the class. As a follow-up, have each student use six sheets of computer paper (still connected) and the steps below to create a booklet featuring a year in her life. Display the booklets on a bulletin board titled "Season To Season."

Figure 1

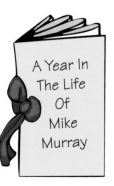

A Year In The Life Of Mike Murray

Figure 2

Steps:
1. Fold each page of computer paper in half lengthwise to create an accordion fold of the stack. This will create 12 pages (Figure 1).
2. Write "A Year In The Life Of [your name]" on the back of the first page.
3. Starting with page 2, label each page with a month, beginning with January.
4. Illustrate each page with something that you normally do during that month.
5. Fold the book back up. Punch a hole in the center of the left margin of the stack (Figure 2). Be sure that the hole is punched through all the sheets of paper.
6. Slip a piece of yarn or ribbon through the hole and tie it to hold the pages in place.

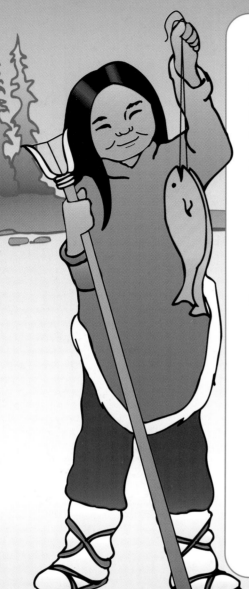

Lucky Charms

The Inuit are famous for their soapstone, animal bone, or ivory carvings. Inuit hunters often wore *amulets*, or charms, carved into the shapes of the animals that they hunted. The carvings were thought to help them in the hunt. Guide students through the steps below for carving their own amulets. Then have each student write a paragraph telling how he hopes his carving will bring him luck.

Materials for each student:

1 bar of soft bath soap   1 pencil
1 plastic knife   permanent felt-tipped pens
1 toothpick   1 damp paper towel

Steps:

1. Decide on an object to carve. Remember, it should represent an area in which you hope to be lucky. For example, carve a football for luck playing football.
2. Use the knife to scrape off any lettering from your bar of soap.
3. Use the pencil to draw the outline of your object on one side of the soap. Draw the object in reverse on the other side of the soap. Then draw the top, bottom, and sides of the object on the soap.
4. With the knife carve away the soap a little at a time until you have the object's basic shape. Continue to carve until the soap is in the desired shape.
5. Engrave and add fine details using the toothpick and felt-tipped pens.
6. When you are finished, rub a damp paper towel all over your carving to smooth it.

Land Of The Midnight Sun

Imagine trying to sleep on summer nights when it's bright as day! Or not seeing the sun for part of each winter! This is what it's like in the Arctic region. Every June 21, the sun never sets. Each following day has a little less light than the day before. By December 21 there is complete darkness and the sun never rises. Every autumn the Inuit played a string game called Cat's Cradle. By playing this game, they hoped to prevent the sun from falling below the horizon, signaling endless winter. The Inuit also made animals out of the string, which were sometimes used to help tell stories and legends.

Have each student tie the two ends of a three-foot length of yarn together to make a loop; then have him follow the steps shown for making a cat's cradle. Next challenge each student to devise his own string design. Have him write a paragraph explaining his design and telling a brief story about it. Then have students sit in a circle on the floor and share their tales just as the Inuit did during the winter months.

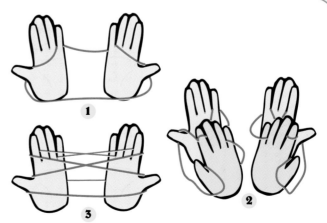

Cat's Cradle

1. Loop the string around your thumbs and little fingers.
2. Put your index finger through the loop across each palm.
3. Spread your hands apart to make the cat's cradle.

Snowy Shelters

Ask students to tell what they know about the Inuit and the word *igloo* will probably come up! To the Inuit an igloo is any house, but an *igluvigak* (eeg-LOO-vee-gack) is a snow house normally used as a temporary shelter when traveling. Because it is such an ingenious shelter, many survival kits give directions on how to make a snow house if you're caught in a blizzard.

Divide your class into small groups. Use the recipe below to make modeling dough for each group. Then give each group the dough, a copy of page 162, and the other materials listed on that page. Challenge the group to complete the model activity as instructed. Display the models in your classroom or school media center. For more information on how the Inuit built snow houses, read *Building An Igloo* by Ulli Steltzer (Henry Holt And Company, Inc.; 1995) and *Houses Of Snow, Skin And Bones* by Bonnie Shemie (Tundra Books Of Northern New York, 1993).

No-Cook Modeling Dough
(enough for one group)
Mix together 2 cups flour, 1 cup salt, and 1 cup water.

Arctic Animals

The Inuit don't live in the Arctic completely by themselves. They share their harsh environment with many Arctic animals. Introduce students to some of these animals by reading *Mama, Do You Love Me?* by Barbara M. Joosse (Chronicle Books, 1991). Then have students create a large mural of Arctic animal life. Start by dividing students into three groups—*ocean, land,* and *sky.* Instruct each group to research the animals that live in its assigned environment during the summer months. Next hang a large sheet of butcher paper across a wall. Use a pencil to divide the paper into three sections: the top for the sky, the bottom left for the ocean, and the bottom right for the land. Finally have each group use a variety of art materials to design its portion of the mural to show the animals that live in its region during the summer. Afterward have each group share information about each animal in its design.

Novel Tie-In

Bring literature to your study of Inuit life with the help of the Newbery classic, *Julie Of The Wolves* by Jean Craighead George (HarperCollins Children's Books). This story follows the adventures of a 13-year-old Inuit girl lost on the treeless tundra. After reading the book, have each student complete the reproducible on page 164. Then, as a class, brainstorm ways that students today can "read nature" like Miyax did.

Building A Snow House

Ever try to build a house out of snow? If so, you probably didn't have much luck! The Inuit use a special process when building a snow house, or *igluvigak* (eeg-LOO-vee-gack). Read the paragraph that explains this process below. After you learn the secret to building a snow house, follow the directions at the bottom of this page to build your own igluvigak.

How To Build A Snow House

The first thing an Inuk does is mark a circle in the snow where he wants the house. It's important to find an area with the right kind of snow—not too hard, not too soft. Then he cuts blocks of snow using a *snow knife*. A snow knife is a long, straight knife made from whalebone. After all the blocks are cut, it's time to start building.

The Inuk places a layer of blocks around the circle in the snow. Then he uses his knife to cut diagonally into a few blocks to form a ramp (see Figure 1). This is the secret to building a snow house. Next he stacks the remaining blocks in a spiral to form a dome-shaped house. He fills in any spaces between the blocks with loose snow. Then he cuts a small opening near the top for air to escape. A block of ice could serve as a window. The Inuk would simply cut a hole in the side of the house and remove the ice block. Finally he cuts a hole for an entrance and adds a porch (see Figure 2). The porch keeps cold air from going inside the igluvigak. It also gives the Inuk extra space for storing things.

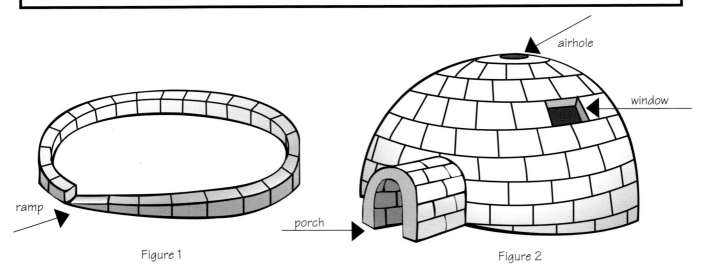

ramp

Figure 1

airhole

window

porch

Figure 2

Materials for each group: modeling dough, a large Styrofoam® ball cut in half, plastic knives, pencil, ruler, white tempera paint, paintbrush, a piece of cardboard to serve as a base for the model

Steps:
1. Place the Styrofoam® on the cardboard.
2. Use a plastic knife to cut several rectangular blocks of dough (about 1" x 2").
3. Place a single layer of dough blocks on the cardboard around the perimeter of the Styrofoam® mold.
4. Cut a few of the blocks diagonally to create a ramp (see Figure 1).
5. Continue adding blocks in a spiral around the Styrofoam® mold until you've created a dome. Pinch the blocks together as you work.
6. Fill in any empty spaces between the blocks with small amounts of dough.
7. Cut a window in the side. Also make a small airhole at the top of your house.
8. Cut a hole for the entrance; then use more dough blocks to form a porch (see Figure 2).
9. Let your model dry overnight; then paint it white with tempera paint.
10. If desired, add model people and animals to your arctic scene.

Season To Season

Snow Blocks

Imagine that you are an Inuk thinking about all you have done over the past year. Cut out each snow block. Then put each block on the month in which you may have completed that activity. When you are satisfied with your arrangement, wait for your teacher to go over the correct answers. Then glue each snow block in the correct month's box.

Hunt whales that migrate north after sea ice melts.	Sea ice melting. Move family inland.	Set up winter camp on sea ice.
Dry seal skin while there is still sun.	Hunt caribou while they are fat and furry.	Start of whaling season. Get new set of clothing.
	Gather berries and roots to eat.	Get ready for constant darkness by end of month.
	Midsummer sun. Wear underclothing with fur turned out.	Hunt seal from kayak.
	Stay indoors and play games and tell stories.	Hunt for seal as they come up through breathing holes.

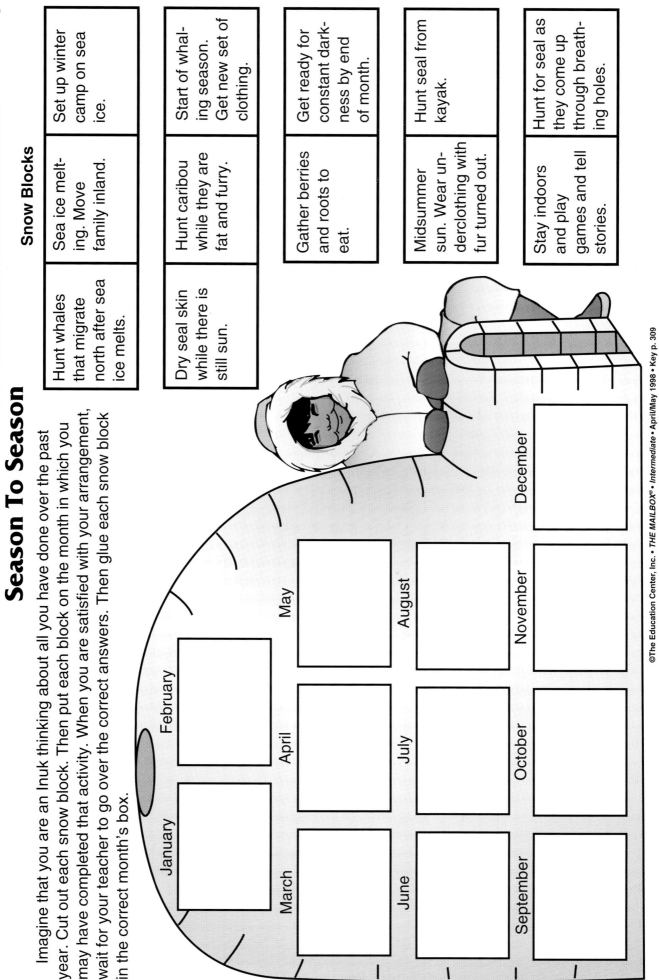

January

February

March

April

May

June

July

August

September

October

November

December

©The Education Center, Inc. • THE MAILBOX® • Intermediate • April/May 1998 • Key p. 309

Note To The Teacher: Use with "Season To Season" on page 159. Provide students with scissors and glue. See page 309 for the answer key. Explain to students that *Inuk* is the singular form of *Inuit.*

Reading Nature

In *Julie Of The Wolves,* the Inuit girl Miyax was able to read signs left by nature. She learned to find food and get around, and was accepted into the wolf pack. Read each sign below. On the line, write the letter of the meaning for that sign according to Miyax.

A. Winter is on the way.

B. Caribou are nearby.

C. Amaroq is the leader.

D. I'm friendly.

E. It is August 24.

_____ 1. A squirrel flicked its tail sideways.

_____ 2. Berry bushes were bending in the polar wind.

_____ 3. A wolf bit Amaroq's chin gently.

_____ 4. Amaroq sniffed the wind, got up, and led his wolf pack down the slope.

_____ 5. The white owl turned his head upside down to get a better look at Miyax.

_____ 6. The sky was lime green.

_____ 7. A snowstorm of cotton-grass seeds flew by Miyax's face.

_____ 8. The sun disappeared below the horizon, only to arise just an hour later.

_____ 9. The fox's brown fur had white patches.

_____ 10. The wolves were pouncing and bouncing.

F. South is that way.

G. It is autumn.

H. It's time for the wolves to hunt.

I. He was suspicious of Miyax.

J. The lemmings are returning.

Bonus Box: On the back of this page, list at least five signs from nature and what they tell you.

©The Education Center, Inc. • THE MAILBOX® • *Intermediate* • April/May 1998 • Key p. 310

164 **Note To The Teacher:** Use with "Novel Tie-In" on page 161. Or use as part of a literature unit on *Julie Of The Wolves.*

SCIENCE UNITS

The Great Powder Puzzle

Introducing The Scientific Method To Intermediate Scientists

Puzzled about how to introduce the steps of the scientific method to your students? Then take a closer look at this "powder-packed" unit that combines chemistry, observation, and fun to produce an exciting back-to-school reaction!

ideas by Gregory Grambo

Background For The Teacher

Chemistry is the study of substances: what they are made of, how they act, and how they change. The most basic of chemical substances are *chemical elements*. When two or more elements combine and create a change, a *chemical reaction* occurs. Since early times, people have made many discoveries by observing elements and the changes they go through. Scientists today seek to understand these substances through *the scientific method* of observation and logic.

The following unit is designed to help your students use the scientific method to experiment with five different powders. During the fun hands-on activities, students will discover what these powders are made of, how they act, and how they change.

Safety First!

Safety should be the first order of business when conducting any science experiment in the classroom. The following tips will help you and your students conduct safe experiments:

- Follow all directions and handle all equipment properly.
- Do not taste any of the chemicals in the experiments.
- Do not touch your eyes, mouth, face, or body when working with chemicals.
- Wash your hands thoroughly after completing the activities.
- Be especially careful with matches and open flames; tie back long hair and roll up loose sleeves.
- Remember fire-drill and other emergency procedures.

Scientific Method

Identify a purpose (Why is the experiment being conducted?)

Gather research (What kind of data is necessary to support the experiment?)

Form a hypothesis (What might happen?)

Perform an experiment (What materials are needed and what steps need to be taken in order to prove the hypothesis?)

Make observations (What happens during the experiment?)

Draw conclusions (Do the results of the experiment prove the hypothesis?)

Materials List

Each group will need the following items:

- five same-sized metal spoons
- pot holder
- one 6-inch candle
- matches
- pie tin
- five clear plastic cups, labeled A–E
- container of water
- five paper plates, labeled A–E
- eyedropper
- iodine (Lugol's solution is recommended and is available at science supply centers and some drugstores.)
- vinegar
- silver nitrate (available at science supply centers and some drugstores)
- about 1/3 cup each of flour or cornstarch, baking soda, sugar, salt, and plaster; each powder in a different container labeled A–E*
- one additional container per group (to hold the sample of the "mystery mixture")

*Make a key for yourself identifying which powder is in each container.

Ready, Set, Experiment!

Give each group of four students a copy of each experiment on pages 168–173 and the materials needed. Discuss the background and safety information on page 166. You may wish to share the names of the five powders being used, but not tell which containers they are in. Continue to stress student safety as some of the experiments involve potentially harmful materials and procedures. After each experiment, have group members wash their hands. Also have them wash any equipment that will be used in succeeding experiments (spoons, plastic cups, eyedroppers).

The Heat Is On! page 168

In this experiment students will use heat to identify one of the mystery powders. Four of the powders (flour, baking soda, salt, and plaster) should turn brown or have no reaction. The sugar will melt, turn brown, then turn black. Sugar is a carbohydrate made of carbon, hydrogen, and oxygen. When heated, the hydrogen and oxygen will evaporate, leaving the carbon behind. Students may also notice a smell like that of marshmallows or caramel emanating from the cooking sugar. Stress that students must be very careful about working with an open flame, and that they must not taste any substance or put it directly under their noses.

Water Wonders page 169

In this experiment students will use water to identify one of the mystery powders. Four of the powders (flour, baking soda, sugar, and salt) will dissolve in water, some more slowly than others. The plaster will not dissolve. After sitting overnight, the plaster will undergo a chemical reaction—it will harden.

Black And Blue All Over page 170

Iodine is used to test for the presence of a starch (like in cakes and cookies). When iodine is put on a starch, a bluish black color will appear. In this experiment, students will use iodine to identify one of the mystery powders. Four of the powders (baking soda, sugar, salt, and plaster) should turn yellowish brown. The flour or cornstarch should turn bluish black. *Remember that iodine is a poison.* Warn students not to touch their eyes, mouths, faces, or bodies when working with the iodine. Also remind them to wash their hands thoroughly after completing the experiment.

Sizzling Stuff page 171

When added to some substances, vinegar (an acid) causes them to react. In this experiment, students will use vinegar to identify one of the mystery powders. Four of the powders (flour, sugar, salt, and plaster) should not react to the vinegar. The baking soda will produce a reaction because it contains carbon dioxide. The vinegar causes the carbon dioxide to bubble and fizz as the CO_2 is released as a gas. (Students may see some fizzing with the plaster since it contains a calcium carbonate, but not as much as the baking soda.)

Heigh-Ho, Silver! page 172

Silver nitrate is a chemical that, when added to a sodium chloride, will produce a chemical reaction. In this experiment, students will add water and then silver nitrate to each powder. Four of the powders (flour, baking soda, sugar, and plaster) should not react. But when the silver nitrate is added to the salt solution, it creates a mixture that will not dissolve in water. The silver nitrate will form a mass and sink to the bottom of the cup. (The nitrate may react with the baking soda solution by bubbling and changing color.) *Remember that silver nitrate is a poison.* Warn students not to touch their eyes, mouths, faces, or bodies when working with the silver nitrate. Remind them to wash their hands thoroughly after completing the experiment.

The Great Powder Puzzle page 173

After each group has discovered the identity of each powder, give students a new mystery mixture to test. Prepare the mixture by combining two or more of the five powders. Give each group a sample of the mixture, a copy of page 173, and the materials determined by the group's members. Instruct students to use the information they learned in the previous experiments to determine which powders are in the mixture. For example, if the new mixture bubbles up when vinegar is added and smells like marshmallows when heated, students can conclude that it contains baking soda and sugar. Evaluate each group's knowledge of the scientific method by observing how its members perform each step of the experiment and by the data they record. 167

The Heat Is On!

Some substances melt, or break down when heated. One of the mystery powders below is a carbohydrate made of the chemical elements *carbon* (like coal), and *hydrogen* and *oxygen* (elements found in water). When heated, the hydrogen and oxygen will evaporate, leaving the carbon behind. Use your powers of observation, knowledge of the scientific method, and heat to discover information about the five different mystery powders.

Purpose: Find the identity of one of the mystery powders by using heat. (**Remember:** Do not taste any substance!)

Hypothesis: What effects do you think heat will have on each powder? What do you think the mystery powder is? _____

_____

_____

Materials:
five same-sized metal spoons (one for each powder)
candle
matches

pot holder
pie tin
five different powders in
    containers labeled A–E

Procedure:
1. Take a spoonful of a powder out of its container. Observe the appearance of the powder.
2. Place the pie tin under the candle to collect the dripping wax. With your teacher's assistance, light the candle and use a pot holder to hold the spoon over it. Observe what happens to the powder once it has been thoroughly heated and after it cools. Record your observations on the chart below.
3. Follow the same procedure for each of the other powders. Be sure to use a different spoon for each powder.

Observations:

Mystery Powders	What changes do you see in its appearance during heating?	What do you smell?	What happens after it cools?
A			
B			
C			
D			
E			

Conclusions: How can heat be used to help identify a substance? Can you identify one of the powders?

_____

_____

©The Education Center, Inc. • THE MAILBOX® • Intermediate • Aug/Sept 1997

Water Wonders

Some substances *dissolve,* or mix evenly with water. Some substances do not; they undergo chemical reactions when mixed with water. Use your powers of observation, knowledge of the scientific method, and water to discover information about the five different mystery powders.

Purpose: Find the identity of one of the mystery powders by using water. (**Remember:** Do not taste any substance!)

Hypothesis: What effects do you think water will have on each powder? What do you think the mystery powder is? _____

_____

Materials:
container of water
five clear plastic cups (labeled A–E)
five same-sized metal spoons (one for each powder)
five different powders in containers labeled A–E

Procedure:
1. Place a spoonful of each powder into its labeled cup. Observe the appearance of each powder.
2. Add water and stir until the powder dissolves or the cup is filled.
3. Observe what happens to each powder; then record your observations on the chart below.
4. Let each powder sit in its cup for the rest of the day. Tomorrow observe each powder; then record your observations on the chart below.

Observations:

Mystery Powders	About how much water is needed to dissolve the powder?	What changes do you see in the powder's appearance?	What happens to the mixture after it sits overnight?
A			
B			
C			
D			
E			

Conclusions: How can water be used to help identify a substance? Can you identify one of the powders?

_____

_____

©The Education Center, Inc. • THE MAILBOX® • Intermediate • Aug/Sept 1997

170

Black And Blue All Over

Iodine is a substance that can be used to test for starch. Starch is found in breads, cookies, and cakes. When iodine is put on a starch, a bluish black color appears. Use your powers of observation, knowledge of the scientific method, and iodine to discover information about the five different mystery powders.

Purpose: Find the identity of one of the mystery powders by using iodine. (**Remember:** Do not taste any substance!)

Hypothesis: What effects do you think iodine will have on each powder? What do you think the mystery powder is?

_____

Materials:
five paper plates, labeled A–E
eyedropper
iodine
five different powders in containers labeled A–E

Procedure:
1. Place a spoonful of each powder on its labeled plate. Observe the appearance of each powder.
2. Use the eyedropper to place three drops of iodine on each powder. (**Remember:** Iodine is a poison! Do not touch any part of your face with the iodine, and wash your hands thoroughly after the experiment.)
3. Observe what happens to each powder after iodine has been added to it. Record your observations on the chart.

Observations:

Mystery Powders	What changes do you see in its appearance?
A	
B	
C	
D	
E	

Conclusions: How can iodine be used to help identify a substance? Can you identify one of the powders?

_____
_____

©The Education Center, Inc. • THE MAILBOX® • Intermediate • Aug/Sept 1997

Note To The Teacher: See "Black And Blue All Over" on page 167 for more information on using this sheet.

Sizzling Stuff

When an acid is added to some substances, they begin to change. When they change, they give off a carbon-dioxide gas. The chemicals will bubble as they give off this gas. Sodium bicarbonate is a substance that reacts to an acid. It is used in cooking and in medicines. Use your powers of observation, knowledge of the scientific method, and an acid (vinegar) to discover information about the five different mystery powders.

Purpose: Find the identity of one of the mystery powders by using vinegar. (**Remember:** Do not taste any substance!)

Hypothesis: What effects do you think the vinegar will have on each powder? What do you think the

mystery powder is? _____

_____

_____

Materials:
vinegar
five clear plastic cups, labeled A–E
five same-sized metal spoons (one for each powder)
five different powders in containers labeled A–E

| A | B | C | D | E |

Procedure:
1. Place a spoonful of each powder in its labeled cup. Observe the appearance of each powder.
2. Pour a spoonful of vinegar into each cup.
3. Observe what happens to each powder once the vinegar has been added to it. Record your observations on the chart below.

Observations:

Mystery Powders	What do you see occurring after the vinegar is added?	What changes do you see in its appearance?
A		
B		
C		
D		
E		

Conclusions: How can vinegar be used to help identify a substance? Can you identify one of the

powders? _____

_____

_____

©The Education Center, Inc. • THE MAILBOX® • Intermediate • Aug/Sept 1997

Name(s) _____

Heigh-Ho, Silver!

Silver nitrate is a chemical that when added to a sodium chloride will produce a chemical reaction. Sodium is an element used to flavor certain foods. Use your powers of observation, knowledge of the scientific method, and silver nitrate to discover information about the five different mystery powders.

Purpose: Find the identity of one of the mystery powders by using silver nitrate. (**Remember:** Do not taste any substance!)

Hypothesis: What effects do you think the silver nitrate will have on each powder? What do you think the mystery powder is? _____

_____

Materials: five same-sized metal spoons (one for each powder); five clear plastic cups, labeled A–E and filled halfway with water; silver nitrate; five different powders in containers labeled A–E

Procedure:
1. Place a spoonful of each powder into its half-cup of water. Observe the appearance of each powder.
2. Mix the solutions with separate spoons.
3. Add a small amount of silver nitrate to each cup. (**Remember:** Silver nitrate is a poison! Do not touch any part of your face with it, and wash your hands thoroughly after the experiment.)
4. Observe what happens to each solution once the silver nitrate has been added to it. Record your observations on the chart.

Observations:

Mystery Powders	What changes do you see occurring in the mixture?
A	
B	
C	
D	
E	

Conclusions: How can silver nitrate be used to help identify a substance? Can you identify one of the powders? _____

_____

Note To The Teacher: See "High Ho, Silver!" on page 167 for more information on using this sheet.

The Great Powder Puzzle

Now that you have tested each of the five powders and discovered its identity, can you now identify a new mystery mixture? This mixture contains two or more of the five mystery powders. Your job is to identify which powders are in the mixture. Fill out each step below as you perform the experiment. Remember to follow the scientific method!

Purpose: Find the identity of the powders contained in the mystery mixture. (**Remember:** Do not taste any substance!)

Hypothesis: Which powders do you think are in the mystery mixture? _____

_____

_____

Materials:
List the materials you need to complete the experiment.

one container of the mystery mixture

Procedure: List the steps you will follow in conducting your experiment.

1. _____

_____

2. _____

_____

3. _____

_____

4. _____

_____

5. _____

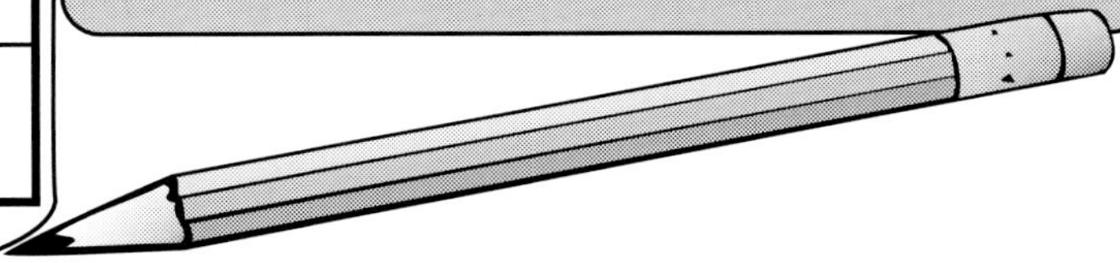

_____

Observations:

 ? ? ? ?	Describe what happens to the mixture after performing each experiment.
applying heat	
adding water	
adding iodine	
adding an acid (vinegar)	
adding silver nitrate	

Conclusions: Can you identify which powders are in the mixture? Explain your choices.

_____

_____

©The Education Center, Inc. • THE MAILBOX® • Intermediate • Aug/Sept 1997

Note To The Teacher: See "The Great Powder Puzzle" on page 167 for more information on using this sheet.

The Most Marvelous Machine

Creative Ideas For Studying The Human Body

Many wonderful inventions have been created throughout our history. But no invention can compare with the most marvelous machine of all time—the human body! Take your students on a guided tour through their amazing body systems with the following creative activities and reproducibles.

by Dana Sanders and Elizabeth H. Lindsay

A String Of Fascinating Facts!

Mesmerize your students with fascinating facts about the body's amazing systems. Duplicate the fact sheet and 12 copies of the pattern on page 177. Cut out each fact and glue it to a cut-out pattern as shown; then place the cutouts in a folder. Stretch a string from wall to wall in your classroom. Then, each day before beginning your body-systems unit, have each of several student volunteers pull one pattern from the folder. Have each student read his fact, then use a paper clip to hang it from the string.

To extend this activity, give your students the opportunity to share some facts of their own. Duplicate multiple copies of the pattern, placing them at a center along with scissors, colorful markers, and reference books about the human body. Encourage students to use their free time to read through the books to find interesting information about the human body. When a student finds a fact he'd like to share, have him write it on one of the cutouts and attach it to the string. Challenge students to fill the classroom with their fabulous facts.

If your intestines were uncoiled, you would be about 33 feet tall.

Thirteen pounds of skin are rubbed away each year by daily activity.

Pam Crane

The Digestion Connection

Give your students a "taste" of the organs of the digestive system with this fun getting-to-know-you activity! Duplicate multiple copies of the nametags at the top of page 178 (one nametag per student). Cut out and mix up the tags. Give one tag to each student along with a copy of the "Digestion Connection Data Sheet" at the bottom of page 178. Direct each student to mingle with the other organs—her classmates—and fill in her data sheet with information about each organ listed (including her own). Afterward use the data collected to discuss the function of each organ in the digestive system.

Body-Book Connections

Connect your students with the following exciting books for an inside view of the human body!

The Body Atlas by Mark Crocker; Oxford University Press, Inc.; 1991

The Body Atlas by Steve Parker; Dorling Kindersley Publishing, Inc.; 1993

The Human Body: An Amazing Inside Look At You by Steve Parker; Harry N. Abrams, Inc.; 1996

Inside The Body by Giuliano Fornari; Dorling Kindersley Publishing, Inc.; 1996

The Magic School Bus® Inside The Human Body by Joanna Cole; Scholastic Inc., 1992

I Wonder Why I Blink: And Other Questions About My Body by Brigid Avison; Larousse Kingfisher Chambers, Inc.; 1993

The Human Body (part of the What If…series) by Steve Parker; The Millbrook Press, Inc.; 1995

A Day In The Life Of A Heart

The heart is a tireless muscle that pumps as much as 2,000 gallons of blood and beats about 103,680 times every day! If this organ could talk, imagine the stories it would tell! Give the heart an opportunity to speak through the voices of your students. After a discussion of the heart's functions, have each student cut a large heart from red paper and use markers to decorate it with facial features. Next brainstorm with students the many things a heart might experience throughout a day, such as waking up to the sound of an alarm clock, running in a race at school, and watching a late-night scary movie. Record students' responses on the chalkboard. Next have each student choose one experience from the list (or create one of his own). Direct the student to write a quotation of what a heart would say in response to the experience on a cut-out speech bubble (for example, "When the alarm clock went off at 6:00 A.M., it made me skip a beat!"). Afterward have each student display his heart cutout and quotation on a bulletin board titled "All In A Day's Work."

When the alarm clock went off at 6 A.M., it made me skip a beat!

Dear Doctor "D,"
I was playing a game of basketball with my friends one day. All of a sudden, I got a really bad cramp in my calf. What is a cramp and why does it happen? What can I do the next time I have one?

Sincerely,
Charlie H.

Dear Charlie,
A cramp is a real pain—especially when it occurs in the middle of a ball game—isn't it? A cramp is when a muscle suddenly feels tight and painful. The muscle stops moving properly and feels stuck. This usually happens when you exercise too hard or for a long time. Doctors aren't exactly sure why a cramp happens, but it is probably from having too much or too little salt in the fluids surrounding the muscle's fibers. The next time you get a cramp, rest for a while and rub the sore spot.

Sincerely,
Dr. D

Ask The Experts

When you have a serious question, whom better to ask than an expert? Give your students the opportunity to become experts in the field of muscular health with the following creative activity. Write each question below on a different index card. Then pair students. Supply each pair with a question card and reference books about the human body. Direct the pair to research the answer to its question, then respond to it in advice-column style (see the example). Finally have each pair of experts share its question and response with its fellow "physicians."

- **Dear Doctor D:** My best friend just told me that I had muscles in my blood vessels! I bet him a soda that he's wrong. Do I win the bet, Doc? Sincerely, Will
- **Dear Doctor D:** What's the big deal about skeletal muscles anyway? Would it be so bad if I didn't have any? I'd think it would make me a more relaxed person, wouldn't it? Sincerely, Avery
- **Dear Doctor D:** I've heard that cardiac muscle is kind of special. What makes it any different from the muscles in my arms or legs? Sincerely, Mary
- **Dear Doctor D:** My sister tore a tendon while playing soccer. Why will this accident keep her on the sidelines for a while? How can I explain to her why it's important for her tendon to heal? Sincerely, Corinne
- **Dear Doctor D:** My neighbor's dad and mom are both bodybuilders. What about bodybuilding makes their muscles SO large? Sincerely, Nathan
- **Dear Doctor D:** I'm doing a report on muscle diseases. What can you tell me about muscular dystrophy and other muscle diseases? Sincerely, Maxie

No Bones About It!

About 206 bones make up the adult human skeletal system. They provide shape and support for muscles, nerves, and other soft parts of the body. Help your students remember the locations and functions of these bones by having them write a class rap. Duplicate the labeled skeleton on page 179. Display it on a wall with a large sheet of chart paper. Pair students; then assign each pair a bone or bone group, such as the skull, face, or shoulder area. Provide each pair with a colorful marker and a reference book about the human body. Direct the pair to write one line for the rap that includes information about the location and function of its assigned bone(s). Then, beginning with the frontal bone, have each pair use its marker to write its rap line on the blank chart. Perform the rap together as a class, having each pair read its own line aloud.

Beyond Belief!

Many of us have read or heard fascinating stories about people who wakened different from the way they were when they went to bed. Challenge your students to conjure up their own unbelievable stories—and review information they've learned about the human body—by using the journal prompts below. Write the prompts on a sheet of chart paper. Have each student choose a prompt and write a story beginning with the phrase "Would you believe that one day I woke up and…" Encourage students to include as much factual information about the human body in their stories as possible. After students have completed their stories, bind the pages between front and back covers. Display the book and invite students to read one another's "beyond-belief" stories.

Would you believe that one day I woke up and…
- I no longer had a skeleton!
- I had muscles the size of a bodybuilder's!
- my brain had doubled in size!
- my stomach was as large as a basketball!
- my heart was talking to me!
- I discovered I had lost my sense of taste!
- I found a note from my respiratory system pinned to my pajamas!

Body-Systems Flip Book

Your students will flip over this unique flip book! Divide students into groups of four. Supply each group with five copies of the pattern on page 180, reference books on the human body, markers or colored pencils, a stapler, and scissors. Direct each member of the group to draw, label, and color an illustration of a different body system on one of the patterns. On the fifth pattern, have one group member draw the outside of a person (face, hair, clothing, etc.). Then have the group compile the pages, putting the clothed drawing on top of the pile. Next direct the group to staple the pages together along the left side of the sheets. Once stapled, have the group cut each page along the dashed cut lines, being careful not to cut the pages apart completely. Finally have the group flip through the pages of its book, viewing the various parts of each system.

Deltoid
Pectoralis
Biceps
Femur
Kneecap (patella)
Fibula
Shinbone (tibia)
Anklebones (tarsals)
Foot Bones (metatarsals)
Toes (phalanges)

I S O F B A L M E T U P N Y

IS OF BAL MET UP NY

The Long And Short Of It

Help students learn more about the nervous system by investigating two types of memories stored by the brain. Explain to students that anything that you can remember for more than a few minutes is in your *long-term memory* (such as how to tie your shoe, how to find your way home from school, the time of your favorite television show, etc.). In fact, by the time a child is eight years old, his brain holds more information than a million encyclopedias! Nothing stays in your *short-term memory* for more than a few minutes. It can only store a maximum of nine things at one time. Most people can't remember more than seven items.

To test this fact, write the following sequence of letters on the board: I-S-O-F-B-A-L-M-E-T-U-P-N-Y. Have students look at the letters for a few seconds; then tape a large piece of paper over the letters. Have each child try to list the letters in order on his paper. (Most will remember only about seven letters.) Explain that you can get more in your short-term memory if you can group the facts to be stored into bigger units. Write this sequence of letters on the board: IS-OF-BAL-MET-UP-NY. Point out that now there are no longer 14 items to store, but only 6. Repeat the viewing and hiding steps above; then see if students do a better job of remembering the second set of letters.

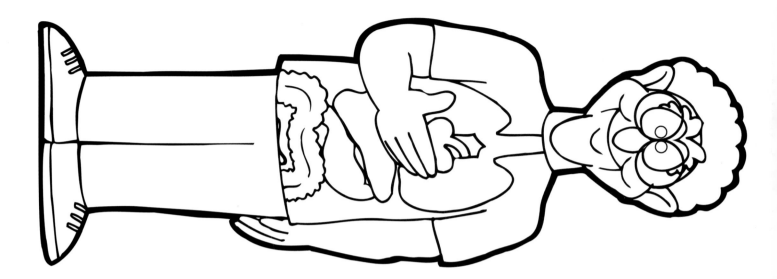

Fascinating Facts

Thirteen pounds of skin are rubbed away each year by daily activity.	If the main "thinking" part of your brain (the *cerebral cortex)* was ironed flat, it would be bigger than a large pillowcase.	If your intestines were uncoiled, you would be about 33 feet tall.
A full stomach holds more than a half-gallon of food and liquid.	When you grow up, you will have enough blood in your body to fill half a bucket. That would fill about five liter bottles of soda!	Babies are born with more than 300 bones, but adults have only about 200. The 100 extra baby bones don't just disappear; the smaller bones join to make bigger bones.
Different nerves in the body send out messages at speeds of up to 400 feet per second.	More than 640 muscles pull your bones so you can move. These muscles make up two-fifths of your body weight.	The average adult stomach processes about 1,100 pounds of food each year.
Your *funny bone* isn't really a bone. It is a nerve along the base of your arm. When you bang your elbow, this nerve may become pinched and create a not-so-funny tingling feeling in your arm.	Your biggest muscles are the ones you sit on.	When you sneeze, air rushes down your nose at over 100 miles per hour.

Nametags

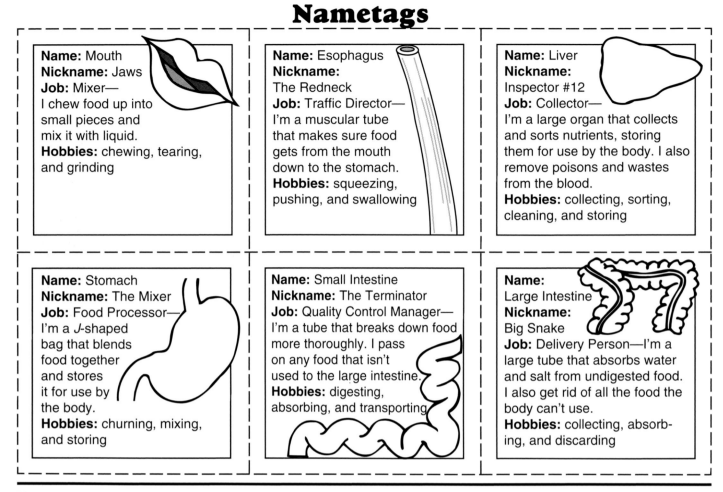

Name: Mouth
Nickname: Jaws
Job: Mixer—
I chew food up into small pieces and mix it with liquid.
Hobbies: chewing, tearing, and grinding

Name: Esophagus
Nickname:
The Redneck
Job: Traffic Director—
I'm a muscular tube that makes sure food gets from the mouth down to the stomach.
Hobbies: squeezing, pushing, and swallowing

Name: Liver
Nickname:
Inspector #12
Job: Collector—
I'm a large organ that collects and sorts nutrients, storing them for use by the body. I also remove poisons and wastes from the blood.
Hobbies: collecting, sorting, cleaning, and storing

Name: Stomach
Nickname: The Mixer
Job: Food Processor—
I'm a J-shaped bag that blends food together and stores it for use by the body.
Hobbies: churning, mixing, and storing

Name: Small Intestine
Nickname: The Terminator
Job: Quality Control Manager—
I'm a tube that breaks down food more thoroughly. I pass on any food that isn't used to the large intestine.
Hobbies: digesting, absorbing, and transporting

Name:
Large Intestine
Nickname:
Big Snake
Job: Delivery Person—I'm a large tube that absorbs water and salt from undigested food. I also get rid of all the food the body can't use.
Hobbies: collecting, absorbing, and discarding

Name _____ The digestive system

Digestion Connection Data Sheet

Welcome to the "Digestion Connection," where meeting and mingling with organs in the digestive system is the name of the game! First fill in the space below with information describing the organ you are. Then "mingle" with the other organs in your class. Find and meet the organs listed in each box below. Fill in each box with the information you gather. Use the back of this sheet if you need more room.

1. Name: Mouth **Nickname:** _____ **Job:** _____ **Hobbies:** _____	**2. Name:** Esophagus **Nickname:** _____ **Job:** _____ **Hobbies:** _____	**3. Name:** Liver **Nickname:** _____ **Job:** _____ **Hobbies:** _____
4. Name: Stomach **Nickname:** _____ **Job:** _____ **Hobbies:** _____	**5. Name:** Small Intestine **Nickname:** _____ **Job:** _____ **Hobbies:** _____	**6. Name:** Large Intestine **Nickname:** _____ **Job:** _____ **Hobbies:** _____

Note To The Teacher: Use with "The Digestion Connection" on page 174.

A Fabulous Framework

The Human Skeleton

Front view

Back view

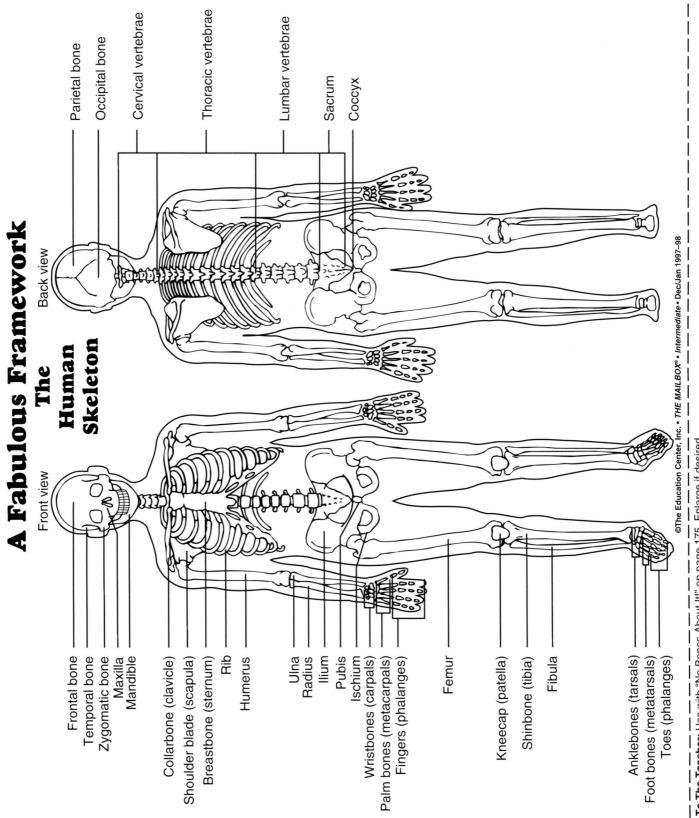

Parietal bone
Occipital bone
Cervical vertebrae
Thoracic vertebrae
Lumbar vertebrae
Sacrum
Coccyx

Frontal bone
Temporal bone
Zygomatic bone
Maxilla
Mandible
Collarbone (clavicle)
Shoulder blade (scapula)
Breastbone (sternum)
Rib
Humerus
Ulna
Radius
Ilium
Pubis
Ischium
Wristbones (carpals)
Palm bones (metacarpals)
Fingers (phalanges)
Femur
Kneecap (patella)
Shinbone (tibia)
Fibula
Anklebones (tarsals)
Foot bones (metatarsals)
Toes (phalanges)

©The Education Center, Inc. • *THE MAILBOX® • Intermediate* • Dec/Jan 1997–98

Note To The Teacher: Use with "No Bones About It!" on page 175. Enlarge if desired.

Pattern

Use with "Body-Systems Flip Book" on page 176.

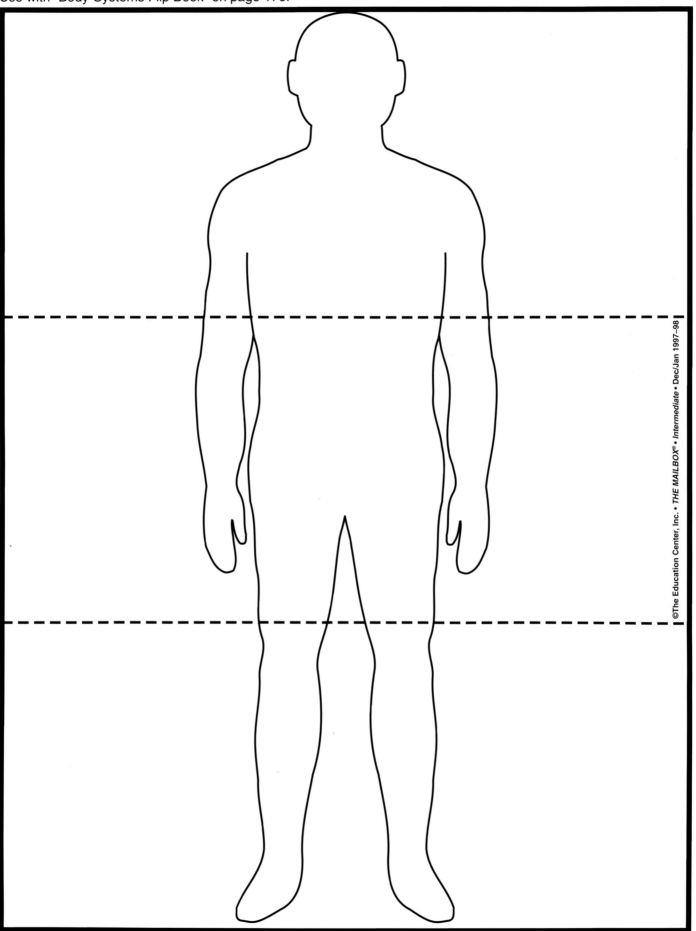

Catch The Electricity Bug!

How do you electrify your students' interest in science? Charge them up, of course! The following how-tos, hands-on ideas, and minds-on activities—plus a class full of "eager Edisons"—will ensure that your electricity unit is wired for success.

by Bonnie Pettifor

Making Electricity Run Smoothly In Your Classroom

- If you don't have enough supplies for the entire class, demonstrate each activity; then undo the activity and put it in a center for partners to visit.
- Pool your supplies with those of colleagues to create one electricity kit to share.
- Choose quality supplies that will last. Lantern batteries will keep for two or three years if stored in a cool, dry place.
- Reduce the chance of burning out lightbulbs by matching the voltage of the bulb to that of the battery.
- Strip one-half inch of insulation off the ends of the wires needed for each experiment. Add alligator clips to the ends of the wires to make them easier to attach and to reduce wear.

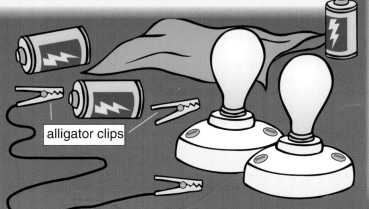
alligator clips

Static Electricity

Introducing Page 184: Rub an inflated balloon on a wool cloth. Ask students if they know why the balloon sticks to the wool. *(Static electricity—the buildup of positive or negative charges on an object—causes the balloon to stick.)* Demonstrate how static electricity works by giving each of eight students a card labeled "+." Give another eight students cards labeled "–." Form two lines, each with four + charges and four – charges. Instruct the lines to walk past each other. As they pass have two of the positive charges from one line switch places with two of the negative charges in the other line. Point out that one line now has more negative than positive charges, and the other line has more positive than negative charges. Explain that this happens when the wool and the balloon are rubbed together. *Electrons* move from the cloth to the balloon, making the balloon negatively charged and leaving the cloth positively charged. Since unlike charges are attracted, the negatively charged balloon is attracted to the positively charged wool, causing them to stick together.

Using Page 184: Divide your class into pairs. Give each pair one copy of page 184, one copy of the horse pattern on page 187, and the materials listed on page 184. Instruct the pair to complete the page as directed. Refer to the answer key on page 310 for the results of each experiment.

Series Versus Parallel Circuits

Introducing Page 186: Select six students. Tape one of six different signs—Battery, Wire, Lightbulb A, Wire, Lightbulb B, and Wire—to each student's shirt. Arrange the students as shown, holding hands, in Figure 1. Direct Lightbulb B to drop her hands. Ask students what would happen to both bulbs. Accept all responses, but do not reveal the answer. Next add another student wearing a Wire sign. Arrange the students as shown in Figure 2. (Have Lightbulb A hold hands with two of the Wire students and touch toes with the other two Wire students.) Again have Lightbulb B drop her hands. Ask students what will happen to the other bulb. Accept all responses, but do not reveal the answer.

Using Page 186: Divide your class into small groups. Give each group one copy of page 186 and the materials listed on that page. Refer to the answer key on page 310 for the results of each experiment. After completing the experiment, repeat the demonstration above, having students explain the difference between a series circuit and a parallel circuit.

Current Electricity

Introducing Page 185: Demonstrate how electrons move, creating a *current,* with this activity. Form your students into a circle. Have each student turn to the right and extend his arm forward until his palm is about one inch from the back of the person in front of him. Select one child to step forward so that his hand touches the back of the person in front of him. Have the person touched take a step forward and touch the back of the classmate in front of her, and so on. After each student has moved, explain that this movement represents *free electrons* (electrons that break away from atoms and wander within the material) transferring energy. The free electrons move forward and bump into other free electrons, creating a current.

Using Page 185: Divide your class into small groups. Give each group a copy of page 185 and the materials listed on that page. Refer to the answer key on page 310 for the results of the experiment.

Extending Page 185: Place one cup of water in a container. Dissolve two tablespoons of salt in a second container filled with one cup of warm water. Then place two tablespoons of salt on a paper plate. Ask students to predict whether each item—the water, the salt water, and the dry salt—is a *conductor* or an *insulator.* Test each as done in Step 5 on page 185. The bulb will only light up when the wires are in the salt water. *Therefore salt water is a conductor, while the dry salt and the plain water are insulators.*

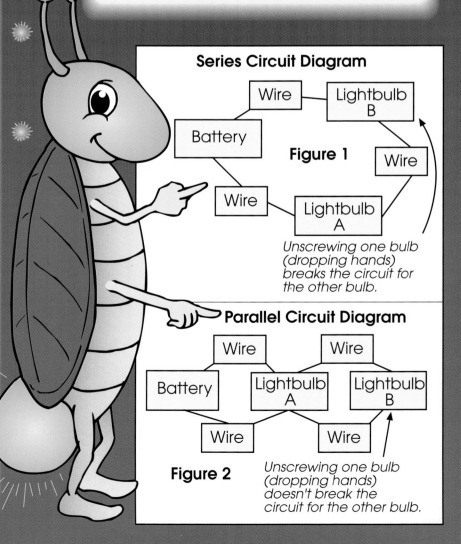

Series Circuit Diagram

Battery — Wire — Lightbulb B — Wire — Lightbulb A — Wire — Battery

Figure 1

Unscrewing one bulb (dropping hands) breaks the circuit for the other bulb.

Parallel Circuit Diagram

Battery — Wire — Lightbulb A — Wire — Lightbulb B — Wire

Figure 2

Unscrewing one bulb (dropping hands) doesn't break the circuit for the other bulb.

182

Electricity And Magnetism

Demonstrate the connection between electricity and magnetism with the following small-group or learning-center activity:

1. Bring a magnet close to a compass. Observe what happens. *(The compass needle will move. Like poles of a magnet repel and unlike poles attract, just as positive and negative electrons do.)*
2. Wrap a coil of wire around a large iron nail or bolt about 20 times; then remove the nail and connect the ends of the wire to a battery.
3. Place the coiled wire close to the compass. Observe what happens. *(The compass needle moves, indicating the presence of a magnetic field created by the electrical current flowing through the wire.)*
4. Insert the nail into the coil. The nail will become magnetized because of the electrical current. Use the magnetized nail (or *electromagnet*) to pick up small metal objects such as paper clips.
5. Disconnect the battery from the electromagnet and try to pick up the same paper clips with the nail. Observe what happens. *(When the battery is disconnected, the nail loses its magnetic force.)*

We All Need Each Other!

Connect your electricity studies to building cooperation in the classroom. Post a battery cutout on a bulletin board. Have each student complete one copy of the lightbulb pattern on page 187. Connect the cut-out lightbulbs to the bulletin-board battery by drawing a black line or by using real electrical wire. Fill the center of the resulting series circuit with photos of students working together. Remind students that if one lightbulb in a series circuit is loose or missing, all the bulbs go out. Likewise, if one student isn't doing his share, everyone is affected.

I can help my classmates learn more by

Name: _____

Get A Charge Out Of This!

Zap! Have you ever touched a door handle and felt a tiny electric shock? If so, you've felt static electricity. *Static electricity* is the buildup of positive or negative charges on an object. Complete each experiment below to get a real charge out of static electricity!

Experiment 1: Electroscope

Materials: flexible drinking straw; one small lump of clay; 1" x 8" strip of tissue paper; inflated balloon; piece of wool, nylon, fur, or flannel fabric; large metal paper clip; one piece of transparent tape; timer or watch with a second hand

Procedure:

1. Bend the straw and push the bottom end of it into the lump of clay. Stick the clay base to the edge of a desk.
2. Fold the tissue paper in half and place it over the straw as shown. Tape it to the straw.
3. Bring the balloon close to the tissue paper. Record your observations. _____
   _____
4. Rub the balloon along the fabric for 30 seconds.
5. Bring the balloon close to the tissue paper again. Record your observations. _____
   _____
6. Why do you think the paper acted as it did? _____
   _____
7. Touch the balloon to the paper clip to clear the balloon of the static electricity.
8. Why do you think the paper clip clears the balloon of its static electricity? _____
   _____

Experiment 2: Jumping Cereal

Materials: handful of puffed-rice cereal, sheet of notebook paper, two-foot length of plastic wrap

Procedure:

1. Ball up the plastic wrap. Place the cereal on a desk.
2. Rub the plastic-wrap ball on the notebook paper several times quickly.
3. Hold the plastic-wrap ball over the cereal. Record your observations. _____
   _____
   _____
4. Why do you think the cereal acted as it did?
   _____
   _____
   _____

Experiment 3: Static Horse Race

Materials for each student: one copy of the horse pattern; scissors; inflated balloon; piece of wool, nylon, fur, or flannel fabric

Procedure:

1. Cut out the horse pattern. Fold it on the dotted line so that it stands.
2. Charge your balloon by rubbing it on the fabric.
3. Hold your charged balloon in front of your horse to pull it along. Then have a race with your partner.
4. Why does your horse follow the charged balloon? _____
   _____
   _____
   _____

Bonus Box: For Experiment 3, does it matter which material you use to charge your balloon? Experiment with different materials. For each material used, record the amount of time the balloon held the charge on the back of this paper. Then explain your observations.

©The Education Center, Inc. • THE MAILBOX® • Intermediate • Feb/Mar 1998 • Key p. 310

Go With The Flow!

Some materials—called *conductors*—allow electricity to flow through them easily. Other materials do not make it so easy for electricity to get through. These are called *insulators*. Complete the experiment below to make a simple circuit. Then use the circuit to test objects to see if they are conductors or insulators.

Materials: one C-size battery; three 5-inch lengths of wire; flashlight bulb in a holder; masking tape; several objects made from various materials including metal, plastic, and wood

Procedure:

1. Tape one wire to each end of the battery as shown.
2. Attach one of the battery's wires to one side of the bulb holder. Leave the other battery wire resting.
3. Attach the third wire to the other side of the bulb holder.
4. Touch the two free wire ends together and the bulb should light. If it does not, check all the connections and try again.
5. Touch both free wire ends at the same time to each object. If the bulb lights, the item is a conductor. If the bulb does not light, the item is an insulator. Record your data in the chart below.

Object	Type of material of object	Conductor or insulator

Observations And Conclusions:

1. From what materials are the conductors made? _____
2. From what materials are the insulators made? _____
3. Look at the wires connecting your circuit. What part is the conductor? The insulator? _____
   _____
4. What purpose do you think insulators might serve? _____
   _____

Bonus Box: On the back of this page, list three places where you have seen insulators being used.

©The Education Center, Inc. • *THE MAILBOX*® • *Intermediate* • Feb/Mar 1998 • Key p. 310

Comparing Circuits

Electrical currents follow paths called *circuits*. A *series circuit* connects everything in a single path. A *parallel circuit* has more than one path for current. Complete the experiments below to make both a series and a parallel circuit.

Experiment 1: Making A Series Circuit

Materials: two flashlight bulbs with holders
three 5-inch lengths of wire
C-size battery

Procedure:

1. Attach the wires to the battery and lightbulbs as shown in the illustration. If the bulbs do not light, check the connections and try again.

2. While the bulbs are lit, unscrew one bulb. Record your observations.

_____

_____

3. Why do you think this happened?

_____

_____

Experiment 2: Making A Parallel Circuit

Materials: supplies listed for Experiment 1
one more length of wire

Procedure:

1. Attach the wires to the battery and light-bulbs as shown in the illustration. If the bulbs do not light, check the connections and try again.

2. While the bulbs are lit, unscrew bulb B. Record your observations.

_____

3. Why do you think this happened? _____

4. Screw bulb B back in and unscrew bulb A. Record your observations. _____

5. Why do you think this happened? _____

6. Which type of circuit do you think is more reliable? Why? _____

Bonus Box: Why wouldn't you want to wire a house with series circuits? Write your answer on the back of this page.

©The Education Center, Inc. • *THE MAILBOX® • Intermediate* • Feb/Mar 1998 • Key p. 310

Note To The Teacher: Use with "Series Versus Parallel Circuits" on page 182.

fold

©1998 The Education Center, Inc.

Use with "We All Need Each Other!" on page 183.

I can help my classmates learn more by

Name:

©1998 The Education Center, Inc.

Buggy 'Bout Ecology

Ecosystems, homeostasis, biomes, food chains—put them all together and you've got a topic kids will go buggy over—ecology! Help students learn how plants and animals interact and depend on one another for survival with the following creative activities and reproducibles.

by Patricia Twohey

Ecosystems Everywhere!

Use this fun, hands-on activity to introduce students to ecosystems! *Ecosystem* describes how a habitat's plants and animals interact with one another and the nonliving parts of their environment. Draw a diagram of the very simple ecosystem shown on the board, explaining each part to the class. Then divide students into groups. Assign each group an ecosystem: mountain, forest, rain forest, desert, savanna, wetland, beach, coral reef, or plains. Have each group research its ecosystem; then have group members prepare a skit—complete with simple costumes—that shows how the plants and animals in the ecosystem interact with one another. Invite each group to share what it learned by performing its skit for the class.

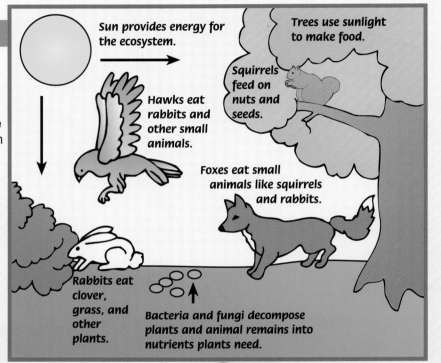

Sun provides energy for the ecosystem.

Trees use sunlight to make food.

Squirrels feed on nuts and seeds.

Hawks eat rabbits and other small animals.

Foxes eat small animals like squirrels and rabbits.

Rabbits eat clover, grass, and other plants.

Bacteria and fungi decompose plants and animal remains into nutrients plants need.

Keep The Balance

Turn to a fast-paced card game to teach students about homeostasis! The number of an ecosystem's plants and animals must stay in balance to survive. This balance is called *homeostasis*. Give each student four index cards; then divide the class into groups. Assign each group one of these ecosystems:

Ecosystem 1—plants, rabbits, foxes, hawks
Ecosystem 2—plants, mice, owls, foxes
Ecosystem 3—plants, deer, wolves, humans

Have the group follow the directions to play the game. Then have each student complete a copy of the reproducible on page 190.

To Play:
1. Print the name of a different organism from your ecosystem on each of your cards.
2. Combine your cards in a deck with your group members' cards and shuffle them.
3. Deal the cards to the group until there are none left.
4. Select one card from your hand to discard and pass facedown to the player on your right.
5. Pick up the card passed to you and look at it; then decide to keep or discard it.
6. Continue passing cards until a player has the four different members of the ecosystem and calls out, "Homeostasis!"

Who's For Dinner?

Challenge students to step up to the plate—the dinner plate, that is—and learn more about food chains. A *food chain* is a group of living things that form a chain in which the first living thing is eaten by the second, the second is eaten by the third, and so on. Write the name of each organism below on a paper plate. Give one plate to each student. Direct the student to research her organism; then have her write about how the organism gets energy on the plate's back and draw the organism on the plate's front.

After each student finishes her plate, have her find the two or three classmates whose organisms are members of her organism's food chain. Have each resulting group use tape and yarn to attach its plates in order to create a food-chain mobile.

	desert	ocean	tropical rain forest	tundra	savanna	grassland
primary producer (mainly green plants)	mesquite tree	shrimp	rain tree	mosses and lichens	African grasses	prairie grasses and plants
primary consumer	kangaroo rat	mackerel	sloth	lemming	zebra	jackrabbit
secondary consumer (predator)	Gila monster	seal	harpy eagle	snowy owl	lion	coyote
tertiary consumer (predator)		shark				

shrimp

mackerel

seal

shark

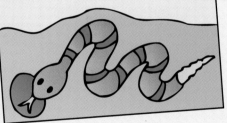

Winter's Coming, Mr. Snake!

Hibernation Pajama Party

Grab those blankets and come to a hibernation pajama party! Read aloud *The Happy Day* by Ruth Krauss (HarperCollins Children's Books, 1989). Then introduce the following terms to your class:

animal hibernation—a sleeplike state that protects an animal from cold or lack of food

animal estivation—a state of dormancy that protects an animal from heat or lack of water

torpor—a hibernation of only a few hours due to cold or lack of food.

Divide your class into groups. Have each group research the hibernating practices and other interesting facts of one of these animals: nighthawk, bat, chipmunk, snail, fat-tailed lemur, marmot, toad, lizard, snake, salamander, turtle, rufous hummingbird. Instruct each group to use the facts it finds to create a simple picture book.

When the books are finished, invite a primary class to your room. Spread out several blankets on your classroom floor. Divide the younger students equally among the blankets; then have each group share its picture book with one group of youngsters. You can bet that this will be a pajama party students won't soon forget!

Animals On The Go!

Travel the globe in a few short minutes with this animal migration activity. Some animals migrate because their environment becomes too harsh for survival at certain times of the year. Have students brainstorm a list of specific reasons that animals migrate *(food, climate, giving birth, breeding)*. Then have them list dangers migrating animals might face *(predators, hunting, fences, lack of food, injury, etc.)*. Next have students list ways people can help protect migrating animals from these dangers. Conclude by having each student complete a copy of page 191 as directed.

Keeping The Balance

Ecologists study how animals and plants interact with one another in their natural setting, or ecosystem. *Homeostasis* is the balance in the number of plants and animals in an ecosystem. When the different plants and animals compete for food, water, light, and other resources, they help to keep the balance. Sometimes natural events (like very cold weather) or man-made events (like the burning of trees) can disturb this natural balance.

Directions: Pretend that you and the members of your group are ecologists. Read each description. Brainstorm and list the possible effects the events taking place in the ecosystem could have on its homeostasis. Then list ways to help to keep the balance in each ecosystem.

ECOSYSTEM 1

Rabbits eat the plants that grow in a large meadow. Foxes eat the rabbits. Last year the weather was so good that there were lots of plants. Also many more rabbits than usual were born. Since there were more rabbits, the foxes had lots to eat and stayed healthy. The healthy fox population had many more babies than usual so their population grew even larger.

Effects On Homeostasis		Ways To Keep The Balance

ECOSYSTEM 2

In the tropical forests, people and animals have lived together with nature for many years. Lately companies have been buying the land. The companies cut down the trees for wood. Or they use the cleared land for farmland to grow crops for money.

Effects On Homeostasis		Ways To Keep The Balance

ECOSYSTEM 3

On a plateau, deer feed mostly on a small supply of grass. Coyotes feed on the deer. Hunters have been killing so many coyotes that very few remain.

Effects On Homeostasis		Ways To Keep The Balance

Bonus Box: On the back of this page, list three natural and three man-made events that can affect an ecosystem.

©The Education Center, Inc. • THE MAILBOX® • Intermediate • April/May 1998 • Key p. 310

Animals On The Go!

Some animals travel the same routes every year. This practice is known as *migration*.

Directions: Pretend that you are a travel agent for the migrating animals listed in the chart below. Your job is to map out each animal's travel route. First color the box to the left of an animal's name in the chart below. Then use the same color to draw a line on the map to show the animal's route. Finally calculate how far that animal travels during a round-trip.

Color	Traveler	Distance (Miles One Way)	Departs From	Destination	Round-Trip Mileage
	1. Arctic Tern	11,250	North Pole	South Pole	
	2. Bat	1,200	Canada	Bermuda	
	3. Golden Plover	9,500	Alaska/Canada	South America	
	4. Monarch Butterfly	1,000	U.S./Canada	Mexico	
	5. Short-Tailed Shearwater	10,000	Australia	Alaska	
	6. Atlantic Salmon	3,000	St. Lawrence River	Atlantic Ocean	
	7. Blue Whale	2,500	Indian Ocean	Antarctica	
	8. Dogfish	1,250	Canadian Coast	Mediterranean Sea	
	9. Fur Seal	4,500	Pribilof Islands, Alaska	California Coast	
	10. Green Turtle	1,500	South America	Ascension Island (Atlantic Ocean)	

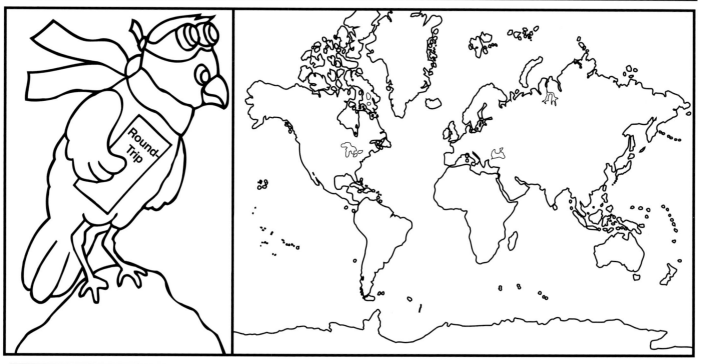

Bonus Box: Based on round-trip mileage, list the animals in order from the one that travels the farthest distance to the one that travels the least.

- -

Note To The Teacher: Use with "Animals On The Go!" on page 189. Provide each student with colored pencils or crayons and access to a world map or globe. Explain to students that the routes they draw will not be exact, but only representative.

Take Action!

Directions: Select one ecology action plan to complete. Then fill in the contract at the bottom of this sheet.

① Water Conservation

- List the ways you use water.
- Make an action plan that explains how you can save water.
- Discuss your plan with your teacher.
- Record your water usage for one week.
- Tell how your plan worked.
- List three reasons people should conserve water.

② Pollution And Waste Reduction

- List examples of pollution and waste found at your school or home.
- Make an action plan that explains how you can reduce pollution.
- Discuss your plan with your teacher.
- Record your pollution-fighting activities for one week.
- Tell how your plan worked.
- List three reasons people should reduce the amount of pollution in the world.

③ Ecosystem Preservation

- Diagram the plants and animals in the ecosystem around your home or school.
- Describe how the living and nonliving members of this system interact with one another.
- List five things that might cause an imbalance in the ecosystem.
- Observe the ecosystem for one week and list any changes that occur.
- List three ways you can help keep the ecosystem in balance.

④ Endangered Plant Or Animal Conservation

- Research and record ten facts about an endangered plant or animal that lives near your home or school.
- Write an action plan describing how you can help to protect this animal or plant.
- Discuss your plan with your teacher.
- Record all of your animal- or plant-saving activities for one week.
- Describe what would happen if everyone were to follow your action plan.
- List three reasons people should protect endangered plants and animals.

I, _____, promise to care about the ecology of my planet by completing

action plan number _____ . I will complete all parts of the plan by

ecology action plan number

date _____

Today's Date _____

_____
Student Signature

©The Education Center, Inc. • THE MAILBOX® • Intermediate • April/May 1998

ECO-EXPERT

Thanks!

_____

is awarded this Eco-Expert Award for successfully completing an Ecology Action Plan.
Our planet thanks you for caring!

Teacher's Signature _____   Date _____

©The Education Center, Inc. • THE MAILBOX® • Intermediate • April/May 1998

Note To The Teacher: Provide each student with a copy of the contract to complete as directed. Award the certificate to each student who successfully completes the contract.

AIN'T NOTHING BUT A ROCKHOUND!

ROCKS AND MINERALS ACTIVITIES THAT CAN'T BE BEAT

Treat students to a rock 'n' rolling science experience with these hands-on activities about rocks and minerals!

by Cindy Mondello

MOVIN' ON:
TEACHER DEMONSTRATION

Erosion is the wearing away and moving of rock materials by natural forces. The main cause of erosion on the earth's surface is running water. To help students understand erosion, pour a mixture of half sand and half soil into an empty aquarium. Pile the mixture high on one end of the aquarium to form a steep hill with a flat top. Use a watering can to sprinkle "rain" softly on the soil. Have students watch what happens. *(The running water carries away some of the soil as it travels down the slope.)* Then have students observe what happens when you make it rain harder. *(More of the soil and sand mixture will be carried down the slope.)* Next plant some grass or plant clippings on the hilltop and hillside, and repeat the sprinkling. Ask students how the plants change the erosion process. *(Plants are the best protection against soil erosion. Plants, grass, trunks of trees, and exposed roots help slow the speed of runoff. When water travels slowly, it has less carrying force.)* As a follow-up activity, have students research to find other causes of erosion.

MATERIALS LIST

- soil
- sand
- watering can
- grass clippings or clippings from a plant or bush
- water
- newspaper
- waxed paper
- dark bread (two slices)
- white bread (one slice)
- scissors
- glue sticks
- gravel

- pebbles
- large jars with lids (one for each group of four)
- plastic drinking straws (one per child)
- modeling clay
- white vinegar
- glass jars (one for each group of four)
- unglazed ceramic tile
- large aquarium (empty)
- marble chips (found at a plant nursery)
- assortment of minerals (collected from nature or purchased at a hobby store)
- rock-and-mineral field guides

MAKIN' DEPOSITS:
STUDENT ACTIVITY

Bank on the fact that students will understand the concept of deposition with the following activity. *Deposition* is the settling of materials carried by the agents of erosion—water, wind, and ice. Have students predict what will happen to rock particles of different sizes when they are deposited by water. Then divide students into groups of four to complete the following experiment:

Materials for each group: equal amounts of sand, gravel, and pebbles; large jar with lid; water

Procedure:

1. Mix together the sand, gravel, and pebbles in the jar.
2. Add water until the jar is about three-fourths full.
3. Secure the lid on the jar.
4. Shake the jar carefully until the contents are thoroughly mixed.
5. Allow the contents to settle.

Have students observe how long it takes for the materials to settle. Then ask: "What happened to the jar's contents when it was set down? Do you see different layers on the bottom? What is different about them? How do you think materials settle in rivers or streams?" Conclude by having each student make a sketch of the jar, labeling each layer correctly.

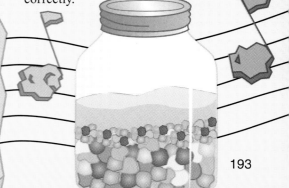

CRYSTAL CONSTRUCTION: STUDENT ACTIVITY

Minerals are the solid materials that make up rocks. One of the properties of minerals is the shape of their crystals. There are six basic crystal shapes. Duplicate the patterns on page 196 for each student. Have students follow the directions on the page to make models of *cubic* and *tetragonal crystals*. Encourage students to use rock-and-mineral guides to find the names of the other four crystal systems and examples of each one. *(The six basic crystal shapes and examples of minerals are* cubic *[halite, galena],* tetragonal *[zircon, chalcopyrite],* hexagonal *[quartz, calcite],* orthorhombic *[sulfur, staurolite],* monoclinic *[mica, gypsum], and* triclinic *[feldspar, rhodonite].)*

STREAK TEST: STUDENT ACTIVITY

Another way of identifying a mineral is by the colored mark it makes when rubbed against a piece of unglazed porcelain. This color is known as the mineral's *streak*. Make a streak test kit with an assortment of minerals and an unglazed ceramic tile. Ask several student volunteers to rub the edge of each mineral along the ceramic tile. Have students compare the colors of the different minerals with the colors of the streaks that were made. *(Color cannot always be used as a clue to the identity of an unknown mineral. Some minerals are always the same color, but the colors of other minerals may vary. A streak test is more reliable than a mineral's color. For example, malachite is a green mineral that makes a green streak, and sulfur is a yellow mineral that makes a yellow streak. Hematite, on the other hand, is a mineral that can be either black or red, but always makes a red streak.)* Have each student or group use a rock-and-mineral field guide to make a streak chart as a reference for further mineral studies.

DIGGING UP ROCKS AND MINERALS

Dig up rocks and minerals for the activities in this unit by contacting the geology departments of local colleges and universities for information. To purchase rocks and minerals that don't occur naturally in your area, check the Yellow Pages for local rock-and-mineral shops or teacher supply stores. The following stores carry rocks and minerals and are located in many areas. To find the stores nearest you, call the home offices listed below:

The Nature Company
750 Hearst Avenue
Berkeley, CA 94710
(510) 644-1337

The Discovery
Channel Store
750 Hearst Avenue
Berkeley, CA 94710
(510) 644-1337

The Nature
Of Things Store
10700 W. Venture Drive
Franklin, WI 53132
(800) 283-2921

World Of Science, Inc.
900 Jefferson Road, Bldg. 4
Rochester, NY 14623
(716) 475-0100

REFERENCE BOOKS FOR ROCKHOUNDS

Rocks And Minerals by Alan Woolley (EDC Publishing, 1992)

The Magic School Bus Inside The Earth by Joanna Cole (Scholastic Inc., 1987)

Adventures With Rocks And Minerals, Book II: Geology Experiments For Young People by Lloyd H. Barrow (Enslow Publishers, Inc.; 1995)

The New York Public Library Incredible Earth: A Book Of Answers For Kids by Ann-Jeanette Campbell and Ronald Rood (John Wiley & Sons, 1996)

Rocks And Minerals edited by Lisa Miles (EDC Publishing, 1997)

ROCKIN' ON THE WEB

For on-line help, check out the Rockhounds Information Page (http://www.rahul.net/infodyn/ rockhounds/rockhounds.html) for links to sites related to rocks and minerals *(valid as of 12/97)*.

ROCK SANDWICH, ANYONE?: TEACHER DEMONSTRATION

One of the three types of rocks is *metamorphic rock.* Help students discover how metamorphic rock is formed with the following demonstration. Place several sheets of newspaper on the floor. Position a sheet of waxed paper on top of the newspaper. Stack three pieces of bread on the waxed paper—a white slice between two dark slices. Cover the bread with another sheet of waxed paper. Walk across the "rock sandwich" several times. Then cut the sandwich in half with scissors. Have each student describe the inside of the sandwich. Follow up the demonstration by having students define the three types of rocks *(igneous, sedimentary,* and *metamorphic)* in their science journals. *(The three slices of bread represent three layers of sedimentary rock. When pressure was applied to the rock, it changed into metamorphic rock. Metamorphic rocks are formed by changes in igneous or sedimentary rocks. These rocks may be changed to metamorphic rocks by extreme heat and pressure. Metamorphic rocks are found beneath the earth's surface and are generally the hardest and densest of the three types of rock.)*

BREAKING UP IS HARD TO DO: STUDENT ACTIVITY

New rocks are formed while others are broken apart and changed. This breakup and change of rocks and minerals is called *weathering.* There are two main types of weathering: *physical weathering* and *chemical weathering.* The simple experiments below will help your students understand the differences in the two.

Physical Weathering: How does freezing water break up rocks?
Materials for each student: 1 plastic drinking straw, modeling clay, water
Procedure:
1. Seal one end of the drinking straw with clay. Make sure the clay does not extend past the end of the straw.
2. Fill the straw with water.
3. Seal the other end of the drinking straw with clay.
4. Place the straw in a freezer for 24 hours.
5. Observe the straw the next day. What has happened? How does this relate to physical weathering? *(The clay plugs have been pushed out of the straw and a column of ice is extending past the ends of the straw. Water expands when it freezes. When water gets into cracks in and around rocks, it can actually move or break the rocks when it freezes.)*

Chemical Weathering: How does rain chemically weather rocks?
Materials for each group of four students: marble chips, glass jar, white vinegar
Procedure:
1. Place marble chips in the glass jar.
2. Fill the jar with white vinegar, a mild acid.
3. Observe and record the effect of the vinegar on the rocks for one or two days. *(Raindrops dissolve small amounts of carbon dioxide from the air. When water and carbon dioxide combine, carbonic acid is formed. Rocks can be weathered by acidic rain. Rocks containing limestone weather more quickly than others. Minerals such as calcite, gypsum, and halite are also dissolved by the carbonic acid in rainwater.)*

Patterns

Use with "Crystal Construction" on page 194
and "On A Roll With Grammar" on page 249.
Provide students with scissors and glue sticks.

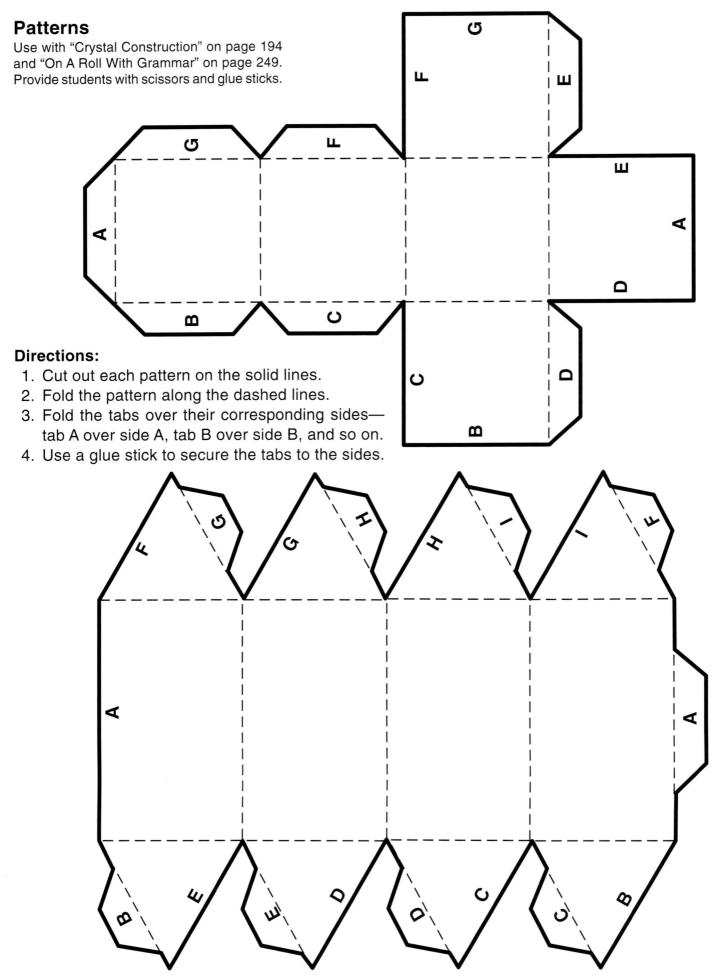

Directions:

1. Cut out each pattern on the solid lines.
2. Fold the pattern along the dashed lines.
3. Fold the tabs over their corresponding sides—
   tab A over side A, tab B over side B, and so on.
4. Use a glue stick to secure the tabs to the sides.

MINING FOR MMM~GOOD MINERALS

Some rocks contain large amounts of minerals. These rocks are called *mineral deposits*. A mineral deposit that can be mined for profit is called an *ore*. Silver, gold, and asbestos are examples of ores. However, there can be problems with the mining of ores. A mine may cover a very large area and may reach deep into the earth's surface. This digging up of very large areas of land can cause environmental problems.

Complete the following activity to help you understand the difficulty in reaching ores. You will also discover how land is lost during mining.

Materials for each student: 1 chocolate-chip cookie, toothpick, plastic drinking straw, paper towel, centimeter ruler, clock

MINING RULES

1. Your mine will earn $1,000 for every 2 cm of straw that is filled with chocolate pieces.
2. The value of your chip mine goes down $100 just for mining it.
3. You will be charged $100 for every five minutes it takes to mine the chocolate.
4. You will be fined $100 for each cookie piece that breaks off. The more damage you cause, the more money you lose.

PART I: MINING & PROCESSING

1. Examine the chocolate-chip cookie mine (your cookie). How many "minerals" (chocolate chips) can you see on the surface? _____
2. Record your starting time: _____
3. Use the toothpick to carefully dig out the minerals. You may *look* at the bottom of the cookie, but you may only mine it from the top.
4. To process your minerals, separate the crumbs from the chocolate you have mined.
5. Record your ending time: _____
6. Record your total mining and processing time: _____ minutes
7. Total Mining & Processing Fee ($100 per every five minutes): $ _____

PART II: LAND DAMAGE

1. Chip Mine Fee: $100
2. Land Damage: Count the cookie pieces that broke off as you worked: _____
   # of cookie pieces x $100 = $ _____
3. Total Land Damage + Chip Mine Fee: $_____

PART III: MEASURE MINERALS

1. Pick up the mined chocolate pieces with the straw.
2. Measure the amount of chocolate in the straw: _____ cm
3. Record the value of your minerals ($1,000 for every 2 cm of straw filled): $ _____

PART IV: COMPUTE PROFIT

Total Mining & Processing Fee $_____ +

Total Land Damage Fee $_____ =

Total Cost $_____

Value of Minerals $_____ –

Total Cost $_____ =

Total Profit $_____

PART V: CONCLUSIONS

Write your answers on the back of this sheet.

1. How is your chip mine like a real one?
2. How is it different?
3. What happened to the land while you were mining?
4. How could you repair the land?

HARD AS A ROCK

Hardness is one way that minerals are identified and classified. Geologists use a hardness scale invented by Friedrich Mohs of Germany. This scale orders ten minerals from softest to hardest, with talc being the softest mineral and diamond being the hardest.

Try the simple scratch test below to determine different degrees of hardness. Use the chart as a guide.

Test Sample	Hardness Value
fingernail	2.5
penny	3.0
nail	4.5
steel file	6.5

Scratch Test Steps:

1. Hold a pencil in one hand. With your other hand, scratch the pencil lead with a fingernail.
2. Observe how easy or difficult it is to make a scratch in the lead.
3. What hardness value would you give the pencil lead? _____
4. Next take a piece of coarse sandpaper and scratch a penny, a nail, and a steel file.
5. What items will the sandpaper scratch? _____
6. What items scratch the sandpaper? _____
7. Where would sandpaper fit on the chart above? _____

LET'S SPLIT!

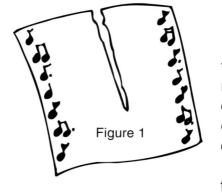
Figure 1

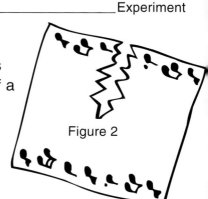
Figure 2

Cleavage and *fracture* are two other ways that minerals are identified. The tendency of a mineral to break along a smooth surface is called cleavage. Some minerals break unevenly or along curved surfaces. This uneven breakage is a fracture.

Create an example of cleavage and fracture with the quick and easy experiment below.

1. Rip a single sheet of a paper towel from top to bottom. What happens? _____

_____

2. Turn another sheet of paper towel as shown in Figure 2 and try to rip it from side to side. What happens? _____
3. Which tear is an example of cleavage? _____
4. Which tear is an example of fracture? _____
5. Use a rock-and-mineral guide to find examples of minerals that cleave and fracture. List them in a chart on the back of this page.

Note To The Teacher: For "Hard As A Rock," provide each student or group with a sharpened pencil, a penny, a nail, a steel file, and coarse sandpaper. The sandpaper will scratch all the items. None of the items will scratch the sandpaper. Sandpaper would fit in the chart below the steel file. The sand of the sandpaper is mostly quartz, which is 7 on Mohs's scale. For "Let's Split!", provide each student with two paper towels. The following are minerals that cleave: beryl, galena, and mica. Two examples of minerals that fracture are obsidian and iron pyrite.

LITERATURE

Novels In A Nutshell

Creative Ideas For Using Novels In Your Classroom

Who knows the best teacher-tested methods for using novels in the classroom? You do! Once again, our subscribers have shared with us the very best of their creative teaching strategies. Use the following collection of novel ideas to keep your students bright-eyed and bushy-tailed down to the last page!

COMPARE AND CONTRAST

1st Character   2nd Character   3rd Character

Top Ten Lists

Your students will definitely rate this activity in the top ten! After reading a few chapters in a novel, ask an important question pertaining to the story. As a class create a list containing the top ten answers to the question. For example, while reading *Number The Stars* by Lois Lowry (Dell Publishing), have students name the top ten reasons why Annemarie and Ellen should be afraid of the Nazi Germans. Record students' responses on a sheet of chart paper; then display the list in the classroom. Students will be demonstrating comprehension without even knowing it!
Lauri Wedel-Isaacs—Gr. 4, L'Ouverture Computer Magnet School, Wichita, KS

Discovery Box

Help your students discover the fun in novels by creating a Discovery Box for the book your class is currently reading. Obtain a computer-paper box or any large box with a lid. Decorate the box by painting it, coloring it, or covering it with wrapping paper. Inside the box place items such as mementos, papers, and any other objects pertaining to your current novel. Invite students to add more items (labeled with their names) to the box—explaining why they chose each particular object. Then display the box and its contents in a special place where students can visit it throughout the reading of the novel.

After completing the novel, divide your class into small groups. Assign each group a section, chapter, or character from the book. Have each group create puzzles, games, and review questions (along with answer keys) for its assigned topic. Combine all the materials into a binder; then place the binder into the box. You'll have a unique method of assessment for your students plus materials to use when you read the novel with your new class next year.
Virginia H. Kotok, St. Margaret School, Greentree, PA

Analyzing Characters

Promote higher-level thinking as well as build comprehension with this characterization activity. Create and laminate a chart similar to the one shown. At the beginning of a novel, use a transparency pen to write the name of a character and your students' impressions of that character in the first circle. As you read further into the novel, add a second character, and then a third. Each day after reading from the novel, add or change any information about each character on the chart. After completing the novel, have each student use the chart as a reference for writing a short essay comparing herself to one of the book's characters. What a great method of assessment!
Lauri Wedel-Isaacs—Gr. 4

Spelling List

cashew

filbert

peanut

almond

macadamia

Pam Crane

Comprehension Checkup

If coming up with materials to check comprehension is making you a little nutty, enlist the help of your faster readers! Instruct each student who finishes early to write five questions (accompanied by an answer key) about the chapters he read. Tell students that their questions may focus on any skill and may be true-or-false, multiple-choice, short-answer, cause-and-effect, or essay questions. Use their questions in a discussion after reading or as a review before the next day's lesson. Upon completion of the book, have each student write two questions and answers related to any part of the book. Choose at least one of each student's questions; then arrange the questions in a test format. Duplicate a class set, and distribute one to each student as a unit test or as a review before a teacher-made quiz. *Michelle Bauml—Gr. 4, Richwood, TX*

Three Times The Learning!

Spelling, reading, writing—finding time for each is a challenge! Incorporate both spelling and writing into your reading program with this time-saving idea. Each Friday help your students choose a list of spelling words from your current novel. Next add frequently misspelled words from your students' writing assignments to the student-generated word list. On Monday give the complete list of words to each student as his spelling list for the week. During the week assign reading activities that will provide writing practice as well as helping students learn their new spelling words. For example, instruct each student to write a letter—containing at least ten of the spelling words—from one character in the novel to another. You'll be able to assess three subjects at one time! *Debbie Patrick—Gr. 5, Park Forest Elementary, State College, PA*

Now That's A Novel Idea!

Use your current novel to teach a variety of skills with this simple idea! Duplicate a page from a novel; then make a transparency of the page. Project the transparency with an overhead projector to model skills such as verb tenses, contractions, suffixes, figurative language, and punctuation. The transparency can also serve as the perfect basis for a writer's workshop minilesson. *Jeanne Randazzo Szczech—Gr. 6, Libby Elementary, Oceanside, CA*

Quick Pop Quiz

Assess each student's comprehension by using a student-generated pop quiz. Give each student a notecard on which to write one question related to the chapter that he just read. Instruct the student to start his question with "Why" to promote higher-level thinking. While each child is getting out a sheet of notebook paper and a pencil for the pop quiz, collect the cards and choose ten of the questions to include on the quiz. Administer the test; then collect the quizzes before discussing the answers. Students will be given instant feedback, and you'll have a quick assessment for each child. *Lauri Wedel-Isaacs—Gr. 4, L'Ouverture Computer Magnet School, Wichita, KS*

Why...?

Digging Into Dialogue

Take advantage of a novel's abundance of dialogue with this simple tip! Duplicate one copy of a page from your current novel. White-out each comma, quotation mark, and ending punctuation used to punctuate dialogue on the copied page. Duplicate a class set of this page and distribute it. Instruct each student to add the appropriate punctuation to the page; then have her check her corrections against the actual novel's page. *Michelle Bauml—Gr. 4, Richwood, TX*

Putting Novels To The Test

Use this assessment idea with your favorite novel to give students practice in test taking, critical thinking, and writing. Create a chapter test that includes multiple-choice questions, spelling and grammar questions, short-answer essays, true-false statements, and fill-in-the-blank questions for your current novel. Make an overhead transparency of the test and display it with an overhead projector. As a class, complete the test and discuss the different forms in which a question can be asked. Next assign a few students to each of the remaining chapters in your current novel. Instruct each group to create its own test for its assigned chapter. Either duplicate a class set or create an overhead transparency of each test for your students to complete. Tests won't seem so bad to your students when they create their own! *Alice Boles—Gr. 5, Riley Elementary, Lakewood, CA*

Group 'Em!

Vary your method of using novels by forming small novel groups. Obtain four to ten copies of each novel that you would like your students to read. Assign each child to one of the novel groups and distribute the books. Allow each group member to read the novel at his own pace during reading workshop. Duplicate and distribute one copy of the list of after-reading project ideas on page 203 to each student. Before passing its novels to another group, have each group choose one project from the list; then have it create the project to motivate the book's next group of readers. Instruct each group to complete a different project for each book that it reads. *Alice Boles—Gr. 5*

Nuts 'Bout Books!

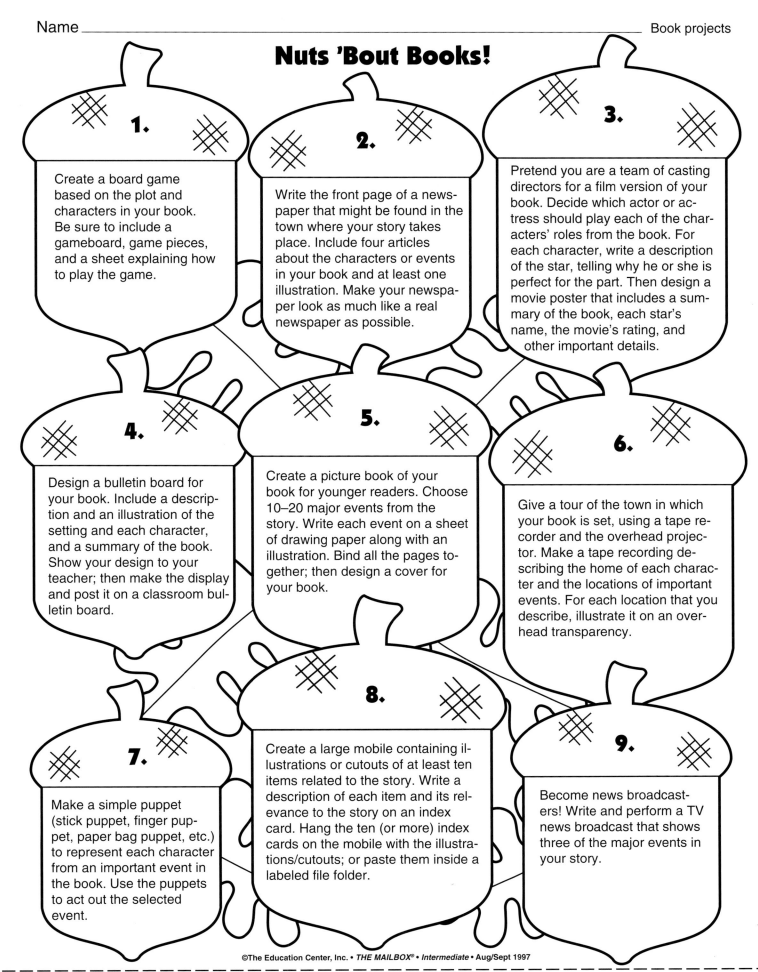

1. Create a board game based on the plot and characters in your book. Be sure to include a gameboard, game pieces, and a sheet explaining how to play the game.

2. Write the front page of a newspaper that might be found in the town where your story takes place. Include four articles about the characters or events in your book and at least one illustration. Make your newspaper look as much like a real newspaper as possible.

3. Pretend you are a team of casting directors for a film version of your book. Decide which actor or actress should play each of the characters' roles from the book. For each character, write a description of the star, telling why he or she is perfect for the part. Then design a movie poster that includes a summary of the book, each star's name, the movie's rating, and other important details.

4. Design a bulletin board for your book. Include a description and an illustration of the setting and each character, and a summary of the book. Show your design to your teacher; then make the display and post it on a classroom bulletin board.

5. Create a picture book of your book for younger readers. Choose 10–20 major events from the story. Write each event on a sheet of drawing paper along with an illustration. Bind all the pages together; then design a cover for your book.

6. Give a tour of the town in which your book is set, using a tape recorder and the overhead projector. Make a tape recording describing the home of each character and the locations of important events. For each location that you describe, illustrate it on an overhead transparency.

7. Make a simple puppet (stick puppet, finger puppet, paper bag puppet, etc.) to represent each character from an important event in the book. Use the puppets to act out the selected event.

8. Create a large mobile containing illustrations or cutouts of at least ten items related to the story. Write a description of each item and its relevance to the story on an index card. Hang the ten (or more) index cards on the mobile with the illustrations/cutouts; or paste them inside a labeled file folder.

9. Become news broadcasters! Write and perform a TV news broadcast that shows three of the major events in your story.

©The Education Center, Inc. • THE MAILBOX® • Intermediate • Aug/Sept 1997

Matilda

An Outrageously Funny Novel By Roald Dahl

Get ready for true adventure when child-genius Matilda Wormwood faces off with her half-witted folks—and then with the formidable school headmistress known as "The Trunchbull." Share this hilarious best-seller—and the following creative activities based on it—with your students for an extraordinary reading treat!

by Beth Gress

Brit Lingo

The author's British background makes for some unfamiliar vocabulary for most American kids (such as *telly, pence, breeches, form, washbasin, headmistress, pound,* and *mummy*). As you read the book, have students pick out words and phrases that are considered more British than American; then have them determine the meanings of most of these words from context. Make a list of the British terms that students find, writing the American equivalent beside each one.

Classifying Character Words

As you share the book, challenge students to name adjectives (other than those included in the book) that describe each main character. As they name these words, list them on a chart. Remove the chart before having each student complete a copy of the vocabulary reproducible on page 208.

After students have completed the reproducible activity, have them think about ways that some of the characters can be compared to animals. For example, Mr. Wormwood is referred to as "ratty" on several occasions in the book. What animal might Miss Trunchbull be compared to? Miss Honey? Matilda? Have small groups of students meet to discuss their animal comparisons; then have each group write its ideas in the form of similes and metaphors that describe each character.

"The Reader Of Books" (Chapter 1)

Matilda—a true book lover—had read some pretty heavy stuff by the time she started school! Have students take a survey of their parents or other adults to see if they have read any of the books listed on Matilda's reading list found in Chapter 1, "The Reader Of Books." Make a class chart to show the survey results. Then ask your media specialist if he or she can provide a synopsis of any of the books on the list. Share these synopses with your students so that they can get an idea of what some of the books are about.

Next have students make recommendations for books they think Matilda would like. Have them write their recommendations, giving reasons why these books might interest Matilda. Bind the recommendations in a notebook to place in your classroom library.

Shady Numbers
(Chapter 5)

Mr. Wormwood is an underhanded used-car dealer. He explains to his son—via math story problems—how he makes money selling cars after "fixing them up." Discuss the British currency terms *pound* and *pence* with your students. (Check the Foreign Exchange listings in the newspaper's business section for the U.S. dollar equivalent of the British pound.) Have student pairs use the equivalences to write more math story problems about Mr. Wormwood's shady deals. The numbers in their problems can represent mileage or profit. Give each pair an overhead transparency pen and a blank transparency on which to write two problems. Then have each pair present its problems to the class for everyone to solve together.

A Honey Of A Teacher
(Chapter 7)

In Chapter 7, Matilda makes up a very clever limerick about Miss Honey. Review the form of a limerick. Remind students that the first, second, and fifth lines rhyme, as do the third and fourth lines. A limerick should also make sense and be humorous. Find and read other examples of limericks. (Ask your media specialist for help in locating examples.) Then have students make up limericks about their teacher—you! Afterward distribute copies of the bottom half of page 207. Have students work independently to complete the reproducible by creating limericks about characters in *Matilda*.

Throw That Hammer!
(Chapter 10)

Miss Trunchbull is touted as being a British Olympian in the hammer throw event. Many students may have never heard of this sport. Show the class a picture of someone competing in the event; then let students try this simplified version. Tie the end of a three-foot-long piece of rope through the holes in a Wiffle® ball. Show it to your students and remind them that the real hammer throw uses a metal ball on a wire. Have students estimate how far they can throw this make-believe hammer. Then accompany your students outdoors. Once outside, have each child throw the hammer and measure the distance of her throw. Have students use the class data to make graphs, find averages, or use as the basis for more student-written story problems.

A Regimented Classroom
(Chapter 13)

Miss Trunchbull's classroom management style is truly regimented. Ask students what they think of having to stand to give answers, or addressing all adults as "sir" or "ma'am." What would they think if their teacher pointed, yelled, ranted, and raved while calling their classmates outlandish names? For an interesting writing assignment, have students write paragraphs that compare and contrast their own classroom with that of Miss Trunchbull's. Then read aloud *Miss Nelson Is Missing* by Harry Allard (Houghton Mifflin Company, 1985)—another story that features a memorable character, substitute teacher Viola Swamp. Have students compare Miss Swamp to Miss Trunchbull.

Miracle #1
(Chapter 14)

In Chapter 14, Matilda's magical power allows her to move objects without touching them. Ask students to imagine what they would do if they had such a power for one day. How would they use that power? How would they use it if they were Matilda? Have each student write a paragraph describing his miracle on white paper; then have him cut around his paragraph to make a thought bubble. Enlarge the art on the top half of page 207. Post the artwork on a bulletin board with students' paragraphs positioned above it. Add the caption "Matilda's Magical Powers Might…"

If I had magical power I might use it to load the dishwasher when it's *my* turn.

Amy

Poor Miss Honey
(Chapter 16)

Miss Honey's living conditions are almost as unbelievable as Miss Trunchbull's punishments. Ask students for ideas on how they might make such conditions more livable if they were in Miss Honey's place. Have students work in groups to make a plan for improving Miss Honey's home. After each group presents its plan to the class, vote on the idea that is the most creative, yet practical.

Principal's Punishments

Miss Trunchbull's punishments for students are severe—even unbelievable! Indeed, their unbelievability is what students at Crunchem Hall say allows "The Trunchbull" to get away with them. List and discuss examples of Miss Trunchbull's punishments; then follow up the discussion by having each student choose one of these topics to write about:

- In what types of cases should the punishment fit the crime—as in Bruce Bogtrotter's cake-eating punishment? In what types of cases should the punishment not fit the crime?
- How could you convince your parents that you were punished by Miss Trunchbull in some unbelievable way—like being put in The Chokey or being swung around by your braids?
- What types of rules might Miss Trunchbull have in her school?
- What do you think would be fair rules for Miss Trunchbull's school?

Journal-Writing Topics

During your reading of *Matilda,* have students respond to any of the following topics in their journals:

- What would you do if you were blessed with Matilda's super-intelligence?
- Matilda gets revenge on her parents in several creative ways. Is seeking revenge always the right thing to do? Is it ever the right thing to do?
- Write a story about an unusual punishment that *you* received from "The Trunchbull."
- Make up spelling rhymes to go with your spelling words, like the one Miss Honey taught her students to help them learn the word *difficulty.*
- After reading Chapter 19: Predict what you think Matilda might do with her special powers.
- Compare Mr. and Mrs. Wormwood's values about children, education, business, TV-watching, and family to your family's values.
- In the last chapter, the Wormwoods move to Spain. Pretend you are Michael and write a letter to Matilda describing your new life.

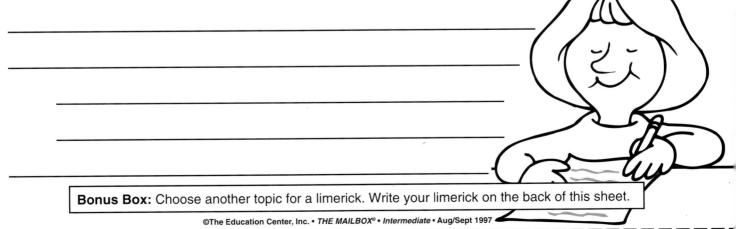

Name_____

Matilda
Writing limericks, character analysis

Poetic Personalities

A *limerick* is a poem with a special rhyme and meter. It usually tells a humorous story about someone. A limerick has five lines: lines 1, 2, and 5 rhyme with each other; lines 3 and 4 rhyme with each other. Limericks often begin with, "There once was a _____ who…," but not always. Sometimes the last line tells something that's unexpected.

Reread the limerick that Matilda wrote about Miss Honey (Chapter 7). Notice how lines 1, 2, and 5 have the same meter with three stressed beats. Lines 3 and 4 have the same meter, but they are shorter than the other lines and have only two stressed beats per line. On the lines below, write your own limerick about one of the characters in *Matilda*.

_____

_____

_____

_____

_____

Bonus Box: Choose another topic for a limerick. Write your limerick on the back of this sheet.

Note To The Teacher: Use with "A Honey Of A Teacher" on page 205.

"Character-istics"

The words listed in the columns on each side of this sheet describe characters from Roald Dahl's *Matilda.* Look up each word in a dictionary; then write a synonym for it in the blank below the word. Finally match each word to a character that it describes. Write the word in the character's box.

	Miss Honey	Miss Trunchbull	
prodigy			genius
tyrannical			gormless
half-witted			fragile
frail			corrupt
gigantic			extraordinary
mild	Matilda	Mr. Wormwood	fierce
precocious			brilliant
formidable			ratty
dishonest			athletic
menacing			impoverished

Bonus Box: On the back of this page, write a paragraph about one of the four characters. Use all of the words in that character's box in your paragraph.

Newts, Newts, Everywhere!

Matilda's first miracle happens when she tips a glass of water containing a newt onto Miss Trunchbull. Use this newt theme to create an eye-catching art project. Then combine your completed project with your classmates' on a bulletin board or wall.

A *tessellation* is a pattern of repeated shapes that completely fill up an area. There are no gaps and no overlapping. You can make tessellations with squares, triangles, rectangles, and hexagons. Or you can create your own shape from one of these geometric figures.

Follow the directions below to make a tessellating newt from a hexagon.

Materials:
scissors
pencil
12" x 18" sheet of white construction paper
transparent tape
pattern on this page

Pattern

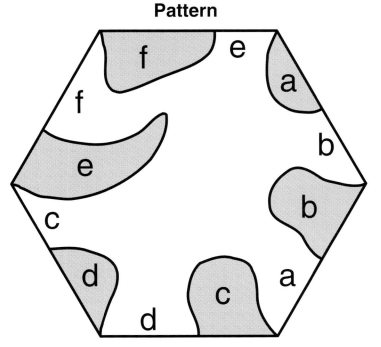

To make your pattern:
1. Cut out the hexagon pattern.
2. Carefully cut out each shaded section.
3. Tape each cut-out section to the edge of the hexagon it matches. *Do not* flip over any of the shaded sections—keep all letters faceup. Use tiny pieces of tape. Don't allow the tape to extend over the edge of the paper.
4. When you're finished, your pattern should look like this:

To tessellate:
1. Trace your completed pattern in the middle of the 12" x 18" sheet of paper.
2. Rotate the pattern so that it fits into the side of the newt already traced—just like a puzzle piece.
3. Trace the pattern again.
4. Continue rotating and tracing until your entire sheet is filled with newts.
5. Trace to the edge of the paper, even the newts whose edges extend off the paper.
6. Decorate each newt with similar eyes, backbones, ribs, color, etc.

SHILOH

A Book Unit On The Newbery Winner
by Phyllis Reynolds Naylor

Eleven-year-old Marty Preston loves roaming the hills of his West Virginia home. But when a young beagle follows him home from the old Shiloh schoolhouse, his life is never the same. Finding the dog abused, Marty refuses to return him to his cruel master and vows he will do anything to save the animal. Invite your students to experience the special bond that exists between a young boy and his dog with the following student-centered activities and reproducibles.

written by Elizabeth H. Lindsay and Hellen Harvey

Before Reading The Book: Key your students into character traits with this book-long character-development project. Draw and cut out a large key; then write each character's name on it as shown. If desired, laminate the key for durability. Use a hole puncher to make a hole below each name; then attach a large paper clip to each hole. Post the key on a wall or bulletin board. Next duplicate multiple copies of the small key pattern on page 213 onto colorful construction paper. Hole-punch each key where indicated; then store the keys in a container near the display. While reading the book, direct each student to label the front of a key with a trait exhibited by one of the characters. On the back of the key, have the student write a sentence from the story that supports the trait. Have the student cut out the key and attach it to the paper clip under the appropriate character's name. Use this information to discuss major and minor characters and how they develop from the beginning of the story to the end.

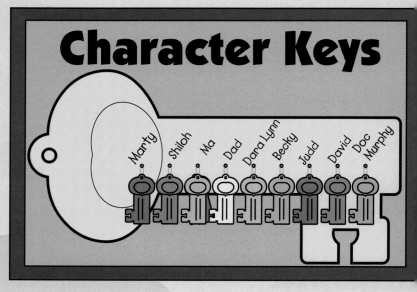

Character Keys

Marty Shiloh Ma Dad Dara Lynn Becky Judd David Doc Murphy

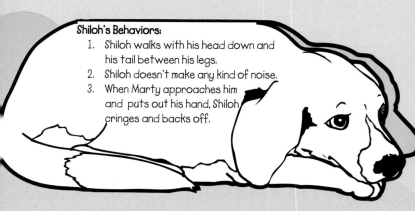

Shiloh's Behaviors:
1. Shiloh walks with his head down and his tail between his legs.
2. Shiloh doesn't make any kind of noise.
3. When Marty approaches him and puts out his hand, Shiloh cringes and backs off.

After Reading Chapters 1–2: When Marty first sees Shiloh near the old schoolhouse, the young beagle is slinking along with his head down and his tail between his legs. As Marty continues to watch the dog, it exhibits other behaviors that lead him to conclude that it has been mistreated. Explain to your students that an author often doesn't directly tell a reader everything he wants to know about a story, but gives clues so that the reader can draw his own conclusions. Distribute a copy of the beagle pattern on page 213 to each student. Then as a class brainstorm a list of these behaviors that Marty sees Shiloh exhibiting. Direct each student to write two or three of these behaviors on the front of the pattern; then have the student draw a conclusion about the possible reason for each behavior, writing each explanation on the inside of the pattern. Have each student share his explanations; then challenge him to continue to read for clues about each character throughout the story.

After Reading Chapters 3–4: After returning Shiloh to Judd Travers, Marty constantly thinks about the dog being back in the hands of his abusive master. Write the word *abuse* on the chalkboard and ask students what they think the word means *(improper treatment)*. Next point out Marty's suggestion that Judd get a subscription to a magazine about dogs so that he can learn how to be kind to them. Have students suggest possible magazine topics related to the proper care of a dog such as housing, feeding, grooming, exercising, training, and providing love and attention. Then divide students into small groups based on the number of topics discussed, and assign each group a topic. Supply each group with a 9" x 12" sheet of white construction paper, markers or colored pencils, glue, and appropriate reference materials. Direct the group to create a magazine page that includes tips and illustrations about its topic such as the one shown. Collect each group's completed page and make a front and a back cover. Bind the pages together between the covers using a hole puncher and yarn or brads. Finally have a student volunteer decorate the cover; then have each group share its page.

After Reading Chapters 5–7: "Oh, what a tangled web we weave, when first we practice to deceive!" Discuss with students the meaning of this quote: how one lie can spread to other lies and affect many people. Then ask students questions such as, "Are there different kinds of lying? Is one kind of lie less wrong than another? Does lying for a good cause make it okay?" Next draw a large spiderweb on a sheet of bulletin-board paper and write "Marty's Lies" in the center of it. Then give each student a marker and have her write a sentence describing a lie that Marty told in the web. Afterward discuss how Marty's initial lie of not telling his parents that he had Shiloh in a pen led to other lies that affected not only him, but his family and others. Finally have each student write a paragraph explaining how Marty could have handled the situation instead of lying.

After Reading Chapters 8–10: Marty learns that his lying about keeping Shiloh sets off a chain of serious events. Discuss with students the chain reaction that often occurs in a *cause-and-effect* relationship: whenever there is a cause, there is an effect; and whenever there is an effect, there is a cause. Draw the cause-and-effect chain shown on a chalkboard. Have students fill in the chain with examples from the story and explain how one cause-and-effect event led to another. Follow up the activity by distributing a copy of page 215 to each student. After each student completes the activity, discuss the answers as a class.

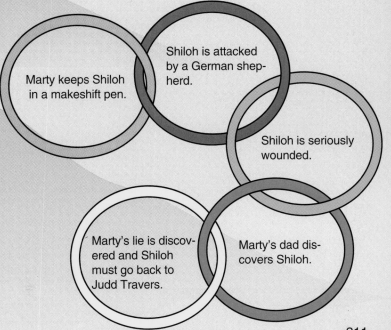

After Reading Chapters 11–12: From trying to prevent Shiloh from being discovered to finding new ways to provide him with food, Marty continues to be a problem solver. Now with Shiloh in the Preston's home while his wounds heal, Marty is more determined than ever to find a way to keep him. Have students identify the various ideas Marty comes up with in his quest to keep Shiloh. *(Marty continues to collect cans; he asks Mr. Wallace to put in his name as a newspaper carrier; and he studies the bulletin board at the back of the store where people put up notices for jobs.)* Then distribute a copy of the problem-solving profile on page 214 and discuss the steps used to make a good decision. Have each student imagine that she, like Marty, has a dog that she must pay for in order to keep. Direct the student to become a problem solver and use the profile to help her make the best choice.

After Reading Chapters 13–14: As Marty is on his way to Judd Travers's home to tell him he intends to keep Shiloh, he sees that Judd has shot a doe. Knowing that shooting a deer out of season is illegal, Marty uses the information to seal a bargain with Judd: he will not tell the game warden about the doe on the condition that he can purchase Shiloh. Even though Marty had admitted that he'd do almost anything for Shiloh, he experiences a dilemma about the situation—he's willing to look the other way about the deer in order to get something he wants. Discuss Marty's predicament with the class—does the fact that he is saving Shiloh justify his actions? If Marty's actions were discovered and he was brought to trial, would a jury find his actions punishable? Divide students into teams of four to ponder this scenario. Have each "jury" list Judd's crime, the facts of the case, and Marty's reasons for not reporting the crime on a sheet of paper. Direct the group to use the information listed to determine if Marty's actions were justified, and in a paragraph explain why or why not. Have each group appoint one member as foreman and read its verdict to the class.

After Reading Chapter 15: Marty's determination to keep Shiloh makes him work harder than ever—even though he fears that Judd may not keep his end of the bargain. Have students give examples from the story of the many things Marty does for Judd. Next direct each student to make a list of the ten most important things in her life, then rank the items in order of importance (1 being the most important, and 10 being the least important). Ask the student to select one of the items on her list. Have her write a paragraph explaining why the item is important to her and what she would do to keep it if she were in jeopardy of losing it.

- Animal rights
- Problem solving
- Achieving goals
- Friendship
- Family
- Helping others
- Honesty
- Law
- Money
- Doing what you think is right

Culminating Activity: Although Marty is just 11 years old, he seems wise beyond his years. Have each student search the novel for a quote that shows Marty's wisdom, such as "Thinking don't cost nothing" or "If some kid was shaking like this dog is, you wouldn't feel no pull for keeping an eye on him?" Discuss with students the meaning of each quote. Next provide each student with a sentence strip and a marker. Write the topics shown at the left on the chalkboard and direct each student to choose one. Then have the student write a "word of wisdom" on his sentence strip based on what he thinks Marty would say about the topic. Have each student share his strip; then post the strips on a wall or bulletin board titled "Words From The Wise."

A Sensational Sequel
Follow Marty and Shiloh's life together—and the continuing tension between Marty and Judd—with Phyllis Reynolds Naylor's sequel, *Shiloh Season* (Atheneum Books For Young Readers, 1996).

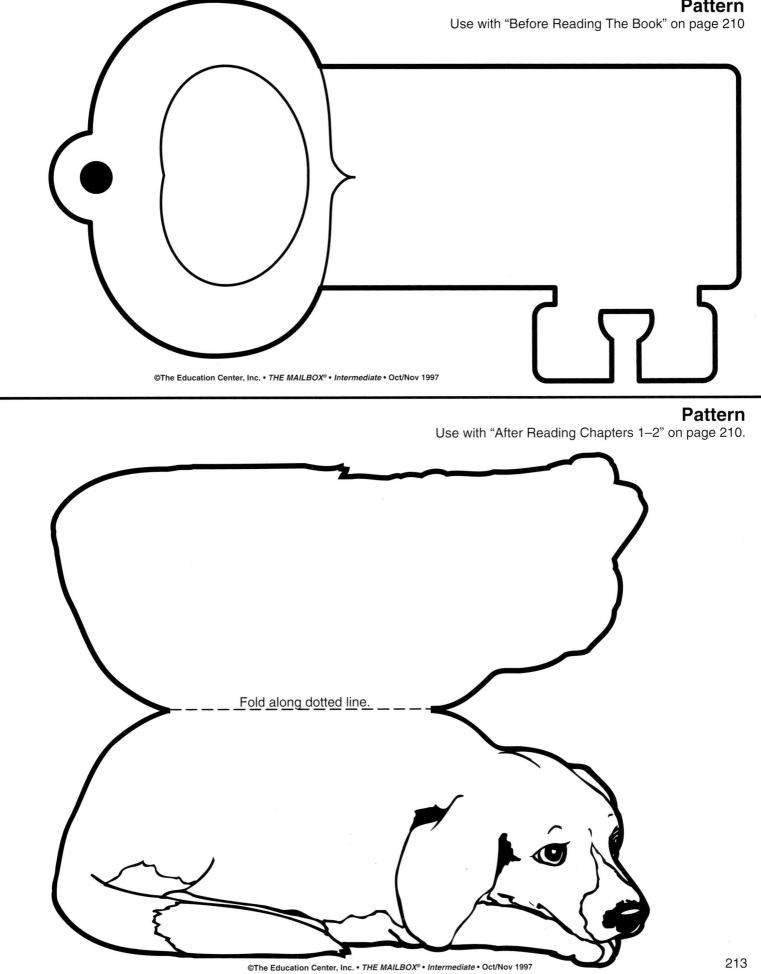

Fold along dotted line.

Pin Down A Solution!

Problems, no matter how big or small, require some decision making. Sometimes the decisions are easy to make, like choosing what to wear to school or what book to read. But some problems, like how to achieve a goal, require a little more planning. Read the profile below and use it to help you pin down a solution to your problem! Use the back of this sheet if you need more space.

Problem-Solving Profile

1. Define your goal—*What is it that I want to accomplish?*
   _____
   _____
   _____

2. List all possible solutions—*What can I do to help me reach my goal?*
   _____
   _____
   _____
   _____
   _____
   _____

3. Study your solutions—*What are the pros and cons of each solution?*
   _____
   _____
   _____

4. Rank the solutions—*How would I rank the options from best to worst, easiest to most difficult, etc.?*
   _____
   _____
   _____
   _____
   _____

5. Choose the best solution—*Which solution will work best for me?*
   _____
   _____
   _____

6. Evaluate your success—*Is my plan working? Should I pick another solution?*
   _____
   _____
   _____

©The Education Center, Inc. • THE MAILBOX® • *Intermediate* • Oct/Nov 1997

214 **Note To The Teacher:** Use this sheet with "After Reading Chapters 11–12" on page 212.

A Perfect Pair

Like a boy—or girl!—and his dog, a *cause* and an *effect* go together. Whenever there is a cause (reason), there is an effect (result); and whenever there is an effect, there is a cause. Read each cause-and-effect phrase below. Match each effect to its cause by writing the appropriate letter in the blank next to each number. Then, on the back of this sheet, use the connecting words shown to write five sentences, each including one of the cause-and-effect matches. (You may need to rearrange, change, or add words to create your five sentences.)

Example: *Cause:* Marty whistles. *Effect:* Shiloh runs toward him.
Because Marty whistles, Shiloh runs toward him.

Causes:

_____ 1. Marty realizes that Shiloh has been abused.

_____ 2. Shiloh returns to Marty's house.

_____ 3. Marty wants to earn the money to buy Shiloh.

_____ 4. Shiloh is happy to see Marty.

_____ 5. Marty tells his friend David that he can't come over to Marty's house because his mom is suffering from headaches.

_____ 6. Marty asks Mr. Wallace if he has any old cheese or lunch meat that he can sell cheaply.

_____ 7. Marty prepares a mixture of sour cream, cut-up frankfurters, and some little chunks of cheese for Shiloh.

_____ 8. Marty continues to feed Shiloh.

_____ 9. Mr. Wallace tells people that the Preston family is facing hard times.

_____ 10. Marty's dad tells his family at dinnertime that Judd Travers wants to hunt on their land.

_____ 11. Ma, knowing that Marty doesn't like squash, notices that he saves it to eat later.

_____ 12. Marty sees that Judd Travers has killed a deer out of season.

Effects:

A. Marty collects bottles for deposits and cans for recycling.

B. Shiloh throws up the first time he eats the mixture.

C. Marty fears that Judd will discover Shiloh.

D. Mr. Wallace thinks that Marty is buying the food for his family.

E. People ask Marty's mother if she is feeling well and tell her what to take for a headache.

F. Ma suspects that Marty may be hiding Shiloh.

G. Marty decides that he has to buy Shiloh from Judd Travers.

H. Shiloh fattens up and his ribs don't show as much.

I. Marty hides Shiloh in the woods up on the hill.

J. Shiloh wags his tail, yips with joy, and licks Marty's face.

K. Judd makes a bargain with Marty.

L. People leave food for Marty's dad in their mailboxes.

Shiloh

Connecting Words

Causes:	Effects:
causes	results in
because	as a result
since	consequently
as	for this reason
whenever	therefore
	so
	so that

Bonus Box: Search through the story for three more cause-and-effect relationships. Then, on another sheet of paper, draw a picture that shows each relationship. Have a classmate write a cause-and-effect sentence for each picture.

Note To The Teacher: Use this activity with "After Reading Chapters 8–10" on page 211.

The Giver
The Newbery Medal-Winning Novel
By Lois Lowry

Jonas's community is perfect. There is no war, hunger, poverty, or pain. The community provides everything for its citizens—including lifetime jobs. Jonas is content until he turns 12 and is selected to be The Receiver Of Memory, whose job it is to hold all the memories of the world that came before. Now Jonas knows the truth. Use the following creative activities as you and your students step inside this mesmerizing science-fiction story.

by Susan Giles and Wanda Humphries

Visualizing A Perfect World
(Use before reading the book.)

What makes a world perfect? Share the statement, "Jonas's world is perfect," with your class. Then have each student imagine what the qualities of a perfect world would be. List students' responses on the chalkboard. Next instruct each student to choose one imperfection—such as hunger or poverty—that she would like removed from today's society. Instruct her to explain in a paragraph how removing that imperfection might change the world. Allow each student to share her paragraph with the class.

Dear Diary...
(Use after chapter 1.)

Encourage students to keep a record of Jonas's endeavors by helping them make one-of-a-kind reading diaries. Ask each student to explain whether he thinks diaries are permitted in Jonas's community. Then guide each student through the steps below to create his own diary. After reading each chapter of *The Giver,* instruct each student to respond to that chapter's events in his diary as if he were Jonas.

Materials: one 7" x 11" sheet of white construction paper folded in half, greeting-card style; one foam meat tray cut into a 5 1/2" x 7" rectangle; several sheets of drawing paper cut into 5" x 7" rectangles; dull pencil; ruler; tempera paint; ink roller or paintbrush; scissors; stapler; marker

Steps:

1. Measure a one-inch frame around the center of the meat tray; then cut out and discard the center piece.
2. Use the dull pencil to press designs into the foam frame.
3. Use an ink roller or a paintbrush to apply paint to the decorated side of the frame.
4. Press the frame—paint side down—onto the front of the folded construction paper.
5. Remove the frame and allow the paint to dry.
6. Stack the sheets of paper inside the diary, staple the book together, and add a title to the cover.

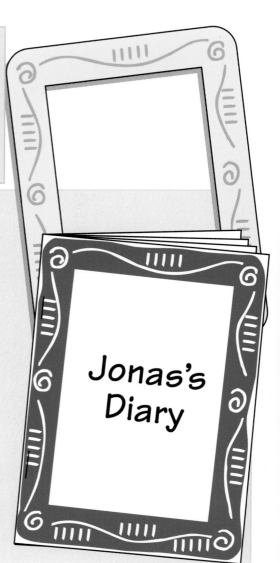

Jonas's Diary

Community Differences

(Use after chapters 2–5.)

After reading the first few chapters, your students will begin to notice many differences between Jonas's community and theirs. As a class, brainstorm a list of those differences. Then have students suggest categories into which the items listed can be divided (for example, home, school, jobs, rules, etc.). Next write each category title on a different section of a bulletin board covered with light-colored paper. Have students decide into which category each item listed on the board should go. Write each item in the appropriate section of the bulletin board. Then, throughout the book, allow students to add new differences to the board as they discover them.

Home	School	Rules	Jobs	Children
• *arranged marriages* • *babies assigned—1 boy, 1 girl* • *dream sharing* • *no cars*	• *chanting hymns* • *ritual apology* • *volunteer hours*	• *no bragging* • *no hoarding food* • *third offense results in "release"* • *announced over speakers*	• *assigned* • *begin at age 12*	• *one "comfort" object* • *given numbers before names* • *get bicycles at age 9*

Community Members

(Use after chapters 6–11.)

What type of person makes a successful member of Jonas's unique community? As a class, brainstorm a list of personality traits—such as *humble, forgiving, self-disciplined, selfish, understanding,* and *curious.* List students' responses on the chalkboard. Have each student study the list; then have her write all those traits that she thinks describe herself on a sheet of paper. Next invite several student volunteers to the board, one at a time. Have each student circle one trait that she thinks describes Jonas, explaining her choice.

On the following day, divide your class into small groups. Have each group imagine that it is the committee responsible for selecting new members of Jonas's community. Instruct the group to create a list of the personality traits it would look for in a community member. Have each group share its list; then use all the groups' responses to create a master list on the chalkboard. Have each student compare this new list to the traits that she previously listed about herself; then have her write a paragraph telling whether she would make a viable member of Jonas's community.

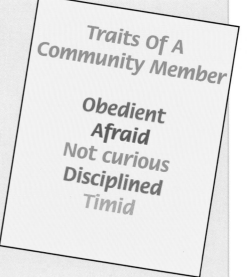

Traits Of A Community Member

Obedient
Afraid
Not curious
Disciplined
Timid

A Black-And-White World

(Use after chapter 12.)

A world without color—such as Jonas's community—is difficult for students to imagine. Load a camera with black-and-white film; then invite student volunteers to take pictures of different places around the school, such as the classroom, library, cafeteria, and playground. Post the developed photographs on a bulletin board titled "A Black-And-White World."

Then use the bulletin board and the questions below to start a discussion about what it would be like living in Jonas's community without color:

• How might the absence of color affect the choices that you made?
• How might your mood be affected?
• What colors would you miss the most and least? Why?
• Would your life be simpler or more complicated without color? Explain.
• How might school be affected?
• Do you think learning would be easier or more difficult? Explain.

Givers And Receivers

(Use after chapter 16.)

Just as Jonas holds the memories of the world before him, senior citizens hold the memories of the world before your students were born. Have each student think of an older person—such as a relative, friend, neighbor, or school staff member—whom he would like to interview. Give each student one copy of page 219; then, as a class, read through the questions and statements. Explain to each student that he will need to choose at least 15 questions from the list on page 219, then use those questions to interview his chosen person. Further explain that he should try to use a tape recorder or video camera to tape the interview, but that the interview can be handwritten if necessary. After the interview, have each student type on the computer or write on paper three favorite memories that he learned during the interview. Bind the class's new memories into one memory book to keep in the classroom. Or duplicate enough copies so that each student can take home his own booklet.

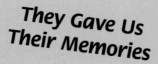

They Gave Us Their Memories

Interviews With Older Friends

written by Mrs. Giles's Class

Picture-Book Projects

(Use after completing the book.)

Strengthen sequencing skills with a fun picture book–publishing project. Challenge students to name the main events in *The Giver*. List their responses on the chalkboard. With help from students, circle the ten most important events and place them in sequential order. Then divide your class into groups of five students. Give each group 11 sheets of black construction paper and a box of colored chalk. Direct each group member to choose two of the events on the board, then use colored chalk to illustrate each one on a different sheet of black paper. Also select one group member to create a cover for the book using the remaining sheet of black paper. Next spray each group's completed illustrations with aerosol hairspray to prevent the chalk from smearing. Finally have each group arrange its pictures in order, punch holes along the left sides of the papers, and use yarn to bind the pages together. Display the books in a reading corner for students to browse through during free time.

A Simulated Community

(Use after completing the book.)

Culminate your study of *The Giver* with this simulation activity. Assign one student to be The Receiver, one to be the Chief Elder, and at least two students to each of the other jobs listed. Present the "community" (your students) with each of the scenarios listed, one at a time. Instruct each student—excluding the Committee Of Elders—to write a paragraph explaining his reaction and possible solution to the problem based on how his assigned character might react. Next have several students share their solutions with the Committee Of Elders, which analyzes the suggestions and makes a final decision. Extend the activity by inviting students to brainstorm other scenarios or problems to present to the community.

Community Jobs:

Laborer	Engineer	Instructor	Director Of Recreation
Nurturer	Speaker	Pilot	Committee Of Elders
Doctor	Caretaker Of The Old	Law And Justice	

Scenarios:
- Some of the Landscape Workers have reported an unusual sighting on the outskirts of town. They described creatures walking through the fields on four legs. On examination, the Elders determined it was a herd of animals.
- Although we have Climate Control, the water level in our river is going down. Because the river is the source of 70% of all the water used in the community, minor problems have already begun to arise.
- A plane from Elsewhere has crashed in one of our community's fields. The Pilot ejected safely and escaped out of the community. His personal belongings—including a wallet, a Bible, clothing, sketchbooks, and a novel—scattered along the ground and are gradually being discovered by children of the community.

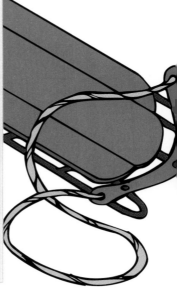

Memories From The Past

Have you ever wondered what life was like when an older relative or friend was your age? Well, now's the time to find out! Choose an older person in your life to interview. Read the questions below; then check at least 15 of them to ask your older friend. After your interview, choose three memories shared by your friend that are your favorites. Describe them in your own words on the notepad.

Name of person you interviewed:

_____

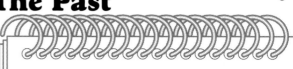

Three Favorite Memories

___ In what year were you born?

___ Where were you born?

___ How many people were in your family?

___ Describe your elementary school.

___ How did you travel to school?

___ Do you remember any of your teachers? Describe one whom you remember.

___ What were some of the rules that you had to follow in school?

___ How were students disciplined in school?

___ How were you disciplined at home?

___ What types of games did you play at school with your friends?

___ Describe one memory of school.

___ Did you have a stuffed animal as a child? If so, what was it?

___ What types of clothes did you wear to school?

___ What memories do you have of your childhood that make you happy?

___ How did you decide on the job you held as an adult?

___ At what age did you finish school and begin work?

___ If you were trained for a lifetime job, what would you want that job to be?

___ What is your favorite color, and why?

___ How does music affect your life?

___ Do you have any memories of extreme weather, such as a blizzard or hurricane?

___ Describe a memory of one of your birthdays.

___ How did you meet your spouse?

___ How did you choose the name(s) for your child(ren)?

___ Have you ever learned a lesson after making a wrong choice? Explain.

___ What is your favorite memory of a holiday?

Note To The Teacher: Use with "Givers And Receivers" on page 218.

219

Think About It

Chapter 1: At the end of the evening meal, each person in the community must share his feelings with the members of his family unit. What is significant about this ritual?

Chapter 2: What do you think are the advantages and disadvantages of being given a lifetime job?

Chapter 3: Do you think public humiliation is a good method of punishment? Why or why not?

Chapter 4: How would you describe *release* in Jonas's community?

Chapter 5: Jonas says that it is better to talk about ways people are the same instead of different. In what ways does Jonas's community try to avoid differences?

Chapter 7: Would you like to be considered an adult and begin training for your lifetime job at the age of 12? Explain.

Chapter 8: Jonas is said to have *intelligence.* He's also told that he will soon gain the *wisdom* he needs for his job. What do you think are the differences between *intelligence* and *wisdom?*

Chapter 9: Do you think lying is necessary to keep a "perfect" society going?

Chapter 11: The Giver tells Jonas that he has great honor, but it is not the same as power. Which do you think is more important: honor or power? Explain.

Chapter 13: Jonas says that he and The Giver have to protect people from making the wrong choices. What do you gain or lose by making a wrong choice?

Chapter 14: Why do you think Jonas loses memories when he shares them with Gabriel?

Chapter 15: If given the choice, would you choose a pain-free life without memories, or a life filled with memories and pain? Explain.

Chapter 17: Throughout the story, citizens apologize for mistakes; but they never say, "I'm sorry." Do you think there is a difference between saying, "I apologize," and "I'm sorry"? If so, what is the difference?

Chapter 18: The author ends this chapter by saying that The Giver's thoughts were elsewhere and his eyes looked troubled. Reread the last paragraph in this chapter. What do you think The Giver is thinking about?

Chapter 19: Jonas's community focuses on sameness; yet they don't believe that there should be two identical people, twins, in the community. What might be the community's reasons for thinking this way?

Chapter 20: What are your thoughts on Jonas's escape plan?

Chapter 21: What do you think will happen in the community now that Jonas has left? What do you think The Giver will do to help?

Chapter 22: Jonas begins to experience some of the things that the community did not have to worry about, such as hunger, pain, and poor weather. Do you see any advantages to a community like Jonas's? Are the advantages worth dealing with the disadvantages?

Chapter 23: Explain in your own words how this book ends.

Note To The Teacher: Duplicate one copy for each student to use for journal questions. Or make a copy for yourself to use as discussion questions after each designated chapter.

Name _____

Colorful Words!

Can you imagine a world without color? The people of Jonas's community don't even know what color is! Just as color adds beauty and detail to our world, words can do the same for writing.

Directions:

1. Use a dictionary to find the definition of each word numbered 1–12. Write the definition on the line.

2. Look for a *synonym*—a word with a similar meaning—for that word in the picture. Write it on the line. (You will probably need to look up the meanings of some of these words too.) Then color the space containing the synonym according to the color in the ( ).

3. When you finish, you will see a memory like the one Jonas shared with Gabriel.

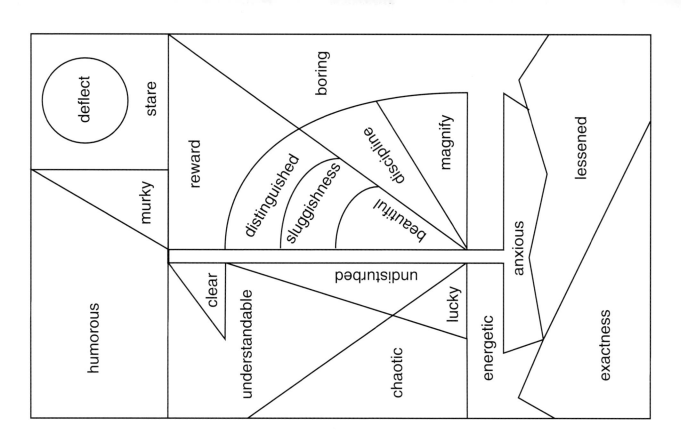

	Word	Definition	Synonym	
1.	apprehensive	_____	_____	(brown)
2.	prominent	_____	_____	(orange)
3.	enhance	_____	_____	(purple)
4.	fortunate	_____	_____	(orange)
5.	chastise	_____	_____	(yellow)
6.	serene	_____	_____	(green)
7.	avert	_____	_____	(yellow)
8.	indolence	_____	_____	(red)
9.	diminished	_____	_____	(green)
10.	conspicuous	_____	_____	(red)
11.	precision	_____	_____	(green)
12.	exquisite	_____	_____	(purple)

Color all remaining spaces blue.

Bonus Box: Choose five words from the picture. Write an antonym for each word on the back of this page.

©The Education Center, Inc. • *THE MAILBOX®* • *Intermediate* • Dec/Jan 1997–98 • Key p. 311

Mrs. Frisby And

Activities For Robert C. O'Brien's Newbery Winner

Mrs. Frisby, a widowed mouse, is in a precarious situation: her son Timothy is sick and too weak to be moved. But if she and her four children don't move soon, they'll be killed by the farmer's plow. Her only hope lies with the mysterious rats of NIMH. Introduce your students to this classic Newbery tale that has captivated readers for years; then follow up reading with the creative activities and reproducibles that follow.

ideas by Jane Robinson, Joy Kalfas, and Elizabeth H. Lindsay

Before Reading: Rats, Mice, And Intelligence

Before beginning this novel, share the book's cover with students. Have them use the cover to predict possible characters, settings, and plot events. Then write each of the following phrases on a different envelope as shown:

Rats are animals that…
Mice are animals that…
Rats and mice are different because…
Being intelligent means…
Animals and people are different because…

Place each envelope—along with five index cards and a pencil—at a different area in the room. Next divide students into five groups, directing each group to a different envelope. Have group members discuss how to best finish the envelope's phrase; then have the group write its response on an index card and place the card in the envelope. After rotating each group to every envelope, share the responses from each one. Discuss with students their perceptions of rats and mice and how they think they were formed. Also talk about what they think are characteristics of someone who is intelligent.

After Chapter 1: Putting Predictions To The Test

Put prediction skills to the test with this ongoing activity! Guide students to understand that when they ask questions, use clues, and guess answers while reading, they are making *predictions*. Model this strategy by reading aloud chapter 1. Stop to ask questions about what you're reading (for example, "Why is Timothy sick? What is moving day? What will Mrs. Frisby do about Timothy's sickness?"). Think aloud about each question, verbalizing clues and possible answers. Afterward ask students what questions they asked themselves. As you record their responses on the chalkboard, have them identify clues and suggest possible answers. Then give each student a copy of page 225 to complete as she reads the book. Throughout the story, have students share the thoughts they have recorded on their sheets.

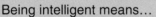

The Rats Of NIMH

After Chapter 1: Building A Better Mouse House

Challenge students to put on the hard hats and build their thinking skills with this nifty homework activity! First have students describe Mrs. Frisby's house (see chapter 1). Discuss how she uses the things she finds around her to furnish it. Then ask, "If you were a mouse, from what materials would your home be made and furnished?" For homework, instruct each student to create a mouse house using materials found in her home. The following day let each student hide her house in the classroom. Then invite students to go "mousing" for the hidden houses. Finally have each student share her house. Extend the activity by challenging each student to choose a classmate's house and write a tale about the mouse who lives in it.

During Reading: Brain Busters

While reading the story, continue building thinking power with these fun-filled brain busters:

- After Chapter 1: Pick a period in history, such as the colonial period, the Egyptian period, or the future. Brainstorm items from that period that a mouse might use in its house, such as a quill pen for a bed.
- After Chapter 14: Brainstorm alternative solutions to Mrs. Frisby's moving-day dilemma. For example, the Frisby family could have moved in with the rats.
- After Chapter 18: Brainstorm a list of imaginary books the rats might want to read, such as *Miniature Gardening* and *Dollhouse Furnishings*.
- After Chapter 18: NIMH is an *acronym* that stands for the *National Institute Of Mental Health*. Brainstorm other acronyms and their meanings, such as *NASA* (National Aeronautics and Space Administration) and *ZIP* (Zone Improvement Plan).

After Chapter 16: "A-maze-ing" Mazes

A *maze* is a place or puzzle with many confusing paths and passageways. They are often used to test skill in problem solving or to test reactions in animals. Provide each student with an 8 1/2" x 11" sheet of drawing paper and a fine-tipped black marker. Direct the student to first use a pencil to draw his design on a sheet of loose-leaf paper. Then have the student use the black marker to carefully trace his maze onto the drawing paper. Laminate the completed mazes. Then give each student a classmate's maze and have him solve the puzzle using a wipe-off marker. If desired, give students a time limit for solving the mazes. Reward each student who finds his way out of a maze with a small prize or treat.

After Chapter 17: Power Prescriptions

The scientists at NIMH created a super injection that turned rats into highly intelligent creatures. It was a prescription that translated into thinking power! What prescriptions would your students write if they could cure anything in the world? Present this question to students; then have them brainstorm problems they'd like to cure, such as pollution and illiteracy. Record students' responses on the chalkboard. Then give each child a copy of the pattern on page 226. Have the student choose a problem from the list, and write the symptoms and a prescription on the pattern. Then have him color and cut out the pattern to post on a display titled "Rx For A Wonderful World."

Symptoms:
littered land
dirty water and air
sick plants and animals
Rx:
Antipollution Pill
Take one tablet daily to eliminate pollution in our world.
Dr. J. Shealy

After Chapter 22: How Would You Use That?

Like the rats of NIMH, good thinkers think about all of the possibilities before making a decision. Have students brainstorm a list of items the rats gathered from the Fitzgibbons' farm to use in their home (Christmas-tree lights, carpet, electrical wire, etc.). Discuss how they used each item; then talk about ways they *could* have used each one. Next place 10–15 everyday items—such as a spool of thread, a bottle cap, and a paper clip—in a bag. Pull out each item one at a time. Have students suggest ways the rats could use each item. Then direct each child to choose the ten most useful items and rank them, with 1 being the most useful and 10 the least useful. Extend the activity by having each student add five other items to the list, explaining the value of each one.

More Fiction About Remarkable Rodents

Put students on the path of some other great rodent thinkers with these fantastic books:
- *Abel's Island* by William Steig (Farrar, Straus & Giroux, Inc.; 1976)
- *Ben & Me* by Robert Lawson (Little, Brown & Company; 1988)
- *The Mouse And The Motorcycle* by Beverly Cleary (Avon Books, 1990)
- *Poppy* by Avi (Orchard Books, 1995)
- *Rasco And The Rats Of NIMH* by Jane L. Conly (HarperCollins Children's Books, 1988)
- *Redwall* by Brian Jacques (The Putnam Publishing Group, 1987)

End Of The Book: A Rats-Of-NIMH Celebration

As a culminating activity, have students plan a feast fit for a beast—a rat or mouse, that is! First have students brainstorm foods that mice and rats might enjoy eating, such as cheeses, crackers, fruits, and nuts. Then divide students into small groups. Have each group plan a party activity like one of the "Brain Busters" on page 223 or a silly "rat-race" relay. Before the big day, ask parents to help supply food, drinks, and paper products. Decorate the room Rats-Of-NIMH style, including items such as a string of Christmas lights, scattered leaves, and buckets of books. Then celebrate the completion of a terrific tale!

Power-Packed Predictions

What does it take to become a super reader? Prediction power! Follow the directions below to help you make some power-packed predictions about *Mrs. Frisby And The Rats Of NIMH.*

Directions:

1. On another sheet of paper, make a chart labeled with the headings shown in the example. (Be sure to make the columns big enough for you to write your answers.)
2. Write each page number and question listed below in the appropriate columns.
3. As you read the book, carefully read the page listed in the chart for each question.
4. Record your prediction for the answer to the question.
5. Write the story clue or clues that helped you make your prediction.
6. Continue reading the story.
7. When you find the actual answer to the question, write a check in the *yes* column if your prediction was correct. If your prediction was not correct, write a check in the *no* column and write the actual answer.

Example:

Page	Question	Prediction	Story Clues	Yes	No	Actual Answer
11	Who is Mr. Ages?					

1. Page 11: Who is Mr. Ages?
2. Page 37: Why are the rats carrying an electrical cable?
3. Page 56: Why is Jonathan Frisby's name so well-known in the woods?
4. Page 57: How do you think the rats will be able to move Mrs. Frisby's home?
5. Page 82: What is the plan of the rats of NIMH?
6. Page 86: What kind of place is NIMH?
7. Page 96: Why do you think Mr. Frisby never told his wife the story of NIMH?
8. Page 111: Why were the rats being injected and tested?
9. Page 125: How is the ability to read going to help the rats?
10. Page 212: How do you think the rats will convince the exterminators that they are not more of the mechanized rats?

Note To The Teacher: Use with "Putting Predictions To The Test" on page 222. (Page numbers are taken from the paperback version published by Aladdin Books, 1986.)

Pattern

Use with "Power Prescriptions" on page 224.

Symptoms:

Rx:

Prescribed by:

Name _____

Mrs. Frisby And The Rats Of NIMH
Journal writing

What Do You Think?

After reading the story, choose _____ of the journal topics listed below. Write your responses in a special journal or notebook of your own.

1. What characteristics would rats need to have to be considered respectable creatures? Explain.
2. Mr. Frisby said to his wife, "All doors are hard to unlock until you have the key." What do you think he meant?
3. After receiving injections at NIMH, the rats became highly intelligent and stopped aging. If you could choose either of these qualities, which would you choose and why?
4. *Intelligence* is the ability to understand, think, and learn. Give three examples from the story that show the rats' intelligence.
5. Jenner and a few others left the main group because they didn't agree that the rats should stop stealing from humans. Which rats do you agree with, and why?
6. Think about the qualities of a good leader. If Nicodemus could no longer be the rats' leader, which rat should replace him? Explain.
7. Many characters in the story show great courage. Which character do you think is the most courageous, and why?
8. Dr. Schultz conducted experiments on the rats and mice in his lab at NIMH. Make a list of the pros and cons of using animals in medical and scientific experiments.
9. Choose one of the situations below. Write what you think happened.
   • why the toy tinker was in the woods
   • which rats died in the tunnel
   • what happened to the six mice lost in the air ducts at NIMH
   • why the seven rats were in the hardware store
   • how the rats will live at Thorn Valley
10. After their experience at NIMH, the rats felt they didn't fit in anywhere. Sometimes people feel this way. Write three things you could do to help a person who feels left out to fit in.
11. Many animals in the story help one another. Write about a time when you and a friend, neighbor, or family member helped each other.

Name_____

Tools Of The Trade

The rats of NIMH are terrific problem solvers. Problem-solving strategies are "tools" that can be used to solve problems. Use one of the strategies listed on the chalkboard to help solve each problem below. Solve the problem on the back of this sheet. Then draw the strategy symbol in the box. Write the answer in the blank.

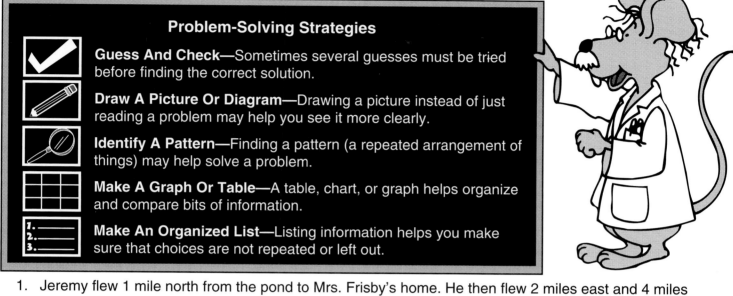

Problem-Solving Strategies

Guess And Check—Sometimes several guesses must be tried before finding the correct solution.

Draw A Picture Or Diagram—Drawing a picture instead of just reading a problem may help you see it more clearly.

Identify A Pattern—Finding a pattern (a repeated arrangement of things) may help solve a problem.

Make A Graph Or Table—A table, chart, or graph helps organize and compare bits of information.

Make An Organized List—Listing information helps you make sure that choices are not repeated or left out.

1. Jeremy flew 1 mile north from the pond to Mrs. Frisby's home. He then flew 2 miles east and 4 miles south to the owl's tree. If on the return trip Jeremy flew 2 miles west, how far and in which direction did he have to travel to get back to the pond? ☐ _____

2. Four rats gathered 12 loads of oats, 19 loads of wheat, 11 loads of barley, and 7 loads of corn. Rita gathered 12. Reggie did not gather 7. If Rhonda gathered 11, how many did Ricky gather? How many did Reggie gather? ☐ _____

3. Each of Isabella's three favorite books has a different-colored cover: red, blue, and gold. How many different ways can she arrange the books on the library shelf? ☐ _____

_____

4. Look at the letter-and-number combination below. What letter and number comes next?
   R 1 A 4 T 7 R 10 A 13 ☐ _____

5. The rats and mice divided their basketball teams based on jersey numbers. Team 1 wore jerseys 3, 6, 12, 24. Team 2 wore jerseys 4, 9, 19, 39. What was the jersey number of each team's fifth player?
   ☐ _____

6. Which group of 3 rats and which group of 3 mice successfully completed the maze an equal number of times?
   Rat A = 24, Rat B = 45, Rat C = 36, Rat D = 75, Rat E = 12
   Mouse A = 32, Mouse B = 19, Mouse C = 29, Mouse D = 24, Mouse E = 43
   ☐ _____

7. Justin had 1 quarter, 3 dimes, 2 nickels, and 5 pennies. If he needed to pay Mr. Ages 63 cents for a powder, which coins did he use? ☐ _____

8. The rats moving Mrs. Frisby's home walked in a single-file line. Arthur was ahead of Alan. Amy was behind Alan. Arthur was behind Alma. Anastasia was between Amy and Alan. Who was last in line?
   ☐ _____

Fudge-A-Mania

It's looking to be a grim summer for Peter Hatcher. He and his little brother Fudge are back in Judy Blume's second sequel to *Tales Of A Fourth Grade Nothing.* This time the Hatchers are sharing a Maine vacation house with none other than archenemy Sheila Tubman and her family! To no one's surprise, Fudge and company stir up some wacky situations over their three-week vacation. Get ready for summer by reading this hilarious novel with your students. Then use the following activities and reproducibles to generate some classroom fun—and learning—that's nothing short of "fudge-tastic"!

by Debra Liverman

Before Reading The Book
Skill: Data collection

How much do your students have in common with the characters in *Fudge-A-Mania*? Find out with this data-collection activity. Draw a large Venn diagram on the chalkboard. Label one circle "younger siblings" and the other circle "older siblings." Give each student a small sticky note to label with his name. Have each student come to the board and place his sticky note in the area of the Venn diagram that applies to him. Next instruct each student to write each statistic on the diagram as a fraction in simplest form. For example, in the illustration *6/26, or 3/13, of the students have both younger and older siblings.* For an added challenge, direct each student to convert each fraction to a percentage rounded to the nearest whole number. For example, in the illustration *3/13, or 23%, of the students have both younger and older siblings.* Record the final statistics on another area of the chalkboard; then repeat this activity with a different category from the list below.

Categories:
Do you have a brother(s) or sister(s)?
Do you have a cat(s) or dog(s)?
Can you turn a cartwheel or stand on your head?
Have you ever baby-sat for a sibling or for another child?

After Reading Chapter 5
Skill: Grammar review

Review a variety of language arts skills with this scavenger-hunt activity. Duplicate one copy of page 231 for each student. Challenge each student to find the items listed on that page within the first five chapters of *Fudge-A-Mania.* Award a small treat, such as a piece of fudge, to the student who finds the most items.

After Reading Chapter 7
Skill: Creative thinking

This creative-thinking activity is a real "rib-tickler"! Reread Peter's poison-gas-in-the-toilets story at the end of chapter 7. Remind students that Peter made up the story to explain to Jimmy why his family is staying with the Tubmans. Then challenge each student to pretend to be Peter and make a list of the top ten reasons why the Hatchers are sharing a vacation house with Sheila and her family. Explain that their reasons can be silly or far-fetched—the more creative, the better! Next have each student read his top-ten list to the class, starting with the number-ten reason and ending with number one. Step aside, David Letterman!

After Reading Chapter 8
Skills: Propaganda techniques, Creative thinking

When Peter hears Mitzi talk about her monster spray, he immediately thinks of how his dad would advertise this product. Refer students to Peter's ad for Mitzi's monster spray in chapter 8, and review propaganda techniques you've discussed this year *(for example, bandwagon, testimonial, repetition, etc.).* Then distribute one copy of page 232 to each student. Have the student imagine that she can create a magical spray that makes something she doesn't like melt away. Then have her brainstorm the spray's abilities and write a mini-advertisement for her new product on the spray-can pattern on page 232. Next have her follow the directions on that page to make her spray can three-dimensional. Pin each completed can to a bulletin board titled "Spray Your Troubles Away!"

After Reading Chapter 10
Skill: Writing a personal narrative

Poor Sheila! First she gets a phone call saying that her friend Mouse Ellis has chicken pox and can't come to Maine for the summer. Then Peter burps while she's crying. And finally Tootsie shoots oatmeal across the table right onto Sheila's face! It was definitely starting out to be "one of *those* days." Everyone has them—as your students will probably agree! After reading this chapter, help students sharpen their personal narrative skills by asking each child to list details about the last time she had "one of those days." After the student has completed her list, have her write and share a personal narrative that begins "It turned out to be one of *those* days!" At the end of your sharing session, have the class vote to pick the story that described the worst of the bad days. Award that child a special prize or class privilege. Then give each child who successfully completed the assignment a small treat—maybe one to save for the next time she has one of *those* days!

After Reading Chapter 11
Skill: Creative thinking

Gag, yuck! Peter unwillingly becomes a member of the I.S.A.F. Club (I Swallowed A Fly Club) while riding his bicycle. Find out how many of your students are eligible for membership in this special club. Then challenge each student to create his own unique club and an acronym for it. Give each student a sheet of light-colored construction paper. Have the student design a badge for his club, including the club's name and an explanation of how he earned membership in it, on an appropriate shape cut from the construction paper. Use a rolled piece of tape to stick each student's badge to his shirt. Next have each student share his badge with the class and find out how many classmates are eligible for membership in his club.

I.B.A.B. Club (I Broke A Bone Club)
I was climbing the tree in my back-yard when my foot slipped. I landed a trip to the hospital with a broken arm.

After Reading Chapter 12
Skill: Creative expression

When Tootsie walked across the canvas leaving a trail of footprints, Mr. Fargo didn't get upset—he got art! Have your students create their own footprint designs with the art project described in the box on the right. Display the completed designs around your room and invite other classes to visit your unusual footprint gallery.

Materials for each student: one 12" x 18" sheet of white construction paper, one copy of the footprint patterns on page 233, scissors, colored pencils

Steps:
1. Carefully cut out each footprint pattern. You will be using these cutouts as templates to trace.
2. Fill the construction paper with footprints by tracing the different-sized cutouts, overlapping them in several places. To make a left footprint, flip a cutout over before tracing it.
3. Color in each enclosed space on your design with a solid color or a pattern. Add depth to your picture by experimenting with light and dark colors.
4. Title your picture, using the word *feet* or *foot* in its name.

Feet Frenzy!

Ryan

After Finishing The Book
Skill: Sequencing

Reinforce students' sequencing skills by having them create illustrated booklets that summarize some of the main events in *Fudge-A-Mania.* Divide your class into groups of three or four students. Give each group one copy of the bottom of page 233, scissors, colored pencils, glue, and 12 sheets of 5 1/2" x 8 1/2" white paper (duplicating paper cut in half). Direct each group to cut apart the events on page 233 and organize them in sequential order. Next have the group illustrate each event on a different half-sheet of white paper, gluing the event strip below the drawing. Have each group make a cover from construction paper, and staple it and the sequenced illustrations together to make a booklet. After groups share their booklets, have students suggest other events that could have been included in their booklets.

Turtle gets sprayed by a skunk.

Skunked

On The Hunt

On your mark; get set; hunt! So what are you hunting? An example of each item below can be found within the first five chapters of *Fudge-A-Mania.* Your job is to find one example of each item from the book and write it on another sheet of paper. Be sure to include the number of the page on which you found each item. Refer to your language arts book if you need help. Good luck and happy hunting!

Find...

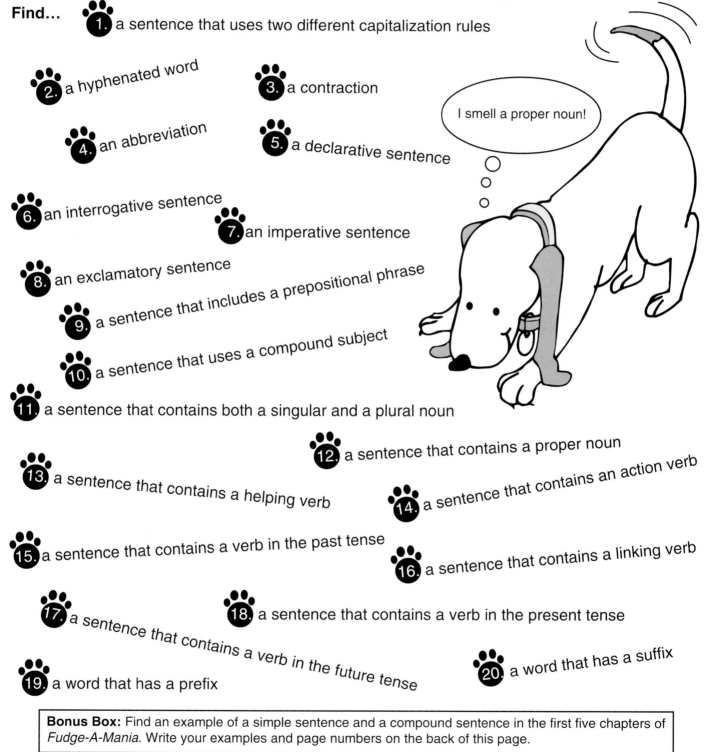

1. a sentence that uses two different capitalization rules

2. a hyphenated word

3. a contraction

4. an abbreviation

5. a declarative sentence

I smell a proper noun!

6. an interrogative sentence

7. an imperative sentence

8. an exclamatory sentence

9. a sentence that includes a prepositional phrase

10. a sentence that uses a compound subject

11. a sentence that contains both a singular and a plural noun

12. a sentence that contains a proper noun

13. a sentence that contains a helping verb

14. a sentence that contains an action verb

15. a sentence that contains a verb in the past tense

16. a sentence that contains a linking verb

17. a sentence that contains a verb in the future tense

18. a sentence that contains a verb in the present tense

19. a word that has a prefix

20. a word that has a suffix

Bonus Box: Find an example of a simple sentence and a compound sentence in the first five chapters of *Fudge-A-Mania.* Write your examples and page numbers on the back of this page.

Note To The Teacher: Use with "After Reading Chapter 5" on page 228. After students are finished, divide them into groups. Have group members work together to check each other's examples for accuracy.

How To Assemble Your Spray Can:

1. Decorate the front of the pattern with the following:
   - Name of your spray
   - Mini-advertisement for your spray
   - Any illustrations
   - Your name
2. Cut out your can along the bold lines.
3. Fold the can along the dotted lines.

4. Glue or tape the top tabs together and the bottom tabs together.
5. Make your can three-dimensional by pushing the sides of the can together in the center.
6. Gently crease the front and back of the can to hold its shape.

Pattern

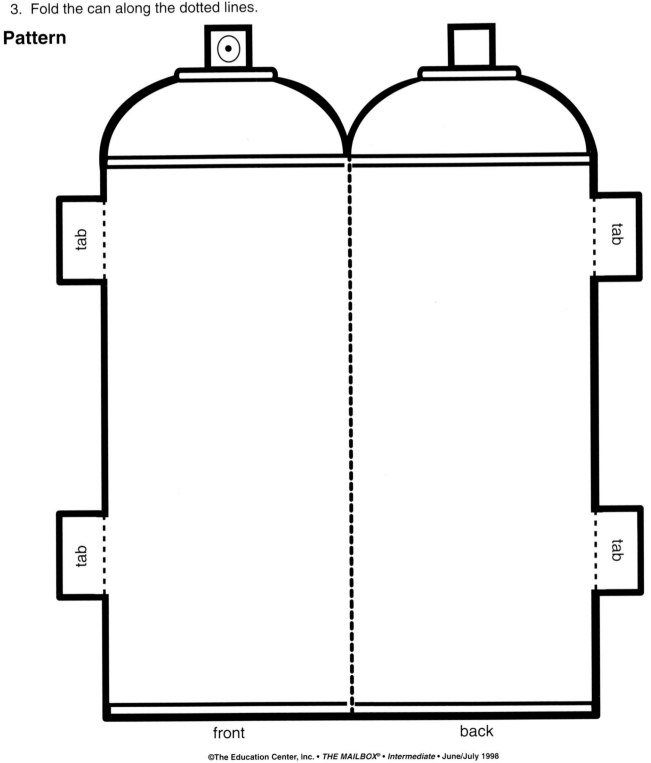

front   back

Note To The Teacher: Use with "After Reading Chapter 8" on page 229. Provide each child with markers, scissors, and glue or transparent tape.

The Tubmans, Jimmy, Peter, Sheila, Grandma, and Peter's dad go sailing.

Big Apfel hosts a baseball game.

Fudge eats almost all the blueberries and gets sick.

Buzzy Senior and Grandma get married.

Peter swallows a fly while riding his bicycle.

Mrs. Hatcher agrees to pay Sheila $7.00 a day to baby-sit Fudge.

Peter's mom tells him about their Maine vacation.

Peter meets Izzy at the library.

Sheila opens all the windows in the house, and Uncle Feather escapes.

Tootsie walks across Mr. Fargo's paint canvas and gets blue paint on her feet.

Turtle gets sprayed by a skunk.

Fudge gets caught in the rollaway bed.

Bound For Oregon

An Unforgettable Novel About One Family's Westward Trek

Between 1840 and 1870, thousands of American families journeyed over the western wilderness for the promise of a better life in the Oregon Territory. Share with students Jean Van Leeuwen's story—based on a true account—of Mary Ellen Todd and her determined family, who left their Arkansas home for a new life out west. Use the following activities to bring your class this thrilling tale of grit and courage.

written by Cynthia Wurmnest

While You Read: Weave a common thread during the reading of *Bound For Oregon* with an ongoing project. Before reading starts divide the class so that each group can be assigned two to three of the novel's 16 chapters. Point out that the book has no chapter titles and few illustrations. Each group's job will be to create a title and an illustration that capture the most important idea in each of its assigned chapters. Have each group start work after an assigned chapter is read. Mount the illustrations and chapter titles in sequence on a long sheet of paper to make a chronological mural of the book's events. Use the mural for review when the book is finished.

Chapter 2: Oregon, Here We Come!

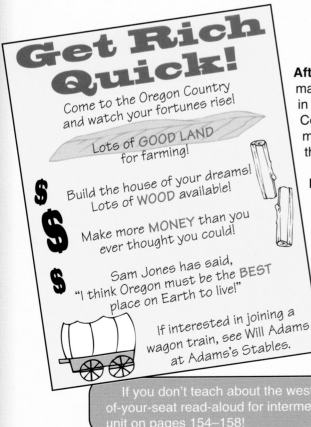

Get Rich Quick!

Come to the Oregon Country and watch your fortunes rise!

Lots of GOOD LAND for farming!

$ Build the house of your dreams! Lots of WOOD available!

$ Make more MONEY than you ever thought you could!

$ Sam Jones has said, "I think Oregon must be the BEST place on Earth to live!"

If interested in joining a wagon train, see Will Adams at Adams's Stables.

After Chapter 1: Mary Ellen's father caught Oregon fever after listening to a man speak about the ease of life in the new territory. Using the descriptions in this chapter, have each student prepare an advertisement for the Oregon Country. Give each child a choice of making a handbill *or* writing a two-minute, street-corner speech to be presented to the class. Give students these guidelines for the projects:

Requirements for a handbill:
1. Use an eye-catching title.
2. Make the handbill title readable from ten feet away.
3. List three reasons to go to the Oregon Country.
4. Include a quote from someone who has been there.
5. Give the name of a contact person and a way to reach him or her.

Requirements for a speech:
1. Start with a catchy introductory sentence like the question, "Would you like to be rich?"
2. Entice the audience with three reasons to go to the Oregon Country.
3. Conclude by asking who's ready to go now to the Oregon Country.

If you don't teach about the westward movement, *Bound For Oregon* is still a fabulous, edge-of-your-seat read-aloud for intermediate students. If you <u>do</u> teach about this time period, see the unit on pages 154–158!

After Chapter 2: Mary Ellen and Louvina were allowed to fill a *reticule* (drawstring bag) with personal belongings to keep them entertained on the trip. Have each student decide which personal items she would pack in her reticule if she were Mary Ellen. Give each child an index card, scissors, glue, a piece of wallpaper or gift wrap, yarn, and a magazine or catalog to cut apart. Have each student cut a large reticule shape (see the illustration) from her wallpaper. Then have her cut out pictures of items to pack in her bag. (Allow original drawings too.) Have the student glue her pictures on the front of the reticule. Then have her list her items—and the reason for bringing each one—on the index card. After the student glues the card on the back of the project, have her glue the yarn to the top of the bag and add a nametag as shown. Post the bags on a bulletin board titled "Packed And Ready!"

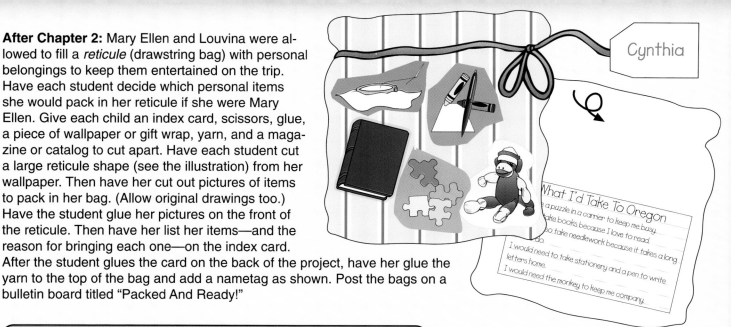

Cynthia

What I'd Take To Oregon
...a puzzle in a carrier to keep me busy.
...take books because I love to read.
...take needlework because it takes a long time to do.
I would need to take stationery and a pen to write letters home.
I would need the monkey to keep me company.

Reasons for continuing on trek
- We've already come this far.
- We'll have a better life in Oregon.
- We can make it if we just keep going.

Reasons against continuing on trek
- We're too tired to keep going.
- We might drown trying to cross the river, like others have.
- We've heard there are raiding Indians on the other side of the river.

After Chapter 6: Crossing the Kaw River was such a risky milestone on the journey that Mary Ellen knew there was no going back. Before the crossing, people argued and discussed the reasons for going on and the reasons for going back home. Instruct each student to refer back to his chapter 1 project (the handbill or speech for going to Oregon). Then have him list three reasons in favor of going on to Oregon and three reasons against continuing the journey. List the students' responses on the chalkboard or on a chart. Discuss the contrast between the hopes and dreams for the future, and the fears and worries of the present.

After Chapter 10: The people who made this dangerous trek west were a special breed. Many people have referred to their characters collectively as "The American Spirit"—the willingness to take risks to better themselves and others. Brainstorm with students those traits that make up this spirit, as shown by Mary Ellen's family and others in the story. List the traits on the board; then have the class select the 12 most important ones. Have each student list these traits on her paper. Next direct each child to choose ten classmates to survey. Tell her to ask each classmate to choose the three most important characteristics for a frontier family to have. Have her record her data and design a colorful bar graph to illustrate her results. Display the graphs on a bulletin board.

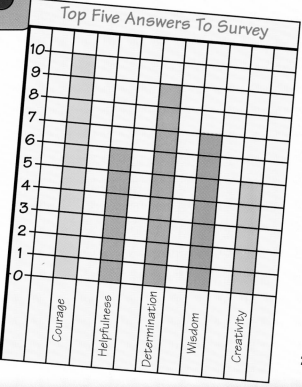

Top Five Answers To Survey

Courage · Helpfulness · Determination · Wisdom · Creativity

After Chapter 13: *Foreshadowing* is used by an author to arouse interest. In foreshadowing the author plants clues about what will happen later in the story. Jean Van Leeuwen does this skillfully for several major events up through chapter 13. List each of the following events on a separate card:

- Louvina's illness
- the Indian raid
- Mr. Grant's disappearance
- Elijah's birth
- the deaths of Captain and Mrs. Clark

Divide students into groups. Hand each group a card to keep secret from the other groups. Ask each group to find the author's foreshadowing hints about the card's event in the pages or chapter preceding it. When a group finds a hint, direct group members to record that sentence or passage on the back of the card. Next instruct each group to write a brief scene based on the hint to act out for the class. Have classmates try to guess the event that is being foreshadowed in the scene. Discuss how the foreshadowing made the reader think before the event happened.

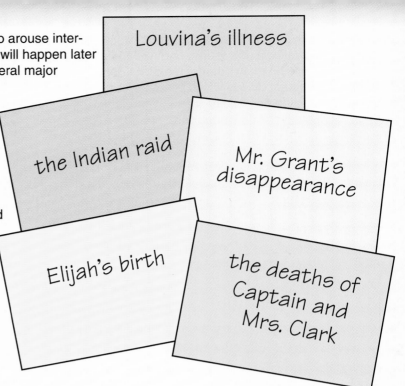

After Chapter 14: The star quilt Grandma made for Mary Ellen was a great source of comfort for the girl. The quilt's comfort came from its association with Mary Ellen's beloved and brave grandma. At the ends of many chapters, Mary Ellen wraps up in the quilt to help herself through various traumas. Direct students back to chapter 2 to reread about Grandma's bravery. Then have each child compose a letter of encouragement from Grandma to Mary Ellen, making Grandma's words fit the terrible situation in chapter 14. Remind students that the purpose of the letter is to provide Mary Ellen with the inner strength to do what she must do. Create a display of the letters, each mounted on a colorful piece of construction paper. Title the display "To My Dearest Mary Ellen."

After Finishing The Book: What's a great way to assess what students know about the book they've just read? Have them speculate about different outcomes with this partner activity. Enlarge the circle shown; then give a copy to each student pair, along with a small cardboard square, a pushpin, and a paper clip. Direct each pair to pin the circle to the cardboard square at the circle's center, placing the paper clip so that it is caught by one end under the pin. Have the partners take turns spinning the paper clip and answering the question. If a question is landed on more than once, rule that each student's answer must be different from his partner's. After each person has answered several questions, bring the class together to share responses.

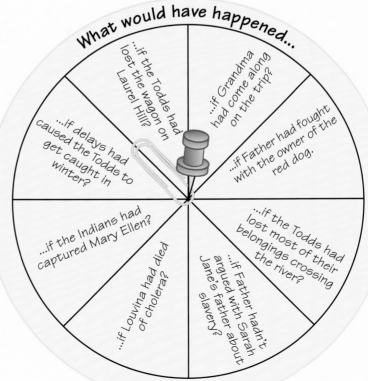

Why? Because!

You know *what* happens in a story. But do you know *why* things happen? If you do, that makes you a good reader! Knowing why things happen is a key to understanding and remembering what you read.

Below are five events from *Bound For Oregon.* They are all *effects* that had *causes.* In each box, write a cause for the boldfaced effect.

Father decides to move his family to Oregon.

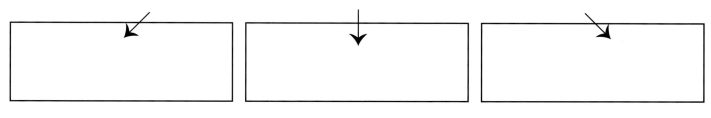

Mary Ellen doesn't want to leave Arkansas.

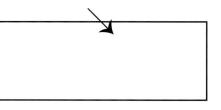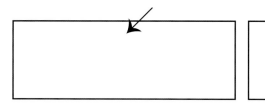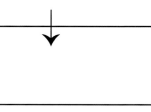

It takes months to get ready for the trip.

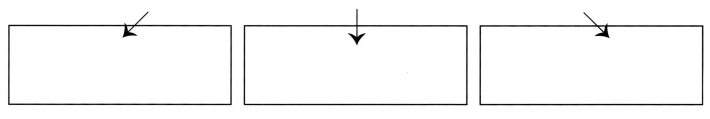

Other families traveling in wagons turn back.

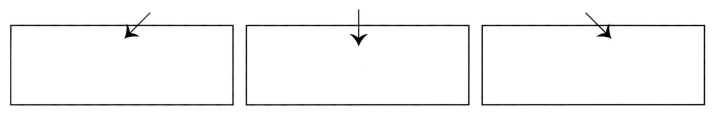

The Christmas celebration is very special.

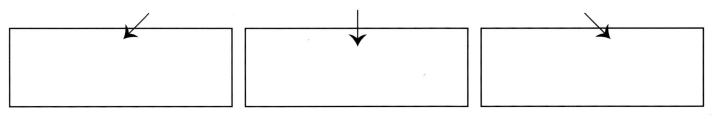

Bonus Box: On the back of this page, write an event that recently happened to you. Draw three boxes below the event. Then fill in the boxes with three causes for why this event happened.

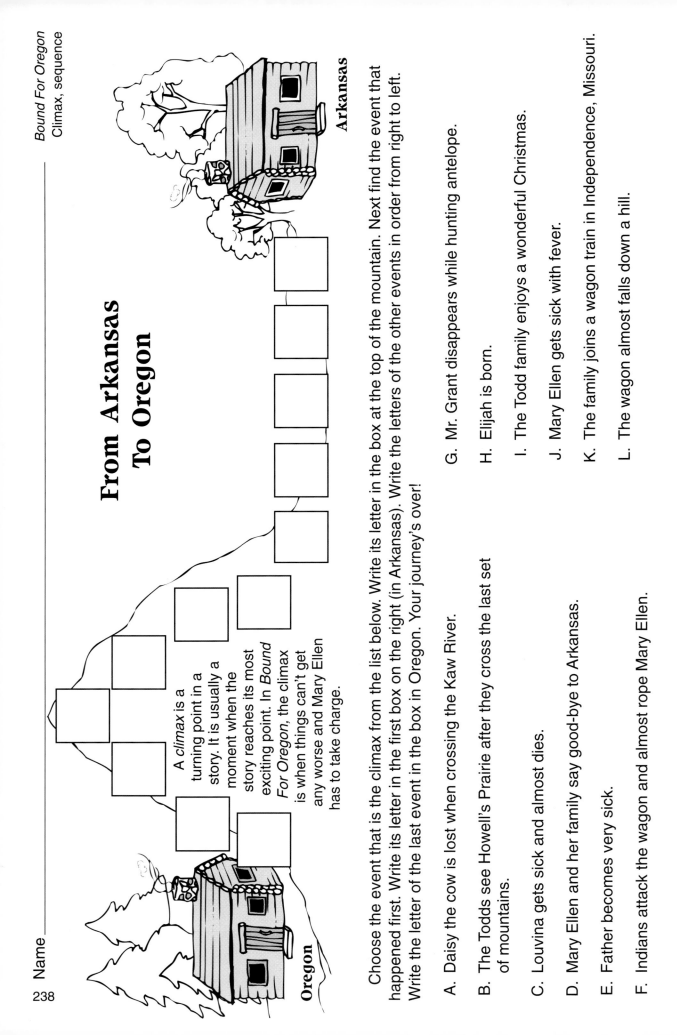

From Arkansas To Oregon

Arkansas

Oregon

A *climax* is a turning point in a story. It is usually a moment when the story reaches its most exciting point. In *Bound For Oregon*, the climax is when things can't get any worse and Mary Ellen has to take charge.

Choose the event that is the climax from the list below. Write its letter in the box at the top of the mountain. Next find the event that happened first. Write its letter in the first box on the right (in Arkansas). Write the letters of the other events in order from right to left. Write the letter of the last event in the box in Oregon. Your journey's over!

A. Daisy the cow is lost when crossing the Kaw River.

B. The Todds see Howell's Prairie after they cross the last set of mountains.

C. Louvina gets sick and almost dies.

D. Mary Ellen and her family say good-bye to Arkansas.

E. Father becomes very sick.

F. Indians attack the wagon and almost rope Mary Ellen.

G. Mr. Grant disappears while hunting antelope.

H. Elijah is born.

I. The Todd family enjoys a wonderful Christmas.

J. Mary Ellen gets sick with fever.

K. The family joins a wagon train in Independence, Missouri.

L. The wagon almost falls down a hill.

Bonus Box: On the back of this sheet, draw a poster to advertise the movie version of *Bound For Oregon*.

Thematic Units

Giants Of The Sea

Whales, gentle giants of the deep, swim through the world's waters with grace and agility that defy their girth. Dive into the activities featured in this whale of a unit and teach your students more about the amazing creatures that have been guarding the deep for millions of years!

by Wanda Helmuth

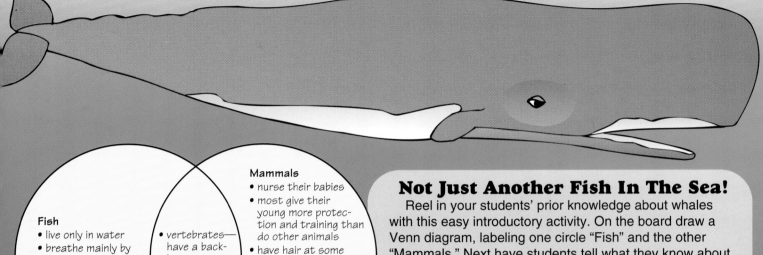

Fish
- live only in water
- breathe mainly by means of gills
- most are cold-blooded

- vertebrates—have a backbone
- some have fins

Mammals
- nurse their babies
- most give their young more protection and training than do other animals
- have hair at some point in their lives
- warm-blooded
- have a better-developed brain than other animals
- breathe with lungs

Not Just Another Fish In The Sea!

Reel in your students' prior knowledge about whales with this easy introductory activity. On the board draw a Venn diagram, labeling one circle "Fish" and the other "Mammals." Next have students tell what they know about each animal category as you write the information in the appropriate circle. Be sure to record characteristics common to both categories in the area where the circles overlap. Conclude by having students point out the many differences between fish and mammals. Then explain that whales are mammals and not fish, as many mistakenly believe.

Visualize The Size

How do whales measure up? Find out with this hands-on activity! Have each student complete page 244 as directed to learn more about different whale species. Write the name and maximum length of each whale listed on page 244 on two 8 1/2" x 11" cardboard sheets; then make two signs by taping a tongue depressor to each sheet at the bottom. Take the signs, a stopwatch, and several yardsticks to your school playground. Have small groups of students measure and mark off the length of each whale; then have them stick each whale's signs in the ground at both ends of its measurement to show its length. Next, time students as they run from one blue whale sign to the other. Repeat this for one of the smaller whales and have students compare the times. Or have each student determine how many kids of his height lying end-to-end would equal a blue whale's length.

Moving In For The Krill

Did you know that the blue whale needs approximately 3 million calories a day to sustain itself? It gets many of those calories from *krill*—tiny marine plankton. Challenge students to calculate a blue whale's mealtime caloric intake based on the traditional three meals a day of humans *(1 million calories per meal)*. Then post the list of caloric values shown. Have students work individually or in groups to write several combinations of foods from the list that equal 1 million calories. Review students' lists and compare them to the amount of food normally consumed by a human during breakfast. Discuss reasons why the blue whale needs so much more food than humans. *(It is the largest animal on earth.)*

Food Item	Calories
1 fried egg	99
2 slices of bacon	86
1 slice of ham	213
1 piece of toast with butter and jelly	179
1 pancake with butter and syrup	178
1/2 grapefruit	58
1 small banana	81
1 glass of orange juice	130
1 bagel	165
1 bowl of Cheerios® cereal with skim milk	198
1 bowl of Cap'n Crunch® cereal with skim milk	239

Where There's A Whale, There's A Way!

Track the migration patterns of baleen whales with this investigative activity. Many baleen whales summer in the cold waters of the Arctic or Antarctic, where they feed and store up blubber. In the winter the whales migrate to the warm waters of the tropics, where they mate or, if already pregnant, give birth. Show students the list of baleen whales below. Then divide your class into small groups. Assign each group one whale from the list. Have each group draw the migration routes of its whale on a duplicated world map. Then give each student a 4" x 6" index card on which to design a postcard showing two locations that the whale might visit during its annual migratory trip. Direct the student to draw pictures of two of the places visited on one side of the card and write a message from the whale to a friend on the other side. Pin the postcards and maps on a bulletin board.

Baleen Whales
black right whale
  (also called right whale)
bowhead whale
pygmy right whale
gray whale
blue whale
Bryde's whale
fin whale
humpback whale
minke whale
sei whale

Dear Nancy,
My pod and I just arrived at our winter lodging off the coast of Baja California in Mexico. The lagoon we will be spending the winter in is beautiful! At the beginning of my trip, I saw many icebergs, but as we swam into warmer waters, they all disappeared. I'll write you again soon!

Your friend,
Gary Gray Whale

Nancy Narwhal
145 Icy Way
Arctic Ocean
North Pole 34890

A Whale Of A Fable

Whales, like many other creatures of the wild, have fascinated people for centuries. Many fables have been written in an attempt to teach lessons and explain things about animals that people did not understand, such as how the leopard got its spots or how the camel got its hump. Share some of these fables with students by reading excerpts from *Just So Stories* by Rudyard Kipling. Then review elements commonly found in fables:

- supernatural events
- a useful lesson or moral
- inanimate objects or animals that speak and have human characteristics

Finally have each student complete a copy of page 243 as directed to create his own whale fable.

Flip Through It

You can bet students will flip over this activity on whale movement! Share the following terms used by scientists to describe whale movement:

breaching—leaping dramatically out of the water
spy hopping—lifting the head out of the water to look around
sounding—diving
head lunging—fighting method in which whales speed toward each other with their heads out of the water
lobtailing—using flukes (lobes at the end of the tail) to splash the water

Next have each student select one whale movement to illustrate. Give each student 10 to 15 pieces of 3" x 4" white paper. Using illustrations from the whale books listed on page 242 as a guide, have each student break down the movement of a whale into sequential steps, drawing a different step on each page. Then have the student stack the pages in reverse order from last to first and staple them along the left edge to make a booklet. Direct each student to begin at the back and quickly flip through her completed book to create an animated effect. There she blows!

Whales On The Web

For more information on whales, check out this exciting Internet site *(valid as of 12/97):*
http://www.whaleclub.com

Wet And Wonderful Whale Books

Explore the wonderful world of whales with these "fin-tastic" books!

reviewed by Deborah Zink Roffino

Humpback Whales

written by Dorothy Hinshaw Patent
illustrated by Mark J. Ferrari and
Deborah Glockner-Ferrari
Holiday House, Inc.; 1989

Engaging readers with fact-filled text and more than two dozen choice photographs, this easy-reading book is perfect for young marine researchers. In her book, Dr. Patent closely examines the habitats and the remarkable features and abilities of different whale species.

Big Blue Whale

written by Nicola Davies
illustrated by Nick Maland
Candlewick Press, 1997

Descriptive text and sensory language allow your kids to get up close and personal with the blue whale. The artistic technique of cross-hatching gives the book's illustrations added texture and flair, providing unusual perspectives of the deep.

The Birth Of A Humpback Whale

written by Robert Matero
illustrated by Pamela Johnson
Atheneum Books For Young Readers, 1996

This chapter book gives the reader a comprehensive look at humpback whales. Accompanied by black-and-white sketches, the narration details the birth, growth, learning, and migration of this one-of-a-kind species of baleen whale.

Whales

written by Lesley A. DuTemple
The Lerner Group, 1996

Packed with interesting facts and photographs, this book provides information about whale classification, family structure, communication skills, traveling patterns, and environmental threats. Zoom lenses capture the myriad textures of the whales, smooth and barnacled. The book's clear, concise information—along with a detailed glossary and index—makes it an ideal choice for whale enthusiasts.

The Whales

written and illustrated by Cynthia Rylant
Scholastic Inc., 1996

Lyrical, imaginative, and artistic, this poetic work is sure to inspire your young writers. Through carefully crafted words and bold paintings, the majesty of the sea's great creatures is captured in a simple yet effective format. More than a dozen different cetaceans—including narwhals and humpback, blue, and gray whales—are mentioned in the poetic text.

The Whale: Giant Of The Ocean

written by Valérie Tracqui
photographed by François Gohier/Jacana
Charlesbridge Publishing, Inc.; 1995

This remarkable series book presents a photographic essay of nature's gentle giants. Included in the book is simple information on whale songs, patterns of migration, pods, and the dangers the animals face.

A Whale Of A Fable

Animals such as whales have fascinated people for centuries. Over time, fables have been written to teach lessons. They have also been written to explain things about animals that people did not understand, such as how the leopard got its spots or how the camel got its hump.

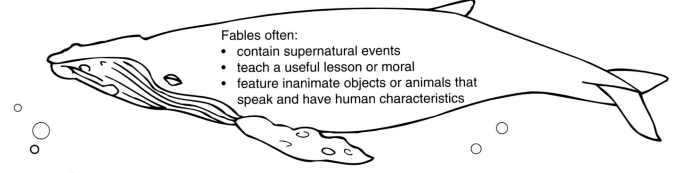

Fables often:
- contain supernatural events
- teach a useful lesson or moral
- feature inanimate objects or animals that speak and have human characteristics

Directions: Select one of the whale facts listed below. Then write a fable that describes how the whale developed that unusual feature.

- The sperm whale is well-insulated. It has a layer of blubber about one foot thick.
- The male narwhal's left tooth is a sharp, eight-foot-long tusk that juts out of its mouth.
- The bottlenose dolphin gets its name from its long beak, which looks like the neck on a bottle.
- Newborn belugas are brownish or gray, but the adult beluga has creamy, white skin.
- The humpback whale sometimes has 1,000 pounds of whale lice on its body.
- Gray whales have the longest migration of any mammal—about 6,000 miles.
- The tail flukes of a whale are so strong that they would not break even if the whale were hung up by them.
- How old is a baleen whale? You can tell by counting the bands of dark and white layers on the ear plugs deep inside its head.
- The sei whale may be the fastest-swimming whale. It has been clocked at 35 miles per hour.
- The bowhead whale produces a V-shaped spray from its blowholes.
- The sperm whale is a champion diver. It has been reported to dive as deep as 1.8 miles.
- The humpback whale is quite a musician. It sings long, complex songs and can make about 1,000 different sounds.
- The right whale has lots of bumps on its head and even has hairs on its chin.
- A sperm whale's head is very large. Inside its head is a huge supply of oil.
- Captured killer whales are usually very gentle. They can be trained to be great performers in marine parks.

Hint: Be sure your fable has a beginning, a middle, and an end. The moral of your fable should end your story.

Bonus Box: On a separate sheet of paper, draw a picture to illustrate your fable.

©The Education Center, Inc. • *THE MAILBOX®* • *Intermediate* • June/July 1998

Note To The Teacher: Use with "A Whale Of A Fable" on page 241.

243

Tons Of Trivia

— baleen whale

— toothed whale

Whales are divided into two main groups: *toothed* and *baleen*. Toothed whales have teeth. They use their teeth to catch their food, which they swallow whole. Baleen whales have long, fringed blades. These blades hang from their upper jaws in place of teeth. The blades help baleen whales strain food from the water.

Directions: Use encyclopedias and other reference books to fill in the chart with facts about the following kinds of whales.

Type Of Whale	Baleen Or Toothed	Maximum Length	Maximum Weight	Type Of Food Eaten	Unusual Features
beluga				fish, squid, crabs	
blue whale	baleen				
bowhead whale					huge head shaped like the bow of a boat
fin whale			152,000 pounds (76 tons)		
gray whale		50 feet			
humpback whale				plankton, small fish	
killer whale			16,000 pounds (8 tons)		
narwhal	toothed				
pilot whale				fish	
sperm whale		69 feet			

Bonus Box: Pretend that a relative just gave you $100 for a birthday gift. That's the exact cost of a ticket to go on a whale-watching expedition. Would you spend your money on the chance to see a live whale out in the sea? Write and explain your answer on the back of this page.

©The Education Center, Inc. • *THE MAILBOX®* • *Intermediate* • June/July 1998 • Key p. 312

Note To The Teacher: Use with "Visualize The Size" on page 240.

Lilliputian Land

Thematic Activities On Giants

Gigantic Gulliver and people 1/12 his size—what intermediate kid could resist that scenario? Read aloud *Gulliver's Travels* or a book that retells its story. Then use the following activities to take a giant step into an adventure your students won't soon forget!

ideas by Dale Smith—Gr. 5, Chukker Creek Elementary, Aiken, SC

Studying The Statistics

Reading about a giant lends itself to studying people's heights. For homework have each student record the height of a parent or another adult relative. The next day tally the measurements on the board in least to greatest order. Direct each student to convert all the measurements into inches, display the data as a bar graph, and find the average adult height. Follow up with the activity below.

Lilliputian Proportions

Combine the activity above with one on ratio and proportion to make a display that really puts things in perspective! Use the average adult height determined in "Studying The Statistics" to make and display a life-sized drawing of Gulliver on a bulletin board as shown. Staple lengths of string to Gulliver to "tie" him down. Next direct each student to use a calculator to divide that average height by 12, then use art materials to make a person that number of inches tall. Have students also make cutouts of details—such as trees, dogs, and ladders—to position on and around

Gulliver. The resulting board will boast an understanding of ratio that reaches gigantic proportions!

Literary Giants

Use *Gulliver's Travels* as a springboard to expand students' knowledge of literary classics as well as other books about giants. Read aloud picture books, folktales, or other books from the list shown, culminating with the book about Beowulf. Then direct each student to write a short story that's a sequel to the Beowulf tale.

Abiyoyo by Pete Seeger (Simon & Schuster Children's, 1994)
The BFG by Roald Dahl (Puffin Books, 1989)
The Great Quillow by James Thurber (Harcourt Brace & Company, 1994)
Jim And The Beanstalk by Raymond Briggs (The Putnam Publishing Group, 1989)
The Mysterious Giant Of Barletta: An Italian Folktale by Tomie dePaola (Harcourt Brace & Company, 1984)
Odysseus And The Cyclops retold by Warwick Hutton (Simon & Schuster Children's, 1995)
Paul Bunyan by Steven Kellogg (Morrow Junior Books, 1992)
Beowulf The Warrior by Ian Serraillier (Bethlehem Books, 1994)

Name _____

A Giant Tale

Not all recipes are found in a cookbook! Here's a recipe for you to use to cook up your own story about a giant.

Directions: Complete each step listed below in that order. Use one or more items from each category box to help you write your tale. Add your own ideas too. Remember to indent when you start a new paragraph.

Steps:

1. Write one or more sentences to introduce your giant.
2. Write several sentences describing your giant's clothing and accessories.
3. Write a few sentences describing your giant's appearance.
4. Write one or more sentences describing the setting of your story.
5. Write several sentences describing the story's problem.
6. Write a few sentences describing how the problem is solved.
7. End the story with a good concluding sentence.

Settings
in a dingy cave
in a mountain meadow
on a grassy hill
on a rocky ledge
in an overgrown forest
near a deep canyon
at a lagoon
outside a village

Clothing
polka-dotted bow tie
green plaid jacket
knotty red sweater
patched overalls
purple tennis shoes
striped wool skirt
blue gingham shirt
dusty gray ball cap

Names
Goophus	Haddenglib
Stiggy	Jergensdorph
Bumblegumph	Ruphus
Theo	Ziggenwerf

Accessories
drum
paintbrush and paint
map
whistle
rope
wooden crate
jug of water
crooked stick

Problems
the absentminded giant
the accident-prone giant
the forgetful giant
the giant who cries all the time
the giant who only eats pickles
the giant who can't stay awake
the lost giant
the terribly bashful giant

Appearance
cheerful eyes
piercing eyes
worried face
wrinkled face
face covered with warts
booming voice
gentle voice
large, red nose
grizzly beard
green eyebrows
18 feet tall
missing tooth

GAME PLANS

Stingless Spelling Bee

Looking for a way to keep even your most challenged speller buzzing with excitement during your next spelling bee? Have each student cut out a large petaled flower from a sheet of construction paper; then have her place it and a pencil on her desk. Next divide your class into two equal hives of worker bees, lining up the hives opposite one another. Begin the game by calling out a word to the first bee in a hive. Allow that bee to request that a sentence including the word be given if she desires; then have her give the first letter in the word's spelling. Continue down the line of bees, having each bee provide the next letter until the word has been spelled. Request that the bee who names the last letter state "end of word" so you know when the word is finished.

If a bee provides an incorrect letter, say, "Go collect some honey." Direct the bee to return to her flower (on her desk) and write the correct spelling of the word and each successive word called on her cutout. Continue alternating from hive to hive until only one bee remains in each line. Crown the remaining bee on each team the queen or king bee of that hive. Direct each worker bee to use his flower word list to study for the upcoming spelling test.

Pat Roberts
Leander Middle School
Leander, TX

Direction Detection

Get your students headed in the right direction with this entertaining game featuring intermediate and cardinal directions. Label each of the four walls of your classroom with a cardinal direction—north, south, east, west. Explain to students that each corner of your room will signify an intermediate direction, such as southwest (the corner between the south wall and the west wall). Choose one student to be a Direction Director. Blindfold the student; then tell the remaining students to move to any of the four corners. Next have the Direction Director call out a specific intermediate direction. Request that any students standing in that corner sit down. Remaining students may then circulate to different corners if desired. Continue the game until only one student remains; then let this student be the Direction Director for round two. What a fun way to review directions!

Dena Chamberland—Gr. 4, St. Joseph's Intermediate School
Woonsocket, RI

Eight Potato

Enhance your students' fluency with this fast-paced game. Direct students to sit in a circle. Select one child to be the caller and have him stand in the middle. Have the caller call out a letter of the alphabet and choose one classmate to be the "potato." Instruct the potato to name any eight words that begin with the letter called. While the potato is calling out words, have the student sitting to his left tag the person to her left. Direct each successive student to do the same. If the potato is tagged before he calls out eight words, he changes places with the caller and assumes his duties. If the potato successfully names eight words before being tagged, the caller remains in the circle's center. Then the game continues with him selecting a new classmate and alphabet letter that has not been previously called.

Caroline Jensen and Janice Holsteen—Gr. 5
American School in Aberdeen
Scotland, UK

Basic Facts Card Game

This fun multiplication review will have your students mastering their basic facts in no time! Begin by making several sets of multiplication flash cards—recording a different problem on the front of each card. Next divide your class into groups of two to four players. Give each group a set of cards. Select one child in each group to be the dealer, evenly distributing the cards in his deck to his group members. Have the player to the left of the dealer begin play by laying down a card from his hand. Direct the next player to lay down a card with a product equal to or greater than the card played before him. Explain that if a player does not have such a card, he doesn't get to lay down a card and he loses that turn. Direct students to continue until a player gets rid of all his cards or no player is able to lay down a card. Then have the last student to play a card collect all the fact cards and begin the game again.

Melinda Salisbury—Grs. 4–6
Baldwin North Intermediate School
Quincy, IL

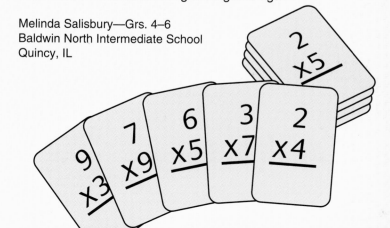

GAME PLANS

On A Roll With Grammar

Roll out plenty of parts-of-speech practice with this fun grammar game! Divide students into groups, and assign a "roller" and a "timekeeper" for each. Give each group three copies of the cube pattern on page 196. Then have groups follow these directions to prepare and play the game:

1. On one pattern, write "noun" in two squares, "verb" in two squares, and "adjective" in two squares.
2. On each square of the second die, write a different commonly used consonant, such as *N, S, T, L, R,* and *P.*
3. Write a different amount of time, such as "15 seconds" or "45 seconds," on each side of the third die.
4. Assemble each of the three dice as directed on the pattern page.
5. To play, the roller rolls the dice and calls out the results. Group members have the time indicated on the die to list words that are the same part of speech and begin with the same letter as shown on the other two rolled dice.
6. At the end of the time limit, group members share their words. Award a point to each player for every correct answer given.
7. At the end of each round, change the roller and timekeeper so everyone has a turn.
8. At the end of the last round, each group member totals his points to see who has the most.

Game Variation: Add an additional challenge to the game by adding "adverb" and "preposition" to the parts-of-speech die.

Marsha Schmus—Gr. 4, Ypsilanti, MI

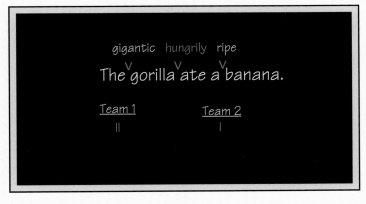

Stretching Sentences

Add muscle to your students' writing with this fun sentence-building game. Divide your class into two teams. Then have each team's members place materials, such as their vocabulary lists and definitions, on their desks for reference. Using white chalk write a very basic sentence, such as "The gorilla ate a banana," on the chalkboard. Then have a student from the first team use colored chalk to insert a vocabulary word or phrase into the sentence. Require that the student also provide the definition for the added word; then award his team a point if the new word makes sense. Continue having teams take turns adding to the same sentence until a team is stumped or has had four turns. Then total the points and marvel at the incredible sentence the class has constructed!

Michelle Bauml—Gr. 5, Gladys Polk Elementary, Richwood, TX

Slam-Dunk Review

Score points with your students with the help of this exciting review game! Write review questions on separate index cards, giving each question a point value from one to three depending on its difficulty. Tape a large embroidery hoop to your chalkboard; then use a foam ball or a wadded-up piece of paper for a basketball. Have your students predict the class's final score for the game. Then have students take turns answering questions. When a student answers a question correctly, allow him to take a shot at the basket for the class. If the student makes the basket, award him the point value indicated on the card and add it to the class score. Conclude play when all questions have been asked; then tally up the points earned and compare the total to the class's prediction. Reviewing key concepts has never been such slam-dunkin' fun!

Sue Mechura—Gr. 4, Ebenezer Elementary, Lebanon, PA

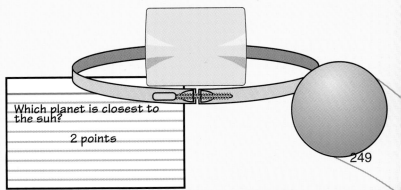

249

GAME PLANS

X-Out

Strengthen basic computational skills with a game of X-Out. Copy the gameboard shown in the illustration onto the chalkboard. Divide your class into four or five teams. Have Team 1 roll three dice; then have it add, subtract, multiply, or divide the numbers until the solution is one of the numerals on the gameboard. Have one member of Team 1 record that number of points and cross out that numeral on the gameboard. Next allow Team 2 to use the same three numbers rolled by Team 1 to arrive at a different solution. Continue rotating turns until all possible solutions have been found for those three numbers; then have Team 2 roll the dice for three new numbers. When all the numerals on the gameboard have been crossed out, tally each team's score. Declare the team with the most points the winner.

Patricia Clancy—Gr. 5
Peter Noyes School, Sudbury, MA

The M&M's® Challenge

Make review time a little sweeter by playing The M&M's® Challenge! Cut out several small circles in the following colors: yellow, blue, orange, brown, red, and green. Place the circles in a bag; then copy the chart below on the chalkboard. To play have your students sit in a large circle. Call on one student and ask him a review question. If his answer is correct, have him pull a circle (to keep until the game is over) from the bag. Refer to the chart and count that many spaces around the circle of students to determine which student gets a chance to answer the next question. If the selected student does not answer the question correctly, call on another child. Continue for as long as desired. At the end of the game, allow students to trade in their paper M&M's® for the real candy.

Jennifer Meyer—Gr. 4
Jeannette, PA

yellow = count one space
blue = count three spaces
orange = count five spaces
brown = count eight spaces
red = count ten spaces
green = reverse four spaces

All colors (except for green) are counted to the right.

Word Up!

This new twist on tic-tac-toe is a great vocabulary-review game! Give each student a supply of index cards. Instruct the student to write a different vocabulary word on the front of each card, then write its definition on the back. To play Word Up, direct the student to place nine of her labeled cards—word side up—in a tic-tac-toe formation on her desktop. Next read a definition. Instruct each student who has that word to call it out, then remove that card from her desk. Have the first student to call out the word announce the next definition (one from her desktop, which she can then remove). Direct the first student to remove three cards horizontally, vertically, or diagonally to say, "Word Up!" Reward her with an inexpensive treat; then prepare for another round, allowing students to rearrange their cards and/or substitute new ones.

Shannon Popkin—Gr. 4
Heritage Christian School, Brookfield, WI

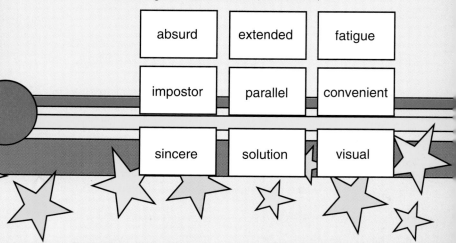

Building Character

BUILDING CHARACTER

Golden 'Grams

To help defray some of the expenses of a field trip, our fourth graders organized a schoolwide fund-raiser. Covered-wagon cutouts with gold-wrapped candy kisses attached were sold during recesses. Students and teachers wrote kind messages to each other on the cutouts. A teacher in charge reviewed the messages, then delivered them to classrooms. As a result of this successful fund-raiser, our students had a great field trip to California's gold country!

Patti Okui—Gr. 4, Hesperian School
San Lorenzo, CA

Mr. Wilson,
Thank you for helping me with my soccer skills.

Greg Taylor

Lending A Hand

Motivate students to serve others with this heartfelt display. Brainstorm with students the different ways that they can help improve the community. List their responses on the board. Have each student trace one hand on construction paper, as shown, and cut out the tracing. Next have him label a cut-out heart with a community service. Display the hands holding the hearts on a bulletin board titled "Lending A Hand In Our Community."

Colleen Dabney—Grs. 6–7
Williamsburg Christian Academy
Williamsburg, VA

Planet Hesperian Celebrities

To help students focus on and develop good character qualities, our school has a program called "Planet Hesperian Celebrities." Each month students work on one of nine character traits, whose first letters form an acrostic of our school name (see the illustration). Students who display these qualities are chosen by their teachers and honored at monthly assembly programs. Certificates are awarded and photos of the winning students are displayed on a hallway bulletin board.

Patti Okui—Gr. 4

Helpful
Effort
Studious
Polite
Enthusiastic
Respectful
Integrity
Attentive
Neat

Super Sellers

Looking for an activity that develops self-esteem and positive feelings in your students? Have each student sign a slip of paper; then collect the slips. Next have each student draw a name, making sure he doesn't draw his own. Explain that the person whose name is listed on each student's slip has been nominated to receive the key to the city. The challenge? The student must "sell" that person by creating a campaign poster. To get more information, each student must interview his nominee, concentrating on positive qualities and talents. Give each student a 12" x 18" sheet of white construction paper on which to design his poster. Then have each student share his poster, explaining why his nominee deserves the key to the city.

Chris Christensen—Gr. 4, Las Vegas, NV

BUILDING CHARACTER

Give Group Work A Hand!

Promote teamwork and cooperative learning in your classroom with this student-made bulletin board. Divide your class into six groups; then instruct each group to work together to trace the outline of each member's right and left hands. Photograph each group working together on this step. Next have each student cut out and write his name on the front of his hand outlines. Collect the hand cutouts. After the film has been developed, have each group staple its hand cutouts in a circle around its photo on a bulletin board. Title the board "A Round Of Applause For Our Group!" When groups change or new students are added to the class, simply move the hands into different circles and take additional pictures.

Terry Healy—Gifted K–6
Eugene Field Elementary
Manhattan, KS

Pat On The Back

Heighten students' self-esteem with this back-pattin' activity! Provide each student with a paper plate and two pieces of masking tape. Have the student trace his hand on the back side of the plate. Assist each student in taping his plate onto his back so that his "pat on the back" (handprint) is showing. Then have students give each other pats on the back by writing specific compliments on each other's plates. Encourage all students to sign all classmates' plates. Before allowing students to remove and read their plates, discuss what it feels like to give and receive compliments.

Kim Marinelli—Gr. 5
La Barriere Crossings
Winnipeg, Manitoba, Canada

I Have Really Blossomed!

Plant a seed of self-esteem and watch students really grow with this end-of-the-year poetry-writing activity. Have each student make a list of all the things she has learned or improved on throughout the year. Instruct the student to use her list to write a poem describing all of the ways she has blossomed this year. Take a picture of each student wearing a paper flower head-piece and a crepe-paper stem that wraps around her body (see the illustration). Have the student share her picture and poem with her parent(s) at an end-of-the-year conference.

Betty J. Bowlin—Gr. 4
Henry Elementary
Ballwin, MO

B.A.T.S.

Keep students from going batty when conflicts arise with this simple self-control strategy. Teach your class this four-step mnemonic device: *B*reathe; *A*sk yourself to count to ten; *T*hink of your favorite place; and *S*ay, "I'm okay; I can handle it!" Write this strategy on several bat cutouts. Then post the bats in various locations around the classroom. When a student is about to lose his self-control, point to a bat or say, "Bats!" The student, as instructed earlier, does the steps silently. Watch the number of problems decline as your students learn that there are other ways to handle conflicts.

Michele Raece—Gr. 4
Maplewood Heights School, Renton, WA

Breathe.
Ask yourself to count to ten.
Think of your favorite place.
Say, "I'm okay; I can handle it!"

BUILDING CHARACTER

Tearing Down The Walls

When the negativity of the world crept into my classroom, I thought my students would benefit from a lesson in love. I gave each student a 4" x 12" strip of red paper to symbolize a brick. I had each student write one reason why friends sometimes don't get along on his brick. We then stapled the bricks on a bulletin board to make a wall (see the illustration). After a few days, my students used 4" x 12" strips of yellow paper to build a ladder of words that can help scale the wall, such as *love, tolerance,* and *communication.* Now my students strive to have attitudes that break down the walls between friends.

Debra Bauer—Grs. 5–8
Hackettstown Middle School
Hackettstown, NJ

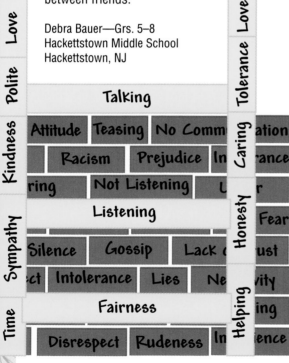

Recipe For Success

Put your class on the lookout for good character traits with this student-made bulletin board. Divide your class into six groups; then assign each group one of the following traits—responsibility, cooperation, diversity, respect, compassion, and honesty. Instruct the group to write the trait along with its dictionary definition, give the group's definition written in its own words, give an example of this trait in use, and draw an illustration on a sheet of tagboard. Post each group's work on a bulletin board titled "Our Class's Recipe For Success." Throughout the year, allow students to share examples of these six character traits in use; then add them to the posters on display.

Jeanne Randazzo Szczech—
   Gr. 6
Libby Elementary
Oceanside, CA

Sidewalk Sweepers

Promote respect and school pride with this simple idea. Invite each class in your school to choose an area of the sidewalk to "adopt." Then have the participating classes sweep their adopted areas daily. Post a small sign that lets everyone know which class is maintaining each area of the sidewalk.

Betty Richardson
Greater Atlanta Christian School
Norcross, GA

In Your Honor

Since you take the time to honor the flag each day, save a few minutes to honor some important people too. Every day after students recite the Pledge Of Allegiance, select one student to choose a person that he would like to honor and explain why he chose that person. Soon your students will be recognizing and honoring parents, coaches, teachers, doctors, and many others who might normally go unnoticed—all in less than one minute a day!

Jean Kelly—Gr. 4
Lackawanna Trail Elementary Center
Factoryville, PA

Lifesavers...
Management Tips
For Teachers

LIFESAVERS...
management tips for teachers

Discipline Tickets

Want to hold your students responsible for their behavior? Duplicate a discipline ticket (as shown) that can be used for both positive and negative behavior. Request that the student fill out and sign the ticket. Discuss the incident with the student, if necessary, before you sign the ticket. Store the tickets in an expanding file folder or binder. When a student accumulates a predetermined number of positive tickets, staple them together and send them home with a reward (candy, bookmark, etc.). When a student accumulates a predetermined number of negative tickets, phone parents and send the copies home. Have parents sign and return the tickets to you. Do this on a weekly basis, so students start fresh each Monday. With this idea, you will have a written record of each student's behavior, which comes in handy at conference time.

Pamela Doerr—Substitute, Elizabethtown School District, Elizabethtown, PA

> **Discipline Ticket**
> Date:_____
> Name:_____
> Behavior:_____
> _____
> _____
> _____
> Student Signature:_____
> Teacher Signature:_____
> Parent Signature:_____

Listening Dial

Motivate your students to tune in to your lessons with a Listening Dial. First model what it means to be a good listener by using the acronym LISTEN: Look at the speaker, Interact in discussion, Sit up straight, Think, Enjoy, No interrupting. Then create a Listening Dial (see the illustration) to let your students know just how well they are listening each day. When the class is displaying good listening skills, place the dial on the character with a wide smile and big ears. When the students need to improve their listening skills, warn them by moving the dial to the character with smaller ears. If the listening improves, move the dial back to its original position.

Joan E. Fate—Gr. 4, Whittier Elementary, Clinton, IA

Permission Slip Relief

Are you sometimes swamped with returned permission slips or book orders? Free up your hands and your desk by pasting your class list to the outside of a large envelope. Laminate the envelope; then use a magnetic clip to hang it on the chalkboard. Tie one end of a length of yarn to the clip and the other end to a transparency marker. Now when a student comes to school with a permission slip, instruct her to put the signed slip in the envelope and use the marker to check off her name. You'll quickly be able to tell which child is missing a permission slip, and all the slips will be in one convenient place.

Diane Moser—Gr. 5, Sangre Ridge Elementary, Stillwater, OK

Field Trip

Sue ✓	Lamont
Rob	James
Antwan	Cindi
Jerry ✓	Shea
Sandy	Debi ✓
Lee ✓	Brad

Bind It!

Does keeping up with your monthly materials have you in a bind? Purchase and label one binder for each month of the school year. Place all your ideas, reproducibles, and bulletin-board materials (placed inside hole-punched Ziploc® bags) for each month in one of the binders. Use dividers to separate the materials inside each binder. Now your materials will be easily accessible and organized!

Tanya Glaser—Grs. 5–6 Special Education
Millard Fillmore Elementary
Moravia, NY

Letters From A Teacher

Relaying all your classroom information to your students' parents can be a challenge. Gather one copy of each of the letters on your homework policy, class schedule, book clubs, and other important items; then place them in a packet titled "Letters From A [your grade level] Teacher." Send one packet home with each of your students on the first day of school. Parents will appreciate having this reference at their fingertips, and you'll feel better knowing that they've been informed.

Ann Redmond—Gr. 4, West Broad Street School, Telford, PA

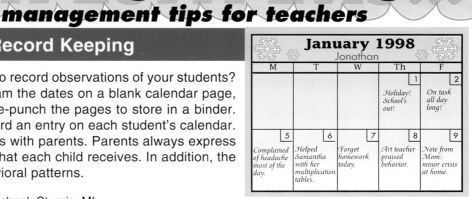

LIFESAVERS...
management tips for teachers

Individualized Record Keeping

Looking for a quick and easy method to record observations of your students? At the beginning of each month, I program the dates on a blank calendar page, duplicate a copy for each child, and hole-punch the pages to store in a binder. Then, each day as it's convenient, I record an entry on each student's calendar. At conference time, I share the calendars with parents. Parents always express appreciation for the individual attention that each child receives. In addition, the calendar often reveals a student's behavioral patterns.

Beth Pratt—Grs. 5 & 6 Multiage, Eastwood School, Sturgis, MI

	January 1998			
		Jonathan		
M	T	W	Th	F
			1 Holiday! School's out!	2 On task all day long!
5 Complained of headache most of the day.	6 Helped Samantha with her multiplication tables.	7 Forgot homework today.	8 Art teacher praised behavior.	9 Note from Mom: minor crisis at home.

Give It Your Best Shot!

Need a simple, inexpensive way to motivate and reward students? How about letting them shoot some hoops! I mount a plastic basketball hoop over a bulletin board in my classroom. Whenever a student answers a question correctly, makes an extra effort to participate in class, or needs recognition in some way, I allow him to take a shot at the hoop with a small soft basketball. The ball and goal are never used for physical education or free time, so students really look forward to the privilege of taking shots. It's a great way to review for tests, reward an individual for a thoughtful deed, or just add some fun to the day.

Pamela C. Broome—Gr. 5, Rockwell Elementary, Rockwell, NC

Hugs, Hugs, And More Hugs!

To encourage good behavior in my class, I arrange my students in six groups of four desks each. Large paper numerals (1–6) hang from the ceiling above the groups so that no matter how often I regroup them, students can easily identify their group numbers. Each group also has a large coffee can covered with bright paper and labeled with the group's numeral. The cans are for storing hugs! My hugs are small strips of colorful paper labeled with the word "hugs." Students earn hugs when any adult compliments their behavior, when they are on task, and when they exhibit good behavior throughout the school. On Monday, the hugs are counted; then students in the group with the most hugs are my helpers for the week. Even though my hugs are paper, students know that this is my way of letting them know how proud I am of their good behavior.

Sandy Carter—Gr. 5, Carpenter Elementary, Deer Park, TX

Assignment Board

No more "Do we have any homework?" with this handy assignment board! Each month I draw a calendar grid on a sheet of poster board. I display the calendar on a bulletin board along with a fine-tipped marker. Each week a student helper records all daily work on the calendar. In addition, each student has a notebook in which he records the assignments. Students who are absent can check the board when they return to school. I save each calendar; then, at the end of the year, I show my amazed students all the work they have accomplished.

Julie Kwoka—Gr. 5, George Southard Elementary, Lockport, NY

Reproducibles At My Fingertips

To help me keep up with my favorite reproducibles, I store them in three-ring binders. Each subject-area binder has dividers labeled with skills, such as Context Clues, Synonyms, Homonyms, Creative Writing, etc. When a student needs extra practice with a particular skill, I simply flip to an appropriate reproducible and copy it for her immediate use.

Cynthia T. Reeves—Gr. 4
Albert Harris Elementary
Martinsville, VA

LIFESAVERS...
management tips for teachers

No-Fuss Lunch Count

Make taking the daily lunch count and attendance a picnic! Hotglue two labeled wicker paper-plate holders to a piece of decorated cardboard as shown. Next attach pinch clothespins—each labeled with a different student's name—along the top of the board. Finally title the board "Lunch Count" and attach it to a wall or bulletin board. As each student arrives at school, have him clip his clothespin to the appropriate plate. The clips that remain on the top of the board identify those students who are absent.

Brenda Fendley—Gr. 4, Blossom Elementary, Blossom, TX

Dear Mom and Dad,

On Thursday, February 19, my class will have a math test. I will need to study pages 124–136 and do the bonus problems on pages 128, 132, and 136. I plan to study very hard.

Love,
Aimee

X *Mr. Johnson*

Keeping Parents Informed

Have students practice letter writing while they inform their parents of upcoming tests. A few days before a scheduled quiz, instruct each student to write a friendly letter to her parents explaining when the test will be given and what she will need to study. Direct each student to have her parent sign the letter and return it the following day. This method keeps both students and their parents informed around test time.

Martha Meadows—Gr. 5, Immaculate Heart Of Mary
Cuyahoga Falls, OH

All In One Binder

Use a three-ring binder to keep your teacher essentials all in one place. Make a lesson-plan template that includes your lunchtime, special times, and other weekly scheduled activities. Duplicate several copies of the template; then place them in a three-ring binder with your grade book, stickers, grading scale, and other important information. Everything you need will be right at your fingertips!

Cathy Stemen, Cardington, OH

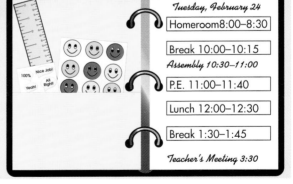

Lesson-Plan Highlights

Help prepare for the day's lessons with this bright idea! Use a highlighter marker to highlight the items in your lesson-plan book that need to be duplicated, prepared in advance, or purchased. You'll know at a glance what needs to be done for each day's lessons.

Patty J. Vermeer—Gr. 4, Galva-Holstein Elementary
Holstein, IA

Super Sub Support

Show support for your substitute with this positive-behavior motivator. Write "There's No Substitute For Cooperation" on the chalkboard. Then leave instructions to have the substitute write the names of the three or four most cooperative and helpful students under the heading. When you return, reward those students whose names are listed on the board with inexpensive prizes. Students will be eager to be put on the list the next time you are absent.

Julia Alarie—Gr. 6, Essex Middle School, Essex, VT

LIFESAVERS...
management tips for teachers

File It Away!

When we do an activity that has several pieces—such as making a food-chain model—I don't want to find the cutouts scattered all over my classroom. So I label each pocket of an expanding file with a student's name. At the end of a period, I pass around the file so each student can place his pieces in his pocket. The next day I pass the file around again so we can pick up where we left off—with no lost pieces!

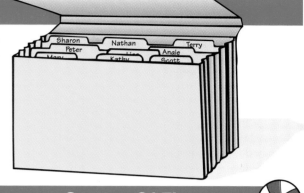

Elizabeth Jamison—Gr. 4, Harman Elementary, Dayton, OH

Drink Passes

Patrol the path to the water fountain with this simple idea! Make drink passes titled "Morning," "Recess," and "Afternoon" from construction paper. Distribute a copy of each different pass to each student. Once he has used his three passes, a student's drink privileges are over for the day.

Patti Eby—Gr. 5
Shalom Christian Academy
Chambersburg, PA

Groups Of Five

The best organizational tool I've found is accomplished in three simple steps. First I place students in groups of five. Then I assign each student a day of the week. Finally I assign a specific class job—such as passing out papers or running errands—to each group. When a student's day of the week arrives, he is the leader of his group and performs his group's job.

Janet Swope—Gr. 4
Midway Heights Elementary
Columbia, MO

Bulletin-Board Letters File

Organize your bulletin-board letters with this easy idea. Obtain a file or large recipe box with alphabetical dividers. Put all the *A*'s behind the A divider, the *B*'s behind the B divider, and so on. Your letters will be right at your fingertips and easy to find when you need them!

Patty J. Vermeer—Gr. 4
Galva-Holstein Elementary
Holstein, IA

The Flip Side

To encourage students to be responsible for their behavior, decorate the front of a three-ring binder with the title "Good Behavior." Flip the binder; then label the blank cover "Behavior That Could Improve." Have each student write her name and "I showed good behavior when…" at the top of a sheet of paper. Bind these pages alphabetically in the front of the binder. Next have each student write her name and "My behavior could improve when…" at the top of a second sheet of paper. Flip the binder and bind these pages inside. When a child demonstrates good behavior, invite her to write about it on her page in the front of the binder. If she displays poor behavior, have the student write about how she could improve on her page in the back of the binder.

Pat Twohey—Gr. 4, Old County Road School, Smithfield, RI

LIFESAVERS...
management tips for teachers

Coffee-Mug Time-Saver

Use old coffee mugs and craft sticks to help with taking lunch and attendance counts. Write each student's name at the end of a different craft stick; then place the sticks in a mug labeled "Extras." Label additional mugs according to your school's lunch choices as shown. Every morning have each student place his stick in the appropriate cup. Just a quick check of the cups by you or a student helper, and your lunch and absentee counts are done!

Bonnie Gibson—Gr. 5, Kyrene Monte Vista School, Tempe, AZ

The Mailbox® Notebook

Want to have all your favorite reproducibles from *The Mailbox®* magazine organized and right at your fingertips? Just tear the reproducible sheets from the magazine, punch three holes in them, and store them in a three-ring binder. Whenever you need a particular reproducible, just remove that page from your personal notebook and copy it.

Christina Bracci—Gr. 6
St. Matthew School
Indian Orchard, MA

Planning As You Go

Take a little time now to save lots of planning time later. Staple copies of the reproducibles used each day directly to that dated page in your plan book. Also jot down notes about any changes you'd like to make in the lessons. When making next year's plans, you can look back at the reproducibles, read your notes, and prepare your lessons in a snap!

Sharon Abell
Mineral Springs Middle School
Winston-Salem, NC

Topics Organizer

Science
Plants
Ecosystems
Energy, Work, And Machines
Light
Sound
The Solar System And Beyond
The Earth And Its Layers
The Skeletal System
The Muscular System

Need help remembering the topics to be taught at your grade level? List the topics for each subject on a different sheet of paper as shown. Laminate these sheets; then place them in a binder. As the year progresses, cross out each topic with a wipe-off marker as you teach it. At the end of the year, simply wipe off the pages to use them again the following year.

Suzanne Hostetler—Gr. 4
Aboite Elementary
Fort Wayne, IN

Assignment Board

Create more chalkboard space by posting daily assignments in another visible spot in the classroom. List the different subject areas on two poster-board sheets. Laminate the sheets and post them on a small bulletin board adjacent to the chalkboard or on the side of a file cabinet. Add seasonal decorations if desired. Each day write the homework assignments on the sheets with a wipe-off marker.

Marilyn Davison—Grs. 4–5
River Oaks School
Monroe, LA

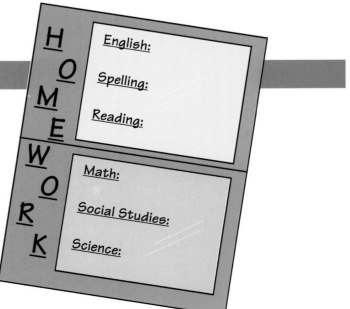

H
O
M
E
W
O
R
K

English:

Spelling:

Reading:

Math:

Social Studies:

Science:

It Computes!
Using Technology In
The Classroom

IT COMPUTES!

Computer Critter To The Rescue

Do you sometimes feel that you have to be a super-person in order to facilitate small-group instruction *and* help those who are working on the computer? Well, have no fear—Computer Critter is here! Place a small stuffed animal by the classroom computer. Tell each student that whenever she has a question while at the computer, she can let you know by quietly placing the critter beside you. While the student waits for your help, let her play a computer game. Then, when there is a logical break in instruction, you can answer the student's question. Using this idea ensures quality student time at the computer without the headache of interruptions.

Cheryl Gjesvold—Grs. K–6 Resource Room
Fairfield, MT

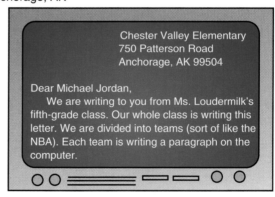

Computer Management

Tired of students fighting over your one and only computer? Then this idea is sure to bring a rousing round of cheers! Divide students into computer teams of five. Encourage each team to create a name for itself such as The Inputs or The Printouts. Then divide an index-card notebook into sections (one per team). On each card of a team's section, write the team's name and one member's name.

Next assign each team a day of the week. On his team's assigned day, have the student whose name is on the first card of his team's section go to the computer. When his time is up, have the student flip the card to the next team member's name. Continue until each member has had time at the computer. On the following day, start with the first card of the next team.

Beverly Langland—Gr. 5
Trinity Christian Academy
Jacksonville, FL

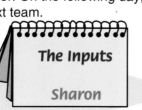

The Inputs

Sharon

Collective Computer Letter

Since computers are such popular learning tools, having only one in your classroom creates quite a challenge! Here's a way to deal with this challenge and encourage cooperative learning at the same time. Have the class choose someone to write a friendly letter to, such as a pen pal, a favorite author, or an athlete. After students have decided to whom they will write, discuss possible topics to include in the letter.

Next divide students into teams, and assign each team a paragraph topic for the letter. Direct one team at a time to go to the computer and write its paragraph. Instruct the first team to set up the letter format and write the first paragraph. Tell each following team to edit the previous paragraph, then write its own. After each team has added its paragraph, direct the first team to edit the final paragraph and add a closing. Students will enjoy this cooperative approach to using the computer.

Sally M. Loudermilk—Gr. 5
Chester Valley Elementary
Anchorage, AK

Chester Valley Elementary
750 Patterson Road
Anchorage, AK 99504

Dear Michael Jordan,
    We are writing to you from Ms. Loudermilk's fifth-grade class. Our whole class is writing this letter. We are divided into teams (sort of like the NBA). Each team is writing a paragraph on the computer.

Scavenger Hunt

If you're searching for a way to introduce your students to a multimedia encyclopedia, look no further! Create a scavenger hunt by listing questions about subjects you are currently studying, such as famous authors, animals, or historical events. Distribute a copy of the scavenger hunt to each student; then direct each student to use the computer's encyclopedia to complete the sheet. For each question, have the student locate the appropriate entry, find the answer to the question, and record the information on his scavenger-hunt sheet. You'll find your students learning to use the computer while enjoying "the thrill of the hunt."

Sue Reed—Gr. 4, Ebenezer Elementary, Lebanon, PA

IT COMPUTES!

Connect The Dots To Print

If the computers in your lab or classroom are connected to different printers, you'll find that this practical idea is right on the dot! To avoid printing confusion, label each printer and its corresponding computer(s) with matching colored dots. Remind each student to look for his printed material at the printer with the same-colored dot as the computer at which he was working. This easy system is sure to save you time and eliminate confusion as students work on projects.

Therese Durhman
Hickory, NC

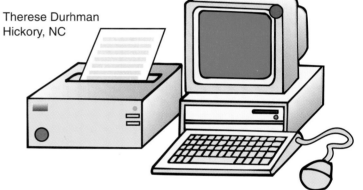

Computerized Pen Pals

Do you like the idea of class pen pals, but dread having to keep up with all the letters and paperwork? Here's a practical solution to that dilemma! Label a disk "Letters To Pen Pals." Direct each child to type a letter to a prospective pen pal and save it on the disk in a file titled with his name. Once each student has typed a letter, place the disk in a disk mailer and send it to another teacher. Ask the teacher to have each of her students read the letters and then select a pen pal. Have the teacher send you a disk with her students' responses. Or, if she has a home Internet account, send her an E-mail with the letter files as attachments. Bye-bye, paperwork!

Dana Sanders
Cartersville, GA

Letters from
Mrs. Spaw's
Class

Tools For Technology

Do your students need help remembering all the functions available on your computer's tool bar? Help them learn to use these handy tools with this creative idea. Locate a small graphic of each tool on the tool bar—the software manual is a good place to look. Duplicate each graphic and its function description; then mount it on an individual index card. Place the cards in a toolbox. Then have each student select a card from the toolbox. Direct the student to read aloud the information on the card; then designate that student as the "expert" on that tool. For example, you might have an "eraser expert" or a "spray can expert." Post the list of experts in your computer lab. Encourage each student to consult a tool's expert when he needs help with a function.

Julie Jo Adamson—Gr. 5
Groveland Elementary
Wayzata, MN

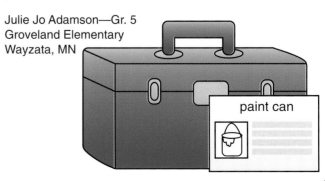

paint can

Interactive Spelling Partner

Use your classroom computer to help students learn their spelling words. Each week tape-record the spelling list; then place the tape and a tape recorder with headphones next to your classroom computer. Instruct each student to play the tape—stopping and rewinding as needed—and type each spelling word on the computer's word-processing program. After the student types all the words, have her use the program's spell-check to identify the words she needs to study and correct her spellings. Then have the student print out a copy of the list to use as a study reference.

Julie Eick Granchelli—Gr. 4
Towne Elementary
Medina, NY

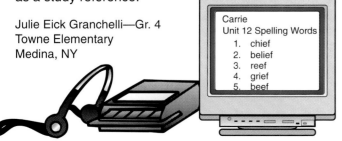

Carrie
Unit 12 Spelling Words
1. chief
2. belief
3. reef
4. grief
5. beef

IT COMPUTES!

Computer Spelling Tutor

Turn your computer-crazed kids into word wizards with this creative spelling idea! Have a student volunteer type a paragraph using your classroom computer's word-processing program. Direct the student to use the program's find-and-replace feature, usually found under "Edit" on the menu bar, to replace each vowel in the paragraph with a blank line. Have the child print a copy of the paragraph; then duplicate it and give a copy to each student. Direct each student to use his spelling skills to fill in the missing vowels.

Julie Eick Granchelli—Gr. 4, Towne Elementary, Medina, NY

Tw_ b_ys w_r_ w_lk_ng _n
_ p_th t_ sch__l wh_n th_y
s_w _ sh_d_wy f_g_r_ r_n
_cr_ss th__ r p_th. Th_ b_ys
w_r_ s_ sc_r_d th_t th_y r_n
_ll th_ w_y b_ck h_m_.

Chip Tip

Cash in on the motivational potential of your classroom computer! Purchase a package of poker chips or make a supply of paper chips from colored oaktag. Reward a student who exhibits good behavior or shows superior effort with a chip. Let a student who earns three chips exchange them for extra computer time. This positive system is sure to supply students with megabytes of motivation!

Pat Twohey—Gr. 4
Old County Road School
Smithfield, RI

Sharing Disks

Not enough disks for each student to have her own? No problem! Gather a supply of floppy disks—one for every three or four students. On each disk's label, list the names of students who are to use that disk. Direct each student to save her work on her assigned disk in a file that begins with two characters: her initials. Have the student fill in the remaining spaces of the file name (the number will vary depending on the computer program being used) with letters of her choice. When a student needs to find a document on the shared disk, all she has to do is look at the file(s) beginning with her initials to locate her document.

Denise Amos—Gr. 4
Crestwood Elementary
Crestwood, KY

We're On The Web!

Use this eye-catching display to help students weave their way through the World Wide Web. Title a bulletin board "We're On The Web!" Draw a web on the board with a black marker as shown. Use white chalk to write the name of each student on a spider cutout. Direct each student to use the chalk to write the URL for a favorite Web site on his spider; then post the spiders on the web. Encourage students to refer to the display for recommended sites as they explore the Web.

Cathy Ogg—Gr. 4
Happy Valley Elementary
Johnson City, TN

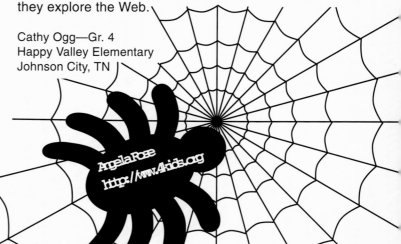

READING ROUNDUP

Reading Roundup

Book Baskets

Motivating students to read while reducing traffic to your classroom library is in the bag—or basket—with this simple idea! Place students' desks in several small-group arrangements; then put a basket on each group's table. Fill each basket with a variety of books that suit the various interests and reading levels of your students. Include picture books, novels, and nonfiction books. Then direct each student to choose a book from his group's basket to read during his free time. Rotate the baskets at the beginning of each week, and replenish them with new books after each classroom cycle.

Sean Moré, Lake Magdalene Elementary
Tampa, FL

Biography Bottles

Here's an idea that's sure to uncork bottles of creativity! Direct each student to choose a biography of a famous person to read. After each student has read her book, provide her with a 4" x 6" index card; an empty, plastic two-liter bottle; a cup of sand or gravel; a medium-sized Styrofoam® ball; yarn; poster board; and various arts-and-crafts materials. Instruct the student to place a small amount of sand or gravel in the bottom of the bottle to anchor it, then decorate the bottle to represent her famous person. Next direct the student to label the top of her index card as shown. Also have her include a brief paragraph that describes her person's achievements and tells why she chose to read about this person. Have each student share her work; then display each biography bottle and its card on a shelf.

Linda Cowell—Gr. 4
Kate Bond Elementary
Memphis, TN

Title: *Where Do You Think You're Going, Christopher Columbus?*
Author: Jean Fritz
Illustrator: Margot Tomes
Publisher: Putnam Publishing Group

Christopher Columbus was a great navigator and explorer. He sailed across the Atlantic Ocean in search of a sea route to Asia. But instead he found the West Indies, and Central and South America. I chose to read about Columbus because he was a courageous explorer.

Monthly Reading Contests

Round up your readers with a school-wide monthly reading contest! Determine a theme and prize for each month. Have each participating teacher choose a reading goal for each of her students to meet by the end of the month. Advertise the contest by displaying banners and posters throughout the school. At the end of each month, reward students who met their goals with the prize for the month. Also have each teacher post the names of students who met their goals; then have the principal read aloud these names on the intercom. Top off the contest by writing each reading goal winner's name on a slip of paper and drawing for individual prizes such as books, markers, and calculators. Vary the contest theme and the prizes awarded each month. Then stand back—you'll soon see a herd of readers heading for the nearest bookshelf!

Lisa Ware and Lisa Mattel—Gr. 5
North Jackson Elementary, Talmo, GA

Verb Volume

Looking for a book full of action? Read aloud *Add It, Dip It, Fix It: A Book Of Verbs* by Richard Schneider (Ticknor & Fields Books For Young Readers, 1996) for a unique look at verbs. After sharing the book, choose a common noun such as *ball*. Then demonstrate how to combine the noun with 26 verbs, each beginning with a different letter of the alphabet. For example, <u>a</u>rch the ball, <u>b</u>ounce the ball, <u>c</u>atch the ball, <u>d</u>ribble the ball, etc. Then pair up your students. Assign each pair a common noun, and challenge the pair to combine that noun with 26 different verbs as in the book and your example. (For a handy list of nouns, see "English Made Easy" on page 306.) Provide each pair with a sheet of chart paper on which to record its noun-verb combinations. Have each pair share its completed list with the class.

Joy Frerichs
Valley Point Middle School
Dalton, GA

Reading Roundup

Best Booklist Ever

Which books would your students rate as hands-down favorites? Find out by having your class develop the Best Booklist Ever for your grade level. Ask each student to name one or two books he enjoyed reading this year. Make a ballot of students' responses. On voting day, give each student a ballot and have him mark his top two choices. Collect the ballots and tally the results on the chalkboard. Have students count the tally marks to rank the top ten books. Then either publish the results in a school newsletter or share the list with a teacher in a grade level just below yours. This is one booklist students won't want to miss!

Terry Healy—Gifted K–6
Eugene Field Elementary
Manhattan, KS

Pog® Book Reports

Students will go Pog® wild over these book reports! Duplicate a copy of page 268 for each student, directing her to label a circle for each of the following:

- each major character (name on one circle, picture on another)
- the main setting in the book (where and when on one circle, picture on another)
- each problem/solution (problem on one circle, solution on another)
- the major climax
- a Slammer (book's title and author on one circle, picture on another)

Next have her glue the completed sheet to poster board, cut out the circles, and glue the corresponding front-and-back circles together. Also have the student label an index card with the book's title and author, a summary, and a personal rating of the book. Instruct her to store the circles and card in a resealable plastic bag.

Elizabeth Zito, Milford, CT

Ben And Me
by Robert Lawson

Slammer

Super Reader Pancake Breakfast

Reward your goal-reaching readers with a special breakfast just for them! At the beginning of each grading period, set a reading goal for each student. Then announce your plans for hosting a before-school breakfast at the end of the quarter for all students who meet their goals. At the end of the grading period, enclose a breakfast invitation in the report card of each qualifying student. The afternoon before the breakfast, set up the serving table in your classroom. That night cook bacon at home and refrigerate it. Also mix pancake batter and store it in a pitcher. The next morning, reheat the bacon in the microwave at school, pour the juice, and cook the pancakes on an electric griddle right at the serving table. Students will become eager readers to chow down such a super meal!

Marilyn Davison—Grs. 4–5
River Oaks School
Monroe, LA

Patterns
Use with "Pog® Book Reports" on page 267.

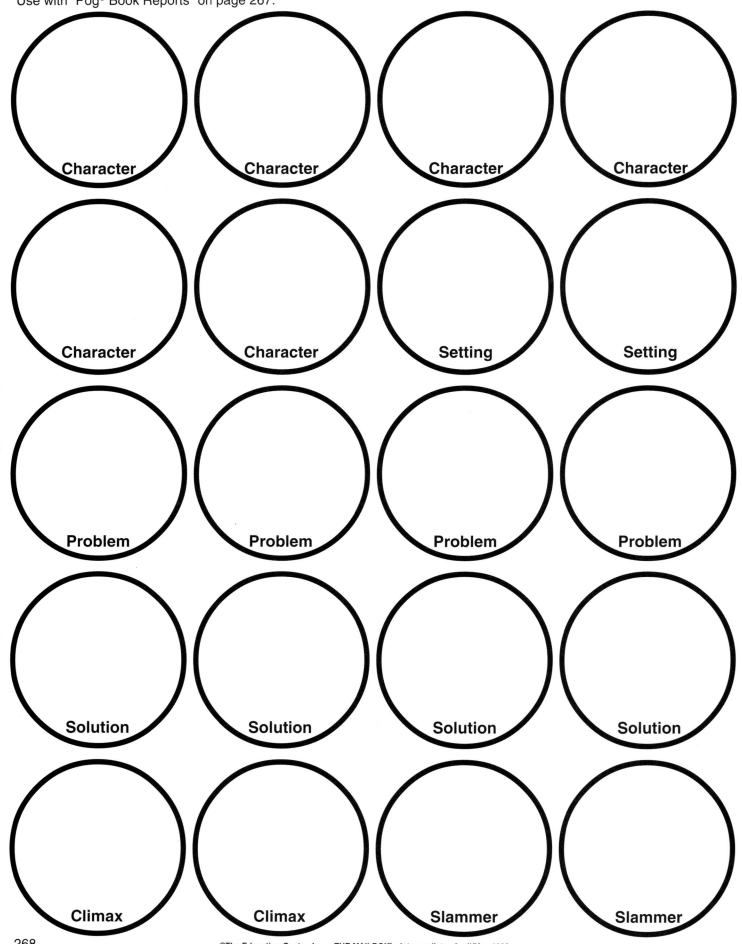

Character   Character   Character   Character

Character   Character   Setting   Setting

Problem   Problem   Problem   Problem

Solution   Solution   Solution   Solution

Climax   Climax   Slammer   Slammer

Seasonal Ideas & Reproducibles

Seasoned To Perfection!

Creative Activities To Spice Up December And January Holidays

You can't ignore them—the holidays that start rolling in around December, that is. And neither can your students. So why not mix their natural excitement about the holidays with the following creative activities? It's a sure recipe for seasonal success!

Christmas Across Cultures

Add a pinch of other cultures to your holiday menu with a fun, grade-level activity. Have each teacher in your grade level select a country (possibly one that fits into a current topic of study) and research its holiday traditions. Also have her post a replica of the country's flag on her classroom door, along with a cut-out character representative of the country.

On the day before Christmas break, have each teacher dress in a costume from her country. Rotate students through the classrooms for 25-minute periods. During each period, the teacher shares her country's holiday traditions with students, takes them through a simple activity, and then serves a snack related to her country. Toward the end of the day, have each student return to her homeroom to enjoy an American Christmas party. What a fun way to experience the holiday traditions of other cultures! *Liz Cooper—Gr. 4, Northside Elementary, Texas City, TX*

Seasoned With Hanukkah Literature

Give students a peek at the traditions of Hanukkah through the pages of outstanding picture books. Divide your class into five groups. Give each group a sheet of art paper, markers, and one of these picture books:

- *A Great Miracle Happened There: A Chanukah Story* by Karla Kuskin (Willa Perlman Books)
- *The Gift* by Aliana Brodmann (Simon & Schuster Books For Young Readers)
- *In The Month Of Kislev: A Story For Hanukkah* by Nina Jaffe (Viking)
- *Inside-Out Grandma: A Hanukkah Story* by Joan Rothenberg (Hyperion Books For Children)
- *The Tie Man's Miracle: A Chanukah Tale* by Steven Schnur (Morrow Junior Books)

Have each group read its story together, then design a poster that summarizes the book's lesson or plot. Provide time for groups to share their books and posters; then have students make tasty Hanukkah treats as described below.

Delicious Dreidels
Push one end of a toothpick through a large marshmallow, then into the bottom of a chocolate kiss. A top-notch treat!

The Greatest Gift

What are the ingredients of a great gift? Get students thinking about the meaning of gift giving with this activity. For homework, direct each student to ask at least five people this question: "What is the best gift you've ever received?" The next day provide students with art supplies, and challenge each child to create a unique ornament for each answer he received. After the student has labeled each ornament with an answer, divide the class into groups. Have the members in each group compare their answers, then make a chart or graph showing the results of the survey. After groups have shared their work, have each student hang his ornaments on a large cut-out tree or a real Christmas tree in your classroom. *Julia Alarie and Jacqueline Schumacher— Gr. 6*
Essex Middle School
Essex, VT

a fresh apple pie on the first day we moved into the neighborhood

A Timely Gift

What gift gives all year long? A calendar, of course! Help each student create a personalized calendar with this easy gift idea. For each child, duplicate 12 copies of the blank month-at-a-glance calendar on page 279. Provide an actual calendar to show the correct placement of months and days for the upcoming year. After students have examined several store-bought calendars and discussed design and monthly themes, have each child glue each month's calendar page on the bottom half of a 12" x 18" sheet of white paper. Next have him illustrate the top portion of each page according to the month. Hole-punch the top of each page; then have the student attach the pages loosely with yarn so that they can be easily flipped. *Diana Auerhammer, Creston Elementary, Creston, MT*

Holiday Coupons

The holidays are wonderful—but they can also be more than a little hectic and expensive. Cut the costs of providing gifts for your students with this simple idea. Duplicate one or more copies of the coupons on page 277 for each child. During your holiday party, have each student cut out, color, and assemble his coupons to make a booklet. While students are working on their booklets, you'll have time to put away your holiday decorations—which means an orderly, neat classroom when you return from the Christmas break. Now *that's* a great gift! *Alice Koziol—Gr. 4, Chesapeake, VA*

Rudolph led Santa's Sleigh, right?

Use this coupon to lead our class line today.

Need the gift of gab?

Enjoy a three-minute uninterrupted chat with your teacher.

Hang in there!

Take ten minutes of free time to enjoy your favorite classroom activity.

Stride Toward Freedom

Dr. Martin Luther King made great strides toward promoting freedom, peace, and understanding among all people. Highlight his accomplishments this January with a student-made display. Back a bulletin board with white paper and the title "Stride Toward Freedom" (which is also the title of Dr. King's first book). Duplicate a class supply of the footprint pattern found on page 280. After students have had a chance to study Dr. King's life, have each child complete a pattern, cut it out, and glue it on a red, black, or green piece of paper. Then have him trim around the pattern to leave a 1/4-inch border of color. Mount the projects on the board, along with a picture of Dr. King or a student-written timeline of his life.

Stride Toward Freedom

Dr. Martin Luther King took a stride toward freedom and peace when he led the bus boycott in the South.

I can follow in Dr. King's footsteps in my classroom by trying to see the good qualities in each of my classmates.

I can follow in Dr. King's footsteps at home by helping my little sister learn to ride her new bicycle.

Name: Evan

Dizzy Dreidels

It's Hanukkah, and that means it's time to play the dreidel game! But while these dreidels were dizzily spinning, the words on them got all scrambled up. First unscramble each word on the back of this page or another sheet of paper. Then read the Hanukkah story and write each unscrambled word in the correct blank. If necessary, work back and forth between the story and the scrambled words to complete the page.

PETMEL
THILGS
TABELT
ELDIRED
DONSTHUA
SHIWEJ

LENCAD
GITHE
VIDAD
KOCEDO
SNAKAPEC
HAMOREN

MEREBERM
CARLIME
STEAKL
LISVFAET
TIFGS
PLAM

Hanukkah is a _____ holiday, also known as the _____ of _____.

The eight days honor an event that took place over two _____ years ago when a small

group of Jewish men fought a _____ to recapture their _____. When it was time to light

the sacred temple _____, only one day's oil was found. But miraculously, the oil lasted for

_____ days!

Today Jewish families _____ this miracle by lighting one _____ for each of

eight days. The special candleholder is called a _____. Houses are decorated with the

Star of _____. _____ are exchanged, and children enjoy playing a Hanukkah game

with a toy called a _____. Potato _____, also called _____, are a

favorite Hanukkah food. They are _____ in oil as a remembrance of the _____

of the lamp.

Bonus Box: How many words of three letters or more can you spell using only the letters in MENORAH (not repeating any letter more than once in any one word)? List them on the back of this page.

©The Education Center, Inc. • THE MAILBOX® • Intermediate • Dec/Jan 1997–98 • Key p. 312 • written by Ann Fisher

Rudolph led Santa's sleigh, right?

Use this coupon to lead our class line today.

©1997 The Education Center, Inc.

Battling the winter blahs?

"Snow" problem!

Present this coupon to your teacher for a special treat.

©1997 The Education Center, Inc.

Interested in "stocking" your desk with school supplies?

See your teacher for a new pencil.

©1997 The Education Center, Inc.

Need a break from "ho-ho-homework"?

Use this coupon to skip this assignment (after getting your teacher's approval):

_____

©1997 The Education Center, Inc.

Need the gift of gab?

Enjoy a three-minute uninterrupted chat with your teacher.

©1997 The Education Center, Inc.

Hang in there!

Take ten minutes of free time to enjoy your favorite classroom activity.

©1997 The Education Center, Inc.

Enjoy a noteworthy day!

Skip the morning assignment today.

©1997 The Education Center, Inc.

Jingle All The Way...

...to the water fountain for a free drink!

©1997 The Education Center, Inc.

Coupon Clipper

Esther—who happens to be a real coupon clipper—is anxious to start her holiday baking. But first she needs to stock up on some ingredients. Esther has coupons for nine items, shown below. Now she must decide which of the local grocery stores to visit. All three stores have the same regular prices on the nine items, but they all have different deals on coupons:

- Little's Vittles honors an unlimited number of coupons at face value.
- Edie's Edibles doubles all coupons that are worth 40 cents or less. It also allows customers to use a maximum of six coupons per visit.
- Chloe's Culinary Corner allows each customer to use a maximum of four coupons. It will also triple any coupon worth 40 cents or less.

Fill out the chart below to list the values of the coupons at each store. Then figure Esther's total savings for each store.

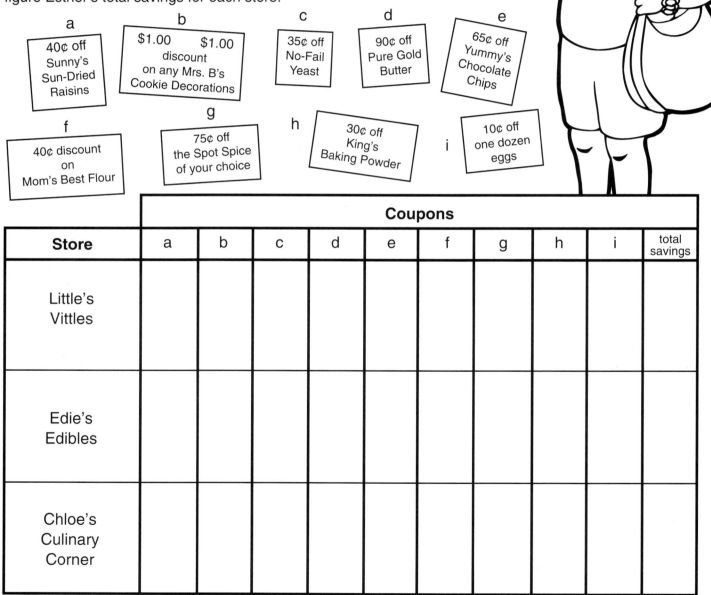

a 40¢ off Sunny's Sun-Dried Raisins

b $1.00 $1.00 discount on any Mrs. B's Cookie Decorations

c 35¢ off No-Fail Yeast

d 90¢ off Pure Gold Butter

e 65¢ off Yummy's Chocolate Chips

f 40¢ discount on Mom's Best Flour

g 75¢ off the Spot Spice of your choice

h 30¢ off King's Baking Powder

i 10¢ off one dozen eggs

Store	a	b	c	d	e	f	g	h	i	total savings
Little's Vittles										
Edie's Edibles										
Chloe's Culinary Corner										

At which store will Esther save the most money with her coupons? _____

Bonus Box: Esther has discovered a fourth grocery store. It will let her use an unlimited number of coupons and will double any coupon under 50 cents. How much money will Esther save at this store using the coupons above? Write your answer on the back of this page.

Sunday	Monday	Tuesday	Wednesday	Thursday	Friday	Saturday

©The Education Center, Inc. • THE MAILBOX® • Intermediate • Dec/Jan 1997–98

Note To The Teacher: Use with "A Timely Gift" on page 275.

Stride Toward Freedom

Dr. Martin Luther King took a stride toward freedom and peace when he _____

_____

_____

_____

_____

_____.

I can follow in Dr. King's footsteps in my classroom by _____

_____

_____

_____

_____.

I can follow in Dr. King's footsteps at home by _____

_____

_____

_____

_____.

Name: _____

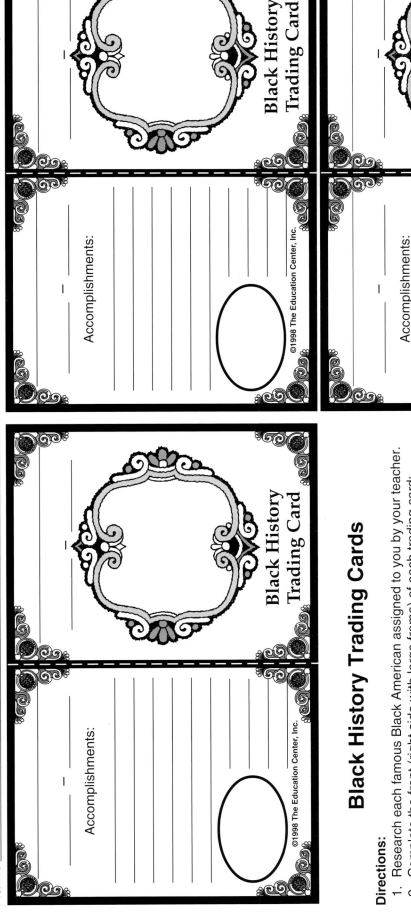

Accomplishments: _____
_____
_____
_____
_____
_____
_____

Black History
Trading Card

©1998 The Education Center, Inc.

Accomplishments: _____
_____
_____
_____
_____
_____
_____

Black History
Trading Card

©1998 The Education Center, Inc.

Accomplishments: _____
_____
_____
_____
_____
_____
_____

Black History
Trading Card

©1998 The Education Center, Inc.

Black History Trading Cards

Directions:

1. Research each famous Black American assigned to you by your teacher.
2. Complete the front (right side with large frame) of each trading card:
   a. Write the person's name in the top blank.
   b. Write the person's year of birth (and year of death if no longer living) below the name. Example: 1924–1995.
   c. Draw a picture of the person in the frame.
3. Complete the back (left side) of each trading card:
   a. Write the person's name and year of birth (and year of death if no longer living).
   b. Briefly list some of the person's accomplishments.
   c. In the oval, draw a symbol that represents this person. For example, a baseball and bat could represent Jackie Robinson.
4. Cut out each card on the bold lines.
5. Fold each card in half on the dashed line.
6. Rubber-cement or tape the two halves together.

©The Education Center, Inc. • *THE MAILBOX®* • *Intermediate* • Feb/Mar 1998 • adapted from an idea by Nancy Curl—Gr. 6, Olson Middle School, Tabernacle, NJ

Note To The Teacher: Provide each student with one copy of this reproducible. Assign each student three famous Black Americans to research. When students are finished, use pushpins to attach each trading card to a bulletin board.

Cupid's Capers

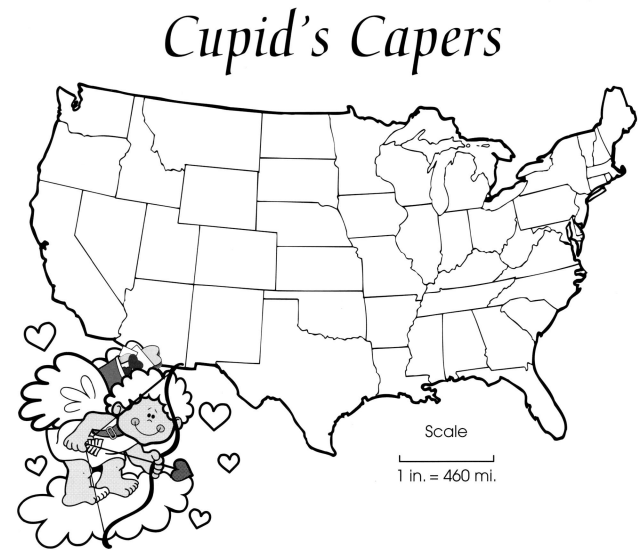

Scale

|———————|

1 in. = 460 mi.

It's Valentine's Day, and Cupid is planning to deliver valentines, sweets, and flowers to several U.S. cities. He chose the cities listed below to visit first. Why? He thinks their names sound "romantic"!

Kissimmee, Florida (FL)	Sweetwater Station, Wyoming (WY)	Loveland, Ohio (OH)
Rosebud, Texas (TX)	Flower Hill, New York (NY)	Paradise Valley, Arizona (AZ)
Sweet Home, Oregon (OR)	Lovingston, Virginia (VA)	Sunset Hills, Missouri (MO)

Directions: Plan the shortest possible route for Cupid. The route must include all nine cities.
1. First find the state in which each city is located.
2. Make a dot in the center of the state; then lightly shade the state with a colored pencil. Write the state's abbreviation beside the dot.
3. Study the map and its shaded states, and then plan Cupid's route.
4. Cupid flies in straight lines, so use a ruler to draw lines from dot to dot.
5. Use the map scale to estimate how far Cupid will travel: about _____ miles.

Bonus Box: At the last minute, Cupid noticed an envelope in the bottom of his bag. It needs to be delivered to Valentine, Nebraska. How much farther must Cupid travel to reach this tenth city?

Top O' The Mornin' To Ye!
Creative Activities For Celebrating St. Patrick's Day

What is green, has an Irish flavor, and is loads of fun? St. Patrick's Day—the perfect holiday to celebrate in your classroom with the following fun learning activities!

You Don't Say!

The Irish seem to have the perfect saying for any situation. Share these traditional Irish proverbs with your students:

- A full cabin is better than an empty castle.
- Don't desert the highway for the shortcut.
- Often a person's mouth has broken his nose.
- The people go, but the hills remain.
- A shut mouth catches no flies.
- The silent mouth is sweet to hear.

Have each student choose a saying from the list and illustrate both its literal and figurative meanings. Post the pictures on a shamrock-decorated bulletin board. *Irene Taylor—Gr. 4, Irene E. Feldkirchner School, Green Brook, NJ, and Karen Richmond, St. Albans, WV*

Instant Irish

Use the following suggestions to get your students in the spirit of St. Patrick's Day:

- Have each student add *Mc* or *O'* to the beginning of her last name when signing her work: McSamuels or O'Samuels.
- Have students write with green pens or markers all day.
- Challenge students to list as many *Pats* or *Patricks* as they can.
- Let the blarney flow! Allow everyone wearing green to have five free minutes of chat time.
- Treat students to a little Irish music. When the music begins, have students stop what they are doing while a volunteer draws a name from a hat. If the student whose name is drawn can tell the class a fact about Ireland, reward her with a St. Patrick's Day sticker or a green lollipop, pencil, or eraser.

Barbara Samuels, Rockaway, NJ

Blarney To The Rescue

Leprechauns are known for using their gift of gab to get out of tight situations! Can your students persuade a leprechaun to listen for a change and alter something about himself? Begin with a brainstorming session; then share the following story starters:

- You're tired of green. Persuade a leprechaun to wear another color—perhaps hot pink!
- Persuade a leprechaun not to play any more tricks on humans.
- Persuade a leprechaun to try living in a condo for a change.
- See if you can persuade a leprechaun to give up his gold.

Be sure to have students include a little blarney to flatter the leprechauns into changing their behavior! *Barbara Samuels*

283

St. "Pat-egories"

Leprechauns have been up to their tricks again. In each box that is labeled with a category, they erased the items! And in each box with a list of items, they erased the category!

Can you complete each box? Use what you know about St. Patrick and how we celebrate his special day. If a category is given, try to list four items that belong in that category. If the items are given, try to decide on a category in which all the items in that box belong. The first one is done for you.

1. _Cities With Large St. Patrick's Day Parades_

   a. New York

   b. Boston

   c. Chicago

   d. Philadelphia

2. St. Patrick's Day Symbols

   a. _____

   b. _____

   c. _____

   d. _____

3. St. Patrick's Day Party Decorations

   a. _____

   b. _____

   c. _____

   d. _____

4. _____

   a. Capital city is Dublin

   b. Located on an island in Europe

   c. Known as the Emerald Isle

   d. Also called _Eire_

5. _____

   a. emerald

   b. olive

   c. chartreuse

   d. celadon

6. Events In St. Patrick's Life

   a. _____

   b. _____

   c. _____

   d. _____

7. Green Things

   a. _____

   b. _____

   c. _____

   d. _____

8. _____

   a. red clover

   b. trefoil

   c. black medic

   d. white clover

Bonus Box: On the back of this page, draw two more category boxes. Leave out the category in one box, but list its four items. List the category for the second box, but leave out its items. Challenge a classmate to fill the boxes.

Nickel Mania

Which U.S. president—born on April 13, 1743—was also an inventor, an architect, and an author, and is also commemorated on the U.S. nickel? None other than Thomas Jefferson! In honor of this famous American, round up a few nickels and complete the fun activities that follow.

1. The *diameter* of a circle is the length of an imaginary line that passes through its center. Look at the diameter of a nickel. Do you think it measures one inch, less than one inch, or greater than one inch? Estimate; then measure the diameter with a ruler.

   Estimate _____   **Answer** _____

2. If nickels were placed side by side along this line, how many would fit? Estimate; then find the actual answer.

   |—————————————————————————————————————|

   Estimate _____   **Answer** _____

3. Look around the classroom. Find an object that fits each measurement below.

   A. the length of 4 nickels   _____

   B. the length of 10 nickels   _____

   C. the length of 20 nickels   _____

   D. the length of 40 nickels   _____

4. Suppose a family member offered you the choice of two amounts of money: enough nickels stacked on top of each other to equal your height, or a twenty-dollar bill. Which offer would you choose? Make a choice; then test your choice following Steps 1–5.

   Your Choice _____

   Test Your Choice:

   1. Make a one-inch stack of nickels. Record how many nickels are in the stack. _____

   2. With the help of your partner, measure how tall you are to the nearest inch. Record your height in inches. _____

   3. Multiply the number of nickels in one inch by your height in inches. This will tell how many nickels tall you are. Record your height in nickels. _____

   4. Multiply your height in nickels by five to get a total number of cents. Place a decimal point two places from the right to get a dollar amount. Record the cents, then the dollar amount.

      _____   _____

   5. Did you choose the best offer? Why or why not? _____
      _____

Bonus Box: On the back of this sheet, write the names of the presidents whose heads appear on the penny, dime, and quarter.

©The Education Center, Inc. • THE MAILBOX® • Intermediate • April/May 1998 • Key p. 313 • written by Ann Fisher

Note To The Teacher: Provide each pair of students with a supply of nickels, a ruler, a yardstick or measuring tape, and pencil and paper.

Recycled Words

Celebrate Earth Day by doing some recycling, but not with trash—with words!

Directions: Use the letters in each recyclable item listed below to spell a word that fits each clue. Write one letter in each blank. Use a dictionary if you need help.

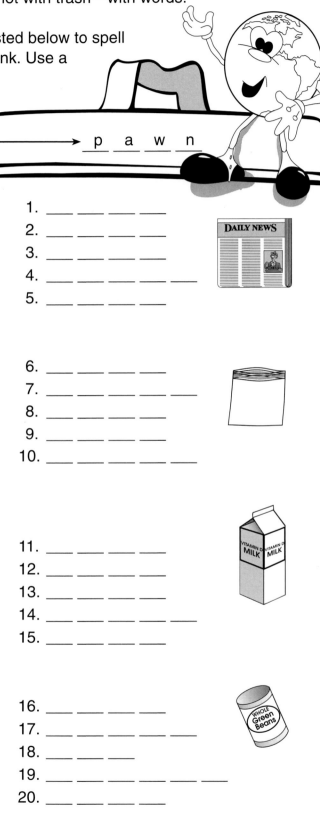

newspaper
Example: a game piece used to play chess ⟶ p a w n

1. a section of glass in a window or door
2. to trade or barter
3. a flying insect that can sting
4. a long, sharp-pointed weapon
5. a large water bird with a long, graceful neck

plastic bag
6. a plaster covering that supports a broken arm or leg
7. an explosion
8. a series of items, names, or numerals often written in a certain order
9. to take in your breath suddenly
10. food made from flour and water, such as spaghetti

milk carton
11. a low, sad sound
12. a place for ice-skating
13. a fastening made by tying a rope or string
14. to follow the tracks of someone or something
15. a ring on a chain

aluminum can
16. peaceful, untroubled
17. a channel dug across land
18. hit, throw, or shoot something in a particular direction
19. any living creature that can breathe and move
20. largest or most important

1. __ __ __ __
2. __ __ __ __
3. __ __ __ __
4. __ __ __ __ __
5. __ __ __ __

6. __ __ __ __
7. __ __ __ __ __
8. __ __ __ __
9. __ __ __ __
10. __ __ __ __ __

11. __ __ __ __
12. __ __ __ __
13. __ __ __ __
14. __ __ __ __ __
15. __ __ __ __

16. __ __ __ __
17. __ __ __ __ __
18. __ __ __
19. __ __ __ __ __ __
20. __ __ __ __ __

Bonus Box: List five more words using the letters of one recyclable item listed above. Write your words on the back of this sheet.

OUR READERS WRITE

Our Readers Write

New Additions

Watch the compliments start adding up for this creative back-to-school display! Cut addition symbols from construction paper; then laminate the cutouts. Use a transparency pen to write one student's name on each laminated cutout. Post the symbols on your classroom door with the title "Check Out The New Additions To My Class!" Use the symbols again next year by erasing the names and reprogramming the cutouts with the names of your new students.

Juliane Wyatt—Gr. 6
Conner Middle School
Hebron, KY

Lara Marshall

Rodney Luck

Back-To-School Breakfast

Get to know your new students and their parents at a back-to-school breakfast. Reserve your school cafeteria or another meeting place for a social breakfast before the start of a selected school day. Contact a few parents to provide coffee, juice, and paper goods. Ask the other invited families to bring one breakfast item to share. The breakfast takes minimal preparation and provides a great opportunity for everyone involved to become acquainted.

Phyllis Ellett—Grs. 3–4 Multiage
Earl Hanson Elementary
Rock Island, IL

Don't Forget Birthdays!

You'll always have a birthday card on hand with this timesaving tip! At the start of the school year, create a list containing each student's birthday. Sign one birthday card for each child in advance; then attach each card to the appropriate page in your plan book for that week. Simple, but effective!

Sharon Abell—Math & Social Studies
Mineral Springs Middle School
Winston-Salem, NC

No-Fuss Calendars

Need an attractive calendar display without the fuss? On the first school day of each month, label a 3" x 3" square of white construction paper for each day of that month. Give each student one square; then have him use crayons or colored pencils to decorate the square with a colorful illustration. Post each date card in its correct place on a calendar skeleton. Your students will be proud to take part in creating this one-of-a-kind classroom calendar!

Page Hardin—Gr. 4
Pocahontas Middle School
Powhatan, VA

Me Boxes

Looking for a unique way to learn more about your new students? Provide each student with an empty cereal box and a variety of art materials. Instruct the student to decorate all six sides of his box so that it looks like him. Next instruct each student to take his box home and fill it with five items that reflect who he is, such as a family photograph or a favorite CD. Tell each student that the items must be small enough to allow the lid to close with all five items inside. Have each student show his Me Box to the class and share the meaning of each item found inside. On the night of Open House, place each student's Me Box on his desktop so that parents can easily locate their child's desk!

Scott Davis
Fairmont Elementary
Pasadena, TX

On The Trail!

Get your students on the right trail with this wall display! Post a cut-out detective holding a large magnifying glass on a classroom wall. Title the display "On The Trail To Good Writing [or any relevant skill]." Each time you teach a new writing skill—such as starting a sentence with a capital letter—write the skill on a footprint cutout and post it on the wall leading away from the detective. Your students can watch the footprints travel up the wall as their writing skills soar too!

Denell Hilgendorf—Grs. 4–6
Osaka International School
Osaka, Japan

Begin every sentence with a capital letter.

Getting-To-Know-You Puzzle

Searching for a first-day-of-school activity? Divide a sheet of poster board into enough puzzle pieces so that each student gets one piece. Write a list of ten questions such as "What makes you happy?" and "What is your favorite hobby?" on the chalkboard. Give each student one puzzle piece; then instruct him to write the answers to five of the questions on his piece. Have each student post his piece to create the complete puzzle on a bulletin board titled "Piecing Together A New Year." What a great way to discuss differences, sharing, and getting along—all at the same time!

Margaret Zogg—Grs. K–6 Substitute
Liverpool Central School District
North Syracuse, NY

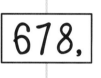

Hanging Names

Guide each new student to her desk with a hanging nametag! Write each student's name vertically so that each letter is connected on a large sheet of construction paper. Cut out each name; then use a hole puncher to make a hole in the top of the first letter. Thread a length of fishing line through each hole and hang the names from the ceiling over the matching students' desks. Learning your new students' names will be a snap with these visual references hanging over their heads!

Sandra H. Dunaway
Stewart County Elementary
Lumpkin, GA

Picturing Larger Numbers

Don't let reading large numbers intimidate your students! Have each student use an index card to create a number frame (see the illustration). Simply have each student place his frame over the first period while reading a large number. Students can read one period at a time, using the comma to remind them to name the period. Make larger frames to accommodate numbers written on the chalkboard or individual slates.

Katherine Gegner—Grs. 3–4
Linkhorne Elementary
Lynchburg, VA

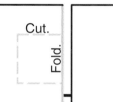

Cut.
Fold.

678,

Classroom Scavenger Hunt

Familiarize your students with their new surroundings this August by sending them on a scavenger hunt. Give each student a list of about 20 items to find in the classroom such as scissors, crayons, and glue. (Number each student's list differently so that everyone won't be hunting for the same item at the same time.) Students will find out where everything is kept in the classroom—all without a single word from you!

Diane Moser—Gr. 5
Sangre Ridge Elementary
Stillwater, OK

We Build Great Kids!

Set up your classroom with a construction theme, and your crew will be anxious to dig into the new year! To start the year with this fun room theme:

- Create a poster (see the illustration) from an old blueprint or light blue paper and post it in the classroom.
- Draw a bricklike pattern on a bulletin board titled "Foundations For Success." On each brick write an important skill such as team spirit, careful listening, and problem solving.
- Hang a "Work Area" sign on the classroom door, a "No Parking" sign at the pencil sharpener, and a "Soft Shoulder" sign near your desk.
- Place a path of orange construction cones made from art paper leading up to the classroom door.
- Place a few toy dump trucks around the classroom filled with goodies such as sugarless candy or popcorn.
- Don't forget to wear your hard hat!

Judy Person
Hockinson Intermediate School
Brush Prairie, WA

Apprentices Wanted

Boys and Girls

Day Shift Only
Hours: 9:00-3:00

Requirements:
Smiles, energy, a positive attitude

Find Me!

This Open House idea doubles as an end-of-the-year activity! Give each student a sheet of drawing paper on which to draw a self-portrait and write three sentences about herself. Instruct the student to write her name in small letters on the *back* of the paper. Place each student's self-portrait on her desk during Open House; then challenge parents to find their child's desk. Save the self-portraits until the last day of school. Read aloud each one; then have students guess who fits the description. How well did your students get to know one another during the year?

Suzanne Crouse—Gr. 5
Deep Creek Intermediate
Chesapeake, VA

Cory

$$3/4 + 1/2 =$$

$$3/4 + 2/4 = 5/4 = 1\ 1/4$$

Practice Papers

Conserve paper with personalized practice sheets. Write each student's name on a separate 12" x 18" sheet of manila paper; then laminate the sheets. Provide each student with one of the laminated sheets and a wipe-off marker for which he should be responsible. Instruct the student to use the sheet to practice math, spelling words, or other skills. Keep a spray bottle full of water and supply of paper towels to use to clean the laminated sheets after each activity.

Janice Mantooth—Gr. 5, Eula ISD, Clyde, TX

Keep Them Listening!

Motivate your students to stay attentive during filmstrips, oral reports, and discussions with this simple idea. Write each student's name on a different Popsicle® stick and place the sticks in a cup. During filmstrips and discussions, ask students to take brief notes about what they are learning. Afterward pull a stick from the cup and have that student share one fact that he learned from the discussion (being sure not to repeat a fact already given by a classmate). If a student catches an error in another student's fact, reward him with a homework pass or small treat.

Linda Mabry—Gr. 6, Triad Elementary, North Lewisburg, OH

Ms. Gough's Class's Science Fair Project

Easel Display

Transform the plastic back from a daily tear-off calendar into a great mini-easel. Use it to show information about projects on display in the media center or around the classroom. Best of all, this mini-easel can be used again and again!

Mary W. Gough—Gr. 4
James River Day School
Lynchburg, VA

Cooperative Spelling

Take the monotony out of a regular spelling routine with this idea. Divide your class into two teams. Give each team a different spelling list for the week. Have the teams work together—completing activities and playing related games—to learn their list of words. At the end of the week, give both teams a spelling test on their words and record the grades. For the next week, switch the word lists for each team and repeat the process. Then calculate each team's grade average for both tests and award the team with the highest average inexpensive prizes or homework passes. Now, that's motivation!

Deena Block—Gr. 4, George B. Fine Elementary, Pennsauken, NJ

ESTIMATE TICKET
NAME: Pam Crane   ESTIMATE: 120 jelly beans

Estimation Contests

Fill your students' free time with enrichment activities that they'll be motivated to complete. Place items such as paper clips, marbles, or beans in a clear plastic container so that students can estimate the number of items inside. Then provide a variety of brainteasers, math puzzles, and mini-research projects that your students can complete to earn estimate tickets. Each estimate ticket is worth one entry in the estimation contest. Have the student fill out the ticket and place it in an entry box positioned near the filled plastic container. At the end of the week, announce the actual total and award a small treat to the student with the estimate closest to the correct one.

Tom Wier—Gr. 4
Godfrey Elementary, Wyoming, MI

Mrs. kane's third-grade class is going to the cincinnati zoo today.

What's In The News?

Help your students keep up with current events while they practice proofreading sentences! Have students tell you facts about what is going on in world, state, community, school, or personal news. Include grammatical and punctuation errors as you record each sentence on a sheet of chart paper. Then have student volunteers use proofreading marks to correct your mistakes.

Michelle Pirog—Gr. 6 Resource
Raritan-Flemington Middle School
Flemington, NJ

Bulletin-Board Remedy

Never have an empty hallway bulletin board again! Cover the board; then label half "Resource Alert" and the other half "Share Board." Attach a pen, an envelope containing index cards, and a supply of pushpins to the board. Invite teachers to request supplies such as empty baby-food jars or egg cartons on the "Resource Alert" side and post their favorite ideas from *The Mailbox®* magazine and other resources on the "Share Board" side.

Cheryl Althouse—Gr. 4,
Kralltown Elementary, East Berlin, PA

A Values Auction

Find out what your students value most with this thought-provoking activity. Tell each student that he has $4,000 to spend at an auction for values. Direct the student to write down how much he would be willing to pay for each value listed below. Then compare student bids for every item and award that value to the highest bidder. Follow up the activity by having each student write his reflections in a journal. *(Values: freedom, high-school education, college education, marriage, family, religious freedom, a good-paying job, lots of friends, one good friend, respect for parents, happiness, being left alone, fancy car, having everything I want, service to others.)*

Diane Ptak, Albany, NY

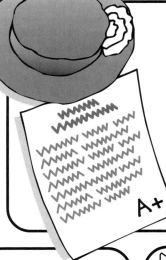

Hats Off!

Tip your hat to great student work with this attractive bulletin board. Have each student contribute her favorite hat to display on a board titled "Hats Off To Great Work!" Post samples of a few students' work next to their hats for about a week. Then return the hats to their owners and refresh the display with a new group of work and hats.

Jennifer Bruce—Gr. 5
East Sparta Elementary, Canton, OH

Self-Esteem Mural

Shower your students in compliments and boost their self-esteem! Assign each student a two-week period to be featured on a classroom bulletin board. Cover the board and label it with the name of the featured student. Keep a supply of markers nearby and invite classmates to visit the board to add as many compliments about the featured student as they choose. Each child in your classroom is guaranteed to feel special!

Judy Foley—Gr. 4, Howe-Manning School, Middleton, MA

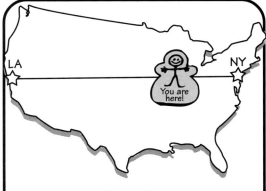

Walkers' Club

Ensure physical exercise for your students by starting a Walkers' Club. Measure a distance around the school for students to walk during recess. Then have your club calculate the distance to a chosen city on a map and set a club goal to walk that same distance around the school. Create a display in the classroom to chart your students' daily or weekly progress. Once your club reaches its goal, reward it with a special treat.

Patricia E. Dancho—Gr. 6
Apollo-Ridge Middle School
Spring Church, PA

In The News

Expand your students' study of science and social studies beyond the classroom walls. Award extra-credit points to students who bring in newspaper or magazine articles that relate to your current units of study. Have each student summarize his article for the class, then post it on a bulletin board titled "In The News." This simple idea helps students see that what they learn in the classroom is also part of the world outside our school.

Debra Garrett—Gr. 4
El Dorado Springs R-2 Elementary
El Dorado Springs, MO

New Medicine Found In Rain Forest Plant

Holiday Doormats

Searching for an inexpensive gift your students can make this holiday season? Visit your local carpet store and ask the manager for discontinued carpet samples. Next make an assortment of seasonal stencils from construction paper. Give each student her own carpet sample; then have her use the holiday stencils and stencil paints to create a one-of-a-kind holiday doormat. Have each student wrap her doormat in seasonal wrapping paper and give it to her parents as a holiday gift.

Shari Medley—Gr. 5
Lakeshore Elementary
Fond du Lac, WI

Popcorn Tins

Looking for something to do with all those decorative popcorn tins left over from the holidays? Use an empty tin to create a supply kit to use during roadside emergencies. Fill the tin with a flashlight, a first-aid kit, a warm blanket, flares, and other emergency gear. Store the tin in your car for emergencies. What an easy way to recycle *and* ensure peace of mind as you travel the winter highways!

Nancy S. Kaczrowski
Luverne, MN

A Grand Entrance

Keep your visitors feeling warm and toasty with this creative door-decorating idea. Cover the door with white bulletin-board paper. Measure the area around the top and sides of the door; then cut strips of white paper to make a fireplace-like frame for the door. Lay the strips flat on a table. Cut two 2 1/2" x 4" rectangles from a sponge. Dip one sponge in red paint and one in black; then make impressions on the strips. Once the strips have dried, tape them around the edges of the door. Add a mantle cut from brown paper; then decorate the fireplace with stockings.

Valerie Ford and Jenell Powell
Tyler Independent School District
Tyler, TX

Paper-Plate Globes

Familiarize your students with the world's continents and oceans with a lesson that's out of this world! Give each student two paper plates and circular outline maps of the Western and Eastern Hemispheres. Have each student glue one map to the bottom of each plate. Direct the student to then color the continents green and the remaining space blue. Have the student put the plates together, matching the Bering Strait/Antarctica areas, and staple them. Punch a hole at the top of each globe and hang it from the ceiling using yarn.

Karen Bellis—Gr. 4
Morgan County R–1
Stover, MO

Great Gift Suggestions

Lend a helping hand to parents and students who are searching for the perfect holiday gift to give a teacher. Have your school advisory council or P.T.A. send a letter to parents offering practical teacher-gift suggestions. List items such as stickers, sticky notes, markers, glue sticks, and other frequently used classroom materials. These gift suggestions make shopping for the teacher much easier and less stressful during the busy holiday season.

John Hagan, Jr.
Grafton Middle School
Grafton, MA

Christmas Catalog Computation

This creative idea adds up to a great consumer-math lesson. Design several denominations of money; then duplicate copies of each bill. Combine different combinations of the bills to make a bundle for each student. Randomly distribute one bundle of money and a Christmas catalog to each child. Direct the student to use the catalog's order form to order items for each of his family members. Remind the student that he cannot spend more money than he has been given. Students will have a great time spending their imaginary fortunes while practicing basic computation skills.

Rusty Fischer—Gr. 6
Cocoa Beach, FL

A "Piece-ful" Holiday Art Project

Piece together a great art project with this activity involving puzzle pieces. Spray-paint large puzzle pieces brown; then provide each student with any three pieces. Have the student glue the puzzle pieces together to make a reindeer, using two puzzle pieces as antlers and one as a face. Give each student two small wiggle eyes and a red pom-pom nose to attach to the face. Then glue a string or ribbon onto the reindeer to use for hanging it on a Christmas tree.

Sonya Franklin, Springville Elementary
Springville, AL

Reach For The Stars

Keep up with current events using this star-studded activity! Have each student bring in a newspaper article detailing a recent news event. Provide each student with a copy of the star pattern shown. Direct the student to complete each section of the star using information from her news article. Then have the student summarize the news-making event in a paragraph with the help of her star organizer. Display the completed stars and paragraphs on a bulletin board titled "Star-Studded Current Events."

Who? What? How? Why? When? Main Idea Where?

Jane Cooney—Gr. 5
Guion Creek Elementary
Indianapolis, IN

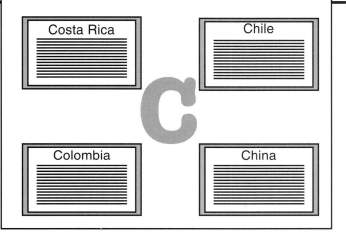

Costa Rica
Chile
C
Colombia
China

Christmas Around The World

This eye-catching wall display and research project makes a great addition to your holiday lesson plans. Write the letters from *Christmas* on nine 11" x 14" construction-paper sheets, writing one letter on each sheet. Then divide your class into eight groups (since the letter *s* appears twice). Assign one letter to each group; then direct the group to research the holiday customs of as many countries as possible that begin with its assigned letter. Have the group find out how each country celebrates the holidays and record that information on an index card. Mount each index card on colorful paper and display it around the letter to which it corresponds.

Pat Thames, Ivor, VA

Christmas-Card Quilt

Make a quilt with a Christmas theme by cutting the fronts from an assortment of Christmas cards (use either only ones with horizontal designs or only ones with vertical designs). Punch a hole in each of the four corners of each card.  Thread four-inch lengths of green or red yarn through the punched holes; then tie the yarn into bows to connect the greeting cards in a quilt formation. Hang the Christmas-card quilt on the wall as a festive holiday decoration.

Andrea Troisi—Librarian
LaSalle Middle School
Niagara Falls, NY

Crystal-Clear Storage

Avoid spending your valuable teaching time searching for frequently used supplies with the help of this practical suggestion. Store all of your small supplies—such as tape, scissors, and markers—in clear, plastic shoeboxes. Stack the boxes on top of one another in a convenient location in your classroom. How's that for an easy way to save time and stay organized?

Sharon Abell
Mineral Springs Middle School
Winston-Salem, NC

Covering All Bases

Keep all your bases covered the next time your class makes salt-relief maps. Before your map-making project, locate the person in charge of stocking your school's soda machine. Request that the cardboard soda trays used to ship soda be saved for you to use as map bases. Then have each student use one of the sturdy trays as a base for his salt-relief map. What a great way to keep dough from getting all over your room!

Susan Sandman—Gr. 5
Parkview Middle School
Creve Coeur, IL

293

Spelling In A Flash

Involve all your students in your next spelling lesson with this flashy idea. Write the letters of the alphabet on 26 index cards; then hand out one or more cards per student. Call out one word from the spelling list; then have each student holding a letter that is used in the word's spelling stand up. Direct the standing students to work together to call out in the correct order the letters that spell the word. Have a student who incorrectly calls out a letter or does not say his letter at the appropriate time write the word on his paper. Direct students to exchange cards frequently so that everyone has an equal opportunity to participate.

Chava Shapiro, Beth Rochel School, Monsey, NY

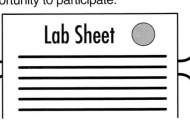

Lab Sheet

Originals Alert

Keep your original reproducibles from disappearing with this simple tip. Using a highlighter, draw a dot in the top right corner of all your original reproducibles. The colored dot on the paper is an easy way to keep from handing out your original.

Beverly Langland—Gr. 5
Trinity Christian Academy
Jacksonville, FL

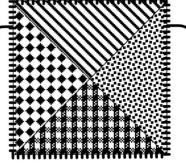

Fractions In Action

Sew up your next lesson on fractions with the help of patchwork quilt patterns. Begin by finding an example of a patchwork quilt in a reference book, or bring in an actual quilt. Have your students look at the quilt and isolate the patchwork squares to discuss halves, fourths, and equivalent fractions. Then provide each student with a 6" x 6" paper square and direct him to design his own quilt square using a fractional design. Now that's a hands-on fraction lesson students will cozy up to!

Sue Reed—Gr. 4
Ebenezer Elementary
Lebanon, PA

Let It Snow!

What better way to motivate children during the winter months than to have a snowball fight?! Cover a door with light blue bulletin-board paper. Post on the display a list of ways to earn snowballs (classroom rules work well). Decorate the door with two characters engaged in a snowball fight. Select one character to represent the class and the other to represent you. Each time you observe the class following a rule, attach a snowball—a white paper doily—by the class's character. If the class breaks a rule, attach a snowball by your character. At the end of the day, count the snowballs to see who has the most. Award that group a win for the day. When the class has earned five wins, give students an incentive, such as extra recess or a night with no homework. What a great way to motivate your class!

Connie Halder—Gr. 4, Christ the King School
Mt. Carmel, IA

Calling Cards

Increase student involvement in classroom discussions with this easy-to-do idea. Write the name of each of your students on a separate 3" x 5" index card. Shuffle the cards before each lesson; then, each time you need a student response, pull a card from the stack and read the name written on it. Return the card to the stack once the student responds. In addition to saving time, the cards offer a great way to ensure that you don't call on the same student over and over again.

Peggy Jo Rose—Gr. 4
Pine Lane Intermediate
Parker, CO

Step Into Learning With Style

If you're looking for a fun way to motivate students, this activity is a "shoe-in"! Have each student bring in an old pair of shoes that he no longer wears. Provide scrap materials and craft supplies; then direct the student to create an object, an animal, or a unique being from the shoes. Once your students have finished designing their shoes, have them complete the following shoe-related activities:

- Write a descriptive paragraph describing your shoes.
- Write a narrative paragraph describing a day in the life of your shoes.
- Create a line or bar graph based on the attributes of the shoes.

As a culminating activity, have your students parade around other classrooms and share their shoe stories!

Linda Cowell—Gr. 4
Kate Bond Elementary
Memphis, TN

Snowball Fight

class

- We will fight every day for snowballs. The one with the most wins that day!
- Miss Halder <u>decides</u>, gives, and takes snowballs.
  - The class can get snowballs by:
  - Miss Halder can get snowballs by:

Every 5 class wins equals a big prize!

Miss Halder

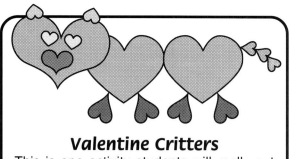

Valentine Critters

This is one activity students will really put their hearts into! Have each child cut out an assortment of hearts from construction paper. Have him glue the hearts on white paper to create a creature. Then have him write a story about his creature, answering questions like these: "Where does the creature live? What does it eat? What do you like best about it?" Post the critters and stories on a Valentine's Day bulletin board.

Sara Floyd
Lomax Junior High, La Porte, TX

Valentine Special Delivery

Make Valentine's Day a special treat for one lucky class this February! Get a class list from a primary teacher in your school. Assign each student in your class one child from the list. Then have the student make a valentine mailbox for the child he selected. Have the student cut one end from a shoebox, then paint the box. After the paint dries, have the student add doilies and construction-paper hearts to the box; then have him attach a flag (cut from red poster board) using a brad. The younger students will love these special deliveries from their older buddies!

Colleen Dabney—Grs. 6–7
Williamsburg Christian
    Academy
Williamsburg, VA

Shamrock Shenanigans

Need a fun activity to get students excited about St. Patrick's Day? Have each child trace a shamrock pattern several times onto construction paper so the tracings do not overlap. Then have the student fill in each shamrock outline with a different pattern. Mount the completed design on construction paper. Try the same activity on Mother's Day by substituting hearts or flower shapes for the shamrocks.

Lori Levings
Cardington, OH

Mental Math Relay

Help your students develop mental math skills with this fun game. Divide your class into Team A and Team B. Have each team stand in a line. Give the first player on Team A a problem to mentally solve. If he is able to give the correct answer in less than 30 seconds, award his team one point, and have him go to the end of his team's line. If he can't give the correct answer, have him go to the end of his line; then ask the first player on Team B. Continue alternating between teams until someone gets the correct answer. Then give a problem to the player at the front of Team B's line. Continue play until each child has had a chance to solve a problem.

Christine Juozitis—Gr. 4
Thomas Jefferson School
Binghamton, NY

Car Rental Maps

When my sister worked for a car rental agency, I noticed that she gave directions to customers on maps that showed our local area on one side and a state map on the other side. I asked the agency to donate 30 maps for my class, which I laminated. These maps are great for individual and group work on map skills.

Cynthia D. Davis
Bonaire Middle School, Warner Robins, GA

The Daily Scoop

Keep students' parents in the know with this newsworthy idea. Every morning give each student a copy of a "Daily Scoop" form like the one shown. Throughout the day have the student write five of the most exciting activities, projects, or special events in which she participated on the form. Have the student take the "Daily Scoop" home for her parents to read and sign. Ensure that the forms get returned on a regular basis by including them as part of your regular homework routine.

Christopher J. Stupak—Gr. 4
Litchfield Intermediate School
Litchfield, CT

The Daily Scoop
Litchfield Intermediate School
Mr. Stupak's Fourth-Grade Class
Date_____
Student _____
Today's Top Five:
1 _____
2 _____
3 _____
4 _____
5 _____
Parent signature _____

Balloon Behavior Bonuses

Inflate your students' self-esteem while promoting excellent behavior with this high-flyin' idea! Cut out a supply of balloons from construction paper. When a student has exhibited excellent behavior for the week, decorate the balloon with eyes, a nose, and the student's name as shown. Hang the balloon from the ceiling outside your room or on a bulletin board to draw attention to the great behavior.

Sandra H. Dunaway
Stewart County Elementary
Lumpkin, GA

Conflicting Accounts

Use this unforgettable activity to help your students see why historical accounts often vary from one source to another. Divide your class into three groups. Take one group aside. Assign a different action—such as marching, clapping, or spinning—for each group member to act out on your cue. Next have the group go to the front of the room. Give the cue, allowing the students to act out their movements for five seconds before stopping. Ask members of the remaining two groups to describe exactly what they saw. Point out that each account—just like those of historians—is slightly different since no one person could see all of the actions in such a short period of time.

Jennifer Bruce—Gr. 5, East Sparta Elementary, Canton, OH

Self-Checking Solution

After each student selects his answers on a multiple-choice or true/false assignment, have him color over his selections with a pink, a yellow, or an orange crayon. Then review the correct answers and have each student check his paper. With this easy suggestion, you won't have to worry about students being tempted to change incorrect answers (since they won't be able to erase over waxy crayon).

Wendy New—Gr. 5
Fairfield South Elementary
Cincinnati, OH

A Pocketful Of Organization

Are you constantly searching for the small pieces that accompany bulletin-board sets? Attach a Press-On Pocket to the back of the largest character in each set. Store the small pieces for the set in the pocket along with the letters for the bulletin-board caption. The next time you get ready to put up that bulletin board, all the pieces you need will be right at your fingertips!

Teena Andersen—Grs. K–6
Wayne County District 25
Pender, NE

A Wise Guide

This is one idea your students are sure to give a hoot about! Make a large cutout of an owl and post it on a bulletin board. Then display the following list and provide each student with his own copy.

Sandra Tatum—Gr. 6
Gatesville Intermediate School
Gatesville, TX

Wise Owl School Survival Skills
Write down assignments.
Ignore distractions.
Set a specific time to study.
Establish a regular place to study.

Organize your materials and time.
When you need help, ask someone.
Listen carefully at all times.

News Across The Country

Explore geography and the latest news from coast to coast! Post a U.S. map in a center. On each of 50 cards, write the name of a different state. Label one folder "Team 1" and another "Team 2." Divide your class into two teams, assigning one team the wall space to the map's left and the other team the space to the right. During free time encourage each student to look through newspapers to find an article mentioning any state. Have the student cut out the article and write a short summary of it to place in his team's folder. Then have him mount the article and the state's card on his team's side of the map, connecting them to the state on the map with yarn. Once an article has been found for each state, total the articles found by each team to determine the winning group.

Teena Andersen—Grs. K–6

Too Much To Teach?

When my three fellow teachers and I realized we wouldn't be able to cover the rest of the science topics for the year, we came up with a unique plan. First we had our students vote as a group on their two favorite topics from the four remaining units. Each teacher then taught one of the two topics in depth to two different groups. Our students loved being able to explore the topics that interested them most.

Phyllis Ellett—Grs. 3–4 Multiage
Earl Hanson Elementary
Rock Island, IL

The ABC Game

When my students have a few minutes to spare, we play the ABC Game. First I select a topic. Then I ask one child to name something related to the topic that begins with the letter *A*. The next student must respond with a related word that begins with *B,* and so on until everyone has had a turn. If you have more students than letters in the alphabet, begin again with *A*. Or reverse and go backwards through the alphabet.

Theresa Roh Hickey—Gr. 5
Corpus Christi Elementary
Mobile, AL

Easy Eyedroppers

Need some quick, inexpensive eyedroppers for science experiments? Cut plastic straws in half. Have each child put a straw half into the liquid, place her finger over the top end, and hold it in place. Then have the student transfer the liquid droplets to the work surface or slide.

Melissa McKown—Gr. 5
Ringgold Elementary
Ringgold, GA

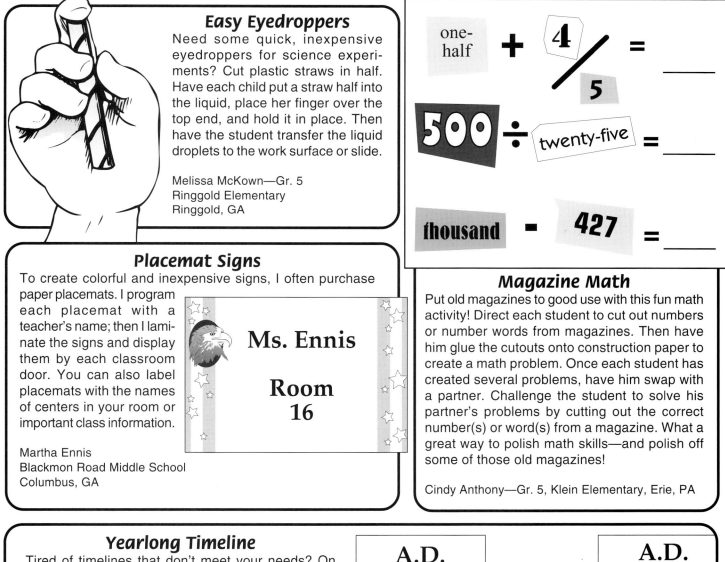

one-half $+$ $\dfrac{4}{5}$ $=$ _____

$500 \div$ twenty-five $=$ _____

thousand $-$ 427 $=$ _____

Placemat Signs

To create colorful and inexpensive signs, I often purchase paper placemats. I program each placemat with a teacher's name; then I laminate the signs and display them by each classroom door. You can also label placemats with the names of centers in your room or important class information.

Martha Ennis
Blackmon Road Middle School
Columbus, GA

Ms. Ennis

Room 16

Magazine Math

Put old magazines to good use with this fun math activity! Direct each student to cut out numbers or number words from magazines. Then have him glue the cutouts onto construction paper to create a math problem. Once each student has created several problems, have him swap with a partner. Challenge the student to solve his partner's problems by cutting out the correct number(s) or word(s) from a magazine. What a great way to polish math skills—and polish off some of those old magazines!

Cindy Anthony—Gr. 5, Klein Elementary, Erie, PA

Yearlong Timeline

Tired of timelines that don't meet your needs? On sturdy cards make a century marker for each year covered in your curriculum (for example, A.D. 1000, A.D. 1100, etc.). Mount the markers in order around your classroom walls. Underneath the markers hang a clothesline. As you study different historical periods, clip cards labeled with specific events and their dates to the clothesline underneath the appropriate markers.

Laura Eberle—Gr. 5, Coronado Village Elementary, Universal City, TX

A.D. 1400

A.D. 1500

Aztec Civilization

Columbus's 1st Voyage

Fishing For Extra Credit

Are your students fishing around for extra-credit points to boost their grades? Collect gift bags decorated with fish. Place several activity cards in each bag. Staple the bags to a bulletin board titled "Fishing For Extra Credit?" When a student finishes classwork early, have him fish an activity card out of a bag and complete the assignment for extra-credit points.

Brandi Lampl—Gr. 4
W. A. Fountain Elementary
Forest Park, GA

Find out how many people currently live in New York City.

Stir-Stick Organizers

Use this teacher-tested idea to keep your classroom library organized. Buy paint stir sticks (one per student) from a local paint or hardware store. Write each student's name on a stick; then store the sticks in a decorative tin. When a student is looking for a book, have her place her stick on the shelf in the book's place while she browses through it. If she decides not to read the book, the student will know exactly where to reshelve it. If she chooses to read the book, have the student leave her stick in place until she finishes reading. No more lost or misshelved books!

Linda Riley—Gr. 5
Dodge Elementary
Grand Island, NE

Stacie

Sweet Treats For Neat Seats

I encourage my students to keep clean desks with the following idea. Periodically I hold an unannounced "clean desk check." Each student who passes the check earns a roll of Smarties® candies taped to an index card that reads, "It's smart to have a clean desk!" Or I attach a fun-size roll of LifeSavers® candies to a note that reads, "A clean desk can be a real lifesaver!" If you want to avoid sugar, try taping two pennies to a card labeled "A clean desk makes 'cents' to me!"

Eileen James—Grs. 3–4
St. Matthews Elementary
Louisville, KY

It's smart to have a clean desk!

The Name Game

To be fair when calling on students to read aloud, decorate a large, empty peanut-butter jar with stickers. Write "Name Game" on the front of the jar. Have each student write his name on a slip of paper. On a few extra slips, write "Choose a friend!", "Read again!", or "Teacher's turn." Place all the slips in the jar. When you need to choose someone to read aloud, have a student draw a slip from the Name Game jar. Who's next?

Ann Scheiblin—Gr. 6
Oak View Elementary
Bloomfield, NJ

Kevin Joah Scott Teacher's turn.

NAME GAME

Read again!

Word-Problem Review

Encourage students to increase their word-problem skills with this simple math activity. Throughout the year duplicate an extra copy of each word-problem sheet you assign. After students complete a page, cut apart the problems on the extra sheet and tape each to an index card. Write the answer on the back of each card. Allow students to use the cards all year long to review previously presented material.

Julie Eick Granchelli—Gr. 4, Towne Elementary, Medina, NY

Border Order

Tired of forgetting which bulletin-board borders you have? Cut a six-inch section off each border and tape it to the inside of a cabinet door in your classroom. When it's time to change bulletin boards, you'll have a quick-and-easy way of selecting just the right border!

Mary Harmon—Gr. 4, Heusner Elementary, Salina, KS

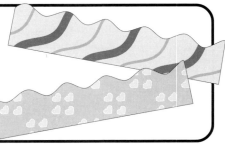

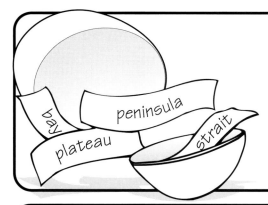

Crack A Word

One of my favorite spring activities is our annual Easter egg hunt. I buy plastic eggs that are readily available during this season. Inside each egg I place a slip of paper labeled with a vocabulary word. I hide the eggs outside; then I send students on a search for the eggs. When all the eggs have been found, we return to class. Each student reads and defines the words hidden inside her eggs. For each correct definition, a student wins a piece of Easter candy.

Dawn Partin, Lugoff Elgin Middle School, Lugoff, SC

Classroom Museum

Don't throw out the old study carrel that no one seems to want—turn it into a classroom museum instead! Select a student each week to display items on the carrel that tell about himself and are special to him. Once everyone has had a turn to prepare an individual display, select a museum committee to be responsible for setting up special-topic exhibits. What a great way to recycle that study carrel and learn about one another at the same time!

Phyllis Ellett—Grs. 3–4 Multiage
Earl Hanson Elementary
Rock Island, IL

It's In The Mail!

Make keeping in touch with parents a little easier this year! Have parents, grandparents, and/or other caregivers send large, pre-addressed and stamped envelopes to school. Let each student put her favorite papers or artwork in her envelope; then mail the envelopes. It's an easy way to make sure a great paper actually makes it home in one piece!

Melinda Salisbury—Grs. 4–6
Baldwin North Intermediate
Quincy, IL

Mr. and Mrs. Ed Blackledge
3412 Forrestgate Court
Butler, PA 15701

Earth Eggs

Conclude your celebration of Earth Day with an "eggs-ellent" art activity! Provide each student with an egg. Help him carefully poke a dime-sized hole in the top narrow end of his egg and remove its contents. Have the student rinse and dry the eggshell, then use permanent markers to decorate it to resemble Earth. Finally direct the student to fill the egg two-thirds full of potting soil and sprinkle rye grass seeds on top. With a little water and sunlight, students' Earth eggs will grow full heads of grassy hair!

Holly Bowser—Gr. 6
Cork Elementary
Geneva, OH

Category Challenge

Challenge students to use their brain power with the following group game. Choose a category such as prefixes, occupations that end in *er,* or words that begin with *qu.* Divide the class into groups. Have each group brainstorm words that belong to the category within a time limit. When time is up, have a student stand and read her group's list of words. Instruct each of the other groups to look at its list and cross off any word listed by another team. The group with the most words at the end of the game is the winner.

Sandra Bartman
Waterloo, Ontario
Canada

Blooming Poetry

Brighten your room with a display that's abloom with student poetry! Have each student cut out a flower shape from loose-leaf paper and write a short poem about spring on it. Then have him color the flower with pastel colored pencils. Mount the poems on a bulletin board decorated with colorful construction-paper flowers. Add cut-out clouds and a sun for a cheerful finishing touch.

Jeannette Freeman—Resource, The First Lady Educational Program, San Juan, Puerto Rico

Springtime

Cookie States

Satisfy students' geography sweet tooth with this tasty lesson on cities and states. Mix up a basic oatmeal or sugar cookie recipe; then shape the dough to make an outline of your state on a large cookie sheet. Give each child an M&M's® candy piece and have her place it on the location of a city. Have her name the city and explain its specific location. After all the cities are located, bake the cookie. When it's done, discuss the map and enjoy your delicious state!

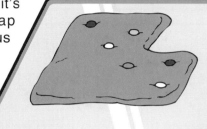

Cathy Ogg—Gr. 4
Happy Valley Elementary
Elizabethton, TN

Sing It Out!

Here's a review idea students will really tune in to! Review major concepts and vocabulary with your class before posting them on a chart or the chalkboard. Divide students into groups; then challenge them to set the information reviewed to music. Encourage groups to use familiar tunes such as "Old MacDonald Had A Farm" or "Yankee Doodle." Have groups write out their songs and perform them for the class. It's toe-tappin' fun that guarantees students won't forget the material they learned!

Patricia Twohey—Gr. 4
Old County Road School
Smithfield, RI

Spelling Relay

Review for a spelling test indoors or out with this fun game! Create two sets of alphabet cards, one written in blue marker and the other in red. Make duplicates and triplicates of high-frequency vowels and consonants. Divide students into two teams. Stand at a designated starting line 30–50 feet away from the two sets of cards; then line up the teams so that they are on your left and right. Announce a spelling word; then say, "Go." Have each team run to its stack of letters, select the needed ones, and hold them in the correct order. The first team to correctly spell the word wins a point.

Gloria Jean Stevens—Gr. 5, Frank Jewett School, West Buxton, ME

A Fantastic Framework

To introduce a study of the skeleton, have student pairs complete the following activity. Engage students in movements that require them to note how their limbs move differently. Next provide each student pair with a large piece of butcher paper. Have one student lie down on the paper; then have the other child trace around her partner. Direct the pair to cut out the outline and draw in the bones as they think they are placed. At the conclusion of your study, have each pair turn over its paper body and draw the bones in their actual locations. Have students compare their original drawings to the newer ones and label the bones. What a "bone-a-fide" way for students to bone up on bones!

Jan Drehmel—Gr. 4
Parkview Elementary
Chippewa Falls, WI

Give Parents A Hand!

Need a handy way to thank your room parents for their yearlong service? Purchase solid-colored canvas or cotton garden gloves. Using fabric paint, have the students decorate the gloves with designs or flowers. Add some seed packages or a small potted plant with a special thank-you note from the class. Your homeroom parents are sure to know how much you appreciate them!

Colleen Dabney—Grs. 6–7
Williamsburg Christian Academy
Williamsburg, VA

Design A Search

At the end of a unit of study, challenge each student to create a word search for his classmates. First have the student write clues that his peers should be able to answer based on the previous week's lesson. Then have him hide the answers on grid paper. When all students have completed their puzzles, have them switch papers for a second review—the solving!

Marsha Schmus—Gr. 4
Ypsilanti, MI

v	t	c	d	k	l	m
n	s	o	e	z	x	o
m	e	u	t	f	a	r
j	r	s	c	s	u	h
e	s	c	i	a	s	o
i	k	o	n	t	d	m
k	t	u	r	b	a	n
r	t	s	m	n	z	y

Clues

1. Common dish in Africa of coarse wheat grains served with a spicy stew
2. Small cap customary among many African men

Trash-Bag Smock

Tired of worrying about paint ruining your students' clothing? Try this simple idea. Give each student a large trash bag. Have her cut one hole in the top for her head and one hole on each side for her arms. Before beginning a painting (or another messy) activity, have the student slip the trash bag over her clothing. After the activity is completed, the bag can be folded and stored in the student's art box for use all year.

Stacey Pardue—Gr. 5
Coosa Valley Academy
Harpersville, AL

Hero And Heroine Awards

Searching for a novel way to honor your students' accomplishments? Look over your class list carefully, thinking about the heroes and heroines that were included in your studies this year. Do you have a "Renaissance Child" who reminds you of Thomas Jefferson? Or an artist whose flowers make you think of Georgia O'Keeffe? If you need help finding the perfect hero/heroine award for a student, consult Joy Hakim's *A History Of Us* (Oxford University Press, Inc.; 1992–95). Present the awards on the last day of school in a special ceremony including students and parents.

Merrill Watrous
Eugene, OR

Thanks For The Memories

Provide your students with a memorable keepsake from the school year with the following activity. Begin by having students brainstorm interview questions to ask each other about the past year (for example, "What was your favorite memory this year?" or "What was the most important thing you learned this year?"). Next have student pairs interview each other using the questions. Direct students to take notes during the interviews; then have each child write a one-page essay on his interviewee. Add a photograph of each child to the final copy of his page before duplicating a class supply. Use the pages and laminated covers to make a memory book for each child.

Carrie Hursh—Gr. 6, Whitewater Valley Elementary
Cleves, OH

"Tee-rrific" Times

Get ready for next year with this year's class! Provide each student with a T-shirt pattern. Have the student draw her favorite memories of the year on the paper shirt. At the start of the new school year, post the completed shirts on a bulletin board titled "We're Going To Have A 'Tee-rrific' Year!" What better way to welcome your new class in August!

Traci Baker—Gr. 4
Brassfield Elementary, Bixby, OK

Teacher Test

Discover how much students have learned about you by challenging them to a game of "How Well Do You Know Your Teacher?" Provide each student with a sheet including 20 questions about situations involving you (see the sample questions). Direct the student to respond to each item as she believes you would respond. Have students exchange papers and check them with you. Award free homework passes to the three students with the highest percentage of correct answers.

Dawn Partin
Lugoff Elgin Middle School
Lugoff, SC

1. Your teacher is thirsty. Which drink will she choose?
   A. water
   B. Mountain Dew®
   C. Coke®
   D. tea

2. What food item would your teacher order from a menu?
   A. beef
   B. bean sprouts
   C. peaches
   D. pizza

3. Your teacher has won a vacation. Where will she go?
   A. Bahamas
   B. Las Vegas
   C. Disney World®
   D. Switzerland

Dream Vacation

Send students on a sensational summer vacation with this fun cross-curricular research activity! Have each student select a state he would like to visit. Instruct him to research and find at least five attractions in the state, such as theme parks, historical sites, museums, or parks. To enhance map skills, have the student plot the route from his home to his vacation attractions. Include math skills by having the child calculate travel time and the cost of fuel. Have the student present his information in the form of a poster, map, or booklet.

Karen Martino
Oxford, OH

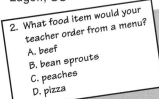

Charming Chimes

Charm students into giving you their undivided attention with this idea. Hang wind chimes from the ceiling. Instead of raising your hand, clapping, or turning off the lights, gently move the chimes. What a soothing way to remind students, "I need you!"

Sue Mechura—Gr. 4
Ebenezer Elementary
Lebanon, PA

Beauty Is...

A camera and one roll of film is all you need for a writing lesson that's a real beauty! Ask students to discuss the question, "What is beauty?" Then walk with students around your school and school grounds to observe. Have each student select one item or scene that he finds beautiful; then have him photograph it. After the film is developed, have each child write a paragraph explaining why he thinks the item he photographed is beautiful. Display the photos and paragraphs with the title "In The Eye Of The Beholder."

Julia Alarie—Gr. 6
Essex Middle School
Essex, VT

Awards Breakfast

Complete the year on a tasty note with an end-of-the-year awards breakfast. Reserve your school cafeteria or another meeting place before the start of a selected school day. Contact a few parents to provide coffee, juice, doughnuts, and paper goods. Award special student awards or plan the breakfast to coincide with the school's award program. The breakfast takes little preparation and provides a great ending to a successful year!

Karen Martino
Oxford, OH

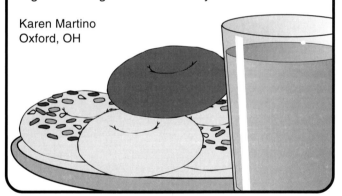

Watch This Sign

An index card and a drinking straw can make mundane math practice a fun game! Provide each student with one card and a straw. Have the student fold the card in half, then write "Yes" on one side and "No" on the other side. Next have the student staple the folded card onto the straw. Write a review problem on the chalkboard, including a correct or an incorrect answer. Have each student work the problem and hold up the appropriate side of her sign. This is a great way to encourage students to check problems carefully!

Julie Eick Granchelli—Gr. 4
Towne Elementary
Medina, NY

Cheap Chart Stand

Transform an inexpensive clothing rack into a chart stand for your classroom. Purchase a clothing rack from a local discount store's housewares department. Add two metal shower-curtain rings for the hangers. Simply punch two holes in the top of each item you want to hang on the stand. What an easy way to display charts and posters!

Susan Lynnette Perkins
Halifax County Middle School
South Boston, VA

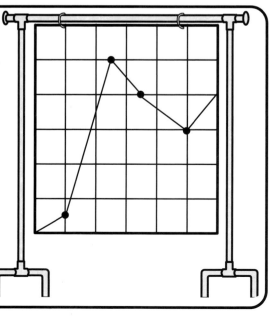

A Year In Review

Throughout the year I use large sheets of chart paper to record class discussions. During the last week of school, I take down all of my bulletin boards and hang the charts from the year's studies. Then the students and I discuss all of the wonderful things they learned during the year. On the last day of school, I take the charts down, roll them up, and award them to students as prizes.

Shari Medley—Gr. 5
Lakeshore Elementary
Fond du Lac, WI

English Made Easy

English Made Easy

Activities For Teaching Correct Word Usage

Preposterous Pictures

Give your students a lesson in word usage while offering them the chance to be a bit silly! Share examples of commonly misused word pairs such as *ant/aunt*, *bare/bear*, and *road/rode*. Then have students brainstorm other misused word pairs while you record their responses on a sheet of chart paper. Next give each student an 8 1/2" x 11" sheet of white paper and assign him a word pair from the list. Challenge the student to write a silly sentence and draw a silly picture that illustrates the correct use of the words. (See the example.) Post the captioned pictures for all to enjoy.

The bare bear was quite embarrassed.

Bingo Blast

dear	night	further	sit
hare	deer	close	farther
heard	reign	clothes	scene
knight	weak	set	you're

Everybody wants to use the *right* words—right? Have students list commonly misused word pairs on the board and identify the correct use of each word. Then instruct each student to write a sample sentence for one of the words on a strip of paper. Place the strips in a container. Next give each student a 16-square bingo sheet and bingo markers. Direct the student to write one word from the list on each square of his card. (If desired, have the student choose 15 words, then fill in a free space.)

To play, pull a strip from the container and read its sentence. If the student has the correct word on his bingo sheet, have him cover the word with a bingo marker. End the game when someone covers four vertical, horizontal, or diagonal squares in a row and calls, "Bingo"; then check the child's answers and start a new game. Follow up the activity by having each student complete a copy of page 305.

Getting The Point

Help students get the point about word usage with the following fun activity. Supply a center with 20 or more playing cards, a dictionary, paper, and a pencil. On each of the playing cards, write a commonly misused word. Next pair students and invite one pair to the center at a time. To play the game, direct one student to draw a card, turn it faceup on the table, and use the word correctly in an original sentence. If the partner agrees that the word was used correctly, the player earns the point value identified on the card. (Determine a point value for jacks, queens, kings, and aces prior to the game.) At the end of the game, have each student add up his points. The student with the most points wins.

Grammar Goofs

Gwen Gogetter has dreams of becoming a gossip columnist. But poor Gwen—she just doesn't know how to use the right words. If she doesn't get help, her gossip-guzzling dreams will be gone with the wind!

You can help Gwen by reading her latest letter to her editor. First circle the 30 words (not names) that she uses incorrectly; then write the correct words on the pencils below. Use a dictionary if you need help. Gwen will be forever grateful for your guidance!

Deer Editor,

Wood you believe that eye, Gwendolyn Gogetter, was invited to the biggest social event of the season? I new that knight I'd have a tail to tell, for the gathering was a see of famous faces! Everybody who is anybody was their—singer Winessa Villiams and movie star Prad Bitt, to name a few. Not even the reign that was pouring down outside could keep these people away (accept for T. J. Thomas—he fell and acquired a reel bad brake in his arm). Four more than an our I talked, ate, and danced with the stars; not for a moment was I board!

Let me tell you about some of the more interesting sites I saw. Rennis Dodman's hare was died blew (a miner offense). Snory Telling shouldn't have been aloud out of the house wearing those close (a capitol offense). But Wobin Rilliams should have one first prize—he past a peace of meet that fell write onto Rinona Wyder's lap. My, what a seen that was!

Now that it's all over, I must say I had a lovely evening. And buy the way, I got lots of autographs!

Sincerely,
Gwen Gogetter

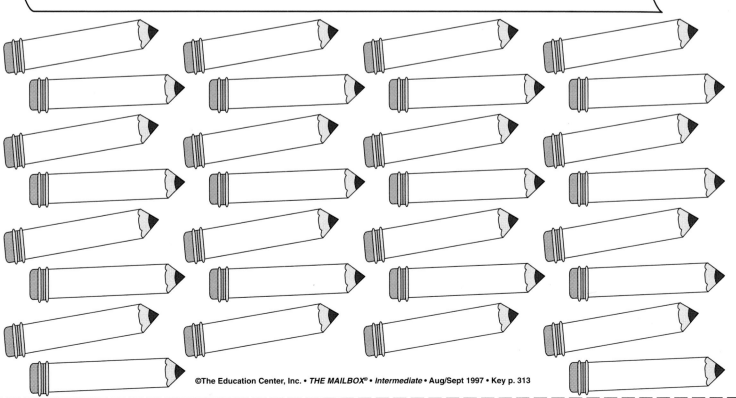

Note To The Teacher: Use with "Bingo Blast" on page 304.

305

English Made Easy

Activities For Teaching Singular And Plural Nouns

Plural Nouns Spelling Bee

Plurals practice is the name of the game with this variation on a spelling bee! Write the rules for forming plural nouns, shown on page 307, on a sheet of chart paper. Label one index card for every student in your class with a noun from the list at the right. Next divide your students into two teams. Direct the teams to stand on opposite sides of the classroom. Shuffle the cards; then have the first student from Team 1 pick a card. Direct the student to read aloud the noun on the card, then spell its plural form. If the student spells the plural correctly, have him keep the card. If not, have him pass the card to the first player on Team 2, who then tries to spell the noun's plural. Direct students to pass the card between each team's players until the plural is spelled correctly. Continue to play until all the cards have been used. Reward the team that has the most cards with bonus points or a special class privilege.

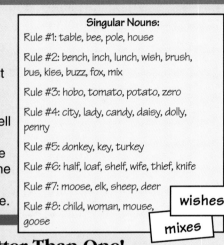

Singular Nouns:

Rule #1: table, bee, pole, house

Rule #2: bench, inch, lunch, wish, brush, bus, kiss, buzz, fox, mix

Rule #3: hobo, tomato, potato, zero

Rule #4: city, lady, candy, daisy, dolly, penny

Rule #5: donkey, key, turkey

Rule #6: half, loaf, shelf, wife, thief, knife

Rule #7: moose, elk, sheep, deer

Rule #8: child, woman, mouse, goose

wishes

mixes

Two Scoops Are Better Than One!

cereals
vitamins
scoops
prizes
flakes

Serve up a lesson on plurals using one of your students' favorite foods—breakfast cereal! Gather six different cereal boxes. Use a bright-colored marker to highlight five singular nouns on each box; then place each box at a different station in the classroom. On a sheet of chart paper, make an answer key that includes the name of each cereal, its five nouns, and the plural of each noun. Also cut 30 paper strips for each of six groups, using a different-colored paper for each group.

Next divide students into six groups. Give each group its 30 strips and direct it to a different station. Instruct the group to write the plural form of each highlighted noun on a different strip, then place the strips in the cereal box. After two minutes have each group rotate to the next station and repeat the process. When all students have been to every station, send one member from each group to a different box; then have that student pull his group's slips from the box. Display the answer-key chart. Direct each student to check his group's answers, putting the incorrectly marked slips back in the box. Tally each group's correctly marked slips; then reward each group that spelled at least 90 percent of the plurals correctly with a special treat.

Picturing Plurals

Your students will identify plural nouns in a snap with this hands-on activity! Cut an eight-foot sheet of bulletin-board paper into one-foot sections. Draw a picture frame around the inside edges of each section as shown. Next divide the class into eight groups. Assign each group a different plurals rule (see page 307). Provide each group with one of the framed sections, a magazine, a newspaper, scissors, glue, and colorful markers. Direct each group to write its rule at the top of its frame, then search the magazine and newspaper for pictures and words that fit the rule (see the examples). Instruct the group to glue its pictures and words inside the frame, writing the plural form of each noun below its picture. Then have the group use its markers to decorate the frame. Finally have each group share its project. Display the pictured plurals around the classroom for students to use as references.

If a noun ends with a consonant before a y, change the y to an i and add es.

puppies

families

libraries bunnies

companies

babies

Packaged Plurals

Preston Peabody is positively puzzled! He knows that a plural noun names more than one person, place, or thing. But sometimes he gets the rules mixed up. One of the nouns he placed in each gift box below does not fit the same rule as the others.

Directions: Use the information on the gift tag to identify the plurals rule for the nouns listed on each box. First write the rule number on the ribbon at the top of each box. Then write the plural form of each noun on the blank provided. Finally circle the noun that does not fit the rule in each box.

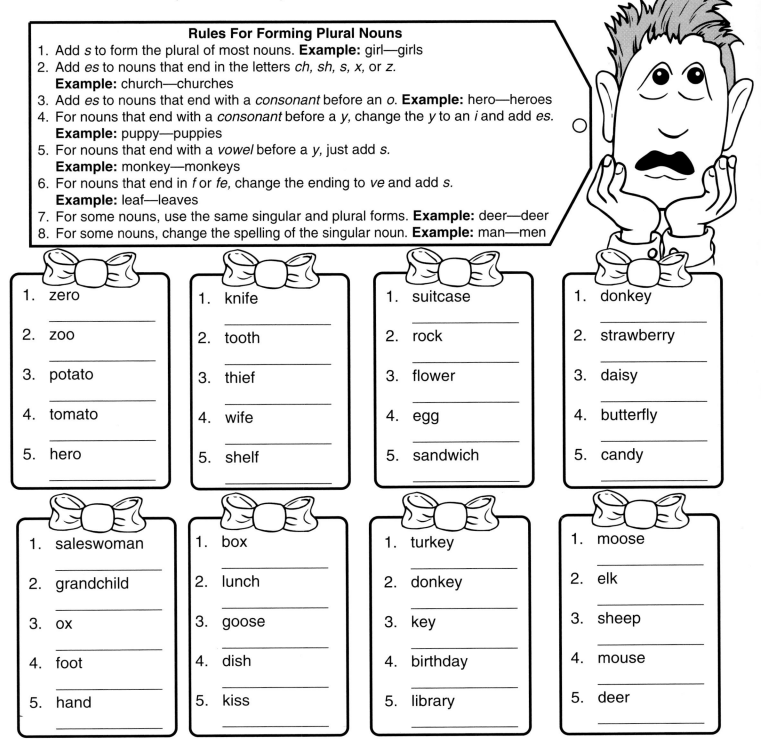

Rules For Forming Plural Nouns
1. Add *s* to form the plural of most nouns. **Example:** girl—girls
2. Add *es* to nouns that end in the letters *ch, sh, s, x,* or *z.*
   Example: church—churches
3. Add *es* to nouns that end with a *consonant* before an *o.* **Example:** hero—heroes
4. For nouns that end with a *consonant* before a *y,* change the *y* to an *i* and add *es.*
   Example: puppy—puppies
5. For nouns that end with a *vowel* before a *y,* just add *s.*
   Example: monkey—monkeys
6. For nouns that end in *f* or *fe,* change the ending to *ve* and add *s.*
   Example: leaf—leaves
7. For some nouns, use the same singular and plural forms. **Example:** deer—deer
8. For some nouns, change the spelling of the singular noun. **Example:** man—men

Box 1:
1. zero
2. zoo
3. potato
4. tomato
5. hero

Box 2:
1. knife
2. tooth
3. thief
4. wife
5. shelf

Box 3:
1. suitcase
2. rock
3. flower
4. egg
5. sandwich

Box 4:
1. donkey
2. strawberry
3. daisy
4. butterfly
5. candy

Box 5:
1. saleswoman
2. grandchild
3. ox
4. foot
5. hand

Box 6:
1. box
2. lunch
3. goose
4. dish
5. kiss

Box 7:
1. turkey
2. donkey
3. key
4. birthday
5. library

Box 8:
1. moose
2. elk
3. sheep
4. mouse
5. deer

Bonus Box: On the back of this sheet, write a silly sentence using at least three of the plural nouns listed above.

Page 110
1. 148; 158; 168; <u>178</u>; 188; 198; <u>208</u> *(add 10)*
2. 605; 705; 805; <u>905</u>; <u>1,005</u>; 1,105; 1,205 *(add 100)*
3. 6,734; 5,734; 4,734; <u>3,734</u>; <u>2,734</u>; 1,734; <u>734</u> *(subtract 1,000)*
4. 76,485; 81,485; 86,485; <u>91,485</u>; 96,485; <u>101,485</u>; 106,485 *(add 5,000)*
5. 18,000; <u>20,000</u>; <u>22,000</u>; 24,000; 26,000; 28,000; <u>30,000</u> *(add 2,000)*
6. 156; 166; 266; 276; 376; <u>386</u>; <u>486</u>; <u>496</u>; 596 *(add 10, add 100)*
7. 85; 185; 285; 385; 1,385; 2,385; 3,385; <u>13,385</u>; <u>23,385</u>; 33,385 *(add 100; add 100; add 100; add 1,000; add 1,000; add 1,000; add 10,000; add 10,000; add 10,000)*
8. 12,612; 12,617; 12,667; 13,167; <u>18,167</u>; 68,167 *(add 5; add 50; add 500; add 5,000; add 50,000)*
9. 1,487,329; 487,329; 387,329; 377,329; 376,329; <u>376,229</u>; <u>376,219</u> *(subtract 1,000,000; subtract 100,000; subtract 10,000; subtract 1,000; subtract 100; subtract 10)*
10. 512,479; 512,478; 512,468; 512,368; <u>511,368</u>; 501,368; <u>401,368</u> *(subtract 1; subtract 10; subtract 100; subtract 1,000; subtract 10,000; subtract 100,000)*
11. 614,375; 614,376; 614,386; 614,486; 615,486; <u>625,486</u>; <u>725,486</u> *(add 1; add 10; add 100; add 1,000; add 10,000; add 100,000)*

Bonus Challenge: 364,237; 364,240; 364,300; 365,000; <u>370,000</u>; 400,000 *(Each value is added to create 0 in the next placeholder: add 3; add 60; add 700; add 5,000; add 30,000.)*

Page 114
1. Since the three letters cannot be repeated, there are only **6** possible combinations:

    ABC, ACB   BAC, BCA   CAB, CBA

2. Since a letter can be repeated within a word, there are a total of **27** possible words. (Tell students that *a tree diagram* would be a good organizer for this problem.)

    AAA ABA ACA   BAA BBA BCA   CAA CBA CCA
    AAB ACB   BAB BBB BCB   CAB CBB CCB
    AAC ABC ACC   BAC BBC BCC   CAC CBC CCC

3. There are **24** different ways that the four cowpokes can line up:

    Dex-Lex-Rex-Tex   Lex-Dex-Rex-Tex   Rex-Dex-Lex-Tex   Tex-Dex-Lex-Rex
    Dex-Lex-Tex-Rex   Lex-Dex-Tex-Rex   Rex-Dex-Tex-Lex   Tex-Dex-Rex-Lex
    Dex-Rex-Lex-Tex   Lex-Rex-Dex-Tex   Rex-Lex-Dex-Tex   Tex-Lex-Dex-Rex
    Dex-Rex-Tex-Lex   Lex-Rex-Tex-Dex   Rex-Lex-Tex-Dex   Tex-Lex-Rex-Dex
    Dex-Tex-Lex-Rex   Lex-Tex-Dex-Rex   Rex-Tex-Dex-Lex   Tex-Rex-Dex-Lex
    Dex-Tex-Rex-Lex   Lex-Tex-Rex-Dex   Rex-Tex-Lex-Dex   Tex-Rex-Lex-Dex

Page 116
A. 1. 7 series
   2. 22 series
   3. New York (A*); 5 *(1949–53)*
   4. American League *(4 of the last 5)*
   5. 1954; 43 years ago *(in 1997)*
   6. 1977 and 1978 *(New York Yankees and Los Angeles Dodgers)*
   7. 5 teams *(Baltimore, Oakland, Cincinnati, New York, and Pittsburgh)*

B. 1. F; B *(Although the table begins with the year 1947, it shows that no series was played in 1994.)*
   2. DK *(The table only includes the years since 1947.)*
   3. T; B
   4. DK
   5. T; T *(1951, for example. In addition, since Brooklyn is a borough of New York City, each series featuring the New York Yankees and Brooklyn Dodgers would have been played in the same city. The Brooklyn Dodgers moved to Los Angeles in 1958.)*
   6. DK
   7. T; T *(The New York Yankees of the American League have played in 20 World Series since 1947.)*
   8. DK *(Although the chart does not show it, the World Series of 1907, 1912, and 1922 each included a tie game that was called because of darkness.)*

Bonus Box answer:
   Jackie Robinson was the first black person to play modern major-league baseball. He joined the Brooklyn Dodgers in 1947 and was named Rookie of the Year. Brooklyn played in the World Series in 1947, as well as five more times during Robinson's ten-year professional career with the team. The Dodgers won the World Series in 1955.
   The World Series of 1947 was shown on television for the first time. The New York Yankees beat the Brooklyn Dodgers in seven games.

Page 133
1. island; F
2. butte; A
3. gulf; E
4. basin; B
5. source; L
6. tributary; N
7. canyon; C
8. mountain; H
9. desert; D
10. strait; M
11. plateau; J
12. plain; P
13. peninsula; I
14. savanna; K
15. isthmus; G
16. valley; O

Page 134

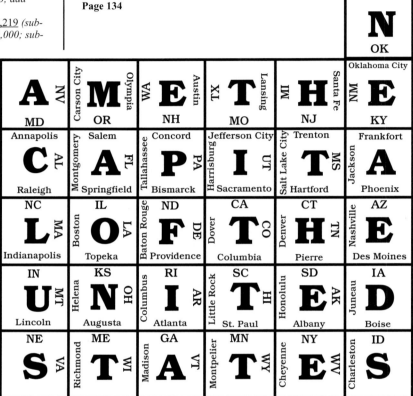

Spelled-out sentence: NAME THE CAPITAL OF THE UNITED STATES.
Answer: Washington, D.C.
Bonus Box: Maryland *and* Virginia

Page 138
1. 2 miles
2. 6 miles
3. 8 miles
4. about 8 miles
5. It is shorter to hike to the hill.; about 2 miles
6. about 16 miles
7. 2 miles
8. 2 miles
9. about 16 miles
10. Your friend is at the river.

Page 139

52°N	4.5°E	Amsterdam, Netherlands
37.5°N	23°E	Athens, Greece
33°N	44°E	Baghdad, Iraq
39.5°N	116°E	Beijing, China
15.5°S	47.5°W	Brasília, Brazil
34°S	58°W	Buenos Aires, Argentina
30°N	31°E	Cairo, Egypt
22°N	88°E	Calcutta, India
53°N	6°W	Dublin, Ireland
64.5°N	147.5°W	Fairbanks, Alaska, USA
55.5°N	4°W	Glasgow, Scotland
17°S	31°E	Harare, Zimbabwe
60°N	25°E	Helsinki, Finland
26°S	28°E	Johannesburg, South Africa
51°N	0.1°W	London, England
40°N	3°W	Madrid, Spain
37°S	144.5°E	Melbourne, Australia
19°N	99°W	Mexico City, Mexico
45°N	9°E	Milan, Italy
45°N	73°W	Montreal, Quebec, Canada
55°N	37°E	Moscow, Russia
18.5°N	72.5°E	Mumbai (Bombay), India
48°N	11°E	Munich, Germany
59.5°N	10°E	Oslo, Norway
41.5°N	12°E	Rome, Italy
33°S	70°W	Santiago, Chile
33.5°S	151°E	Sydney, Australia
35°N	51°E	Teheran, Iran
48°N	16°E	Vienna, Austria

Page 143

1. The Etruscans lived in Italy before the rise of the Roman Empire.
2. Romulus and Remus founded Rome in 753 B.C.
3. The city-state of Carthage was located on the continent of Africa.
4. The Roman Empire surrounded the Mediterranean Sea.
5. The Forum was used for business, government, religious, and social activities.
6. The Roman Empire included England.
7. Julius Caesar was assassinated on March 15 in 44 B.C.
8. The main road that led out of Rome was called the Appian Way.
9. Roman public bathhouses were heated by hot air from furnaces channeled beneath the floors.
10. The volcano that buried Pompeii was Mount Vesuvius.
11. Aqueducts were used to carry water from the mountains to homes and other buildings.
12. Gladiators were slaves or warriors who fought to the death for the entertainment of the Romans.
13. A Centurion was a Roman soldier who was in charge of a group of soldiers in the Roman army.
14. The animal used to pull a chariot was a horse.
15. Trajan's Column is a famous stone monument illustrating the history of the emperor Trajan's military conquests.

Page 148

Answers will vary.
1. Abigail Adams, the wife of John Adams, influenced her husband to consider the rights of women.
2. John Adams was one of the first to propose independence and helped write the Declaration of Independence.
3. Samuel Adams led Boston's resistance to the Tea Act.
4. Ethan Allen was a patriot of the American Revolution and leader of the Green Mountain Boys.
5. Crispus Attucks was the first man killed in the Boston Massacre.
6. George Rogers Clark was an American soldier who prevented the British from claiming what later became the Northwest Territory.
7. Margaret Corbin took her husband's place when he was killed during battle and continued to fight until she was seriously wounded.
8. William Dawes rode with Paul Revere and Samuel Prescott to warn colonists that the British were coming.
9. James Forten was captured in the war at the age of 15 and spent seven months on a British prison ship.
10. Benjamin Franklin persuaded the French to help the colonists during the war.
11. Nathanael Greene was a revolutionary soldier who was responsible for victories in the South.
12. Nathan Hale became a hero when he volunteered to spy on the British for George Washington.
13. John Hancock was the first to sign the Declaration of Independence.
14. Mary "Molly Pitcher" Hays carried pitchers of water to her husband and other soldiers during the Battle of Monmouth.
15. Patrick Henry spoke the words, "give me liberty or give me death!"
16. Thomas Jefferson wrote the Declaration of Independence.
17. John Paul Jones was an American naval captain who captured 16 ships on his first cruise aboard the *Providence* in 1776.
18. Marquis de Lafayette was a French military leader who served as a major general in the Continental Army.

Page 148 (cont.)

19. Richard Henry Lee was a leader of the American Revolution who proposed a resolution restricting the importation of slaves.
20. Francis Marion, nicknamed "swamp fox," commanded the capture of British forts in Charleston, South Carolina.
21. Thomas Paine wrote *Common Sense*, a document that helped persuade colonists to push for independence.
22. Samuel Prescott warned the colonists of Lincoln and Concord that the British were coming after Revere was captured and Dawes was forced to retreat.
23. Paul Revere rode with Prescott and Dawes to warn Concord colonists that the British were coming.
24. Deborah Sampson disguised herself as a man and fought in the American Revolution.
25. Roger Sherman was appointed to the committee to write the Declaration of Independence.
26. Friedrich von Steuben was a Prussian-American general who reformed the army to make it more disciplined and efficient.
27. George Washington led Americans in their fight for independence.
28. Phillis Wheatley was a slave who wrote a poem about America's struggle for freedom.

Bonus Box answer: Benedict Arnold became the most notorious traitor in U.S. history.

Page 149

1. Philadelphia
2. Baltimore
3. Boston
4. Newport
5. Charleston
6. New York City

Page 158

1. May was the best time to start if pioneers were leaving from Independence, Missouri. If pioneers started too early, the rainy spring left mud that would trap wagon wheels. Also the grass wouldn't be tall or thick enough to feed the cattle on the trip. If they started too late, the winter snowfall could trap them in the mountains.
2. *Scows,* large flat boats, took wagons across the Missouri River at the start of the trip. Once into Indian territory, some Indians would use rafts to help the pioneers cross if they paid them. Some pioneers would work together to build rafts from willow branches and long grasses to get the wagons across. Other times pioneers took the wheels off their wagons and floated them across after their boards had been sealed watertight with tar or wax mixed with ashes. It could take a large wagon train five days to get everyone across the river.
3. Some pioneers put the eggs in the flour barrel.
4. The pioneers learned from the Indians how to dry the meat through a process called *jerking*. These dried meat strips kept for a long time.
5. The pioneers burned dried buffalo droppings—called *buffalo chips*—for their fires. In the Rocky Mountains, the pioneers burned sagebrush branches and roots.
6. There were a few forts and trading posts along the trail where wagon trains could stop. Here the pioneers could buy or trade for items, such as sugar, flour, coffee, and leather. However these supplies were not always available.
7. Sometimes pioneers had to borrow a neighbor's oxen to help get a wagon up a high mountain. Once at the top, the pioneers would send the oxen back down the mountain to bring up the next wagon. Some people left large items and boxes along the trail because they just couldn't get them over the mountains.
8. The pioneers put poles between the wheel spokes to prevent the wheels from turning too fast. Also they tied one end of a rope to a large tree at the top of the mountain and the other end to the back of the wagon. This allowed the pioneers to loosen the rope slowly and ease the wagon down the mountain.

Bonus Box: Many westward travelers—including children—kept diaries while on the trails.

— —

Page 163

The following is one way that the snow blocks can correctly be arranged. Italicized information indicates other months during which this information could be correct.

January: Stay indoors and play games and tell stories. *(February)*
February: Hunt for seal as they come up through breathing holes. *(January)*
March: Start of whaling season. Get new set of clothing.
April: Hunt seal from kayak. *(March, May)*
May: Sea ice melting. Move family inland. *(June)*
June: Gather berries and roots to eat. *(July, August)*
July: Midsummer sun. Wear underclothing with fur turned out.
August: Hunt whales that migrate north after sea ice melts. *(March, April, May, June, July)*
September: Dry seal skin while there is still sun. *(June, July, August)*
October: Hunt caribou while they are fat and furry. *(September, November)*
November: Set up winter camp on sea ice. *(October)*
December: Get ready for constant darkness by end of month.

ANSWER KEYS

Page 164
1. D (I'm friendly.)
2. F (South is that way.)
3. C (Amaroq is the leader.)
4. B (Caribou are nearby.)
5. I (He was suspicious of Miyax.)
6. H (It's time for the wolves to hunt.)
7. G (It is autumn.)
8. E (It is August 24.)
9. A (Winter is on the way.)
10. J (The lemmings are returning.)

Page 184
Experiment 1: Electroscope
3. The tissue paper doesn't move.
5. The ends of the tissue paper move apart when the charged balloon comes close.
6. The tissue paper is negatively charged, just as the charged balloon is. Since like charges repel, the ends of the tissue paper move away from the balloon and one another.
8. Metal is a good conductor of electricity. If an extra electric charge (such as the extra negative charges of the balloon) is applied to a conductor, the charged particles don't stay in place but spread over the paper clip's surface. Therefore the balloon loses some negative charges to the paper clip, and once again has an equal number of positive and negative charges.

Experiment 2: Jumping Cereal
3. The puffed rice sticks to the plastic-wrap ball.
4. Rubbing the plastic ball on the paper gives the ball an excess of negatively charged electrons. The extra negatively charged electrons attract the positively charged cereal.

Experiment 3: Static Horse Race
4. After rubbing the balloon on the fabric, it has an excess of negatively charged electrons. These electrons attract the positively charged paper horse.

Bonus Box: Answers will vary. The number of negatively charged electrons on the different fabrics varies. Therefore the length of time the balloon holds its charge will vary.

Page 185
1. Answers will vary. Most conductors are made of metal.
2. Answers will vary. Possible answers include plastic, rubber, and wood.
3. The metal is the conductor and the plastic coating is the insulator.
4. Insulators are used to prevent electricity from flowing into places where it is not wanted or can be dangerous.

Bonus Box: Possible answers include the plastic covering on electrical cords and plugs, plastic handles on metal tools, and rubber-soled shoes.

Page 186
Experiment #1: Making A Series Circuit
2. Both lightbulbs will go out.
3. Series circuits use a single path to connect the battery or other electrical source. Therefore, if one lightbulb is unscrewed or burns out, the circuit is broken and all the bulbs go out.

Experiment #2: Making A Parallel Circuit
2. The unscrewed bulb goes out, but the other one stays lit.
3. Parallel circuits use more than one path to connect the battery or other electrical source. Therefore, if one lightbulb is unscrewed or burns out, the current can still travel to the other lightbulb along another path.
4. The unscrewed bulb goes out, but the other one stays lit.
5. See the answer to #3.
6. The parallel circuit is more reliable because it will work even if one or more bulbs in the circuit are disconnected or burn out.

Page 190
Answers will vary. The following are suggested answers.

ECOSYSTEM 1:
Effects On Homeostasis: The large fox population will consume more rabbits, reducing the rabbit population. Eventually some foxes will starve because there will not be enough food.
Ways To Keep The Balance: Reduce the fox population or increase the rabbit population.

ECOSYSTEM 2:
Effects On Homeostasis: The continued destruction of the tropical forest habitat will cause many animals that live in these areas to lose their homes and die.
Ways To Keep The Balance: Prohibit the destruction of tropical forests.

ECOSYSTEM 3:
Effects On Homeostasis: Because there are fewer coyotes, the deer population will increase. The more deer there are, the less grass there will be to go around, so some of the deer will starve.
Ways To Keep The Balance: Prevent the hunters from killing the coyotes, increase the supply of grass for the deer, or encourage hunters to hunt the deer.

Bonus Box answers:
natural events: forest fires, volcanic eruption, drought
man-made events: deforestation, hunting, expansion of urban areas into natural habitats

Page 208
Students' synonyms for the words will vary. The order of the words in each box will vary.
Miss Honey: frail, mild, fragile, impoverished
Miss Trunchbull: tyrannical, gigantic, formidable, menacing, fierce, athletic
Matilda: prodigy, precocious, genius, extraordinary, brilliant
Mr. Wormwood: half-witted, dishonest, gormless, corrupt, ratty

Page 237
Answers may vary.
Father decides to move his family to Oregon.
- He heard a stranger talk about Oregon.
- He believes the Indians won't bother them.
- He's heard that many people have made it safely to Oregon.
- Times in Arkansas are hard.
- People in Arkansas are too poor to buy Father's pottery.
- The government is giving away good land.
- Many other people are making the trip.
- There are guidebooks to show the way to Oregon.

Mary Ellen doesn't want to leave Arkansas.
- She'll miss Grandma.
- She hears the journey will be dangerous.
- She's afraid of the Indians.
- She'll miss going to school, which she loves.
- She'll miss going to the meetinghouse on Sundays.
- She loves her life in Arkansas.

It takes months to get ready for the journey.
- The Todds have to do a lot to prepare for the trip.
- The family has to have enough food, clothing, medicines, and tools for the trip.
- Mother has to spin and weave strong cloth to make clothes for the trip.
- The girls sew bags for their belongings.
- Father has to buy the wagon and get it ready for the trip.
- The wagon has to be carefully packed with all the family's belongings and supplies.

Other families traveling in wagons turn back.
- They are afraid of Indian raids.
- They are too tired or afraid of disease to continue the trip.
- There is not enough food or water.
- Someone in the family gets sick or dies.
- They miss their lives back home.
- They are afraid to cross the Kaw River.

The Christmas celebration is very special.
- The family is settled into their new home.
- Mother surprises Louvina and Mary Ellen with mittens.
- They have a wonderful Christmas dinner.
- It is baby Elijah's first Christmas.
- Mary Ellen realizes that Mother cares for her.

Page 191
1. Arctic Tern: 22,500 miles
2. Bat: 2,400 miles
3. Golden Plover: 19,000 miles
4. Monarch Butterfly: 2,000 miles
5. Short-Tailed Shearwater: 20,000 miles
6. Atlantic Salmon: 6,000 miles
7. Blue Whale: 5,000 miles
8. Dogfish: 2,500 miles
9. Fur Seal: 9,000 miles
10. Green Turtle: 3,000 miles

Bonus Box answers:
1. Arctic Tern
2. Short-Tailed Shearwater
3. Golden Plover
4. Fur Seal
5. Atlantic Salmon
6. Blue Whale
7. Green Turtle
8. Dogfish
9. Bat
10. Monarch Butterfly

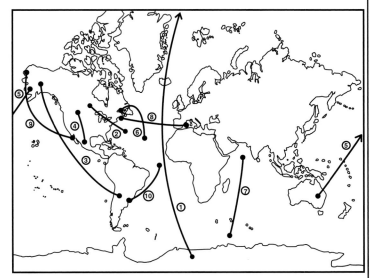

Page 215
1. G
2. I
3. A
4. J
5. E
6. D
7. B
8. H
9. L
10. C
11. F
12. K

Students' sentences will vary. Below are possible answers for sentences 1–5.
1. Marty realizes that Shiloh has been abused. Therefore he decides to buy him from Judd Travers.
2. Shiloh returns to Marty's house, so Marty hides Shiloh in the woods up on the hill.
3. Because Marty wants to earn the money to buy Shiloh, he collects bottles for deposits and cans for recycling.
4. Since Shiloh is happy to see Marty, he wags his tail, yips with joy, and licks Marty's face.
5. Marty tells his friend David that he can't come over to Marty's house because his mom is suffering from headaches. Consequently, people ask Marty's mother if she is feeling well and tell her what to take for a headache.

Page 221
1. apprehensive: anxious (brown)
2. prominent: distinguished (orange)
3. enhance: magnify (purple)
4. fortunate: lucky (orange)
5. chastise: discipline (yellow)
6. serene: undisturbed (green)
7. avert: deflect (yellow)
8. indolence: sluggishness (red)
9. diminished: lessened (green)
10. conspicuous: clear (red)
11. precision: exactness (green)
12. exquisite: beautiful (purple)

The spaces containing *humorous, murky, stare, understandable, chaotic, energetic, reward,* and *boring* should all be colored blue.

Page 225
Accept reasonable answers.
1. Mr. Ages is an older white mouse who was at NIMH with Mr. Frisby and the rats. He is helping the rats carry out their plan.
2. The rats are carrying an electrical cable to tap into a current and bring electricity to their home.
3. Mr. Frisby is well-known because he, like the rats of NIMH, was highly intelligent. While helping the rats put a sleeping powder in Dragon's dish, he was killed.
4. The rats are able to move Mrs. Frisby's home by using a series of pulleys, scaffolding, and logs.
5. The rats' plan is to live on their own—without stealing—in a place called Thorn Valley.
6. NIMH stands for National Institute Of Mental Health. The mice and rats were taken to a laboratory at NIMH.
7. Answers will vary.
8. The rats were being injected, trained, and tested to increase their intelligence.
9. The ability to read helped the rats escape from NIMH.
10. The rats convince the exterminators that they are not more of the mechanized rats by making their tunnel-like home appear to be an ordinary rat hole.

Page 227

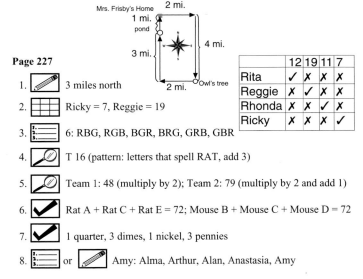

1. ✏️ 3 miles north
2. 📋 Ricky = 7, Reggie = 19
3. 📋 6: RBG, RGB, BGR, BRG, GRB, GBR
4. 🔍 T 16 (pattern: letters that spell RAT, add 3)
5. 🔍 Team 1: 48 (multiply by 2); Team 2: 79 (multiply by 2 and add 1)
6. ✔️ Rat A + Rat C + Rat E = 72; Mouse B + Mouse C + Mouse D = 72
7. ✔️ 1 quarter, 3 dimes, 1 nickel, 3 pennies
8. 📋 or ✏️ Amy: Alma, Arthur, Alan, Anastasia, Amy

Page 233
1. Peter's mom tells him about their Maine vacation.
2. Turtle gets sprayed by a skunk.
3. Sheila opens all the windows in the house, and Uncle Feather escapes.
4. Mrs. Hatcher agrees to pay Sheila $7.00 a day to baby-sit Fudge.
5. Peter meets Izzy at the library.
6. Fudge gets caught in the rollaway bed.
7. Peter swallows a fly while riding his bicycle.
8. Fudge eats almost all the blueberries and gets sick.
9. The Tubmans, Jimmy, Peter, Sheila, Grandma, and Peter's dad go sailing.
10. Tootsie walks across Mr. Fargo's paint canvas and gets blue paint on her feet.
11. Big Apfel hosts a baseball game.
12. Buzzy Senior and Grandma get married.

Page 238

| I | B | L | E | H | J | F | G | C | A | K | D |

Page 244

Type Of Whale	Baleen Or Toothed	Maximum Length	Maximum Weight	Type Of Food Eaten	Unusual Features
beluga	toothed	20 feet	3,000 pounds (1 1/2 tons)	fish, squid, crabs	creamy, white skin
blue whale	baleen	102 feet	392,000 pounds (196 tons)	plankton	largest whale
bowhead whale	baleen	65 feet	244,000 pounds (122 tons)	plankton	huge head shaped like the bow of a boat
fin whale	baleen	82 feet	152,000 pounds (76 tons)	krill, anchovies, other small fish	can blow a cone-shaped jet of water vapor up to 20 feet in the air
gray whale	baleen	50 feet	56,000 pounds (28 tons)	plankton, fish	makes the longest migration of any mammal
humpback whale	baleen	62 feet	106,000 pounds (53 tons)	plankton, small fish	sings songs
killer whale	toothed	32 feet	16,000 pounds (8 tons)	fish, seals	the only whale that attacks and kills other whales
narwhal	toothed	20 feet	4,000 pounds (2 tons)	squid, crabs, fish	male usually has a single tooth that sticks out in front like a horn
pilot whale	toothed	28 feet	8,400 pounds (over 4 tons)	fish	is classified as a dolphin
sperm whale	toothed	69 feet	120,000 pounds (60 tons)	squid, sharks, octopus, fish	has a very large head

Page 270

Answers will vary. Accept words that are in correct alphabetical order, and that would appear between the guide words on each page. Suggestions:

vacant	**wafer**	**wrap**	**yearn**	**zany**
vacation	waffle	wrapper	yeast	zero
valley	wag	wreath	yell	zigzag
vegetable	wagon	wrench	yellow	zing
vehicle	waist	xylophone	yet	zone
veil	wait	yacht	yolk	zoo
velvet	war	yam	yonder	zoom
very	**warm**	**yarn**	**you**	**zucchini**

Bonus Box answers: Answers will vary. Accept answers that are in correct alphabetical order. Suggestions: vain, vapid, vary; wind, withe, witty; yam, yawl, yellow; zeal, zebu, zinnia

Page 271

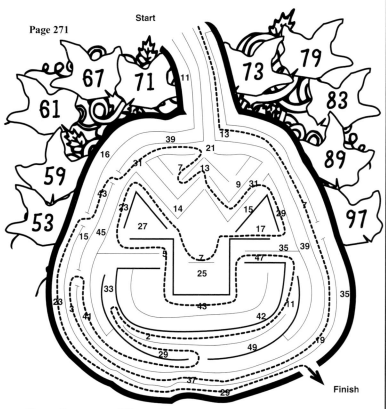

Start

Finish

Bonus Box answer: 990 pounds

Page 273

b	1.	h	5.	e	9.
d	2.	k	6.	i	10.
f	3.	c	7.	g	11.
j	4.	l	8.	a	12.

Page 276

Hanukkah is a ___Jewish___ holiday, also known as the ___Festival___ of ___Lights___.
The eight days honor an event that took place over two ___thousand___ years ago when a small group of Jewish men fought a ___battle___ to recapture their ___temple___. When it was time to light the sacred temple ___lamp___, only one day's oil was found. But miraculously, the oil lasted for ___eight___ days!

Today Jewish families ___remember___ this miracle by lighting one ___candle___ for each of eight days. The special candleholder is called a ___menorah___. Houses are decorated with the Star of ___David___. ___Gifts___ are exchanged, and children enjoy playing a Hanukkah game with a toy called a ___dreidel___. Potato ___pancakes___, also called ___latkes___, are a favorite Hanukkah food. They are ___cooked___ in oil as a remembrance of the ___miracle___ of the lamp.

PETMEL—temple   LENCAD—candle   MEREBERM—remember
THILGS—lights   GITHE—eight   CARLIME—miracle
TABELT—battle   VIDAD—David   STEAKL—latkes
ELDIRED—dreidel   KOCEDO—cooked   LISVFAET—festival
DONSTHUA—thousand   SNAKAPEC—pancakes   TIFGS—gifts
SHIWEJ—Jewish   HAMOREN—menorah   PLAM—lamp

Bonus Box answer:
Possible answers include:

men	mane	mar	eon	near	omen	ram	are	hoar	hear	hone	hen
moan	man	morn	era	norm	one	ream	arm	harem	harm	hem	horn
more	mean	ear	name	ore	roam	Rome	amen	hero	ham	homer	hare
mare	manor	earn	nor	oar	ran	roan	ahem	her	home	hoe	

Page 278

Store	Coupons									Total savings
	a	b	c	d	e	f	g	h	i	
Little's Vittles	40¢	1.00	35¢	90¢	65¢	40¢	75¢	30¢	10¢	$4.85
Edie's Edibles (Choose the six coupons with *s.)	80¢*	1.00*	70¢*	90¢*	65¢	80¢*	75¢*	60¢	20¢	$4.95
Chloe's Culinary Corner (Choose the four coupons with *s.)	$1.20*	1.00*	$1.05*	90¢	65¢	$1.20*	75¢	90¢	30¢	$4.45

At which store will Esther save the most money with her coupons? ___Edie's Edibles___

Bonus Box answer: $6.40

Page 282

Answers will vary, depending on the route that each student chose. One possible route: Oregon-Wyoming-Arizona-Texas-Missouri-Ohio-New York-Virginia-Florida. This route is approximately 5,000 miles.
Bonus Box answer: If the route ends in Florida, like the sample above, then the distance from Florida to Nebraska is approximately 1,380 miles.

Page 284

1. Cities With Large St. Patrick's Day Parades
2. Possible answers include shamrock, leprechaun, pot of gold, and rainbow.
3. Answers will vary.
4. Facts About Ireland
5. Different Shades Of Green
6. Answers will vary. Some possible answers include his capture by pirates at age 16, his escape from slavery, his study in a French monastery, and his founding of more than 300 churches.
7. Answers will vary.
8. Names For The Shamrock Plant

Page 285

1. less than one inch
2. six nickels
3. Answers will vary.
4. Answers will vary. Thirteen nickels measure one inch. The dollar amount that a student measuring 60 inches (five feet) would receive is $39.00. Therefore, this would be the better choice.

Bonus Box answers: penny = Abraham Lincoln; dime = Franklin D. Roosevelt; quarter = George Washington

Page 286

1. pane	11. moan	**Bonus Box answers:** Accept reasonable answers. Possible answers include:
2. swap	12. rink	
3. wasp	13. knot	**newspaper:** pare, pear, snap, span, spawn, ware, warp, wear, wrap
4. spear	14. trail	
5. swan	15. link	**plastic bag:** clasp, clip, gala, glib, last, past, scab, stab, stag
6. cast	16. calm	
7. blast	17. canal	**milk carton:** clam, clan, rail, rain, tail, track, train, trim
8. list	18. aim	
9. gasp	19. animal	**aluminum can:** maul, clan, clam, an, man, nun, I'm, inn
10. pasta	20. main	

Page 305

The order of answers will vary.

dear	rain	sights	won
would	except	hair	passed
I	real	dyed	piece
knew	break	blue	meat
night	for	minor	right
tale	hour	allowed	scene
sea	bored	clothes	by
there		capital	

Page 307

rule 3	rule 6	rule 1	rule 4
1. zeroes	1. knives	1. suitcases	1. donkeys
2. zoos	2. teeth	2. rocks	2. strawberries
3. potatoes	3. thieves	3. flowers	3. daisies
4. tomatoes	4. wives	4. eggs	4. butterflies
5. heroes	5. shelves	5. sandwiches	5. candies

rule 8	rule 2	rule 5	rule 7
1. saleswomen	1. boxes	1. turkeys	1. moose
2. grandchildren	2. lunches	2. donkeys	2. elk
3. oxen	3. geese	3. keys	3. sheep
4. feet	4. dishes	4. birthdays	4. mice
5. hands	5. kisses	5. libraries	5. deer

Deer Editor,

Wood you believe that eye, Gwendolyn Gogetter, was invited to the biggest social event of the season? I new that knight I'd have a tail to tell, for the gathering was a see of famous faces! Everybody who is anybody was their—singer Winessa Villiams and movie star Prad Bitt, to name a few. Not even the reign that was pouring down outside could keep these people away accept for T. J. Thomas—he fell and acquired a reel bad brake in his arm). Four more than an our I talked, ate, and danced with the stars; not for a moment was I board!

Let me tell you about some of the more interesting sites I saw. Rennis Dodman's hare was died blew (a miner offense). Snory Telling shouldn't have been aloud out of the house wearing those close (a capitol offense). But Wobin Rilliams should have one first prize—he past a peace of meet that fell write onto Rinona Wyder's lap. My, what a seen that was!

Now that it's all over, I must say I had a lovely evening. And buy the way, I got lots of autographs!

Sincerely,
Gwen Gogetter

Index